The Madman and the Nun and Other Plays

The Madman and the Nun

and Other Plays by

Stanisław Ignacy Witkiewicz

TRANSLATED & EDITED

BY DANIEL C. GEROULD

AND C. S. DURER

WITH A FOREWORD

BY JAN KOTT

UNIVERSITY OF WASHINGTON PRESS

SEATTLE AND LONDON

COVER PHOTOGRAPH: Wiesław Gołas and Lucyna Winnicka as Walpurg and Sister Anna in *The Madman and the Nun,* Teatr Dramatyczny, Warsaw, 1959; Wanda Laskowska, director; Józef Szajna, designer. Photograph from *Theatre in Modern Poland* (Warsaw: Wydawnictwa Artystyczne i Filmowe, 1963). ENDPAPER: another scene from the same production. Photograph from Zenobiusz Strzelecki, *Polska Plastyka Teatralna* (Warsaw: Państwowy Instytut Wydawniczy, 1963).

Foreword

I MET Stanisław Ignacy Witkiewicz five or six years before the Second World War. I was then a student, and Witkiewicz sometimes dropped by as a guest to the seminars given by the Philosophy Department of Warsaw University. I knew his two novels and some of his plays that had been published in magazines or were circulating in manuscript copies. I saw many of his paintings; Witkacy (the name he created for himself from the first part of his last name and the last part of his middle name) was very popular as a painter. He was making portraits at a low price, and he often gave them away free of charge. Later on I met some of his personal friends, or rather his "ex-" friends; Witkacy called them his "ideological enemies." He had the practice of keeping a numbered list of his acquaintances, and whenever he lowered the position of one of them, he would inform him about it with an "official" letter. Once as an annual, or semestrial, assignment, I wrote about his theory of Pure Form. Later on he invited me to his house. He showed me his collection of canes of famous women, artists, and politicians. There was among them, if I remember correctly, the little cane of Marie Curie-Skłodowska and the umbrella of the great pianist Ignacy Paderewski who, after the restoration of Polish independence, became the prime minister of the first Polish government.

I was under the spell of Witkacy; however, I was more fascinated by his personality and himself than by his creative work. I knew that he was an extraordinary and splendid man, but at the same time I did not have the slightest doubt that his extraordinariness and splendor belonged to another epoch. To the future? No! To the past. Witkacy as a man, writer, and artist seemed to me like a dazzling relic from the beginning of the twentieth century who had strayed into contemporary times.

It would not be worth mentioning this opinion of a young student from thirty years ago were it not for the fact that it was currently shared both by young intellectuals and by mature writers. By definition a precursor is one who swerves away from his own times. As a precursor of the Theater of the Absurd, Witkacy was the most eminent playwright in Poland and one of the most interesting in Europe. But he was also—and this may be most astonishing—one of the most original precursors of what might be called the intellectual and artistic climate of the sixties, of its style of life and of thinking. And not only in Europe, but in America as well. Witkacy, who came too early, seemed to his contemporaries to be a man who came too late. It would be worth while to devote some attention to this very phenomenon of the precursor who swerves away from his time or, to be more precise, to the problem of the dialectic of anachronism and innovation.

Let us begin with the simplest question, with Witkacy's painting. Witkiewicz had the rare gift, even among painters, of a rapid grasp of resemblances. His portraits resembled their models, even those paintings—the most expensive according to his price list—which were made under the influence of narcotics, and which were visionary and deformed. At that time the leading school of painters in Poland were the postimpressionists, for the most part students of Bonnard. The younger or more "modern" painters continued the experiments of the constructivists and cubists; they rigorously practiced abstract painting. Max Ernst and the surrealists were still at that time almost unknown in Poland. Witkiewicz was somewhat slighted by painters; they considered his painting "literary," and this "literariness" was very badly regarded by artists at that time. The postimpressionists and the postcubists as well were preoccupied with form, quality of color, and composition; they were not interested in qualities that were extrinsic to the painting. According to them, Witkacy—the theoretician of Pure Form —was painting old-fashioned, figurative pictures. For them even his visions were illustrations.

I think that the painters were quite right. Today, from a greater perspective in time, the connections that link Witkacy's painting with the English pre-Raphaelite school and with the Viennese Secession are obvious. The cold blue tones, the violet and rose colors in Witkacy's pastels, his unreal, ghostly lighting derive from Arnold Böcklin's painting; his thin, vanishing, and undulating stroke, like the unfolding coils of a snake, is more ornamental than pictorial and comes closest to the style of Edward Burne-Jones. But what was generally considered in the twenties and thirties to be passé became a live inspiration a quarter of a century later.

The Viennese Secession, anathemized as the epoch of the decline of taste, has come back triumphantly into fashion with the revival of the Art Nouveau influence in furniture and perhaps most of all in posters. It has become a new tenet of style. Witkacy's portraits and compositions often strikingly call to mind the psychedelic posters which have become a new art form for collectors. Witkacy's faces, which emerge from a colorful mist with their magnified eyes, their grimacing mouths, and all their striking resemblance to their models, are first of all psychological portraits. There is always tension and anxiety in them, a kind of tragic absence; they are faces from a narcotic "trip."

Witkacy used the term Pure Form for the particular metaphysical quality in painting and poetry which cannot be analyzed into its primary elements; he called it "unity within diversity" or "the mystery of existence." It is not astonishing that this was not understood by painters; for them, form consisted in lighting on a surface and the composition of masses, and not in any "metaphysical qualities."

Witkacy was undoubtedly one of the precursors of the philosophy of "existence," but although he introduced symbols and quasi-mathematical formulas into his argumentation, his language recalled that of the nineteenth-century spiritualists rather than that of the twentieth century's precise and technical philosophizing. To the Marxists, to the phenomenologists, and most of all to the neopositivists, Witkacy's theories were "metaphysics"; they were an accumulation of "empty" propositions which did not permit verification, that is, they were neither true nor false, and did not observe the formal rules of the manipulation of propositions.

For philosophers, Witkacy was an interesting, sometimes fascinating amateur; for writers and men of the theater, he was a painter who, as an amateur, dabbled in literature and the theater. Today Witkacy is more and more often described as a "Renaissance man," as one of the most universal European minds. In his own time, despite the great spell and fascination which he exerted, he was considered a dilettante; he did not fit into the intellectual and artistic community, which was rigidly compartmentalized and highly specialized. Nobody scoffed at the pretensions of artists to superhumanity and independent morality with more force than Witkacy. But in life, especially for the benefit of his friends, Witkacy often very readily put on the mask of a demon. He proclaimed in his theory that modern art is more and more compelled toward perversion, which, translated into more normal language, meant the necessity of formal refinement and of shock-producing means of expression. In addition, he defended the right to perversion in life. This "demonism," which was so characteristic of many generations of the European bohemia, seemed, in the years between the two wars, frightfully old-fashioned.

As a young man, Witkacy walked through the streets of Zakopane in a harlequin's costume; he liked to disguise himself until the end of his life. He adored all forms of social and intellectual provocation; he treated life as a game and a play; certainly he had much in common with Oscar Wilde. But now, from the perspective of a greater distance of time, it becomes obvious that although he lived his life as a play, the genre of the play was tragedy.

Witkacy was, or acted (the adopted mask is also the face) the role of, an aristocrat of the spirit and the intellect, of a bohemian and, most rarely, of a dandy. All these personal patterns—of a liberated artist, of

an artist at odds with society, of an artist misunderstood by the philistines—seemed in the interwar period extremely "nineteenth century."
In the period between the Spanish Civil War and the outbreak of the
Second World War, intellectuals began to be fascinated by political
movements and by the idea of "engagement." For all its naïveté, the
diagnosis by Julian Benda in his well-known book, *The Treason of the
Intellectuals*, was basically accurate. Of course the "engagement" was
understood by intellectuals in various ways. Some considered that the
function of a writer was that of agitator; some, of an ideologist; others
thought, finally, that the preparation of a revolution or a *coup d'état* is
the only important intellectual and moral experience of a twentieth-
century writer. The best examples of these attitudes were: the adher-
ence of the majority of the French surrealists to the Communist party,
the participation of André Malraux and many Anglo-Saxon writers in
the Spanish Civil War, Bertolt Brecht's political and didactic theater,
and, on the side of the "Establishment," Jean Giraudoux as minister and
Paul Claudel as the French ambassador in the United States. Just as
Witkacy did not fit into any of the professional compartments of
intellectual and artistic milieux that were becoming more and more
technical, so he did not fit into the division of the political left and
right. Nor did he have any liberal illusions. His basic nonconformism
resulted from various historical experiences and implied something
different. Once again, this particular nonconformity diverged from the
attitudes of his epoch. It occurred earlier, and it will occur later.
Witkacy's nonconformism was probably closest to that of Alexander
Blok, Leo Shestov, and a large part of the pre-Revolutionary Russian
intelligentsia. Today we can find a similar type of nonconformity and
rebellion against the establishment in the posture of Dylan Thomas,
John Arden, and Allen Ginsberg.

The main road of the Berkeley campus of the University of California ends at the intersection of two streets: Bancroft and Telegraph. On
this corner, a man with a hoarse voice and a middle-aged woman sing
psalms every day at about noon. Next to them barefoot girls and
long-haired, disheveled boys wearing strings of beads over colorful
shirts sell the *Berkeley Barb*. Two hundred feet toward the center of
the campus there is a square with a fountain between the Student
Union and the wide, amphitheatrical steps of the administration building; here stand the tables of the various student groups and organizations. And here you can buy a red booklet with Mao Tse-tung's
thoughts, sign a protest against the war in Vietnam, enroll in several
political parties or in the sexual freedom league. Psychedelic leaflets
with the same flowery, serpentine designs invite you to attend a Baptist

service, to join a nudist group, to take judo lessons, or to devote yourself to either Christian or Buddhist meditation. This little square on the Berkeley campus, where every day numerous scenes from Witkacy's plays are performed with few changes by young boys and girls who have never heard of their author, is one of the most sensitive barometers of the intellectual ferment of American youth. One can find similar squares, although perhaps less intense and colorful, on other American campuses also; and similar symptoms of ferment can be found in Swedish, English, and German universities. The atmosphere of the Berkeley campus resembles most, I think, the Russian universities before the 1905 revolution. Not only were the long locks of the boys and the short hair of the Russian female revolutionaries and suffragists similar, but also the furs worn over shirts, trousers tucked into high boots, or, in summer, sandals on bare feet—of course, taking off their student uniforms was a form of protest. But all these similarities are not the most important; each generation of artistic bohemia since Romanticism has performed some kind of a masquerade. The costume was like a uniform; it attested membership in a clan. The cape has been for a long time the uniform of a painter, just as the bowler has been the uniform of a London stockbroker.

More important than clothes and hair-do are the similarities of intellectual and ideological propositions. In the Russian universities at the beginning of our century, the followers of Tolstoy's belief in nonresistance to evil attempted to convince the apologists for terror that any form of violence is immoral. Socialists disputed with anarchists the need for the political activization of the masses and scoffed at individual herosim as if it were without political significance. The Russo-Japanese War laid bare the weakness of Tsarist Russia. The old religions were coming back, and new ones were born; the adherents to Buddhist Nirvana tried to convince the Old Believers of the new light coming from the East. At the universities the causes of free love and equality of sexual rights for women were advocated; hashish was smoked, ether was inhaled, and the first drug mystics appeared. Most of the time they drank, of course, vodka; but it was a Slavic way of drinking vodka: full of passionate discussions, of "stripping one's soul" and intimate confessions—drunken nights like trips down to the bottom.

At that time Witkacy was at the Academy of Fine Arts in Cracow. Cracow's bohemia was meager and provincial, but the Polish students who had gone to Russian universities violently radicalized somnolent Cracow and its artistic, "aesthetic" milieu. Witkiewicz saw the "naked soul" in its Russian version, a new Apocalypse and one of the ends of the world, only ten years later when he was a cadet in Pavlovski's regiment of the tsar's bodyguard and then the political commissar of a revolutionized division.

All historical analogies are true only up to a point, and are only one means of interpretation. History does not repeat itself, or repeats itself each time in a different way; and if outlived social forms, as Marx wrote, die twice, first as tragedy, then as farce, the grotesque is always both farce and tragedy, a third death of old forms.

It is easier, however, to understand Witkacy's swerving from his time and the contemporaneity of his theater—so striking today—if we compare even for a moment the ideological ferment of the sixties with the Russian universities at the beginning of the century, the similar revolt against the establishment by the children of the same establishment, the contempt of the intellectuals for professional politicians, and the basic nonconformism of the artistic milieux.

It may be that, in the United States, these similarities are especially emphatic, and Witkacy's plays have not only their Polish or European contemporaneity but also their very special American contemporaneity. I realized this while directing *The Madman and the Nun* at San Francisco State College in 1967. A few small changes in the references to books that had been read by the hero were sufficient to make him appear as an incarnation of an American beatnik shut up in an insane asylum after a "bad trip." He had been put there as a dangerous madman, but his madness was, in fact, simply protest, contempt and hatred for the society of satisfied and obedient men. The hero is a madman for the physicians; but truly mad are the physicians themselves, and the whole world is insane.

If we consider the Theater of the Absurd, the Theater of Cruelty, and the Theater of Happenings as the most significant theatrical phenomena of the fifties and sixties, it no longer seems difficult to draw their historical genealogy. But this is true only today, because ten years ago the history of twentieth-century European theater seemed quite different. It was Martin Esslin who first drew the outline of this genealogy.

The origins of this modern theater go back to the scandal at the opening night of Alfred Jarry's *Ubu the King* in Paris in 1896, to Frank Wedekind's grotesque and demoniac tragedies, and, later on, to August Strindberg's works, especially *A Dream Play* (1902) and *The Ghost Sonata* (1907).

The second stage of development comprises German Expressionist drama from Oscar Kokoschka, Yvan Goll, and Georg Kaiser to Brecht's early plays, the literary cabarets in Berlin and Munich, and the Dadaist Cabaret Voltaire in Zürich during the last years of the First

World War. The third, most important stage was Antonin Artaud's *Theater of Alfred Jarry* (1926–28), and the theater of Witkiewicz, who wrote almost all his plays between 1918 and 1925.

> LEON But let's not have any dramas à la Ibsen, with all that tragedy business about the various professions and the shortcomings of each. I'd rather have a cold-soup tragedy or a meat-with-all-the-juices-cooked-out-of-it tragedy à la Strindberg.
> MOTHER Nothing's sacred to you. You treat Ibsen and Strindberg just the same way you treat me. Is there any greater work of genius in the whole world than Strindberg's *The Ghost Sonata?*
> [*The Mother*, Act I]

One of the first plays performed in Artaud's theater was Strindberg's *A Dream Play*. But even a very superficial analysis of Witkacy's *The Mother* and *The Water Hen* reveals that their author continues the destruction of naturalistic theater exactly from the point where Strindberg stopped. The same was true for Artaud. In both Artaud's and Witkiewicz' plays, even before the body of a character who has died has time to cool down, he stands up and walks.

There is a long theatrical history behind characters who, after their death, come back on stage in order to haunt living people or to give them moral lessons; this should become the subject of a separate book. The dead come back on stage both in Shakespeare and in Elizabethan drama, both in Romantic and in modern drama. The dead come back either as ghosts or as hallucinations. The ghost is a metaphysical premise; the hallucination is a psychological situation. But both imply, in the properly theatrical sense, that the ghost or hallucination can be seen only by some of the characters on the stage, that it behaves in a different way from the "living" characters, it speaks differently, it moves differently, it often wears the costume of a ghost or hallucination, and if it does not have a costume, then it still must have some special traits or marks. The theatrical tradition of the behavior of ghosts was probably undermined for the first time by Strindberg. In *The Ghost Sonata* the dead Consul, wrapped in a winding sheet, comes out of the door of the house where he died the day before to look at the flag flying at half mast and to count the poor who came to his funeral. Only the Student, however, sees him. A young girl, whom many years ago Company Director Hummel had seduced and drowned, appears as a Milkmaid in the first scene; she does not speak, but she behaves normally. She even gives a cup of water to the Student. At the beginning only he sees her. The Milkmaid will, however, appear in the same act for a second time; she will raise her arms like one who is drowning and gaze fixedly at her murderer. The metaphysical premise of these apparitions is ambiguous in Strindberg's play; maybe they are ghosts, maybe only hallucinations. From the theatrical point of view, however, they no longer have otherworldly attributes.

But it is only in the plays with "corpses" of Artaud and Witkiewicz that the dead characters come back on stage in an ordinary manner. In *The Water Hen* the heroine who is shot in the first act comes back in the second act as if nothing had happened. In the third act, she is shot once again, but this time definitively. In *The Mother*, old Mrs. Eely dies in the second act. In the third act she lies in state, but this does not hinder her from appearing simultaneously as a person thirty years younger and, moreover, pregnant, expecting the birth of the hero of the play. The "first" Mother who is lying in state turns out to be a dummy. In *The Madman and the Nun* the corpse of a murdered psychiatrist, which has been removed by hospital attendants, comes back after a while, smiling, with the murderer who had hanged himself in the previous scene. His corpse is still on stage and is, of course, a dummy. The same thing happens in Artaud's pantomime *The Philosopher's Stone*, where Harlequin, who has been cut in pieces a moment ago by the jealous Doctor, jumps up from the operating table and immediately has sexual intercourse with the Doctor's wife, Isabella. After a while a baby is shaken out from her skirt who resembles the doctor as closely as two peas in a pod. The Harlequin who was tortured on the operating table was, of course, a dummy. The resemblance between Artaud's and Witkiewicz' plays using corpses is all the more surprising since Artaud could in no way have known Witkacy's plays. This theatricalization of corpses is very important in the history of the contemporary, avant-garde theater; the centuries-old convention of portraying the return of the dead in European theater was completely broken.

In the Chinese theater, when the hero dies or is killed he drops and lies flat for a moment and then runs off the stage. He has died, thus he has ceased to exist, and consequently he cannot be present on the stage. For a European spectator this convention seems surprising at first, yet it does not lack theatrical logic. The actor acts the role of a character, but it is impossible to act the role of a corpse; at most it is possible to simulate it. But to simulate a corpse means, in theatrical language, to pass from the technical means of "acting" to the technical means of "pantomime." The only difference is that it is a pantomime with no gestures. After the performance and after the curtain calls, the corpses get up to bow before the audience; they might just as well have got up earlier.

In the Japanese Nō theater, also, the dead—who return to haunt those who are alive, or to revenge themselves, or to reward their benefactors—do not follow the theatrical premise of a European "ghost." They behave, as far as I know, like characters who are alive, that is to say, according to the same theatrical convention of gestures and without any change in make-up. In the Bali theater, ghosts and demons are represented as huge and lurid puppets. Artaud wrote about the Bali theater:

> There is in the truly terrifying look of their devil (probably Tibetan) a striking similarity to the look of a certain puppet in our own remembrance, a puppet with swollen hands of white gelatine and nails of green foliage, which was the most beautiful ornament of one of the first plays performed by Alfred Jarry's theater.[1]

The theater in which the dead are puppets and in which the dead get up and walk—the theater which breaks away from the convention of European drama—originated in the fascination with the Oriental theater. Artaud experienced this fascination when he saw the Bali theater during the colonial exposition in Paris. The Chinese opera and the Japanese Nō theater fascinated Brecht, too. From the Oriental theater he adopted the ways in which the mask was used, symbolical make-up, and pantomime elements in acting as the basic means of theatricalization and of producing the effect of alienation.

We do not know anything about Witkacy's theatrical experiences during the time when he traveled in Australia and Malaysia. It seems unlikely, however, that when he accompanied Malinowski to New Guinea in 1914 and passed through India, Ceylon, and the Malayan archipelago, Witkacy did not take an interest in or see any Oriental theater. For a foreigner who does not know the language this is primarily a visual theater, a theater of gesture, costume, and movement, a true theater of Pure Form. But this theater of Pure Form is at the same time a ritual and a liturgy. Antonin Artaud understood this theater in exactly the same fashion, as pure spectacle and as ritual, and he opposed it to the deadness of European theater. In the chapter "Metaphysics and the *Mise en Scène*" from *The Theater and Its Double,* he wrote: "In any case, and I hasten to say it at once, a theater which subordinates the *mise en scène* and production, i.e., everything in itself that is specifically theatrical, to the text, is a theater of idiots, madmen, inverts, grammarians, grocers, antipoets and positivists, i.e., Occidentals." [2] In its formulation, even in its style, choice of words, and terms this statement surprisingly resembles Witkacy's theories about the theater of Pure Form.

[1] Antonin Artaud, *The Theater and Its Double,* trans. M. C. Richards (New York: Grove Press, 1958), p. 56.
[2] *Ibid.,* p. 41.

"The last part of the spectacle," wrote Artaud about the Bali theater, "is—in contrast to all the dirt, brutality, and infamy chewed up by our European stages—a delightful anachronism. And I do not know what other theater would dare to pin down in this way as if true to nature the throes of a soul at the mercy of phantasms from the Beyond." [3]

These "throes of a soul at the mercy of phantasms from the Beyond" are like expressions Witkacy might have used, and they could characterize his painting and his theater. Witkacy's Theater of Pure Form and Antonin Artaud's Theater of Cruelty were to serve as the last places where metaphysical experiences which had been banished from philosophy and had become dead in religion could be expressed. Artaud wrote: "In our present state of degeneration it is through the skin that metaphysics must be made to re-enter our minds." But Witkacy would have said: only through the perversion of form.

It may be most significant that in both Witkiewicz and Artaud we find the same infernal fusion, the same explosive combination of two notions, or rather of two visions, of the theater. One of them is the theater of ritual and liturgy, the theater of metaphysical transports, the theater in which—as Witkacy thought—the "Mystery of Existence" will shake even the unbelievers. Or, as Artaud wrote, which "will restore to all of us the natural and magic equivalent of the dogmas in which we no longer believe." The other is the theater of violent physical action, the theater in which gestures, words, movements, and objects are not only a system of signs, but have their own pure theatrical value, just like a hieroglyph or Chinese ideogram which not only has a meaning but is an image as well.

In fact, these are two entirely different notions of theater, although both in Artaud and in Witkiewicz they are tightly interlaced like two fibers in one cord. From the perspective of another twenty-five years, it becomes clear that one of these visions of theater was an illusion. The magic counterpart of dogmas does not exist once you cease to believe in them. Ritual and liturgy in theater are either provocation or profanation of ritual and liturgy. This very profanation of ritual we can find in the theater of Genet, who is the only one to draw all of the consequences from Artaud's Theater of Cruelty.

In one of his rare moments of lucidity Artaud, however, was conscious of his illusion. In 1927 he wrote: "It is certain that if I had created a theater, what I would have done would have had as little relation to that which we are in the habit of calling 'theater,' as the representation of some obscenity resembles an ancient religious mystery." [4]

[3] *Ibid.*, p. 64.
[4] Antonin Artaud, *Oeuvres complètes* (Paris: Gallimard, 1961), II, 26.

In the real theater created by Witkiewicz, there are no metaphysical transports, nor is there any mystery of existence. And perhaps that is the reason why this theater became understood so late. Witkiewicz' theater is sometimes bitter, but always scoffing. The unquestionable greatness of this theater consists in its historical perspective, in the perception of the end of contemporary civilization which was fatally threatened both by the egalitarian revolution coming from the East and by Western mechanization. This mechanization not only produces a society of automatons, but also impels the automatons to direct even those who had invented them. Witkacy's catastrophism only apparently belongs to the nineteenth century. In fact, it was the perspicacious and appalling vision of an inevitable clash between the civilization of computers and the levelers' revolution. For Witkacy the nineteenth century ended once and for all in 1917. In this perspective, all that followed was grim and grotesque.

> EVADER Have you gone out of your mind? To play cards at such a critical time?
> FATHER At our age it's the only way of whiling away the time during a social upheaval. What else could we do? Whist or auction bridge? "That is the question." . . .
> TYPOWICZ One club.
> EVADER Two clubs.
> FATHER (*sitting down*) Two diamonds. (*A red glare floods the stage, and the monstrous boom of a grenade exploding nearby can be heard.*) Banging away in fine style. Your bid, Mr. Specter.
> SPECTER (*in a quivering, somewhat plaintive voice*) Two hearts. The world is collapsing. (*Fainter red flashes of lighting, and immediately afterward two shells exploding a little farther off*)
> TYPOWICZ Pass.
>
> [*The Water Hen*, Act III]

Until the outbreak of the Second World War, Witkacy was understood only by a few—maybe, because we were all still *before*, while he was already *after*.

JAN KOTT
Translated by Bogdana Carpenter

Acknowledgments

INTRODUCING Witkiewicz to the English-speaking world has been a truly cooperative venture, and we owe a debt of gratitude to our many collaborators, both here and in Poland. We especially wish to thank: Mr. Konstanty Puzyna, editor of the Polish edition of the plays, for originally suggesting the idea of translating Witkacy into English and for much helpful advice, as well as for his own excellent introduction and notes, on which we drew heavily; Professor Henry F. Salerno, editor of *First Stage*, for first publishing several of the translations and encouraging us to continue; Professor and Mrs. Jan Kott, for long hours of stimulating consultation about both the translations and the introductions and also for the first very important production of Witkacy in English; Professor Grzegorz Sinko of Warsaw University, for his constant encouragement and brilliant interpretatons of Witkacian ambiguities; Miss Danuta Żmij of *Dialog*, for her splendid cooperation and support at every stage of the project; Professor and Mrs. Alfred Tarski, for sharing their reminiscences about Witkiewicz with us and providing much new information about his life; Professor Czeslaw Milosz, for his help in solving difficult problems of translation and for his own important critical work on Witkiewicz which was invaluable to us; Mr. Karol Laszecki and Mrs. Krystyna Tarasiewicz of *Radar* and Miss Celina Wysocka, for dedicated assistance in obtaining production photographs; Miss Aldona Pruchnicka of the Polish Centre of the International Theatre Institute, for generous aid in tracking down self-portraits and production photographs and for verifying performance dates; Professor Andrzej Wirth, for offering detailed and perceptive comments on all the translations and for directing *The Crazy Locomotive*; Mr. Erik Bauersfeld of KPFA and Professor William Sharp of Stanford University, for suggestions about *The Crazy Locomotive* as they were preparing it for radio and stage performance; Professor Bernard Dukore, for his careful reading and thoughtful discussion of all the translations; our friends and colleagues at San Francisco State College—Professor and Mrs. Joseph Axelrod, and Professors Richard Bratset, Donald Doub, Nello Carlini, Ruby Cohn, John Fell, Leon Katz, Richard Waidelich, Rudy Weingartner, Roger Williams—for suggestions and comments, many of which are now incorporated in the text; Mrs. Jadwiga Brady, for thorough checking of *The Shoemakers;* Mr. Laurence Southwick, for special assistance with *The Water Hen;* Mrs. Karolyn Durer and Mrs. Virginia Gerould, for their good offices throughout the project.

The English versions of the songs in *The Mother*, *They*, and *The Shoemakers* are by Eleanor Gerould, who also played an active role in the polishing and refining of all the translations.

Acknowledgment is made to the following periodicals in which several of the translations and some of the critical introductory material first appeared:

First Stage: The Madman and the Nun, "The Non-Euclidean Drama: Modern Theatre in Poland" (Winter, 1965–66); *The Water Hen*, "*The Water Hen:* Creation and Revolution" (Summer, 1967); *The Crazy Locomotive*, "Introduction to *The Crazy Locomotive*" (Winter, 1967–68).

Drama Survey: "On a New Type of Play" (Fall, 1967).

Permission of the editors of these periodicals, Henry F. Salerno of *First Stage* and John D. Hurrell of *Drama Survey*, is gratefully acknowledged.

A Note on the Names in Witkiewicz

The names in Witkiewicz' plays are often bizarre comic inventions, polyglot and cosmopolitan in tone and etymology, befitting representatives of the world of international depravity. We have attempted to reproduce this atmosphere by retaining Witkacy's names wherever they are intelligible and pronounceable in English and, in other cases, by creating new names along the lines suggested by the Polish. For example, in *The Madman and the Nun*, Grün and Walldorff remain unchanged, whereas in *The Water Hen*, Elżbieta Flake-Prawacka (*flaki* = tripe and *prawiczka* = virgin) becomes Elizabeth Gutzie-Virgeling.

Contents

Illustrations

Introduction

PROLOGUE: WITKIEWICZ AND
THE AVANT-GARDE

THE DISCOVERY of an unknown dramatist of major stature is an exciting process, particularly when it comes thirty years after his death and when the reasons for both his initial obscurity and his subsequent fame are curiously intertwined with the history of European drama and civilization in the twentieth century. In the case of Stanisław Ignacy Witkiewicz (1885–1939), there are reasons for unusual excitement that go beyond his importance to the theater.

Witkiewicz is one of the most amazing artistic geniuses and personalities of the modern period. His range and productivity are incredible; playwriting was only one of the many artistic careers in which he excelled. Painter, playwright, critic, aesthetician, novelist, philosopher, and authority on drugs—Witkiewicz was a Renaissance man of the avant-garde who threw himself into art and life with a flamboyance and a fury unmatched except perhaps by Strindberg. His personal drama was as bizarre and colorful as any of his portraits or plays. His fantastic life and tragic death make him an almost mythical prototype of the artist in the twentieth century, the hero of one of his own dramas.

His creative versatility is a main source of his theater's originality and vitality. Witkiewicz was a superb painter, and his theater is strongly oriented toward painting, a fact which liberates it from the purely literary and gives it tremendous visual vividness and immediacy. His plays are composed as pictures, by colors, shapes, and lines. Witkiewicz was able to bring the experimental daring of modern painting to the theater and break through the purely imitative surface of drama —one of the major aims of the avant-garde in European theater. His many-sided genius and wide-ranging curiosity enabled him to explode the normal boundaries of the theater and bring the drama into line with the other arts and intellectual developments of the modern age.

Witkiewicz is unique in his ability to combine successfully three aspects of twentieth-century avant-garde drama which are rarely found together: fantasy, dreams, and a sense of the mystery of existence; penetrating social and political vision about the workings of history; and, finally, a mocking, irreverent humor and grotesque style built on parody and irony. In other words, Witkiewicz treats revolution, political and scientific totalitarianism, and the collapse of mechanized Western civilization with the poetic atmosphere of Cocteau's *Orpheus* and the breakneck comic verve of the Keystone Cops. Witkiewicz' theater goes far beyond categories such as expressionism and surrealism; his great strength as a playwright lies in his synthesis of different kinds of experience, different genres, and different styles.

To portray an international world of insanity where duchesses and policemen, gangsters and surrealist painters, psychiatrists and locomotive engineers wander in and out, kill one another, and carry on philosophical conversations at the same time, Witkiewicz developed a dramatic technique equally mad and free, full of sudden discontinuity, jerky motions, anticlimaxes, nonsequiturs, chases, free-for-alls, and rapidly accelerated tempos, as in a silent film.

Witkiewicz is a thoroughly original and underivative playwright. His "comedies with corpses," as he called them, present fantastically ludicrous visions of the violent self-destruction of mechanized Western civilization. Now Witkiewicz takes his place along with Strindberg, Alfred Jarry, and Artaud as one of the most original and powerful creative forces in the modern avant-garde theater, although his life ended in violent self-destruction and seeming total defeat. His triumph over oblivion has only been posthumous. Witkiewicz fought an endless battle with chaos, desperately trying to create something out of nothingness before it overpowered him. He lost—at least at first, in one dimension.

CREATION AND REVOLUTION

Stanisław Ignacy Witkiewicz was born in Warsaw on February 24, 1885. He started life as a Russian subject, since at that time Poland did not exist as an independent country, and Warsaw belonged to the tsar. Fifty-four years later, on September 18, 1939, Witkiewicz committed suicide as the new Polish state, a creation of Woodrow Wilson and the Treaty of Versailles, collapsed in defeat after only twenty years of life, attacked from the West by the Germans and from the East by the Russians. Within this period Witkiewicz led a life of the most frenzied artistic activity, trying to create against the chaos without and within that menaced him.

WITKIEWICZ, FATHER AND SON

His birthright was that of an artist. Helena Modjeska, the famous Polish actress who made her later career in America, was his godmother. His mother, Maria Pietrzkiewicz, was a music teacher, and his father, Stanisław Witkiewicz, a famous and influential painter, architect, and art critic—an aggressive exponent of realistic technique, celebrated for his dictum that it was better to paint a head of cabbage accurately than the head of Christ badly, no matter how devoutly. As a theorist, the elder Witkiewicz was opposed to patriotic historical subjects and helped to dispel hazy romantic notions about the nature of painting by his insistence on disregarding all that was extraneous to the work of art.

Disillusioned with the results of industrialism and in reaction against the positivists and positivism, the playwright's father advocated a return to the people and their culture and art. He was one of those responsible for discovering the beauty of the Tatra mountains south of Cracow and making them popular as scenic attractions. As an enthusiast for folklore, the elder Witkiewicz admired the picturesque qualities of the native peasant arts and crafts of the mountain region and introduced a new house design based on the highlanders' log cabins, called the Zakopane style of architecture after his favorite retreat in the Tatras which has since become an internationally known tourist resort. He found further outlet for his energies in mountain climbing, a sport which he popularized in Poland.

Stanisław Ignacy Witkiewicz was an only son, and the relationship between father and son was a close and friendly one. The father took great interest in his son's talents and actively promoted his career in the fine arts. For his part, young Witkiewicz always maintained intimate ties with his father. After Witkiewicz, senior, was forced to leave Poland and settle in Lovranno, Italy, in 1908 because of a tubercular condition, his son came to visit him frequently until his death in 1915.

However, the lasting effect of such a dominating, successful father on his less pragmatic son appears to have been something other than their externally harmonious relations would indicate. Their interests and attitudes to the world were diametrically opposed. The son was addicted to other ways of seeing and other forms of exercise than his father; he could not take things for what they are with his father's brisk, clear-sighted vision—he looked within and beyond. He could not abide the regional, the national, the exclusively Polish, and wanted to get out and see the world. He reacted against the peasant art and highlanders dear to his father's heart and regarded folklore with suspicion as a fraud devised by intellectual artists. In almost all his plays up to *The Shoemakers* in 1934, there is more of the atmosphere of tropical islands and the jungle than of the Tatra mountains.

To the end of his life, Stanisław Ignacy Witkiewicz remained the son of a more famous father, both in his own eyes and in the eyes of society. Early in life, he created the name Witkacy to distinguish himself from his father; he painfully felt the necessity to be great in his own right and the need to create a life and art of his own. He adored his mother and may have resented his father's treatment of her.[1] The family plays like *The Water Hen* and *The Mother* reflect these complexities and suggest that when Witkacy wrote, he tapped his deepest feelings about his father.

In 1890, when Witkacy was five years old, the family settled in Zakopane permanently for the sake of the elder Witkiewicz' health. Until the end of his life, Witkacy considered the small mountain retreat his home, the place to which ultimately he returned after his many travels. He remained the *enfant terrible* of Zakopane for the rest of his life, terrifying tourists with his striking appearance and his eccentric behavior.

Since in these early days there was no school in Zakopane, Witkacy was educated privately at home by a whole circle of tutors, usually friends of his father from the artistic and literary community. He was exposed to everything and allowed to pursue all that interested him. He never did receive methodical schooling or acquire academic discipline; he was self-taught as writer, painter, and philosopher, more an uncontrolled force of nature than a product of technical training. His lack of formal education simply served to heighten his vast intellectual curiosity and to increase his hunger for things of the mind. Insatiability was to become one of the key concepts in his philosophy of art and of life. As a child he was insatiable in his pursuit of knowledge in all fields.

His father's library and studio, his mother's piano and musical scores, and the circle of family friends, were his true education. As the only son of culturally eminent parents, Witkacy was brought up almost exclusively in the company of adults, for the most part artists and intellectuals. From an early age he listened to their talk and participated in it himself. He was raised in an atmosphere where he was special, where his talents could develop freely, where he could become an artist. His friends and contemporaries made up a remarkable group of the best talents of the time, many of whom were soon to gain fame far eclipsing his: the composer Karol Szymanowski, the pianist Artur Rubinstein, the anthropologist Bronislaw Malinowski, and the painter and philosopher Leon Chwistek.

Young Witkacy was a prodigious reader; as a child, he was allowed to read whatever he wanted, encouraged and helped by his father. He was first exposed to Shakespeare at a time when his father was working on an essay on *Hamlet;* the impact on his young imagination was

[1] Zbigniew A. Grabowski, "S. I. Witkiewicz: A Polish Prophet of Doom," *The Polish Review*, XII, No. 1 (Winter, 1967), 43.

obviously strong—his plays are full of Shakespearean quotations, references, parodies, and parallels, ranging from the appearance of Richard III as a major character in *The New Deliverance* to the description of Jeanne Cackleson, the railway guard's wife in *The Crazy Locomotive*, "dressed all in white, decked out in flowers like Ophelia."

His childhood interests were not confined to the arts; he was a voracious reader of scientific works as well. Once one of his aunts stopped at Cracow, on her way to Zakopane, to buy the young Witkacy a present. She had decided to give her precocious nephew a popular book on the natural sciences, but the owner of the bookstore told her that she had better buy a specialized, scholarly study instead, since Staś had already consumed all the elementary works. His plays reflect his interest in science, especially the revolutionary discoveries of modern mathematics and physics which have changed our ways of seeing and understanding the world. Occasionally, as in *Tumor Brainard* (1921), instead of an artist, a mathematician as original as Einstein becomes the defiant hero-genius at odds with society.

Another type of reading furthered young Witkacy's imaginative journeys out of the world around him into other possible worlds of adventure and daring. From the number of references in his works, it would appear that *Treasure Island* and *Robinson Crusoe* were two of his favorite books. A childhood fascination with pirates, a mysterious island, and its dangerous games carries over into Witkacy's creative life as a playwright and becomes a model for his view of society. He retains his child's sense of fantasy and wonder about the strange and sinister operations of the international world of crime and debauchery which he invents as his Europe.

Robinson Crusoe offers Witkacy another key image: man alone on his desert island, confronted with himself and a hostile outside world —the terrifying adventure of being alive. Speaking of their engine-island, the engineer in *The Crazy Locomotive* tells his fireman: "We're on our desert island again: Robinson Crusoe and his man Friday. We're playing the Robinson game the way we did when we were children." H. G. Wells and Jules Verne provided another kind of travel, into the world of the future and of scientific technology which was to obsess Witkacy and become one of the major themes in his drama and fiction.[2] From childhood on he was in search of other worlds and other islands.

Art was his principal means, and Witkacy began to engage in artistic creation very early. He started to paint under his father's tutelage, and by the time he was eight he had already written many plays, of which five very short examples survive. Witkacy's juvenile dramas

[2] Czeslaw Milosz, "S. I. Witkiewicz, a Polish Writer for Today," *Tri-Quarterly*, No. 9 (Spring, 1967), p. 150.

could be called a child's theater of the absurd. They reveal a number of traits characteristic of his mature dramaturgy: bizarre titles, subtitles, and names of characters; wildly accelerated action; fantasy and the grotesque; ludicrous dialogue; and concern with philosophical issues. In *Comic Scenes from Family Life*, an ironic picture of the Witkiewicz home life, puppetlike characters speak in clichés comparable to the language in the first draft of Ionesco's *The Bald Soprano*.[3] Scene I opens on the porch as Mrs. Dungly enters:

> MAMA Good morning.
> MR. DUNGLY Quite a storm we're having!
> MAMA Yes, indeed! (*Enter Papa*)
> PAPA Good morning.
> MRS. DUNGLY Good morning. Well, I really must be going now.
> PAPA Couldn't I lend you an umbrella? (*Mama and Papa go to get the umbrella.*)
> MRS. DUNGLY Well, yes, thank you.
> MAMA I'll get it for you.
> PAPA It is raining. (*Exit Mrs. Dungly. Thunder and lightning*)[4]

In *Menagerie, or the Elephant's Prank*, the elephant misbehaves and attempts to take advantage of the lion, ape, and wolf, but is punished at the end and weeps penitently. *Cockroaches* is a play of terror tracing the reactions of the characters to the impending invasion of the castle by a swarm of cockroaches. *Princess Magdalena and the Overinsistent Prince* can be seen as a further, oblique comment on Witkacy's relations to his parents. It is a drama of thwarted love due to the opposition of the lovers' parents. King Wistilius' son commits suicide in despair, followed shortly by his father who has caused all the trouble. The play is an instant *Romeo and Juliet* in which everything happens with great rapidity. The son quotes Juliet's words, "O happy dagger! / This is thy sheath; there rust, and let me die," as he kills himself, in a combination of parody and unwitting prophecy.

Witkacy's first and last official sign of systematic study was the high-school diploma he was awarded in Cracow in 1903 on the basis of special examinations for nonattending students. Following his father's wish to make him a painter, Witkacy studied in a desultory fashion from 1904 to 1905 at the Cracow Academy of Fine Arts, where he was an unreceptive pupil. In his own painting and in his own theories, he rejected his father's ideal of fidelity to physical reality in favor of extreme distortion and inner truth. He preferred to paint fantastic por-

---

[3] Anna Micińska, "S. I. Witkiewicz, Iuvenilia," *Dialog*, No. 8 (August, 1965), p. 16.

[4] S. I. Witkiewicz, "Komedie z życia rodzinnego" ("Comic Scenes from Family Life"), *Dialog*, No. 8 (August, 1965), pp. 17–18.

traits rather than submit to the academy's discipline and stress on diligent copying. Whereas Witkiewicz the father battled against romanticism in the name of truth, the son declared war on realism and naturalism and all that is rational, symmetrical, and predictable.

From this point on Witkacy began a career of frenzied artistic activity—insatiable pursuit of form, as he called his never-ending search for the essence and the absolute. He soon abandoned landscape painting, which was his father's preferred genre; the son felt that competition with nature was both naïve and impossible as an artistic goal. Undoubtedly competition with his father seemed equally futile. In his portraits Witkacy attempted to portray his subject's inner self and penetrate into the subconscious. His art is a revelation of what lies beneath the surface of appearance and convention. In both painting and theater, Witkacy takes joy in ripping off masks; startling disclosure of hidden identity is one of his favorite dramatic techniques. "And now let's take off our masks" becomes the cry aboard *The Crazy Locomotive;* the engineer turns out to be Prince Tréfaldi, king of murderers, and his fireman, Travaillac, "sought in vain by the police all over the world."

Witkacy was a strikingly handsome man: tall, lean, with penetrating eyes and an intense, haunted look. Volatile and moody by nature, he swung between ecstasy and despair; he loved extremes and wanted all or nothing. An eccentric and a dandy, colorful, unpredictable, impossible to get along with, Witkacy was an individualist of gigantic proportions, an anarchist, a child in an alien world. Women adored him. "He was beautiful like an Archangel with those gray-green eyes of his. When he entered a cafe, my knees shook. And I guess all the women felt the same." These were the impressions of someone who knew him in Zakopane before the First World War.[5]

In his many self-portraits painted in a variety of different styles, the artist presents himself as demonic or demented. In a characteristic Mephistophelean pose, sharp, vicious lines create devilish brows, pointed ears, and a lean, fierce face. The eyes are almost squinting; a sinister hand with long, bony fingers dominates the foreground. In other, later self-portraits, Witkacy takes off this mask and reveals the anguish beneath. A shattered expression, crushed eyes, and terrible suffering emerge from a few rapidly drawn lines.

JOURNEYS TO OTHER WORLDS

Most important for Witkacy's development as an artist and philosopher were his travels outside of Poland—to the art museums of West-

[5] Czeslaw Milosz, "S. I. Witkiewicz, a Polish Writer for Today," p. 144.

ern Europe, to the South Sea Islands, and to Saint Petersburg at the time of the Revolution. The imaginary adventures of his childhood became real journeys of discovery.

Galleries

Witkacy's travels first opened his eyes to new ways of seeing and experiencing life and gave him the tools for portraying this vision. Not the Tatra mountains or the Cracow Academy of Fine Arts, but galleries in Paris were his inspiration both as a painter and as a playwright. In frequent trips to France, Germany, and Italy in the period before the First World War, Witkacy discovered the revolutionary movements in modern art that were rejecting naturalism and impressionism for abstraction. He visited the Gauguin exhibition in Vienna in 1907, seeing firsthand the works of an artist whose interest in the South Sea Islands anticipates Witkacy's own fascination with the primitive and exotic and whose rejection of Western civilization and its naturalistic tradition was congenial to his own point of view.

In Paris in the period from 1905 to 1913, Witkacy was exposed to the Fauves, the Futurists, and early cubism. His enthusiasm for the Fauves and for early Picasso is reflected in *They* (1920), one of his many plays devoted to art. The distortion, flat patterns, and violent colors of the Fauves indicate the direction that Witkacy himself was to take in his mature work both in painting and in the drama. His theater grows directly out of what he saw in the galleries in Paris; the inspiration of his dramas is pictorial, not literary. Because he was the dramatist as painter, he succeeded at a very early date in creating a nonrealistic dramaturgy based on a full-fledged and coherent nonrepresentational theory of the drama. Witkacy's work as a playwright springs directly from his experience of discovering Gauguin, Matisse, Derain, Picasso, and the other revolutionary masters of modern art, and from his own work as a painter and aesthetician.

Australia

Before becoming established as a painter in the period between the two world wars, Witkacy undertook two more trips that had far-reaching influence on his development as an artist and as a thinker. His next journey was to the South Seas with Bronislaw Malinowski, his childhood friend from Cracow who at the age of thirty was beginning his illustrious career as an anthropologist which would ultimately bring him to the United States in 1938 and a position at Yale University where he is buried. In the spring of 1914, the British Association for the Advancement of Science sent Malinowski to Australia and then to Papua (New Guinea) to work among the Mailu people, as a guest at the expense of the Australian government. Witkacy accompanied his friend in the capacity of photographer and draftsman.

The trip had been suggested and arranged by Witkacy's mother as a voyage of convalescence and recuperation from the tragic experiences of the preceding year. In 1913 his fiancée committed suicide, and he came down with typhoid. The expedition, which went via India, Ceylon, and the Malayan archipelago, was not always restful. There were endless quarrels and misunderstandings between Witkacy and Malinowski, neither of whom was willing to compromise or adapt to the other's stubbornness. By the outbreak of the war, the two friends had finally broken with one another for good, and Malinowski later recorded his anger and resentment in his diary:

> The Staś problem torments me. In fact his conduct towards me was impossible. . . . His complaints were unjustified, and the way he expresses himself precludes any possibility of reconciliation. *Finis amicitiae*. Zakopane without Staś! Nietzsche breaking with Wagner. I respect his art and admire his intelligence and worship his individuality, but I cannot stand his character.[6]

Their disagreements were often comic, the petty bickering of geniuses. One of these squabbles took a bizarre turn and had unforeseen complications as grotesque as in a Witkacy play and a surprising comic denouement like one of his own *coups de théâtre*. During a journey through the wilds of Australia, they came unexpectedly to the shores of a lake that cut off their projected route. They would have to skirt the lake in order to resume their cross-country travels, but, faced with the decision of whether to go to the right or the left, they simply could not agree. After a heated argument, they stubbornly insisted on their original positions and decided to split up temporarily, go their separate ways, and meet on the other side of the lake.

Malinowski was delayed in reaching the meeting place and therefore grew alarmed when he got there and found no trace of Witkacy. The anthropologist searched the surrounding bush, where he came upon a group of excited natives chanting and shouting. Malinowski's fears increased when he drew nearer and saw that the aborigines had a white man tied between two poles, stark naked, and that they were holding him high up over a small bonfire. When he recognized his friend Witkacy as the victim about to be roasted, Malinowski reached for his gun, but the next moment Witkacy yelled to him that the natives were helping him. On the trip around the lake, Witkacy had become cov-

---

[6] Bronislaw Malinowski, *A Diary in the Strict Sense of the Term* (New York: Harcourt, Brace & World, 1967), p. 34.

ered with ticks, and the natives with whom he quickly made friends were giving him the traditional heat treatment to get rid of ticks.

In such ways Witkacy acquired a taste for the exotic which is reflected in the descriptions of jungles and tropical scenery that occur in many of his plays and that he actually utilizes as the setting for several of his works. *Mister Price, or Tropical Madness* (1920) takes place in Rangoon where a heat wave drives the Europeans out of their minds, and *Metaphysics of a Two-headed Calf*, "A Tropical-Australian Play in Three Acts" (1921), has as its setting the royal governor's mansion in British New Guinea. The virility of the primitive races is contrasted with the decadence and intellectual dishonesty of the white Europeans. Although Witkacy always considered himself one of the last of an effete dying race, his energy and vitality gave him strength more in keeping with his picture of primitive man than with his own decadent heroes.

Witkacy's travels to the South Sea Islands had an effect beyond providing an exotic setting for several of his plays. His glimpses of the aborigines and the coral reefs and his personal contact with primitive societies influenced all his thinking about man's culture. Witkacy's attitudes to life and society are something experienced and felt, not simply intellectualized.

His anthropological journey with Malinowski enabled Witkacy to see Western civilization from the outside and to approach its customs and its natives as something as strange as anything New Guinea could offer. Subsequently Witkacy draws analogies between the petty tribal chieftains of the Papuans and the rulers of Europe and studies the common origins of strongmen and power politics the world over. From the perspective of the Australian bush, he perceives the relativity of all values and all ethical systems—civilization is simply a game. "Ethics is only the consequence of a large number of people thinking the same way. A man on a desert island wouldn't have any notion of what it means," the hero of *The Water Hen* declares.

A tribal squabble in another hemisphere at the opposite end of the world, the outbreak of the First World War on July 28, 1914, brought the expedition with Malinowski to a premature end. As an Austrian subject, Malinowski was interned in Australia and was then allowed to proceed with his anthropological studies. Despite the fact that the elder Witkiewicz had moved from Warsaw to Zakopane in the Austrian sector twenty-four years before, neither he nor his son had ever changed from Russian to Austrian citizenship. Witkacy was sent from Australia to Saint Petersburg; and here begins the third and by far the most important of his travels—the journey to Russia and through the Revolution.

Russia

Although only sons were exempt from military service in Russia at that time, Witkacy entered an officer's training school to avoid having to serve as an ordinary soldier later on when there was general conscription. Further, still stunned by his fiancée's suicide, he seemed indifferent to whatever happened to him and readily threw himself into the turmoil around him. Through an uncle's influence, he was commissioned an infantry officer in a regiment of the Imperial Life Guard. He was sent to the front in 1915, wounded at the battle of Molodechno, and decorated for bravery.

Witkacy remained in Russia until after the armistice and the formation of the new independent Polish state in 1918. He experienced many of the crucial events of the Russian Revolution firsthand, "swimming in the black sea of a mob gone mad," and witnessed the creation of a revolutionary new society, as he had previously seen the creation of revolutionary new art in Paris. Creation and revolution—these are the two poles on which everything revolves for Witkacy: the destruction of the old, the ceaseless change and flux, the endless battle to create something new out of the void. From the Papuans to the Bolsheviks, from Australia to Saint Petersburg—such sudden displacements and strange juxtapositions of violent experience could not but deepen the sense of metaphysical wonder at the plurality of phenomena which Witkacy felt was the essence of life and art. From the bonfire in Australia to the larger flames in Petersburg, Witkacy circled the globe in such a way as to make men seem insects in relation to infinity. "People are like insects, and Infinity surrounds them and summons them in a mysterious voice," observes the precocious small son in *The Water Hen.*

The Russian journey was rich in experience. More astounding even than the adventure with the ticks and the aborigines—and a further proof of his popularity with "natives"—was the fact that Witkacy was elected political commissar by the soldiers of his regiment after the revolution had started. He lived through one of the crucial moments of history from both sides; the collapse of the Russian Empire became his model for the disintegration of the whole world that he knew and of which he was a part. As an officer in the Tsarist army, Witkacy heard the last gasps of the *ancien régime;* then, as political commissar, he watched the subterranean forces burst forth from below.

The effect of these experiences on his art is incalculable. In virtually all his plays Witkacy portrays a crumbling world perched on a volcano or on an earthquake fault; tottering from the start, ready to collapse at the slightest push, this old order is doomed and dangerous. As the play unfolds, the tension mounts; the first tremors are felt, the eruption begins, and by the end of the last act there is either chaos or something new and frightening thrust up out of the upheaval. The excitement of a Witkacy play springs from the fact that history, both personal and world, is out of control; it works by dynamite.

> Everything in history has to blow up and can't move smoothly into the future along the well-greased tracks of reason. . . . No one individual is going to come up with a new utopia—the new social order will come about all by itself, by spontaneous combustion, explosion, eruption, forged out of the dialectical struggle of everyone's guts in the human boiler; we're sitting on the lid [*The Shoemakers*].

During his time in the fashionable regiment of the Imperial Guard, Witkacy threw himself into the decadent life of the upper classes and participated in the last days of the old depravity and intellectualism. He experimented with life and with art, taking cocaine and peyote for the first time and becoming involved in the excitement over abstract art. In Moscow he saw more Picasso. He began studying philosophy and aesthetics seriously and started to formulate his own ideas about modern art. He painted portraits of his fellow officers in the regiment and soon was selling them to make money for the expenses such a life entailed.

At the same time, Witkacy saw the rottenness and inequities of this world and knew that the masses would tear it down and reduce everything to the same level. He had long believed that Western civilization was in its final stages and that revolution was necessary and unavoidable, but that its tragic corollary was the subordination of the individual to society and the coming "dusk of mechanized grayness." The Russian Revolution convinced him that the greatest happiness of the greatest numbers meant total social conformity, and with it the end of the world to which he belonged and the destruction of the individual. For the author of *The Shoemakers*, the only hope for mankind lies in the regeneration of all of society and of the entire human race—the creation of a new species of man.

Yet despite his contempt for the new anthill society and his worship of individuality, Witkiewicz never romanticized the past or idealized strong men of any age; he was not a believer in an aristocratic elite or in fascist or totalitarian techniques for regenerating mankind. He remained skeptical and ironic about schemes for the rapid transformation of mankind, although he was sympathetic to radical change and felt it was necessary if man was to survive. If he was hostile to communism and feared its leveling effects, he despised the existing regime and regarded liberal democracy as a fraud and capitalism as a cancer on the body politic.

In his personal attitudes and behavior, Witkacy was generous and free from religious and racial prejudice. In the 1930's he befriended the Jewish writer Bruno Schulz, whose work he influenced, and helped him get his stories published. Nor was Witkacy a snob; his natural informality and man-to-man directness obliterated class distinctions. After he completed *The Shoemakers*, he read the play aloud to a group of specially invited guests: his maid, two neighborhood shoemakers, and a couple of young university students, one of whom was Jan Kott. As for the superman, the hero of *The Cuttlefish* (1922) exposes the fraudulent pose of his antagonist Hyrkan IV and kills him just before the play ends.

> You're only great given the extremely low level of civilization in your country. Nowadays Nietzsche's superman can't be anything more than a small-time thug. And those who would have been rulers in the past are the artists of our own times. Breeding the superman is the biggest hoax I've ever heard of.

Witkacy maintained a dialectical view of the relation between the individual and society which is one of his strengths as a dramatist, even if it led him to a position of despair and defeat in his personal views. He can argue both sides and be critical of each, seeing the defects of each position: on the one hand, the arrogant individualist isolated in his power and privilege, and, on the other, the faceless millions reduced to so many cogs and spokes in the wheels of society, which turn without their conviction or consent.

Out of these unresolved and unresolvable oppositions grows Witkacy's apocalyptic vision of life: there are no choices left, there is no way out. In *The Anonymous Work*, "Four Acts of a Rather Nasty Nightmare" (1921), the hero Plazmonik cannot identify with either side in a revolution that is neither entirely right or entirely wrong and decides to go back to prison and spend the rest of his days there: "In our times there are only two places for metaphysical individuals, prison or the insane asylum."

Witkacy is a product of the Russian Revolution. As a result of his personal and historical experiences, he acquired a prophetic sense of the ideological conflicts that came to dominate European history in the next forty years and still obsess us today. "I like you because of the seismograph you carry around in your head," the locomotive engineer Tenser tells his fireman Nicholas in *The Crazy Locomotive;* "you don't even know it's there, but all the time it's recording obscure tremors." Witkacy had a seismograph in his head attuned to the tremors of history. He had a terrible presentiment of the disaster and catastrophe that would overtake all of Europe; in his plays and novels he foresaw the future as dissolution and destruction.

CREATION

Witkacy the artist was born in revolutionary Russia.[7] His creativity as a painter and writer bursts forth like an explosion as a result of living through that shattering upheaval. When he returned home from his Russian journey in 1918, he came back to a new creation—Poland, a country which had not existed for over a hundred years and had only now become a modern state as a result of the Treaty of Versailles. From this point on, the ex-Russian officer and commissar became Witkacy, superartist from Zakopane, turning out dozens of plays, paintings by the cartload, hundreds of articles on art, literature, and philosophy, two vast novels, an original aesthetic theory of painting and theater, an existentialist philosophy, and miscellaneous writings on demonism and drugs. In the period between the two wars—from the time he was thirty-two years old until his self-inflicted death at the age of fifty-four—Witkacy produced a series of improvised masterpieces in the many genres and forms of art which he pursued simultaneously. He began his productive career relatively late, after years of dissipation and adventure, and even then he was unable to settle down to any one art, but threw himself into all at once. Like Leon in *The Mother,* he remained something of a willful dilettante, a type he defended in an age of overspecialization.

A Theater of Amateurs

From 1918 to 1926 Witkacy devoted much of his energies to the theater and to the theory of the drama, writing over thirty plays and developing an original poetics. His fertility is astounding. In 1920 he wrote at least five plays, including *They,* and in 1921 he increased his production to at least six, of which *The Water Hen* is the most famous. It is impossible to be sure exactly how many plays Witkacy actually wrote since most of them remained only in manuscript and many were lost during the ravages of the Second World War.

Of the thirty plays Witkacy wrote during this eight-year period, only seven were ever published in his lifetime, and the dozen or so that were staged were given occasional performances, most often by amateurs, and received little favorable critical comment. We know by title only eleven plays which were presumably destroyed in the holocaust; others have been discovered and recovered due to the efforts of Kon-

---

[7] Andrzej Mencwel, "Witkacego jedność w wielości" ("Witkacy's Unity in Plurality"), *Dialog,* No. 12 (December, 1965), p. 85.

stanty Puzyna, who brought out the first edition of Witkacy's plays in 1962. *Sluts and Butterflies*, "A Comedy with Corpses in Two Acts" (1922), turned up for the first time as late as 1958; the text of *The Crazy Locomotive* (1923) had to be pieced together from two different French translations since the Polish original is lost; and *The Terrible Tutor* (1920) survives in only two of four acts. The thought that one of the lost plays (with titles like *A Superfluous Man, Hangover,* and *The Baleful Bastard of Vermiston*) may still be found in an attic somewhere in the south of Sicily or in an old sea chest in a fishing ship off the coast of Madagascar is an intriguing Witkacian possibility.

Except by a coterie of friends, Witkacy was not taken seriously as a dramatist in his own time, but rather was regarded as an eccentric dilettante and decadent practical joker out to *épater les bourgeois* with absurd titles, preposterous characters and settings, and wildly incoherent plots and dialogue. Witkacy attempted to stage some of his own plays in Zakopane and established the Formist Theater in the ballroom of the Sea Watch, the most expensive hotel in town. However, the local paper, the *Voice of Zakopane,* and the public at large were hostile to these efforts. The casts were amateur, and Witkacy himself designed the scenery and directed. A contemporary has described the spirit of these productions:

> Witkacy's theater was amateur in the true sense of the word. Those who acted in it were dentists and painters, government weather forecasters, that is, employees of the National Meteorological Institute, and women with green eyes. Most important of all were those who spoke Polish with difficulty, with an English, Byelorussian, or Russian accent.[8]

In 1926 the actors in a Warsaw theater simply refused to take part in the production of *Tumor Brainard,* and the play had to be withdrawn. Witkacy's theater was appreciated only by a few of the most intelligent critics, notably by Tadeusz Boy-Żeleński, the poet, critic, and translator who is mentioned a number of times by Witkacy in *The Shoemakers.* Boy characterized Witkacy's theater as metaphysical buffoonery and supercabaret, presenting the sadness, boredom, and despair of modern civilization with a spasmodic laugh. However, most audiences found the plays incomprehensible and the author mad or at least on the verge of madness. As a playwright, Witkacy was a quarter of a century ahead of his time; not until after the revolution brought about by Beckett and Ionesco in the 1950's did such a vision and such dramaturgy become acceptable to even the sophisticated spectator.

[8] Rafał Malczewski, quoted in Konstanty Puzyna, "Nota" ("Appendix"), in *Dramaty,* by S. I. Witkiewicz (Warsaw: Panstwowy Instytut Wydawniczy, 1962), II, 638–39.

Toward the end of the 1920's, discouraged by lack of understanding, Witkacy virtually abandoned playwriting, returning to drama for the last time in the mid-thirties with *The Shoemakers*, a work more somber in outlook than his other plays, and different in technique. Witkacy complained bitterly and blamed both the public and the critics for their stupidity.

> In my opinion the position of artists here in our country is, with a few exceptions, extremely bad. The basic attitude of our society toward those who create something new in art is hostile. If they are not treated as enemies (supposedly) of all constructive patriotic social values, and as enemies of art (conceived as realism) which really isn't art at all, they are at best treated as harmless buffoons who can at least be ridiculed. The blame for this must also fall on the shoulders of the critics who are not at all interested in artistic problems and who don't want to learn anything about them, as can be shown by the reaction to my theoretical works (*New Forms in Painting* and *Aesthetic Sketches*) and the controversy about my book entitled *The Theater*. Putting aside for the moment the question of the critics' lack of training in aesthetics, their greatest fault is their inability to follow an argument logically, which makes it impossible to carry on a discussion with them and renders the fight fruitless. In the old days a Polish artist could at least count on his death to bring him recognition. But since the death of Tadeusz Miciński, who was forgotten in spite of it, it is clear that such a comparatively speaking risky experiment does not have the desired results any more.[9]

Tadeusz Miciński was a symbolist poet and expressionist dramatist and novelist, whose plays and novels with their imaginative mixture of different epochs and countries had great influence on Witkacy. They were both in Russia during the war and visited art galleries together. Witkacy refers to Miciński and his play *Basilissa Teophan* (1909) frequently in his own works, and Miciński's bizarre death and lack of recognition haunted him and served as an example of the grotesque workings of the world: Miciński was killed in 1918 in Russia, as he was returning home, by an irate mob who took him for a tsarist general.

The S. I. Witkiewicz Portrait-Painting Firm

Even during the period of Witkacy's greatest creativity in the drama, it was not as a playwright that he was best known, but as a painter and aesthetician. While rapidly tossing off thirty plays as an amateur, he made his living as a portrait painter and devoted his professional energies to art. Here he was even more productive than in

[9] "Interview with S. I. Witkiewicz," *Wiadomości Literackie* ("Literary News"), No. 15, 1924. Quoted in the program of Teatr Polski, Warsaw, No. 24, season 1965–66, p. 8.

the drama, regarding much of his work in painting not as art, but simply as a job and a means of earning his living. His total output in landscapes and portraits probably runs into the thousands. In 1916 alone, while he was in Saint Petersburg and discovering what a profitable business painting could be, he is reputed to have turned out over two hundred portraits at the same time that he was carrying out his duties as an officer. The large exhibition of his paintings in Cracow in 1967 consisting of 261 canvases and drawings showed only a fraction of his work. Many of the portraits were lost during the Second World War, others have never been identified, and still others are scattered about the world in private homes from Warsaw to Berkeley, California.

His portraits became popular with the well-to-do, especially in Cracow and Warsaw, and the demand was great. From 1923 Witkacy approached much of his portrait painting as a money-making industry, and he finally printed a prospectus called *The Rules of the S. I. Witkiewicz Portrait-Painting Firm* (Warsaw, 1928, reissued in 1932), setting down the regulations governing those who commissioned him to paint their portraits. The Firm's motto was: "The customer must be satisfied. Misunderstandings are unimaginable."

The always-satisfied customers were required to make a down payment, usually one third of the total fee, before work on the portrait was begun, and to pay the rest when the portrait was completed. The number of sittings varied, but a great number of portraits were done by Witkacy at high speeds rivaling his own crazy locomotive. It was not at all unusual for him to finish a portrait in two or three hours. The Firm offered customers a choice among seven types of portraits, ranging from simple and complimentary to the sitter (Type A) to those containing more and more "character study" with accompanying deformation, elongation, and enhancement of particular features. Types C, C & Co, Et, C & H, C & Co & Et, and so on, were executed by the Firm with the help of quality narcotics, and the more expensive the drugs, the more expensive the portrait. The customer was free to choose whether he wanted a flattering portrait or a psychological study; even abstractions were available, as was feminine beautification that would make the subject appear more demonic.

According to the rules, the customer was not allowed to express any opinion about the work commissioned, although he was required to pay the fee whether he liked the finished product or not. Sometimes his customers, many of whom were wealthy society women, got into unpleasant quarrels with Witkacy when they found that their portraits were not sufficiently flattering and true to life. Faced with acrimonious protests, the painter either coaxed, remained utterly silent, or flew into a rage, depending on his mood. Paragraph 3 of the Firm's bylaws was designed to prevent such scenes, but did not always succeed.

> Any kind of criticism on the part of the customer is *absolutely* ruled out. The customer may not like the portrait, but the Firm cannot permit even the slightest comment without a special dispensation. If the Firm had allowed itself the luxury of listening to the customers' views, it would have gone out of its mind a long time ago. WE PUT PARTICULAR STRESS ON THIS PARAGRAPH, SINCE IT IS EXTREMELY DIFFICULT TO RESTRAIN THE CUSTOMER FROM MAKING COMMENTS WHICH ARE REALLY QUITE UNCALLED FOR.

If the customer simply could not stand his completed portrait, he had the option of paying one third of the fee only and leaving the portrait behind as property of the Firm. What Witkacy wanted to avoid at all costs was too close human contact with his customers. As he explains in the final clause of Paragraph 3, "The Firm's nerves must be respected, considering how extremely difficult its job is." Paragraph 10 laid down further laws: "Customers have the obligation to show up for the sittings punctually, since waiting upsets the Firm and may have a negative influence on the execution of the work."

If Witkacy turned into the impersonal, legalistic Firm for his paying customers, a second group of people who sat for their portraits received a quite different kind of treatment. These were his friends and acquaintances, who did not have to pay anything for their pictures and who even had the right to argue with the painter about how he was depicting them. These friends simply donated their time to sitting for Witkacy and in return received free of charge not only a portrait, but hours of brilliant conversation full of characteristic Witkacian irony and self-depreciation.

In the first category of portraits, Witkacy was painting for money and turned out work that sometimes tended to be conventional and perfunctory; in the second category of paintings, he was working to please himself and his friends, and he felt free to indulge in experiments and to push creativity to its limits. In the mid-twenties Witkacy began to experiment with painting under the influence of drugs.

Nicotine, Alcohol, Cocaine, Peyote, Morphine, and Ether

Hundreds of the amazing portraits which he painted bear mysterious letters and numbers next to the signature; these symbols indicate the amounts and kinds of alcohol and drugs he took for each creative effort. Painting under the influence of drugs was one of Witkacy's many attempts to go beyond the normal bounds of everyday experience and to break through objective reality into the inner world of metaphysical feelings. The anguished distortion, terrifying colors, and broken lines of these portraits painted under the influence of drugs are uncontrolled plunges into the irrational. Like the surrealists at about the same time and Henri Michaux, André Masson, and many other artists since, Witkacy by his use of drugs as a creative stimulant wanted to bypass the will and intellect and tap the subconscious.

Witkacy may have needed drugs to go on creating at such an intense rate. In *The Madman and the Nun* (1923), the poet Walpurg explains why he took cocaine and morphine: "My nerves weren't strong enough to resist that damnable something or other that compelled me to write. I had to poison myself. I had to gain strength." Like Walpurg, Witkacy lived at the edge of his nerves, without any sense of moderation, not conserving his strength, but trying desperately to expend it to the full at every moment of his life. Drugs made it possible for him to live and create beyond the limits of his strength and to perceive the universe with heightened intensity. Narcotics were a liberation from normal vision, a mystical experience, a derangement of the senses that revealed inner reality—the world of Pure Form. Morphine and cocaine enabled him to depict, not the accurate head of cabbage his father championed, but a world of fantasy and madness.

Despite his experiments with drugs, Witkacy does not see the liberation they provide as anything but a dangerous delusion. As usual, he grasps both sides of the situation dramatically and presents the negative consequences with great force. Drug addiction figures in many of Witkacy's works whose heroes often hope to transcend reality and achieve instant happiness and perfection through narcotics and pills. In plays like *The Madman and the Nun* and *The Mother*, addiction is linked to insanity and ends in self-destruction. The cocaine party in *The Mother*, which leads to a disruption of normal spatial and temporal relationships and allows the characters a glimpse of a fourth dimension of reality, is presented as something grotesque and frightening—the vision it produces is a nightmare.

Rather than offering a solution to the overwhelming metaphysical questions: What sense does anything make? Why are things the way they are and not some other way? Who am I? Why do I exist?—drugs and pills simply lull our basic human anxieties to sleep like those other "drugs," the various social and political "isms," or else create still worse insatiability. Witkacy's interest in drugs and pills is again prophetic. Since all of life is becoming artificial and synthetic, he fears that the authentic human response to the universe will be replaced by the ersatz and automated. In *Sluts and Butterflies, or The Green Pill*, "A Comedy with Corpses in Two Acts and Three Scenes" (1922), one of the demonic heroines explains the new discovery: "Pills—that's the ultimate mystery . . . We have a new drug which creates such an awful insatiable craving that Messalina would be a perfect angel in comparison to the addicts who'll take it."

In this play the white race, civilized but impotent, has to resort to pills to survive; the savage primitive race of Mandelbaums (the cast of characters includes forty characters all named Mandelbaum, of various sizes and ages) living in the tropics proves superior to the degenerate, drug-addicted Europeans. Pills and drugs are mechanical substitutes designed to render unnecessary the genuine feelings, purposes, and beliefs which have been destroyed in the chaotic absurdity of twentieth-century civilization. In his works, Witkacy does not romanticize drugs or drug addicts, nor does he present pills and stimulants as the solution to the loss of meaning in our lives. These are at best desperate artifices, usually leading to disaster; at worst they can be sinister tools in the hands of the secret forces working to reduce mankind to mechanized docility.

Witkacy the drug addict is another aspect of the legend which he himself helped to perpetuate. In 1932 he published a book entitled *Nicotine, Alcohol, Cocaine, Peyote, Morphine, and Ether*, describing his experiences with drugs and stimulants and the advantages to be had from each. Cocaine appears to have been his favorite.

Pure Form

Throughout the 1920's, concurrent with his work as dramatist, painter, and novelist, Witkacy the critic and aesthetician was busy battling the artistic and cultural establishment and arguing for his own theory of Pure Form in painting and drama. He wrote dozens of polemic articles defending his own works and ideas for various literary weeklies and journals and developed his own aesthetic theory in *New Forms in Painting* in 1919, *Aesthetic Sketches* in 1922, and *An Introduction to the Theory of Pure Form in the Theater* in 1923.

Upon his return to Poland from Russia, Witkacy became a member of a group of painters and writers called the Formists. This group had an important influence on the development of Witkiewicz' aesthetic theory, especially Leon Chwistek and his doctrine of the plurality of realities, to which there are many references in the plays. Chwistek (1884–1944) was the son of a Zakopane doctor and, like his friend Witkacy, a genius of many talents. He was a mathematical logician, philosopher, aesthetician, essayist, and painter. His theory of realities, developed in *The Plurality of Realities* (1921) and *The Plurality of Realities in Art*, criticized the idea of a single, uniform reality and postulated four different realities: (1) the reality of natural objects; (2) the reality of matter as studied in physics; (3) the reality of impressions and appearances; and (4) the reality of images created by us. Applied to aesthetics, these four different realities produce four different kinds of art: (1) primitive art where each object is given its own basic primary color; (2) realism where the physical reality of a particular time and place is depicted; (3) impressionism in which sensations are treated psychologically; and (4) futurism or expressionism in which free images are fantastically created. According to Chwistek's theory of formism, the artist is only obliged to give perfect form to what he has created—each style is equally valid. The form, not the reality portrayed, is all that can be judged.

Witkacy's pure form is closely related to Chwistek's formism. Further, his plays are based on the notion of the plurality of realities and the corresponding modes of depicting each. Often a single play will shift from one reality to another and move from one style to another, taking the spectator on a jolting ride into new dimensions, as in *The Madman and the Nun* or *The Mother* in which we go from the psychological impressionism of the early acts to the fantastic expressionism of the denouements. The plurality of realities is also one of the prime sources of the metaphysical feeling of the strangeness of existence, attacking as it does the whole idea of one's own unity and identity.

Bafflement in the face of an inexplicable universe is the metaphysical feeling which Witkacy claimed the theater should arouse in the audience. In *An Introduction to the Theory of Pure Form in the Theater,* Witkacy proposes a new kind of play which will be liberated from the confines of imitating life and instead make a synthesis of all the elements of the theater—sound, setting, gesture, dialogue—for purely formal ends. Freed from the demands of consistent psychology and logic, the dramatist will be able to use his materials as the musician uses notes and the modern painter colors and shapes. The meaning of such a work lies in its internal construction, not in the discursive content of its subject matter. We are transported into an entirely new world that is free and unpredictable.

> On leaving the theater, the spectator ought to have the feeling that he has just awakened from some strange dream, in which even the most ordinary things had a strange, unfathomable charm, characteristic of dream reveries, and unlike anything else in the world.

Since human beings are the chief elements in drama, Witkacy maintained that theater can never be perfectly abstract like the pure arts of painting and music. The form may be pure, but the materials are the impure facts of life in the twentieth century. The elements of reality are present in Pure Form, but transposed into a new dimension. Ever since his Russian adventures, art was for Witkacy the expression of metaphysical feelings, and not the presentation of reality through either naturalistic means or symbols. Form and content were inseparable.

Witkacy's heretical views kept him constantly engaged in controversy. He was outspoken in his rejection of the two respected "isms" of his day, realism and symbolism. "I'm not condemning either realistic painting or realistic theater—I'm simply saying *it is not art*," he wrote in the *Zakopane Voice* in 1925 at a time when he was trying to stage his own plays in the local theaters.[10] The older generation totally failed to understand his position and regarded him as the brash, irresponsible son of a distinguished father.

It was not only Witkacy's views on art which aroused the hostility and suspicion, and sometimes the metaphysical wonder, of his elders and contemporaries. His life seemed an experiment in Pure Form. His demonic poses, his eccentric habits, and his disdain for social conformity made him the source of much curiosity and the subject of many anecdotes.

Signs over the door of his Zakopane apartment gave detailed information about exactly when he would receive different tradesmen and when he would see his friends: from 3:30 to 4:00 A.M. for his tailor, from 4:00 to 4:30 A.M. for the butcher, and so on. Apparently no one paid any attention to these rules, least of all Witkacy himself. When he did receive guests, he was often in his bathrobe or stark naked. He collected walking sticks that had belonged to famous men (perhaps his response to his father's hobby of mountain climbing) and love letters and other amorous materials. He had an album of what he called "curiosities," including mementos from Australia, an autographed picture of the young Artur Rubinstein, and Rita Sacchetto's garter. He was accused of being a sex maniac and of appearing drunk when he lectured on art, philosophy, and literature.

His dealings with his friends were often tempestuous. He assigned each of his friends a number to indicate where this individual stood in his esteem at any given moment, and he kept a running record of the standings. If a friend did something that displeased Witkacy, he would be informed that he had been dropped from position 17 to position 88 as punishment; other, temporarily favored friends would be advanced into more coveted places. Along with the rules of the Portrait Painting Firm and the signs above his door, Witkacy's ranking of his friends in a constantly shifting order of priority indicates his fondness for playing games. He also liked to stage situations in which total strangers would be brought together purposely so that he could guide the conversation along some previously planned and appropriately mysterious course

[10] Puzyna, "Nota," p. 638.

that would completely baffle the participants. He delighted in making private jokes when he was out in company, bewildering the majority of guests who had no idea what he was talking about.

His fondness for playing games and his desire to impose some bizarre personal order on the world, or perhaps to transform life into a game, are part of the fundamental inspiration for his plays and a source of their originality and spontaneity. Pure Form is another such invented system. In the Preface to his play *The Marriage* (1946) Witold Gombrowicz, who carries on the Witkacy tradition in both drama and fiction, refers to the world he is depicting as "this world of games and eternal artifices, of eternal imitations and mystifications." [11]

Witkacy never outgrew the world of games and mystifications. Rather than a source of weakness, his refusal to take the theater altogether seriously, his flippant attitude to his own medium, his indulgence in self-parody and self-irony, and his treatment of art as a stunt and an extended gag help to give his plays much of their contemporary flavor. In this respect his work has much in common with Jarry's *Ubu the King*, the schoolboy prank with which modern avant-garde drama starts.

Life and art have both become too preposterous to take seriously—they can only be treated as burlesque, parody, and mystification. At the end of *The Water Hen*, as grenades explode and machine-gun fire can be heard, the Father organizes a card game; in the face of protests from his friends, he explains: "It's the only way of whiling away the time during a social upheaval. What else could we do?"

Novels

By the latter half of the 1920's Witkacy had virtually abandoned the theater and pure form and created a new artistic role and personality for himself, that of novelist or rather antinovelist, since he regarded the novel as outside the realm of art and a kind of grab bag into which the most heterogeneous material could be stuffed. He had already written *Bung's Downfall 622 Times, or a Demonic Woman* in 1910, an unpublished and unfinished work. Now he produced two vast works of fantastic fiction, *Farewell to Autumn* (begun in 1925, published in 1927) and *Insatiability* (1930), both of which portray the collapse of Western civilization in nightmare visions of the future where the sexual, political, and philosophical are grotesquely intermingled.[12]

[11] Witold Gombrowicz, *Théâtre* (Paris: Julliard, 1965), p. 88. Gombrowicz refers to Witkiewicz and his theory of Pure Form in the Preface to *The Marriage*.
[12] We are indebted to Czeslaw Milosz' discussion of Witkiewicz' novels in *The Captive Mind*, chap. i, "The Pill of Murti-Bing" (New York: Alfred A. Knopf, 1963), pp. 3–24, and in "S. I. Witkiewicz, a Polish Writer for Today," pp. 143–54.

Witkacy was indeed insatiable in his pursuit of new artistic forms, and in the nonart form of the novel he found a perfect receptacle into which to pour satire, literary criticism, philosophical treatises, footnotes, personal invective, digressions of every sort, apocalyptic visions of disaster, and all kinds of verbal games, ironies, and parodies reducing the novel form itself to absurdity. The characters' names continue the multilingual anagrams and crossword puzzles found also in the cast of characters in the plays. The style is a bizarre mixture of philosophical language, polyglot puns, exaggerated grandiosity, invented words, and convoluted syntax. The world portrayed is the decadent artistic and intellectual circle on the verge of collapse; religion and philosophy are dead, art is growing more and more perverse and insane.

In *Farewell to Autumn,* two revolutions take place, the first bourgeois-liberal; the second, totalitarian, reducing all to the same level and bringing about universal grayness and social mechanization. The hero Atanazy Bazakbal, a would-be artist, comes home from India at the time of the revolution, becomes a petty functionary, and like Leon in *The Mother* becomes obsessed with the seemingly irreversible process of socialization which is destroying the individual and the mystery of life. After taking cocaine, he decides to escape across the mountains near Zakopane, but finally returns to alert others to their plight and to the necessity of doing something about it. He is shot at the border as a spy.

Insatiability presents an even more phantasmogoric picture of times to come, in which the world is divided up into warring factions dominated by different ideologies. Communist China is threatening to conquer all of Europe, having already taken over Russia. Witkacy's usual group of neurotic artists and demonic women suffers from a total sense of futility and metaphysical insatiability and is unable to do anything to resist the coming catastrophe. At this point, mysterious vendors start selling a magic pill, devised by the Malayan-Chinese philosopher Murti-Bing and called the Murti-Bing pill. The pill is a condensed form of the philosophy that has made the Sino-Mongolian army so successful; it brings perfect contentment and makes all metaphysical questioning disappear. More and more people take the pill and become converted to Murti-Bingism, which solves all their problems and lulls their anxieties. Ultimately the armies of the East occupy the West after the surrender of the Western general, and Murti-Bingism triumphs. The old neurotic heroes no longer write dissonant modern music but joyful marches and no longer paint abstractions but socially useful pictures, all under the auspices of the Ministry of the Mechanization of Culture.

Witkacy deplored all substitutes for metaphysics, whether a pill or a

materialistic totalitarian philosophy. Mankind looked for answers to the
basic questions about existence first in religion, then in philosophy and
art. Religion was dead, philosophy was dying. Only art survived to deal
with metaphysical questions, but, cut off from the once orderly picture
of the universe formerly supplied by religion and philosophy, art could
no longer be harmonious. As a substitute for religion and philosophy,
modern art was forced to go to greater and greater extremes and artists
were driven to madness in their quest to satisfy man's metaphysical
longings. Modern artists were the last spokesmen for the old world of
suffering from metaphysical anguish; soon they would be put into
insane asylums. Socialization would turn theaters into foundling homes
for retarded children. The new social order would make all mankind
happy, without religion, without philosophy, without art. These are
the two extreme positions: art grows more and more desperately mad;
the forces for social mechanization and conformity become more and
more powerful. Only philosophy could save mankind, and philosophy
was bankrupt.

> Every epoch has the philosophy it deserves. In our present phase we
> deserve nothing better than a drug of the most inferior kind, to lull to
> sleep our metaphysical anxiety which hinders our transformation into
> automatic machines.[13]

Philosophy and Shoemakers

Discouraged by lack of interest in and understanding of his theories,
plays, and novels, in the face of frustration and defeat and increasingly
disastrous forebodings of what was soon going to happen to civilization, Witkacy gradually withdrew from the world, abandoned literature, and devoted more and more of his time and energies to a new role
and a new game: philosophy. Like Edgar in *The Water Hen*, Witkacy
was a man always desperately searching for a new career and an
ultimate meaning: "I should have been somebody, but I never knew
what, or rather who." Philosophy more than art or anything else
seemed capable of providing answers and solutions.

Witkacy took philosophy more seriously than either fiction or
drama. He was fascinated by logic and logicians and corresponded with
many, both Polish and foreign, including men like Edmund Husserl
and Rudolf Carnap, and he attended many philosophical congresses.
Although his interest in philosophy went back to his stay in Russia and
he began working on his major philosophical work as early as 1917,
Witkacy only began to devote his full attention to the subject late in

---

[13] S. I. Witkiewicz, quoted by Czeslaw Milosz in "S. I. Witkiewicz, a Polish
Writer for Today," p. 146.

life, as a nonprofessional without any formal training and discipline. He was aware of his amateur status and commented on it ironically; in a lecture at Zakopane, attended by the local intellectual elite and visitors from Cracow and Warsaw, many of them professors, Witkacy called attention to the fact that he was a man without a university degree lecturing to professionals.

In academic and professional philosophical circles he was most often patronized as a self-taught dilettante, despite his vast reading in Russian, German, French, and English, as well as Polish. On the other hand, two important philosophers who knew Witkacy at this period, Tadeusz Kotarbiński and Roman Ingarden, esteemed him highly as a thinker. Ingarden points out that Witkacy was concerned with different issues from the technical logical problems with which Polish philosophy was preoccupied at that time.

> Why was Witkiewicz valuable in our philosophical milieu? Did he stand out by the range of his philosophical education? Was he better than the others by the precision of his reasoning and his exactness in formulating results? It seems to me that in these respects he was not an equal of his various peers, particularly those younger than himself, professionally trained philosophers from the Lvov or the Warsaw school. . . . And yet—this is my firm conviction—he was more of a philosopher than many of those who looked down their noses at him, treating him at best as a philosophizing literary critic, and not a scholar.[14]

Ingarden goes on to praise Witkacy as an existentialist philosopher long before Sartre.

> He was in all of this, in his fundamental position, an existentialist many years before the movement appeared in France, and was probably contemporary with Heidegger. But, so far as I know, he never read Heidegger. So far as phenomenologists are concerned, he knew only Husserl's *Logische Untersuchungen*, but the problems of the philosophical bases of logic he never considered essential, and he also had no understanding of phenomenological analyses. He differed from the French existentialists—despite his profound pessimism—because he had more elemental dynamism and primordial autogeny, and philosophically he had greater ambitions to create a complete metaphysical system.[15]

[14] Roman Ingarden, "Wspomnienie o Witkacym" ("My Reminiscences about Witkacy"), in *S. I. Witkiewicz, człowiek i twórca*, Commemorative Volume edited by Tadeusz Kotarbiński and Jerzy E. Płomieński (Warsaw: Panstwowy Instytut Wydawniczy, 1957), p. 173.
[15] *Ibid.*, p. 175 fn.

In 1935 Witkacy published his only book of philosophy, *Concepts and Principles Implied by the Concept of Existence,* which he had been working on for years and which represented the summation of his philosophical studies beginning at the time of the Russian Revolution. He continued writing articles on philosophical subjects and publishing widely in scholarly journals until his death.

Concepts and Principles is a work of technical philosophy in which Witkacy attempts to solve a whole series of philosophic problems— mostly metaphysical, but also epistemological—in a systematic way. His aim is to develop a single coherent system, and his essential position is pluralist, in the manner of Aristotle and somewhat reminiscent of John Dewey, rather than monistic (Spinoza, Hegel) or even dualist (Descartes). As a philosopher, Witkacy is fundamentally a realist, rather than an idealist. Although he uses the term "improved monadology," there is really little of Leibniz in *Concepts and Principles,* except for the pluralism, since there is interaction among existences. In his approach to philosophy, Witkacy is a talented eclectic attracted by the tough-minded, rather than by the romantic, tender-hearted philosophers.

Witkacy remained an amateur all his life in the sense that he cultivated philosophy and the arts to satisfy his own personal needs. He was bound to no one particular school of thought, nor to any single discipline. In everything he did he concerned himself with the fundamental problem of existence and its meaning, trying to encompass all the fields of human endeavor and to comprehend the totality of life.

From 1933, Witkacy lived more and more in isolation in the mountains at Zakopane where he pursued his work on philosophy. His only imaginative work from this period, *The Shoemakers* (1931–34), reflects his growing pessimism and sense of defeat. "A Theoretical Play with Songs," *The Shoemakers* is like his novels in spirit and technique, an abandonment of pure form for a more direct assault on the world around him by means of a fantastic hodgepodge of political and philosophical arguments, rhetoric, literary parody, comments on his friends, jokes in mock Russian, invented insults and obscenities, imaginary menus, and frightening prophecies of disaster.

Much more than the Pure Form plays, *The Shoemakers* reflects directly Witkacy's own times, the political situation in Poland, and the rise of totalitarian dictatorships in Europe. In his artistic development, Witkacy moves from the esoteric pursuit of pure form in art with its promise of a new cultural era to a bitter denunciation of the present which no art, pure or otherwise, can redeem, and which is culturally and politically doomed. His belief in the power of the human intellect to arrest the disastrous course of history has been destroyed by what he sees around him.

In *The Shoemakers* all causes and philosophies prove impotent and in their profusion cancel one another out; every belief contains its opposite, and parody and irony undermine faith in the very bases of life in such a world. The humor in Witkacy's last play has grown corrosive and self-destructive; *The Shoemakers* turns into a frightening mockery of everything, including the audience, the author, and the drama. A sign saying BOREDOM appears several times in the last act—the playwright is destroying the form of the drama, writing an antiplay that is the end of the line. Throughout his career, Witkacy had thrown himself desperately into creation as a battle against the void—like so many of his heroes, he had wanted to play himself out. Now he began to lose faith even in this possibility.

Witkacy's growing gloom was by no means simply a personal neurosis; he was concerned with deteriorating conditions in Europe and deeply disturbed by the spread of fascism. "What awaits us is one gigantic concentration camp," he predicted.[16] His whole life and work had been dedicated to individuality, freedom, creativity, and the expansion of the human mind; he saw that all of this would be destroyed and that he was powerless to do anything about it.

In late 1938, he was one of a group of distinguished guests at a private party in Warsaw. The occasion was the conferring of an honorary degree from a German University on a Polish scholar. At this time an intellectual flirtation was going on between the German ambassador von Moltke and some Polish intellectuals and university professors, and von Moltke was treated with much more deference than the state of affairs in Europe warranted. Witkacy listened to the billing and cooing as long as he could, and then turned to a friend next to him and said: "Either I'll have to get up and scream that this is disgraceful—or I'll have to go into the other room and take some cocaine." On the advice of his friend, Witkacy followed the latter course, impotent to stop the catastrophe he knew was coming soon by an outburst of temper, falling back on drugs to pacify his anger and anguish.

His friend Jerzy Płomieński, coeditor with Kotarbiński of the memorial volume of 1957 devoted to Witkiewicz, describes their last meeting in Zakopane toward the end of August, 1939, a few days before the war and only a few weeks before Witkacy's suicide. Witkacy was nervous and pessimistic; his face was haggard and gaunt. He

[16] Jerzy E. Płomieński, "Polski *pontifex maximus* katastrofizmu" ("The Polish *Pontifex Maximus* of Catastrophism"), in *S. I. Witkiewicz, człowiek i twórca*, p. 265.

pointed through the window toward the Tatra mountains and said that
he would have to leave all this very soon. He then began to talk about
the war that was imminent and dwelt at length on the horrors the war
would bring.

> You can't even imagine the kind of hell that's about to fall on our heads.
> Few of us will live through it. Not one stone will remain standing that
> our generation and our age knew as its own. We are a new Atlantis
> which the wild flood will engulf with all our theories, theories which
> failed to master life and discover its mysterious mechanism accurately
> enough, with all our hysterical forebodings of disaster, too refined and
> sterile, like all this decadent era of ours, a cursed era, with its
> *Schöngeist* hopelessly inadequate for man in the modern world. I feel I
> am nearing the end, together with this era.[17]

An aristocratic superman who ridiculed supermen and realized the
aristocracy had outlived its day, a Renaissance man who knew the Renaissance was long over, a prolific creator who did not believe in the
powers of creation, a flamboyant individualist who knew the individual
would be swallowed up in the social revolutions that must destroy the
rotten old order to institute the mechanized world of the future:
Witkiewicz was a tragic victim of his times, viewing even his own
self-irony ironically, with belief in neither past, present, nor future. For
almost fifty years he had driven himself to create, so as not to face the
ultimate horror, absurdity, and despair.

When the war broke out on September 1, 1939, Witkiewicz was in
Warsaw. Along with many others, he left the capital and moved
toward the eastern provinces where the second line of resistance was to
be organized against the Germans. On September 17, the Russians
crossed the border claiming the eastern provinces which before the
First World War had been part of the tsarist empire. On September
18, Witkiewicz killed himself; he took sleeping pills in a forest, woke
up and cut his wrists with a razor, against a magnificent natural background as in *Farewell to Autumn*.[18] His last words, spoken to a woman
who was with him at the end, were in Russian: *"Ya ne budu zhit' pod
merku"* ("I won't go on living as less than myself").

In his apartment in Warsaw he left behind a chest full of essays and
plays, all of which were presumably lost during the war when the city
was razed to the ground by the Germans. The title of one of these
plays destroyed during the holocaust was *The End of the World*.

---

[17] *Ibid.*, p. 264.
[18] Czeslaw Milosz, "S. I. Witkiewicz, a Polish Writer for Today," p. 153.

EPILOGUE

If the story ended there, it would be possible to say that Witkiewicz died a frustrated and tragic victim of his own and of his age's violent, self-destructive impulses. He would be nothing more than a might-have-been, who anticipated by a generation the theater of the absurd and the theater of cruelty, but who drew an unlucky number in the lottery of history and had the misfortune of being a Pole—he would never come into his own as an artist. In fact, for many years after his death it seemed highly improbable that his bizarre works would ever be anything but a curiosity for a select group of connoisseurs, especially in Poland after the socialist revolution.

However, Witkacy was never content with conventional tragic endings, and his own story has, like many of his own plays, a fantastic epilogue where the principal character, seemingly dead, comes back to life and proves to his disparagers that he is full of vitality. Like Walpurg, dead by his own hand, Witkacy suddenly re-enters with a yellow flower in his buttonhole to become a major force in the modern Polish avant-garde and from there to be recognized in Europe and America as one of the giants of twentieth-century experimental theater.

But it took another revolution to make this possible. As long as socialist realism held sway in Poland, Witkiewicz remained a forgotten figure, but with the October revolution of 1956, the Polish theater returned to its native traditions of fantasy and metaphor and entered into a period of feverish avant-garde experimentation. Along with Beckett and Ionesco, Witkacy was discovered and given recognition as a precursor of the contemporary avant-garde theater.

He was more than a dead ancestor, he was a living creator. His plays were first performed by student theaters as part of the movement against the confines of socialist realism and censorship and for greater freedom of expression, and then, with the performance of *The Madman and the Nun* at the Narodowy Teatr in 1959, Witkacy started to be performed in the professional theaters, where he has now achieved the position of a modern classic. Without Witkacy, modern Polish avant-garde drama would simply not exist as we know it, nor would it have the importance and influence in the world that it enjoys today.

Another, although not final, stage in this unpredictable story came in July, 1967, with the production of *The Madman and the Nun* at the San Francisco State College Theater. After first stirring up some controversy on campus and fears of hostile community reaction to Walpurg's strange adventures, *The Madman and the Nun* proved to be tremendously successful with both the critics and the public. Almost three thousand spectators saw the play in four nights; only *West Side Story* has ever equaled its popularity in the history of our college theater.

This was the first production of Witkacy in America, or for that matter in the English language. It was directed by Jan Kott, who over thirty years ago as a young student sat in Witkiewicz' Warsaw apartment with the two shoemakers and the maid listening to Witkacy read *The Shoemakers*.

The Madman and the Nun and Other Plays

The Madman and the Nun

INTRODUCTION

The Madman and the Nun (Wariat i zakonnica, 1923) serves as the best introduction to Witkiewicz' theater since it presents in compact form the major themes and techniques found in all his plays. Witkiewicz calls *The Madman and the Nun* a short play, and in performance it runs no more than ninety minutes. The cast is small, the single set a simple one: a bare cell for maniacs in a lunatic asylum. Brevity and condensation not only make *The Madman and the Nun* easy to perform, they also explain much of its impact. Restrictions give Witkiewicz a subject and a dramaturgical method. *The Madman and the Nun* contains charges of powder that are all the more explosive for being tightly packed. The madhouse is rocked by a chain of smaller blasts that finally set off the dazzling fireworks display of the final scene.

Witkiewicz makes confinement—and the resulting desire to break out of it—both the theme of his play and its form. The mad poet Walpurg (from Walpurgis Night in *Faust*) is confined in a cell in an insane asylum against his will and put into a straitjacket. Walpurg is looked after by psychiatrists in white uniforms and sisters in nuns' habits. The only window in the cell has twenty-five small, thick panes divided by metal bars; the door creaks on its heavy hinges each time it is unbolted and then bolted again. Walpurg is not allowed to write or do anything, except think endlessly. The tighter his confinement, the more intensely his mind works. Under the pressure of these physical restrictions, it seems to Walpurg that he is about to burst apart. Soon either he will break out, or his heart will burst.

Space on the stage becomes the total space in which all his life is lived. An intense struggle goes on in a small, enclosed area. Walpurg wants to be released from society's care and coercion in the name of benevolence, as well as from his own obsessions. He wants to escape imprisonment within the walls of society and of his own mind. Freedom is what he seeks, both from others and from himself. Even in his straitjacket, Walpurg constantly transcends the narrow space of his cell by his feverish reflections on art, poetry, and love. The juxtaposition of the imprisoned body and the mind roving far and wide generates dramatic tension.

The cell in the madhouse is also the cell of Walpurg's brain. We witness the workings of his mind as he struggles to break out of the mental straitjacket that has been put on him, both by society and by himself. Józef Szajna, the famous stage designer for the Warsaw production of *The Madman and the Nun* in 1959, describes how he made the cell into the interior of Walpurg's mind:

> The cell in Witkacy's *The Madman and the Nun* is represented by a wall that surrounds the hero of the play and the objects in the niches, a large moving head that spies on him, an automatic clock with the mechanism pulled out of it and the swaying symbol of unspecified biological form.
>   The rocking lamp and the turned-up volume of the ticking of the clock are attuned to the mounting frenzy of the "madman's" monologue. They help define the emotion indirectly and by allusion. Acting on the principle of psychograms, the props penetrate to the levels that often escape direct and rational rules, increasing tension.[1]

In the 1967 production at San Francisco State College, Jan Kott used slide projections to penetrate into Walpurg's mind and Sister Anna's as well; clocks running backward and at different speeds created the sense of deranged time within the confines of the cell, cut off from all contact with normal life.

As well as transcending space, Walpurg ranges about in time, returning often to the past with a vision of an earlier stage of society, before science and technology existed, when an individual could rise above the common herd.

> Before, art wasn't perverted, there was no "insatiable craving for form." Life wasn't the aimless movement of soulless automatons. Society was not a machine. There was a soft, pulpy mass of suffering cattle, and out of it grew wonderful flowers of lust, power, creativeness, and cruelty.

A madman like Walpurg is still an individual and will not conform. Madness is a highly explosive, unpredictable force that cannot be controlled by abstract theories such as Grün's. Lust is another high explosive that can blow open the doors and windows of the asylum, and the introduction of Sister Anna, a deeply sensual woman who has become a nun only because of an unhappy love affair, sets off the dynamite already present in Walpurg. Deeply frustrated himself as a result of not seeing a woman for two years, the mad poet finds in Sister Anna an escape from himself, from his obsessions, and from his prison and his jailers. Sex is a creative and liberating force; Walpurg becomes Sister Anna's lover and starts to write again at the same time. However, as long as he is in the asylum, Walpurg is constantly being untied from his straitjacket and then tied up again by Sister Anna; his

[1] Józef Szajna, "Stuff the Stage Is Made Of," *Poland* (American Edition), No. 12 (December, 1965), p. 42.

enslavement is only interrupted from time to time by moments of secret freedom.

In *The Madman and the Nun* society is seen as not only a machine, but a machine with no one really in control. "Imagine a long row of machines in a huge factory without any engineer in charge. All the pointers on the dials have already gone beyond the red arrow, and everything rushes madly on." Those who have placed Walpurg in the asylum and are so sure of the distinction between sanity and madness are only cogs in the lunatic machine that first drives people mad and then locks them up. To Walpurg the whole world has been turned into a prison–lunatic asylum by figures of authority and power who crush life in the name of abstractions: science and religion. Dr. Grün and Sister Barbara are caricatures, grotesque puppets mouthing theories that break down in the face of the multiplicity of life. They are the absolute automationists who want to regiment life and lock up as lunatics those who think and feel differently from the way they do; theirs is a government by psychiatric dictatorship, declaring insane those who dare disagree with it.

The costumes indicate how Walpurg and Sister Anna have been confined; the straitjacket keeps Walpurg from writing and from embracing her, and Sister Anna's wimple and habit prevent her from responding to him until he has torn them off. The dramatic action develops by a series of disrobings and sudden violent outbursts releasing Walpurg from the confines of life as defined by the laws and regulations of the reigning scientific and religious establishment. Sister Anna first starts the process by untying his straitjacket; then Walpurg goes into his ascending spiral. He rips off Sister Anna's wimple and seduces her, kills Bidello with a pencil, threatens Grün with a penknife, breaks the windowpane and hangs himself with his straitjacket—a fitting revenge against the rational society that kept him alive benevolently so that he would not stop suffering prematurely.

But the play does not end there on a tragic note with the defeat of the mad poet at the hands of an evil society. Witkiewicz parodies such stereotypes. Even Walpurg and Anna are treated ironically. Walpurg is a parody *fin-de-siècle* poet who mocks his own calling and fatal passion and transcends his earthly sufferings. Enough forward motion and upward thrust have been generated by the early constrictions of space and time to catapult Walpurg into a world free of space and time—the world of his own dreams.

The last acts of Witkiewicz plays are often the strongest theatrically —the shortest, swiftest, and most startling, full of electrifying *coups de théâtre*. The volcano erupts. The imminence of revolution and the sudden explosive upheaval of subterranean forces—on both the personal and the social level—are axioms in Witkiewicz' analysis of man and society that make possible a maximum of unpredictability in the last half of his dramas, whereas in traditional dramaturgy the probabilities become more restricted as the play progresses, once certain premises have been established. In Witkiewicz, as in war and revolution, the longer the action goes on, the more the improbable and even the impossible become probable and possible.

In a state of insurrection, all the normal laws are suspended: anything can happen. The denouement of a normal play is the outcome of what has gone before and what the audience has been led to expect; in *The Madman and the Nun* the denouement is an insurrection against the whole established order—an insurrection against the laws of time, space, and motion, as well as against society and its rules. The uprising in *The Madman and the Nun* is against everything that has gone before; the denouement is not a consequence of what preceded it, but a refutation of it. Witkiewicz' *coups de théâtre* are like real *coups d'états*—they overthrow the preceding regime and undo a previous period of history.

Walpurg's return to life is a spectacularly comic *coup de théâtre*, exploding both the confines of the asylum and the expectations of the audience. His sudden re-entrance into the cell after he has hanged himself in everyone's presence is the opening blow of the revolution against the automated establishment. Its time-honored notions crumble; the earth begins to tremble for Grün and Sister Barbara—perhaps they are the ones who are insane.

Paradoxically, impossibly, yet appropriately, the mad poet and the debauched nun triumph and go into life and into town, escaping from the prison that man's science and religion have constructed. Dressed in new clothes, born anew, Walpurg and Sister Anna go free, liberated from morality and the laws of biology and physics. Time and space, which pressed so hard on Walpurg before, are totally extendable. The clock stops ticking in his head; he goes out the creaking door.

Arbitrary power is defeated by the revocation of the laws of matter; the victim escapes the victimizers, who are left to pummel one another and roll about on the floor with Walpurg's corpse, as he walks merrily out the door. The ending is a mock transcendental escape, a comic apotheosis; Walpurg's body is subject to all the laws of the physical world, but he himself transcends necessity as in a dream.

The rhythm of the play slowly mounts to this frenzied staccato. After the slow close-ups of Walpurg and Sister Anna in Act I, the action of the last two acts goes faster and faster, like the unattended machines described by Walpurg. In the final act all the movements are exaggerated; the characters hurl themselves about the stage and fling themselves at one another. Alfred and Paphnutius dash about the stage with the frantic, speeded-up rhythms and motions of the Keystone Cops.

The movements of the two attendants and Grün become more and more jerky and mechanical, as they succumb to the mechanistic theories in which they believe. They are the machine-driven, soulless automatons described by Walpurg at the beginning of the play. The victimizers become their own victims; they end up in a pulpy mass of struggling bodies, whereas Walpurg and Anna rise out of it, "wonderful flowers of lust, power, creativeness, and cruelty," like the fashionable yellow boutonniere in Walpurg's lapel. They are free.

Walpurg has fulfilled his earlier dream and gone back in time to a period when the artist was elegant, irresponsible, and free—above the groaning masses. The establishment, the madhouse managers themselves, go mad and sink back into primeval chaos in "the churning pulpy mass of bodies." "We're the madmen now. They've locked us up for good," one of the attendants cries out. The final grotesque fight between the psychiatrist and the Mother Superior and their minions is the result of their sudden discovery in themselves of all the insanity and aggression they had before tried to put onto Walpurg. A complete transfer has taken place: the mad are sane, and the sane are mad.

The Madman and the Nun

or, There Is Nothing Bad Which
Could Not Turn into Something Worse

A SHORT PLAY IN
THREE ACTS AND FOUR SCENES

Dedicated to all the madmen of the world

(y compris other planets of our system

and also planets of other suns in the Milky Way

and of other constellations)

and to Jan Mieczysławski

Alexander Walpurg	*29 years old. Dark-complexioned, very handsome, and perfectly built. Disheveled beard and mustache. Long hair. Dressed in a hospital gown. Straitjacket. Madman. Poet.*
Sister Anna	*22 years old. Very light blonde and very pretty, and to anyone who had "known" her, rather ardent. Fantastic nun's habit. A large cross on a chain on her chest.*
Sister Barbara	*Mother Superior. Dressed in the same costume as Sister Anna. 60 years old. A matron in the style of the Polish painter Matejko.*
Dr. Jan Bidello	*35 years old. Non-Freudian psychiatrist. Dark-complexioned with a beard. White uniform.*
Dr. Ephraim Grün	*Psychoanalyst of the Freudian school. A swarthy cherub in the Semitic style. White uniform.*
Professor Ernest Walldorff	*Jovial old boy, aged 55–60. Long white hair. Clean-shaven. Gold pince-nez. English sports jacket.*
Two Attendants	*Wild bearded beasts. Alfred—Bald, black beard. Paphnutius—Red hair and beard. Both dressed in hospital uniforms.*

The action takes place in a cell for raving maniacs in the lunatic asylum, At the Sign of the Jugged Hare.

ACT I

The stage represents a cell for raving maniacs. To the left there is a bed in the corner. Above the bed the inscription: Dementia Praecox, *Number 20. Opposite there is a window made up of twenty-five small, thick panes divided by metal bars. Under the window a table. One chair. To the right a door with creaking hinges. Alexander Walpurg is sleeping on the bed, tied in a straitjacket. A small light hangs from the ceiling. Dr. Bidello brings Sister Anna in.*

BIDELLO There's our patient. He's sleeping now after a large dose of chloral hydrate and morphine. Poison the hopeless cases slowly is our secret motto. However, perhaps Grün is right. I'm not one of those stubborn psychiatrists who are unwilling to accept anything new. I consent to this experiment, especially since Professor Walldorff and I have exhausted all other means. Dementia praecox. If you, Sister, could—although I very much doubt it—resolve the patient's "complex"—as the psychoanalysts call it—and penetrate, with the help of your feminine intuition, into the dark spot in his soul, the forgotten place, the "psychic wound," as they say, I would be only too delighted with Grün's success. As far as psychoanalysis is concerned, I acknowledge its diagnostic techniques, but have no confidence whatsoever in its therapeutic value. It is fine for those people who can devote their entire lives to being cured. Here's a chair. (*He offers her a chair.*)

SISTER ANNA Very well, Doctor, but what am I actually to do? How am I to go about it? I had almost forgotten to ask you the most important question.

BIDELLO Please don't attempt to do anything out of the ordinary, Sister. Behave quite naturally and directly, in accordance with your own intuition, as your conscience dictates. However, under no circumstances should you gratify his wishes. Do you understand, Sister?

SISTER ANNA Doctor, I should like to remind you that you are speaking to a member of a religious order.

BIDELLO Please don't be offended, Sister. A mere formality. Well, I'll say good-bye to you now. Something else: please remember that the most important thing is to bring to light his "complex," stemming from a forgotten incident in his past which has disturbed him ever since.

(*Sister Anna nods. Bidello leaves, bolting the door. Sister Anna sits down and prays. A pause. Walpurg wakes up and raises himself on the bed. Sister Anna trembles. She gets up and stands quite still.*)

WALPURG (*in a sitting position*) Is this a hallucination? This has never happened to me before. What the devil? Answer me.

SISTER ANNA I am not a phantom. I have been sent to take care of you.

WALPURG (*getting up*) Aha. This is a new device on the part of my noble torturers.

> Devilish devices
> Impinge on our senses.
> But the soul lies concealed,
> No one wants it revealed.

What's your name? I haven't seen a woman for two years.

SISTER ANNA (*trembling*) My religious name is Anna.

WALPURG (*with sudden lust*) Well then, Sister, give me a sisterly kiss. Kiss me. I can't kiss you. You're so pretty. Oh! What agony! (*He draws nearer to her.*)

SISTER ANNA (*moving back, she speaks in a cold and distant tone of voice*) I am here to bring peace to your tortured soul. I, too, am beyond life. Don't you see my nun's habit?

WALPURG (*controlling himself*) Oh—I can't go on this way. I must control myself. (*In a different tone of voice*) Sister Anna, I'm a living corpse. I don't need help, only death.

SISTER ANNA I'm more dead than you. You will be cured, and then your whole life will lie before you. (*Walpurg gazes at her intently.*)

WALPURG Why are you a nun? You're so young, so beautiful.

SISTER ANNA Let's not talk about it.

WALPURG I must talk about it. You're very much like a woman who once was everything to me. Perhaps I'm only imagining it. She's not alive any more.

SISTER ANNA (*trembling*) Not alive?

WALPURG You, too, must have experienced something similar in your life. I felt it at once. He's not alive either, is he?

SISTER ANNA Oh, merciful God, let's not talk about that. I am now in a different world.

WALPURG But I am not. I envy you your other world; you've chosen your own home. But I have to live here, in this terrible prison, in a world my torturers have forced on me, in a world I hate. But my real world is this clock which is constantly ticking in my head— even while I'm asleep. I'd prefer death a thousand times. But I can't die. That is the decree for all of us madmen who suffer without being guilty. We're tortured as if we were the worst criminals. And we're not allowed to die because society is benevolent, so very benevolent that it doesn't want us to stop suffering prematurely. Ha! Please get me out of this damned straitjacket. I'm suffocating. My arms are pulling loose from their sockets.

SISTER ANNA I can't. The Doctor didn't give his permission.

WALPURG So you're in league with my executioners? All right! Sit down. Let's talk. We have time. Oh! I have so much time! Only I don't know what to do with it. And I can't stand my own thoughts —I can't stand—(*Stifling sobs*) . . . My thoughts go in circles, as if driven by a machine. There's an infernal machine going in my head. It's been set, but I don't know for what hour of what day. I don't know when it will go off. And I wait, I wait endlessly. At times I think that such torture cannot go on any longer. But no—a day passes, a night, another day, and then chloral hydrate, morphine, nightmares when I'm asleep, and that terrible sensation on waking up that everything is beginning all over again. And so on and on . . .

SISTER ANNA Please don't talk that way. Please, I beg you; calm yourself. If I can't help you at all I'll have to ask the doctor to relieve me of my duties here.

WALPURG (*wildly*) O no! You'll never get out of here! (*He controls himself; Sister Anna retreats in fear.*) Excuse me, Sister, I'm in full possession of my senses. Let's go on talking. I'll be calm now. Try to understand that I haven't seen a woman for two years . . . What were we talking about? Aha—you lost some one. So did I. Tell me about it. Please allow me to introduce myself. (*He bows.*) Walpurg. Alexander Walpurg.

SISTER ANNA (*reeling*) Walpurg? So it was your poetry my fiancé and I read together. Oh, how dreadful! And yet I'm grateful to you. How many beautiful moments I owe to you. And everything has ended so horribly.

WALPURG Perhaps because the two of you read my poetry together. And besides nothing has come to an end. The world goes on as if nothing had happened. But my third volume is not bad at all. I know what I'm talking about. After the third volume I decided to check into this hotel. Alcohol, morphine, cocaine—the end. And, to top it all, disaster.

SISTER ANNA How could you, with such talent! What happiness to be an artist like you!

WALPURG Happiness! Agony! I wanted to write myself out, to the very marrow, and die. But no. Society is benevolent. They saved me so that I could end my life being tortured here. Oh, their damn medical ethics! I'd like to murder that entire race of butchers. (*In a different tone*) Do you know, Sister, when I was in school, I studied Henrik von Kleist's biography. "*Er führte ein Leben voll Irrtum. . . .*" I didn't understand it then. Now I understand it perfectly.

SISTER ANNA Why have you poisoned yourself with drugs? Tell me, please, I can't understand it at all. A genius like you.

WALPURG What? You don't understand? *"Meine Körperschale konnte nicht meine Geistesglut aushalten."* Who said that? My soul's fire has burned away my earthly shell. Now, don't you understand? My nerves weren't strong enough to resist that damnable something or other which compelled me to write. I had to poison myself. I had to gain strength. I didn't want to, but I had to. And once the whole machine, that old, weak machine starts its lunatic motion, it has to go further and further, whether I'm still creative or not. The mind's exhausted, but the machine goes on and on. That's why artists have to do insane things. What can you do with a senselessly accelerated motor which no one can control? Imagine a long row of machines in a huge factory without any engineer in charge. All the pointers on the dials have already gone beyond the red arrow, and everything rushes madly on.

SISTER ANNA (*listening with her arms crossed*) But why does it always end exactly like that nowadays? It used to be different.

WALPURG Before, art wasn't perverted, there was no "insatiable craving for form." Life wasn't the aimless movement of soulless automatons. Society was not a machine. There was a soft, pulpy mass of suffering cattle, and out of it grew wonderful flowers of lust, power, creativeness, and cruelty. But let's not pursue this conversation any further. Let's talk about life—about our life. I have as much compassion for you as you have for me.

SISTER ANNA My God, my God, my God . . .

WALPURG That's enough. There's only one thing certain: today the greatest art is found only in perversion and madness—I'm talking, of course, about form. But for the true creative artists, not the jackals, the forms they create are intimately connected to their lives. And now tell me about yourself, Sister. Who was he?

SISTER ANNA (*trembling and speaking mechanically*) He was an engineer.

WALPURG Ha, ha, ha, ha! And what happened?

SISTER ANNA (*offended*) Why are you laughing?

WALPURG I wasn't laughing at all. I only envy him. He was one of the small cogs in the machine, and not a demented pebble among meshed iron gears. Go on.

SISTER ANNA He loved only me, but he couldn't break off with a certain . . . woman. And finally he had to end it all. He blew out his brains. Then I entered the convent.

WALPURG What a lucky man! Don't feel sorry for him. So nowadays even engineers can have problems like that. And that's why you entered . . . Oh, how absurd. Why didn't I meet you first?

SISTER ANNA And what would have happened? You would have tortured me to death, the way you did that other woman . . .

WALPURG How do you know about that? Tell me this instant, how do you know that? No one knows anything about it. Who told you, Anna?

SISTER ANNA Please address me as Sister.

WALPURG (*quite coldly*) How does Sister know about it, then? That's interesting. I'm quite calm.

SISTER ANNA (*brutally*) Can't you understand? I'm talking to you, I know your poetry. I know who and what you are now.

WALPURG Oh, yes: I'm a madman in a straitjacket. It's that simple. But it isn't simple to torture someone to death the way I tortured her. I don't know which one of us killed the other. She sacrificed herself. In the final analysis I'm not guilty. She died of brain fever. I don't know if I killed her or if she is actually torturing me to death now—every day—systematically. After she died I read through her diary and then I understood with what dreadful, diabolical skill I had been tormenting her. But that's what she wanted. That's how she killed herself, and now she's killing me. Oh! (*He struggles in the straitjacket.*)

SISTER ANNA And how did you get in here?

WALPURG On account of my weak nervous system. Cocaine. The clock in my head. And that eternal question of whether I killed her or she killed me. Even in the fraction of a second I think two thoughts as different as God and Satan. What else is left? A few poems. They must have been published by now. My sister will make a little money from them. I have a sister whom I hate. What else is there? A little violence. And so I ended up here. But no one gets well here. You can see that for yourself. As a matter of fact I'm in full possession of my senses, I just happen to have a tiny machine in my head. Whoever comes here is finished. Because their type of cure only pushes you further and further into madness; you can try to tell them lies, but eventually you do something stupid, you make one false step, and then you're locked up forever.

SISTER ANNA Everything I've gone through seems so petty now. I used to believe that whatever happened to me was important and unique. Now there's nothing, only a terrible, hopeless emptiness. I don't exist now; he abandoned me forever.

WALPURG (*pleased*) He abandoned you, but only out of shame. For your sake he couldn't even give up some common slut, some demonic old bag, some obscenity or other. Yes, I'm sure. There's nothing at all important or unique in that. His death was proof of his despicable weakness. He couldn't do anything for you. But what about me? (*He falls on his knees before her.*) Please put your hand on my head. Perhaps the clock will stop ticking, at least for a moment. I'm composing poetry again now. But I think my poems are getting worse. I can't write any more. But then you can also use a pencil to kill yourself. I'll never improve, and yet new ideas come to me all the time. Sister, please hold my head in your hands. Oh, if only I could unscrew my head and put it away in a chest of drawers so that it could have a little rest. Then I could rest too.

SISTER ANNA Yes, yes, rest. Just a little. Like this. There. (*She takes his head in her hands and sinks into the chair. He puts his head on her knees.*)

WALPURG Untie my hands, would you? Really, I'm in full possession of my senses.

SISTER ANNA I can't. Please don't ask me to. The Doctor told me . . .

WALPURG (*without rising from his knees, he lifts his head up and looks at her wildly*) The Doctor? Do you want me to fly into a rage? It's always the same story here. You're their accomplice. First they drive you into a state of frenzy and then they put you in a straitjacket. And so it goes on endlessly. (*He pronounces these last words in a desperately hopeless way.*)

SISTER ANNA (*getting up*) Yes, yes . . . I know . . . Nothing else matters. I'll do anything for you. (*She lifts him up, turns him around so that his back is toward her, and unties the straitjacket. Walpurg turns around to face her and stretches out his arms, unrolling the sleeves of his straitjacket up to his elbows. He looks like a boxer getting ready for a fight.*)

WALPURG So—now I'm free.

SISTER ANNA (*fearfully*) Give me your word that nothing else will happen.

WALPURG Nothing else, only let's be happy even if it's only for a moment. You're the only woman in the world. Not because you simply happen to be the first woman I've seen for two years, but because you really are. When I'm with you, nothing else exists for me: my whole past, this prison, the tortures—it all disappears. I feel that I'll still write something more. Everything still lies before me. (*He draws quite near her.*)

SISTER ANNA (*not moving from where she is standing*) I'm afraid. It's all so horrible. Don't come any nearer.

WALPURG Do you think I'm going to hurt you? Do you think I'm going to humiliate you by forcing you to kiss me? I love you. You can trust me. I'm in full possession of my senses. (*He takes her hand. Sister Anna trembles as if she had touched red-hot iron.*) You are the only one. This moment, too, is the only one. It will never come back, nothing ever comes back. We live only once, and whatever is destined to happen on this earth must happen. Any other way, it's a crime which will poison future generations with its venom. Kiss me. What's your real name?

SISTER ANNA (*with no will of her own*) Alina.

WALPURG (*bringing his face close to hers*) Lina, I'm sure you love me. Don't imagine that I've always been this ugly. I didn't have a beard or mustache before. But once I tried to impale myself on the razor, and they stopped shaving me.

SISTER ANNA Oh—don't talk that way. I love you. Nothing exists in the whole world except you. Even eternal damnation . . .

WALPURG (*taking hold of her head in his hands and looking into her eyes*) There is no eternal damnation, the only rewards and punishments are right here in this world. Kiss me. I don't dare . . .

SISTER ANNA (*tearing herself away from him*) No, not that, not that! I'm afraid . . .

WALPURG (*tears off her wimple and clasps her in a wild embrace*) You must, you must. This moment is the only one . . . (*He kisses her on the lips, bending her backward. Sister Anna yields without any resistance.*)

ACT II

The same setting. Very early the next morning. It grows lighter and lighter, but the sky is overcast. A storm is approaching. Thunder and lightning become more and more intense.

SISTER ANNA (*putting on her wimple*) Now I have to tie you up again. How ghastly! But this is for you. I'm giving it to you as a talisman. (*She unfastens the iron cross from the chain she wears on her breast and gives it to him.*) I don't have the right to wear it any more. I had special permission from Mother Superior to wear it. My mother gave me this cross.

WALPURG Thank you, Lina. Thank you for everything. (*He takes the cross and puts it in a crevice in the slats of his bed.*) There was supposed to be a pencil and paper in there, but I never could find them. (*He comes back to her and kisses her hand.*) You know, it's only now that I realize how utterly miserable I've been—now that you love me. Yesterday simply to kiss your hair seemed beyond human happiness. Today, now that you're mine, nothing else matters. I want to get out of here, write, work, shave off my beard and mustache, dress well again. I want to live, to live a perfectly ordinary life. I must get out of here. You'll see. You've given me the strength to overcome anything. Let's both get out of here.

SISTER ANNA (*kissing him*) I feel exactly the same. I'm not a nun any more. I want to lead a normal, quiet life. I've gone through so much.

WALPURG (*gloomily*) Yes, of course, you'll get out. You're not in prison. (*With sudden anxiety*) Lina, don't betray me. That Doctor Bidello is my worst enemy. I prefer Grün, even though he's a disgusting pig, too. You won't betray me? I fear I've awakened your desires, and if you don't see me for a couple of days, someone else might begin to look attractive to you.

SISTER ANNA (*throwing her arms around his neck*) I love you. Only you forever and ever. I'd stay here myself if only you could get out. I love you for what you are. You must fulfill your destiny.

WALPURG Poor thing. I'm afraid for you. There's some violent force in me that I can't control. Necessity rules our lives. I have no will of my own, in the usual sense of the word. There's some higher power, above me or in me, whose orders I'm forced to follow.

SISTER ANNA That's creativity. Perhaps it's God. He will forgive us. And my mother will forgive us also, even though she was a saint.

WALPURG Wait just a minute, I haven't told you everything. It seems to me that maybe I did kill her. But you don't know . . .

SISTER ANNA (*tearing herself away from him*) Don't talk, don't say anything. Put this on quickly. They may come any minute. (*He stands with his back to her; she ties the sleeves of the straitjacket.*)

WALPURG But nothing's changed, has it? You're talking so strangely, as if you'd suddenly stopped loving me.

SISTER ANNA (*finishing tying him into the straitjacket*) Nothing's changed. It's just that I'm afraid. I fear for our happiness. (*She turns him toward her and kisses him quickly.*) And now lie down and pretend to be asleep. Hurry! (*She pushes him toward the bed.*)

WALPURG (*lying down*) Remember, don't betray me. There are so many attractive men in the world—so many scoundrels.

SISTER ANNA You're talking nonsense. Sssh! I think they're coming. (*Walpurg lies down and pretends to be asleep. Sister Anna sits down on the chair and prays. A pause. The door is unbolted and Dr. Bidello enters. Sister Barbara and Grün follow her.*)

GRÜN (*in the doorway, speaking to someone who is outside*) You can wait there. (*Bidello approaches Sister Anna and speaks with her in a low voice.*)

BIDELLO Well? How's it going? (*Sister Barbara kisses Sister Anna on the forehead, and Sister Anna kisses her hand.*)

SISTER ANNA All right. Everything is fine.

BIDELLO Has he been asleep the whole time? (*Grün listens attentively.*)

SISTER ANNA No. He woke up once. He talked quite coherently. He told me about his life. I didn't know that this is the famous Walpurg. Then he fell asleep peacefully. He didn't wake up a second time.

GRÜN Didn't I tell you so! He's beginning to resolve his complex. He fell asleep the second time without chloral hydrate. Has that ever happened in your experience, my dear colleague?

BIDELLO It's never happened to me at all. I never use chloral hydrate. But it's a curious phenomenon—the more so during a period of hysteria. Listen, Grün: I have no prejudices. If you want to try your methods further, go ahead. I consent. To tell the truth, I'm even beginning to believe in psychoanalysis. I'll turn my patient over to you. There's a little too much of the sexual in your theories. That's the only thing I still find questionable.

GRÜN But my dear colleague, the sexual drive is the most important thing in life. All complexes originate there. If you don't mind, I'll wake the patient up.

BIDELLO Go ahead. (*Bidello joins Sister Anna, and they move to stage right. Sister Barbara watches as Grün wakes Walpurg.*)

GRÜN (*waking Walpurg up*) Hello! Walpurg! Listen, it's me, Dr. Grün. (*Walpurg pretends that he is waking up. He stretches out on the bed and then sits up. A pause.*)

WALPURG Ah, it's you, Doctor. I haven't seen you for a long time. I enjoy our conversations together. Why don't you come more often? I suppose Bidello has forbidden you to?

GRÜN Nothing of the sort. He's entrusted you completely to my care. I'm certain that I can cure you. How did your conversation with Sister Anna affect you? That was my idea.

WALPURG It was miraculous. She's a saint. I never felt better in my whole life. I'd like to write again.

GRÜN Splendid. Today you will be given pencil and paper. Books too. What kind of books do you want?

WALPURG The complete works of Tadeusz Miciński and the second volume of Husserl's *Logische Untersuchungen*. Perhaps also Moréas. And the third volume of my own works. I feel so wonderful. Perhaps you'll be so kind as to introduce me to that tall lady dressed in a nun's habit. Duchess Vertigossa, I presume—if I'm not mistaken. (*He stands up.*)

SISTER BARBARA Mr. Walpurg, I am Sister Barbara, Mother Superior of the Convent of Voluntary Lady Martyrs. Please do not forget that.

GRÜN There's no need for me to introduce you if you two already know each other . . .

WALPURG Grün, perhaps you could take off my straitjacket? I'm stiff as a board, and besides, I'm in full possession of my senses now. I couldn't possibly have another attack of hysteria. I give you my word of honor. I slept like two tops . . .

BIDELLO (*breaking off his conversation with Sister Anna*) No, no, no! What's honor to a madman? No one knows. Hysteria when repressed breaks out every so often with redoubled strength. I can't give my consent. (*Walpurg controls a surge of hatred.*)

WALPURG But sir, Grün is willing to vouch for me with his life. Isn't that so, Grün?

GRÜN Yes. Listen, Bidello: it's either or—either he's my patient or he isn't. Halfway measures will get us nowhere.

BIDELLO Well, all right. Go to it. But what will Professor Walldorff say?

GRÜN In view of such good results, I'll answer for the Professor as well. Walpurg, I'll take off your straitjacket, and from now on I'm going to treat you as a convalescent. Turn around. (*Walpurg turns around so that he has his back to Grün. Grün unties the sleeves of his straitjacket.*)

SISTER BARBARA Isn't it somewhat premature, Dr. Grün?

GRÜN Sister Barbara, don't meddle in other people's business. If I were to analyze you, you'd leave the convent immediately. You have a penitence complex because of your guilt feelings toward your husband. Every minute he was alive, you tormented him in the most sadistic manner. I know everything.

SISTER BARBARA Do not forget yourself, Dr. Grün. Do not repeat vulgar town gossip in my presence.

GRÜN This isn't gossip. I know what the facts are. Walpurg, you're free. In six months we'll all leave here together and go into town. Look here, don't be so stubborn. Have confidence in me for once.

WALPURG (*shaking hands with him*) Thank you. (*To Sister Barbara*) At last I've found someone who can recognize a madman for what he is. I've had enough recognition as a poet. (*He shakes hands with Sister Barbara who looks at him disapprovingly.*) Grün, give me a pencil and a piece of paper. I must write down the first stanza of a new poem. The idea came to me in my sleep. I'll do wonderful things with it. (*Grün gives him a pad and pencil. Still standing, Walpurg begins to jot things down.*)

GRÜN (*to Sister Barbara*) You see, Sister, that's how one should treat the sick. Our hospitals are worse than medieval prisons. Only psychoanalysis will free mankind from the atrocious nightmare of the lunatic asylum. What I'm saying is that prisons would be empty if every one—from childhood on—were subjected to compulsory analysis which would eradicate all complexes. I can assure you that this man (*he points at Walpurg*) has a twin sister complex dating back to the time when he was still an embryo. That's why he cannot really fall in love. Subconsciously he loves his sister, although in his normal state of consciousness he feels genuine hatred for her. Walpurg, what's the first thing you associate with "sister"?

WALPURG (*crossing slowly to stage right*) Sinister—a cave—two orphans on a desert island—Vere Stacpoole's novel *Blue Lagoon*.

GRÜN Can you follow all that, Sister? The cave is the mother's womb. So is the desert island. I've resolved his complex. Now, on the second level, the novel—by the way, Sister, have you read it?—has penetrated into his already developed psychic placenta. Walpurg, in two weeks time you'll be fit as a fiddle.

WALPURG (*speaking to Bidello without paying attention to Grün*) Doctor, in my opinion it isn't right to flirt with a nun for quite such a long time.

SISTER ANNA (*Hurriedly*) We were only talking about you.

WALPURG What I told you was just between the two of us.

GRÜN (*to Sister Barbara*) You see, Sister, how rationally he's talking now? He's developing a healthy instinct for life. He's jealous—he can fall in love.

BIDELLO Really—at times I have to laugh at all this psychoanalytic nonsense. Ha, ha, ha! (*Walpurg seizes Bidello by the hair and gives him a terrible blow with his pencil on the left temple. Bidello falls to the ground without a groan.*)

WALPURG (*quietly*) That's for your flirtations with women in religious orders. (*He kicks Bidello with his foot.*) Croak, you filthy executioner! I'm only sorry I couldn't put him through a few tortures before he died. You see, that's a healthy instinct for life. Grün, lend me your penknife. My pencil is broken. That moron had a hard skull, but you don't have a rival any more.

SISTER ANNA (*who has been standing frozen with fear*) What have you done? It's all over now. (*She faints and falls to the ground.*)

GRÜN (*running up*) Walpurg, have you gone mad? I have a weak heart. O my God! Poor Bidello. (*He feels Bidello's pulse.*) He's dead —he hit him right in the temple.

WALPURG I'm completely cured now. First I identified him with my sister, and then I killed them both with one blow. I'm sure she died at that very moment. Ha, ha! My complex is resolved. If psychoanalysis is worth anything at all, I should be let out free at once. I'm not dangerous any more.

GRÜN Come now, Walpurg, aren't you making fun of me?

WALPURG No—I'm speaking quite seriously: I'm cured. That blow to the skull cured me. That's why I'm not responsible for the murder, but from now on I will be responsible for everything I do in the future. Mother Superior, you're in a daze—wake up; I was simply defending the honor of a member of a religious order from the advances of an ordinary Don Juan in a doctor's uniform. Isn't that so? I'm sure this psycho-expert has had any number of love affairs in the women's ward.

SISTER BARBARA These are untimely jokes. You are an utter madman. And if not, you are an ordinary criminal. (*She goes to Sister Anna and revives her.*)

GRÜN This is unheard of! So you really feel all right?

WALPURG (*impatiently*) I said so already. I'll consider my personal enemy anyone who treats me like a madman. I'd like some breakfast —I'm hungry. And please: look after Sister Anna. Can't you see that she's not altogether well? The Duchess can't revive her.

GRÜN I can't believe it. He's resolved his complex all by himself, just as easy as falling out of bed! It's quite incredible! (*He goes toward the door.*)

SISTER ANNA (*coming to*) Oh! What will happen now?

SISTER BARBARA (*angrily*) Things will go on much the same as before. We must not question the will of God. What have you done with your cross?

SISTER ANNA Everything happened the way it did because today I left my cross in the cell. My mother's cross was my only protection.

GRÜN (*shouting through the door*) Alfred! Paphnutius! Breakfast for Number 20. (*The attendants appear.*)

SISTER BARBARA (*to Sister Anna*) You should be ashamed to believe in such superstitions. Go at once to confession. (*The attendants come in and are dumbfounded at the sight of Bidello's corpse.*)

SISTER ANNA Perhaps I'll go tomorrow. After what has happened, I am unworthy. I must examine my conscience.

SISTER BARBARA (*pushing her toward the door*) Go this very minute! Do you hear me?

WALPURG (*to Sister Anna*) Get a good rest, Sister, and come again this evening. Our talks do wonders for me. After all, I couldn't talk about myself with an idiot like Grün.

SISTER BARBARA (*turning around*) No—this must come to an end now. I will not have my sisters turned into victims for murderers.

WALPURG Grün, your penknife.

GRÜN (*giving him the penknife without thinking*) But Sister Barbara, he will be tied up in his straitjacket, to be on the safe side. I can assure you there won't be any more crimes. (*To the attendants*) What are you blinking at? Bring his breakfast immediately. (*The attendants leave.*) He's almost completely cured. Jung describes a similar case. His patient became a model husband and an excellent architect after he butchered his aunt when she came to visit him. He had an aunt complex, and he resolved it. Psychoanalysis alone enabled him to do that.

SISTER ANNA (*not quite herself*) I am ready to sacrifice even my life, if that is necessary. Sister Barbara, I implore you, do not deny me penance for my grave sins.

SISTER BARBARA So be it—I consent. Perhaps God wills it. Perhaps in all of this there is some higher meaning not intelligible to us—the poor in spirit. Go to bed, Sister Anna, and do not go to confession today. And this evening you will come on duty at ten o'clock. (*Both of them leave, passing the attendants who are bringing in breakfast. Walpurg has sharpened his pencil and is writing.*)

GRÜN Eat, Walpurg. You deserve a decent meal after all this. As a psychoanalyst I understand and forgive everything. There is no crime without a complex, and a complex is a sickness.

WALPURG Just a moment—don't interrupt me. The last line . . . I need one more word . . . (*He writes.*)

GRÜN (*to the attendants*) Why are you just standing there, you blockheads? Take the Doctor's body to Section 7. (*The attendants take up Bidello's corpse and leave.*)

WALPURG There, I've finished. Now I've finally cleared my brain of the last trace of madness. The clock has stopped ticking. I have no pangs of conscience whatsoever. (*He attacks his breakfast with enthusiasm. The storm is gathering momentum. Green shafts of lightning intermittently pierce the dark gray shadows. Rain beats against the window.*)

GRÜN A wonderful lesson for the old psychiatric school. I'll write a monograph about you. I'll be world famous.

WALPURG (*sitting and eating with a hearty appetite*) Psychiatry received its best lesson in the person of Mr. Bidello. I never liked that idiot or his manners toward women. I've known him for a long time. For the last five years he saw me as a victim. But when he began to interrelate with sister, then I couldn't stand it any longer. Ha, ha, ha!

GRÜN (*rushes to Walpurg and gives him a hug*) Walpurg! You're the greatest genius in the world! I love you. Together we've created something wonderful.

WALPURG (*suddenly stands up and pushes Grün away. Grün*

staggers.) Enough of your familiarity! Don't pester me! Idiot! He's grown as familiar with me as he would with any of his psychiatric cases. Keep your distance! Do you understand?

GRÜN (*jumping back*) Give me back my penknife! Give me back my penknife!

WALPURG (*throws the penknife on the floor for him; Grün picks it up*) There you are, you coward! One murder per day is quite enough for me. It isn't my custom to trample on cockroaches. Get out!

GRÜN (*retreating toward the door, he opens the penknife*) Paphnutius! Alfred! (*The attendants rush in.*) Put Number 20 in his straitjacket! Quickly! (*With phenomenal speed the attendants throw themselves upon Walpurg, put him in the straitjacket, and tie the sleeves. Walpurg doesn't resist at all.*)

WALPURG Ha, ha, ha, ha! A game of make-believe. We madmen are the shrewdest people. Our instincts are so wonderfully acute that even animals seem stupid in comparison.

GRÜN (*closing his penknife*) Laugh, Walpurg, laugh. No matter what you do, you'll be cured. I'm not interested in you or your silly versifying. The only important thing is that "dementia praecox," as it is called, can in fact be cured by resolving complexes. Let's go. (*He goes toward the door, and the attendants follow him.*)

ACT III

The same setting. The light which hangs from the ceiling is burning. Sister Anna unties Walpurg's straitjacket.

SISTER ANNA You must be very tired, my poor dear.

WALPURG Not at all, not at all. I slept like a log all day long. I slept away fifteen years of sleeplessness. I feel splendid. (*Sister Anna takes off his straitjacket. He turns around and faces her.*) And do you actually know, after all that's happened, I think there's no place on earth worthy of me except this cell. I don't even have any desire to leave it. Read my poem. I have stage fright—I can't.

SISTER ANNA (*reading*) Oh—it's absolutely marvelous!

I am reading the Bible under a tree, and time is fleeting,
Narcotics lurk among the shrubs covered with sun, dew, and flow-
ers,
In the midst of the breath of the morning breeze,
Give me milk—milk straight from the cow,
And eggs—straight from the hen;

I want to be healthy, one of the good guys,
I want to hold my head up high.
But suddenly the simple question: "What for? Is it worth it?"—
And mouth wide open
I've sucked in every drug at once,
And pale as paper, sheet, or handkerchief
I've plunged into the whirlpool of an unknown battle with an un-
   known foe
Who may be Satan, who may be God.
This is no battle
Only: "Draw in the reins! Ready arms! March!"
Only: the stuffing of my brains rammed into other men's skulls.
Superb! But when you're with me, everything will be different. Isn't
that so? No more drugs. I'll be everything to you.

WALPURG Perhaps so. But first of all—come what may—we must get
out of here as soon as possible. Only don't go into excessive ecstasies
over my works. This is the beginning of something entirely new,
but in itself it's nothing.

SISTER ANNA (*sitting down beside him*) You know—I'm so happy I
feel guilty. Oh—if only I could suffer a little. Life beyond this cell
has no meaning for me either. If we were left here for all eternity, I
would be perfectly satisfied. It's so absolutely marvelous to be with
you. Everything has meaning now. And to think that I lived a
completely senseless life for so long! Darling, I must confess when
you killed Bidello, you aroused my desires to the point of madness.
You excite me tremendously! It's monstrous.

WALPURG (*embracing her with sudden lust*) My perverse darling! (*In
a different tone*) If only I were allowed to write when I'm here
alone! I must keep myself completely in check so that that nitwit
won't have me put back in the straitjacket. Yesterday I couldn't
control my emotions: I had to kill that hideous brute.

SISTER ANNA Don't talk about it, Alex. Rest. Lean against me, and let's
forget all that. I'd like to make up for those two agonizing years
you've gone through. We have no idea what awaits us.

WALPURG Everything will be all right now. We'll go somewhere far
away, as far as the tropics. I was there once with her. In Ceylon. But
her ghost won't disturb us now. That was madness, the same as your
love for your idiot. We are destined for each other. We're that ideal
couple whose meeting the universe demanded. Oh—why didn't it
happen sooner!

SISTER ANNA But perhaps it's better this way? Otherwise we never
would have been able to understand each other.

WALPURG Let me kiss you. I love you. You and you alone are an intimate part of me and of what I have to write. For you I can create things I never could have expressed at all without your love.

SISTER ANNA My one and only . . . (*They kiss for a long time, more and more passionately. There is a sudden click of the door being unbolted, and in rush Grün, the two attendants, and Sister Barbara. Walpurg and Sister Anna jump up.*)

WALPURG Too late! (*He stands with his arms crossed on his chest. Sister Anna sits frozen with fear and shame.*)

GRÜN Ha, ha! Too early, rather. So that's how it is, is it, my good Sister! So that's the secret of your successful treatment of my patient. (*They all stand in such a way that Grün is nearest Walpurg and Sister Anna; Sister Barbara is farther away, and the two attendants are still farther away. They make a row parallel to the footlights.*) The late Bidello was right after all. (*Sister Anna throws herself toward Grün, but faints and falls.*) But psychoanalysis can cope even with this.

SISTER BARBARA This is horrible! A criminal and a wanton in a nun's habit! This will be my death blow. (*She covers her eyes with both hands.*)

GRÜN (*to the attendants*) Put him in the straitjacket! I'll show him! He concealed from me a complex I didn't know about. And he pretended that he had a sister complex. But there must be repressed truth even in lies. That's Freud's fundamental position. (*The attendants throw themselves at Walpurg.*)

WALPURG (*in a ghastly voice*) Everyone stay where he is! Not one step! (*Startled by his screaming, they all come to a standstill in rigid poses and "freeze." With frantic speed Walpurg pulls the cross out of the crevice in the bed and shouts*) Now I'll show you something, you psychic murderers! (*As if hypnotized, all the others remain frozen in the furtive and stealthy movements they were making.*) Scum! (*He jumps up on the table, knocks out two sections of the window with the cross, and ties one sleeve of his straitjacket to the bar between them. He ties the other sleeve around his neck and stands up on the table, facing the audience with his arms spread out like a cross, bending forward with a gesture as if he were going to throw himself down.*) And now see what is going to happen, and may my blood be on you! (*He starts to throw himself down.*)

Scene 2, without any intermission

While the curtain is down (*which should be as short a time as possible*), *the actor playing Walpurg unties himself and goes off quickly to the dressing room, and stagehands tie to the sleeve of his straitjacket a dummy which closely resembles Walpurg (a good sculptor must make the mask), but in a hanged condition. When the curtain goes up, everybody on stage should stand in the same positions as in Scene 1. All of this lasts only a moment (1–2 seconds).*

GRÜN (*throwing himself toward Walpurg's corpse*) Cut him down! (*The attendants rush forward and take down Walpurg's corpse from the sleeve of the straightjacket. Grün examines him. Sister Anna jumps up.*)

SISTER ANNA What has happened?

SISTER BARBARA Your lover has hanged himself, you shameless creature! That's what has happened! May God forgive you . . . I cannot. I'm going to lock you up for your entire life. You'll rot in a dungeon . . . You . . . (*She chokes with rage and indignation.*)

SISTER ANNA Oh! Oh! Oh! (*In a sudden rage*) All of you killed him—you criminals! (*She throws herself upon the corpse.*)

GRÜN (*getting up*) Dead. His spine is broken. The epistropheus has penetrated the medulla oblongata. We've lost our guinea pig. The question is: did he die a sick man, or was this, so to speak, the final action of a sick man whereby he would have become cured? Or perhaps he hanged himself already cured? That would be dreadful!

SISTER ANNA (*by the corpse*) Save him instead of spouting nonsense! He's still warm.

GRÜN I said he's dead. You don't know anything about anatomy. His breathing has stopped. Not even psychoanalysis can help him now. But what has he got in his hand? What did he knock out the pane of glass with? I completely forgot about that problem. (*He approaches the corpse.*)

SISTER ANNA (*she wrenches the cross out of the corpse's clenched fist*) It's mine! I won't give it to you! I gave it to him as a talisman!

GRÜN Give it to me this very minute, Sister. (*He grabs the cross out of her hand.*) A cross. The one she always wore on her breast. (*He turns to Sister Barbara.*)

SISTER BARBARA Yet another sacrilege. *Quelque chose d'énorme!* It's her mother's cross, which I allowed her to wear as a favor in view of her irreproachable conduct. (*Sister Anna gets up and, staggering as if she were drunk, approaches Sister Barbara.*)

SISTER ANNA I beseech you! Forgiveness! I shall die in despair. I have nothing at all now: not even the possibility of penance. (*She falls on her knees before Sister Barbara.*)

SISTER BARBARA Your place is in the streets! Slut! Oh, *quelle salope!* Away from me! (*Still on her knees, Sister Anna lowers her face to the floor and freezes in that position. Her hands sink spasmodically*

into her crumpled headdress. Sister Barbara kneels down and prays.)
GRÜN Well—Alfred! Paphnutius! Take corpse Number 20 to the dis-
secting room. That idiot Professor Walldorff will undoubtedly want
to perform an autopsy and look for brain damage. Ha, ha! Let him
look! (*Meanwhile the attendants pick up Walpurg's body and start
to carry it toward the door. To Sister Anna*) Well—Sister Anna,
pull yourself together and let's get out of here at long last.

(*At this moment the door opens and Walpurg comes in. He is
clean-shaven, mustache y compris. His hair has been trimmed. He
is dressed in an impeccably tailored cutaway coat. He wears a
yellow flower in his lapel. Bidello, dressed in a black frock coat,
comes in after him. On his arm he is carrying a woman's dress in
dark colors, blue and violet, and also a woman's hat. Professor
Walldorff can be seen behind him.*)
WALPURG Lina! Get up! It's me, Alex.

(*They are all dumbfounded. Sister Barbara springs up off her
knees. Grün stares at Walpurg with his mouth open and is not able
to catch his breath. The attendants drop Walpurg's body which, in
the stillness of the room, crashes to the ground with a bang. Sister
Anna springs up and looks at Walpurg speechlessly.*)
SISTER ANNA (*throwing herself at Walpurg*) Darling! Is it really you?
And what's that? (*She points at the corpse.*) Oh—what does it
matter, I'm so happy I'll probably go mad. You're so attractive! My
one and only! (*She falls into his arms. They kiss.*)
BIDELLO We're going into town. Oh—here's a dress for you, Miss
Alina, and a hat. Alexander and I picked these things out in a hurry.
At first glance. You'll have to change your clothes. Perhaps these
will do for the time being.
WALPURG Let's go. I'm really completely sane now: sane and happy. I'll
write something marvelous. (*He leads Alina out. Bidello follows
them.*)
BIDELLO Keep well, Grün. And after this, analyze yourself thoroughly.
(*He leaves. Professor Walldorff sticks his head in the door.*)
WALLDORFF Well, ladies and gentlemen? Hee, hee, hee!
GRÜN (*his lips blanched*) Pro-fess-or . . . I . . . I don't know . . .
(*Suddenly he begins to shout in a terrible voice.*) I don't know what
the hell is going on here! (*He approaches the door slowly, clutching
his head in his hands. Sister Barbara stares straight ahead, fiercely and
madly. The attendants look alternatingly at the corpse and at Wall-
dorff.*)
WALLDORFF Oh, it doesn't matter. I'm through with psychiatry. I'm
going back to surgery. Brain operations once made me famous. And
I am taking Bidello as my assist——

GRÜN (*throwing himself toward him*) Aaaaa! That's blackmail!

WALLDORFF Oh no! (*Pushing him away*) Hop! Skip! And away! (*He shuts the door and bolts it from the outside. Grün stands helplessly and stares wildly about at the others.*)

GRÜN Now—oh—suddenly I feel a new complex coming on. But what kind of a complex? (*He screams.*) I don't know what any of this is all about! (*The attendants suddenly spring away from the corpse and, roaring with terror, fling themselves at the door and feverishly attempt to open it.*)

SISTER BARBARA (*in a state of wild despair*) That's all your psychiatry is! (*Sobbing*) In my declining years I cannot tell any more who is mad—you or I or those people. Oh, my God, my God! Take pity on me. Perhaps I've already gone mad. (*She falls on her knees, stretching out her hands to heaven.*)

ALFRED We're the madmen now. They've locked us up for good. And this guy here, he's still lying there right in front of us, but that same Number 20 without the beard, he got up and went out there.

PAPHNUTIUS (*pointing at Grün*) He's the one—he's the worst madman. Hit him, Fred! Give it to him! Harder! Till you can't lift your arm any more!

GRÜN Stay where you are! I can explain it all to you. Perhaps at the same time it will become clearer to me too.

PAPHNUTIUS Explain it to yourself if you're so smart. Take that!

(*He starts to beat him. Alfred throws himself at Grün also, and they both thrash him. In order to save Grün, Sister Barbara throws herself forward and becomes intertwined with the fighters. There arises a so-called "obshchaya roukopashnaya schvatka à la manière russe" [a rough-and-tumble, hand-to-hand free-for-all in the Russian manner], reminiscent of so-called "samosoude" [mob law]. All four of them roll on the floor, hitting one another right and left. Walpurg's corpse becomes absorbed into this heap of thrashing bodies, and it rolls about among them passively. Blinding blue light, from above, fills the stage. Other overhead lamps are turned off, and in a bright elliptical circle of light the only thing visible is the churning pulpy mass of bodies. The curtain drops slowly.*)

7 January 1923

The artist-painter Iwo Gall devised an absolutely diabolic scheme for the scenery for this play. Anyone planning to produce the play should get in touch with him. This is the author's formal stipulation: otherwise nothing doing. [Author's note]

The Water Hen

The Water Hen (*Kurka Wodna*), written in 1921, was performed once during Witkiewicz' lifetime, at the Słowacki Theater in Cracow in July, 1922. The critics were hostile, and Witkiewicz responded with one of his typical polemic defenses of his own theories in an essay called "Some Unessential Remarks about *The Water Hen*." First he denies that the play is in any way autobiographical, as had been suggested by a friend during the intermission of the first performance. Then the playwright predicts his own vindication as an artist in ages to come:

> It's possible not to like me as an artist, but to say that I'm not an artist at all I consider something of an exaggeration, and I'm afraid that the judgment of future generations about some of my critics will not be particularly flattering.

Although he was not totally satisfied with the production because of the inadequate sets, Witkiewicz holds up *The Water Hen* as a good example of Pure Form in the theater. Along with the Epilogue to *The Mother*, *The Water Hen* in its entirety serves as the best illustration of Witkiewicz' theory. When the play is seen as Pure Form, the feeling of bewilderment it arouses in the audience can be accepted as the new theatrical effect the playwright is aiming for and understood and appreciated as such.

At the beginning of Act II of *The Water Hen*, the Duchess of Nevermore cautions her precocious stepson Tadzio: "No one knows why things are the way they are and not some other way. You can ask such questions endlessly and never find any answers." Like Tadzio, we are endlessly trapped into asking unanswerable and possibly irrelevant questions. Why is the Water Hen a water hen? Where does Tadzio come from? Who is the Lamplighter? Is Edgar Tadzio's father? Or is he really Edgar Nevermore? What does any of it mean? Witkiewicz' art lies in the creation of a feeling that there are questions without answers. The play confronts us with another world—a world of strange dreams and unfathomable mysteries—which compels us to wonder why things are the way they are and not some other way.

This metaphysical feeling of wonder and stupefaction is precisely what Witkiewicz argues the theater should create in the spectator. The new type of play Witkiewicz proposes in *An Introduction to the Theory of Pure Form in the Theater* will imitate not real life, but the pure arts of painting and music. Unhampered by such obsolete notions as believable characters and consistent plots, the dramatist will be free to deform reality for purely formal ends and use all the elements of theater as the musician uses notes and the modern painter colors and shapes. The spectator will be transported into a new dimension of thought and feeling, a world of "nonsensicality" where everything is free and unpredictable. *The Water Hen* seems to fit admirably Witkiewicz' suggestion that the new type of play is like "some strange dream, in which even the most ordinary things had a strange, unfathomable charm, characteristic of dream reveries, and unlike anything else in the world."

According to Witkiewicz' own theory, it might seem futile to try to discuss the meaning of *The Water Hen*, rather than simply to admire its brilliant design. After all, we do not ask what Bach's *Chromatic Fantasy and Fugue* means. However, the structure of each is explicable; internal construction, not subject matter, discloses the formal meaning of such art. If it is impossible to say why eight concentric rays of intense green light fill the stage when the Lamplighter appears after Edgar kills the Water Hen, at least it is clear that his reappearance in Act III takes us back in time and place to the beginning of Act I. His octagonal lantern lights the way for Edgar to shoot the Water Hen again. These sudden changes in perspective are part of a formal pattern of recurrence and inversion, giving the play both a pictorial and a musical quality.

Yet beneath its beauty as mystification and formal exercise, its brilliant surface, we begin to detect shapes and reflections if we peer long enough into its depths. Since human beings are the chief elements in drama, Witkiewicz maintained that theater can never be perfectly abstract like the pure arts of painting and music. Even though each element from real life is used only as a splash of color in the composition, *The Water Hen* paints man against the background of the universe, state, society, revolution, time, sex, money, art. The form may be pure, but the materials are the impure facts of life in the twentieth century.

So, if *The Water Hen* asserts nothing, it still says something about a strange world, which is not our world, but which resembles it seen from a great distance. In this "spherical tragedy," man sees himself as the universe sees him. It is a nonhuman drama about humans: "People are like insects, and Infinity surrounds them and summons them in a mysterious voice." The Witkacian world is little and lost in the cosmos. "Our small globe" the Duchess of Nevermore calls it—it is only one among many possible worlds, creations, planets, stars, spheres rolling and spinning in the void. Man is alone, forced at each moment to create himself and his world: every morning Edgar must start the day from scratch. On a new and unfamiliar shore each character has to create a life (or lives) for himself. Witkiewicz sees Robinson Crusoe and his desert island everywhere.

The Water Hen is a play about creation. The Father is a creator, trying to make an artist out of his son. Tadzio wants to create a mother and father, but he is at home nowhere; even the accordion-playing gangster Korbowski has equal rights at Nevermore Palace. Edgar labors to invent some sort of life for himself: "I should have been somebody, but I never knew what, or rather who." He is not even sure if he exists until he can climb inside other people's lives. "My friend's wife—my mistress' son. At last I've created a family for myself!"

Edgar even has to create his own fake penance and suffering with the aid of an obsolete torture machine from the Nevermore museum. In this world, everything—above all, human emotion—is synthetic and secondhand. Edgar looks back to the past for scraps to hold on to: a costume, a phrase, a murder, someone else's wife and son. He has no future, no present; he is nothing and has nothing, except scraps. He is a ham with a few fake grandiloquent gestures and phrases from the past —but with no identity. Even at Nevermore Palace he is only a transient lodger, a fraudulent hero in a sham world.

Tadzio has had enough and accuses his elders of too much creativity: "Manufacturing artificial people, artificial crimes, artificial penance, artificial everything." The play abounds in unnatural concoctions. The Water Hen fed the ginger cat lemons. The Duchess and the Three Old Men—the aristocracy and the money interests—create an incongruous amalgam of classes and races in the Theosophical Jam Company, blending the spiritual and the material in a sticky mixture. The names of the characters—Ephemer Typowicz (an ephemeral type), Specter, Evader—indicate that the speculation is risky and the boom will not last.

New groupings, hybrid graftings, preposterous fusions—the play's motion is generated by the odd malleability and mutability of matter. At the end of the play, an uprising occurs, a new revolutionary society is in the process of creation, as makeshift, insubstantial, and inauthentic as Edgar's calling, marriage, and paternity. Manikins and marionettes: this is the second Genesis of trash and dummies, parodies of true creation. In *The Street of Crocodiles* (1934), Bruno Schulz gives the Father the views of his friend and mentor Witkiewicz: [1]

[1] Henryk Bereza, "Bruno Schulz," *Polish Perspectives*, IX, No. 6 (June, 1965), 37–39.

Demiurge was in love with consummate, superb and complicated materials; we shall give priority to trash. We are simply entranced and enchanted by the cheapness, shabbiness and inferiority of material. . . . Can you imagine the pain, the dull imprisoned suffering, hewn into the matter of that dummy which does not know why it must be what it is, why it must remain in that forcibly imposed form which is no more than a parody? [2]

Parody and improvisation are Witkiewicz' weapons in devising a cosmogony of trash and a metaphysics for manikins. Compared to those two older birds, *The Wild Duck* and *The Seagull,* with their ornate symbolic plumage, *The Water Hen* is a wooden decoy. In "Some Unessential Remarks" Witkiewicz explained: "Unquestionably there is some kind of analogous meaning to the words Water Hen and Wild Duck—both signify birds. But what else there might be in common with Ibsen's play I really could not say."

Witkiewicz' plays often start as gags parodying drama in the older style of creation; titles, characters, and situations from other works kindle his imagination, and he experiments deforming them and pushing them into a new dimension. For a willfully distorted view of an ersatz world, clowning and pranks are indispensable. The names of his characters often contain ingenious private jokes: the Water Hen (*Kurka Wodna*) is a secret anagram for an obscene word for whore (*kurwa*). Sometimes the names are international literary parodies in foreign languages. Instead of being the refrain of Poe's Raven, Witkiewicz makes the Nevermores into characters and continues his bird lore. Like his frequent garbled quotations, misattributions, and invented citations, Witkiewicz' playing with names and titles is a purposeful prank in Pure Form. Everything is haphazard and chaotic and turns into something else: "Art, philosophy, love, science, society—one huge mishmash," in the words of the hero of *The Cuttlefish.*

"A Spherical Tragedy" is the subtitle of *The Water Hen.* All points on its surface are equidistant from its center. Like our small globe, it has no beginning, middle, or end; its structure is circular, finishing where it began with the shooting of the Water Hen. Such a sphere is a separate world, whirling about in space. Witkiewicz brings drama into the world of modern physics and mathematics (as well as of modern painting). The Hungarian mathematician János Bolyai, author of the *Science of Absolute Space,* wrote to his mathematician father: "*from nothing I have created another wholly new world!*" So another son to another father about his new creation. Witkiewicz calls one of his plays written at just this time a "non-Euclidean drama." *The Water Hen*

[2] Bruno Schulz, *The Street of Crocodiles,* translated by Celina Wieniewska (New York: Walker and Company, 1963), pp. 51, 54.

likewise rejects classical geometry for the spherical variety in which the shortest distance between two points is a curve, and parallel lines always meet.

The play moves from zero to infinity, both of which are spherical. Edgar is nothing, a void everyone tries to fill. Tadzio discovers Infinity after Edgar has killed the Water Hen—and she claims she does not exist at all. Spheres and numbers: the construction of artificial worlds. The Duchess' former husband Edgar was reading Russell and Whitehead's *Principia Mathematica* after his entrails had been devoured by a tiger in the Janjapara Jungle. At the beginning of Act II, Tadzio is putting together some kind of mechanical device, and after he has grown up, he studies mathematics. In Witkiewicz, figures and machines start to replace life; the world will soon become totally automatic. The card game (vint in the original) at the end of the play is another construction, paralleling, with its astronomical scores, the heaps of corpses in the streets and all the confiscated property. Matter is endlessly pliable. Even Korbowski rolls up into a ball and becomes a world.

But it is all lies—everything men say and do and all the roles they invent. "Truth is what is actually happening," according to the Water Hen. Suddenly the scene changes: two walls are slid in from the sides, and the field becomes the courtyard of a barracks; or the cherry-colored curtain is drawn, and the landscape with pole and lighted lantern appears between the columns. A rapid shift in perspective, a lifting of the veil, the painted scene is pulled apart, and something strange appears behind it. The colored fragments in the kaleidoscope are shaken; we look through to the view cards of revolution in the background.

The exotic world of international finance, sex, art, and politics—crossroads of different races and peoples—finally blows up. The social spheres—duchesses, artists, sea captains, detectives, crooks, and Russian nannies—are spinning out of control too. Edgar's father will turn into a revolutionary admiral; Edgar and the Water Hen have been transformed into corpses, along with the others in the streets. *The Water Hen* is not only a "spherical tragedy," it is also a "comedy with corpses," another genre invented by Witkiewicz.

It is an a-realistic world, an animated still life of ginger cats and lemons. The outbreak of revolution is no more or less surprising than anything else, and the corpses, "the really frightful things," Witkiewicz, like Tadzio, paints only through a prism of vivid color. The red glare of exploding shells lights the whites and grays and blacks of the mustaches, beards, and hair of the four elderly gentlemen playing cards during the revolution. They are playing-cards themselves—kings and jacks. The bombs are their lantern.

The Water Hen is the painting of a collective dream, a playful excursion into a new dimension of cataclysmic science fiction. It is impossible to do anything with such a society—life cannot become any more artificial, automatic, and false. Here is a cardboard universe for which there is no bid, simply "Pass."

Despite Witkiewicz' strictures, Pure Form cannot explain all of *The Water Hen*, especially not its strong emotional force and its richness as a personal, social, and political statement. It is a family tragedy, dealing with "three abortive generations" and two sets of fathers and sons; their refined, anguished world is on the brink of disaster, and they face emotional and social bankruptcy. From this perspective, *The Water Hen* is surrealistic Chekhov, a fantastic *Cherry Orchard* with gangsters. Instead of the mysterious sound of a harp string snapping and the chopping down of the cherry trees, the rattle of machine guns punctuates the collapse of Witkiewicz' vanishing world.

Like Chekhov, Witkiewicz portrays with poignancy and humor in the first two acts of *The Water Hen* the leisurely life of the upper class on a country estate, attended by servants and consumed by a sense of futility and boredom that is only temporarily relieved by pointless love affairs. As in Chekhov, too, there is a considerable interval of time elapsing between the next to last act and the last act so as to permit the initial situation to deteriorate. However, Witkiewicz deliberately pushes this technique to extremes. Whereas in Chekhov there is simply a gradual and deepening sense of frustration, regret, and futility after the passage of several months, in *The Water Hen* ten years elapse suddenly. In a startling parody of stage servants conveying necessary information to the audience, the Footman announces to Tadzio: "Sir, the Lady who was here ten years ago wishes to speak to you." The changes that have resulted are drastic; the world and the people in it have grown hard, violent, and sick.

The enigmatic Hen who was once so close to Edgar has become a coarse and unscrupulous seductress sticking her claws into Tadzio. Edgar has aged prematurely, and his dissatisfaction with life and search for identity have turned to a hopeless despair driving him to suicide. Tadzio has gone from a dreamy and precocious child, deeply devoted to the father who adopted him, to a brash, bitter young man who hates Edgar and chooses Korbowski as his ideal. Korbowski himself has ceased to be simply the ridiculous kept man paid by the Duchess and has become a hardened criminal and ruthless opportunist. The rhythm of life has utterly changed. Mid-twentieth-century nervousness and tension have replaced the old leisurely ennui; Tadzio's schedule is so busy that he even forgets that women exist, and Edgar has been thrown into the business world: "board meetings at banks, the stock exchange, negotiations with wholesalers and big accounts." The new science is mathematics, and the new world no longer has time for amorous or metaphysical pursuits. Family relations degenerate into a bitter struggle between the new father and new son, Edgar and Tadzio, ending with a physical fight between the two. The decay of the bonds of personal relationships has gone so far that the collapse of society in revolution seems surprisingly convincing, even though it has never been hinted at. Witkiewicz has a Shakespearean grasp on the interrelationship between public and private disaster; when father and son come to blows, it is symptomatic of violence on a broad scale.

The old sea captain is the only character who does not change. His boundless optimism and lack of neurosis make him at first seem the only sane person in a crowd of madmen; his humor and bluntness cast him in a role of a comic chorus, particularly when he talks of his favorite subject, his son's artistic vocation. But, in the last act, his heartiness and lack of concern in the face of disasters that overtake his son and family are a frightening kind of moral insensitivity or something worse. His failure to change or stop joking and his assurance that he will become a "revolutionary admiral" are cynical examples of the power of the human animal to survive. The more sensitive go under.

The Water Hen

A SPHERICAL TRAGEDY

IN THREE ACTS

Father	*Albert Valpor, an old man, former skipper of a merchant ship. Short, broad-shouldered, but not obese. Nautical garb. Beret with a light blue pompon. White Vandyke beard. White mustache.*
He	*Edgar Valpor, his son. About 30 years old. Clean-shaven. Good-looking.*
Small Son	*Tadzio, a boy 10 years old, with long blond hair.*
Lady	*Duchess Alice of Nevermore, a tall blonde, rather majestic and very beautiful, about 25 years old.*
Water Hen	*Elizabeth Gutzie-Virgeling, a person of unknown origin, about 26 years old. Flaxenhaired. Light eyes. Average height. Very pretty, but not at all seductive. Nose turned up just a little bit. Lips very wide, thick, and liver red.*
Scoundrel	*Richard de Korbowa-Korbowski, recte* * *Tom Hoozy, good-looking, dark-haired, very scoundrelly, about 20 years old. Looks like Edgar Valpor.*
Three Old Men:	
a. Ephemer Typowicz	*A businessman, clean-shaven, short gray hair, grown corpulent with power.*
b. Isaak Specter	*Tall, thin, grizzled Semite, with a black mustache and a Vandyke beard. Refined gestures, an Assyrian type.*
c. Alfred Evader	*Nervous, red-haired Semite, with gold pince-nez. Skinny and tall. A mustache, no trace of a beard, a typical Hittite.*
Footman	*Jan Parblichenko, an ordinary flunkey. Reddish-brown hair, pimply. Completely clean-shaven.*

* Witkiewicz uses the Latin *recte* and *false* throughout the play to indicate Hoozy's true and assumed names. [Translators' note]

Four More Footmen	*With long hair, two dark, two albino. All of them (including Jan) dressed in blue frock coats, shirts with ruffled fronts, and white stockings. They wear a great many military medals on their frock coats. Middle-aged. Jan is distinguished from the others by red aiguillettes.*
Three Detectives	*Head detective, Adolf Orsin, blond hair and a big mustache. One of the other two has a mustache and wears glasses. The other has a long black beard. They appear artificial and banal.*
Nanny	*Afrosia Yupupova, an old woman with a heart of gold. A fat blonde 40 years old.*
The Lamplighter	*A bearded individual in a workman's blue coat.*

Supplementary instructions from the central authority: speak without affectation and not from the guts, even at the worst moments.

ACT I

An open field, sparsely overgrown with juniper bushes. Some of the juniper bushes are shaped like cypress (two to the left and three to the right). Here and there bunches of yellow flowers (something in the poppy line). The horizon meets the edge of the sea. In the center of the stage a mound a little over three feet high. A crimson-colored pole (five feet high) rises from the mound. Hanging from the pole there is a very large octagonal lantern with green glass (the lantern may be silver and ornate). The Water Hen, wearing a chemise, stands under the pole. Her arms are bare. She has rather short hair, tied with a blue ribbon, forming a large topknot; the rest of her hair falls loosely around her head. A sheer black crinoline petticoat shows beneath her short skirt, and her legs are bare. "He" stands to the left, dressed in the style of the three bound men in the illustrated edition of Robinson Crusoe. *Three-cornered hat, boots with very wide tops turned down (eighteenth-century style). He is holding a double-barreled shotgun of the worst make. At this very moment he is loading it, with his back and side almost turned to the audience. To the left, a red sunset. The sky is covered with fantastic clouds.*

WATER HEN (*gently reproachful*) Couldn't you be a little quicker about it?

EDGAR (*finishing loading*) All right—I'm ready, I'm ready. (*Shoulders the gun and aims at her—a pause*) I can't. Damn it. (*He lowers the gun.*)

WATER HEN (*as before*) You're wearing us both out quite unnecessarily. We've already decided everything. I thought that after so much anguish we'd finally understood each other. And now you're hesitating again. Be a man. Hurry up and aim!

EDGAR (*raising his shotgun*) There's one thing I hadn't thought of. But what does it matter? (*Shoulders the gun and aims; a pause*) I can't. No, I can't pull the trigger. (*Lowers the gun*) The difficulty is that I won't have anyone to talk to any more. Who will I talk to if you're gone, Lizzie?

WATER HEN (*sighing*) Oh! You'll spend more time in your own company then. It will be very good for you. Be brave. Only for a moment. Afterward you'll be able to figure it out.

EDGAR (*sits on the ground in Turkish fashion*) But I don't want to be by myself.

WATER HEN (*sits resignedly on the mound*) You liked solitude in the old days. Do you remember how you used to run away from me? What's happened to you now?

EDGAR (*angrily*) I've grown accustomed to you. It's awful. I feel that there's a special kind of elastic band between us. I haven't been alone for the past two years. Even when you were far away, the elastic stretched, but never broke.

WATER HEN Well, try something different for once. I have nothing new to offer you. Your chances will be better without me. I'm not talking about women, but about things in general.

EDGAR You're trying to work on my baser instincts. Just like a woman. (*He jumps up.*) You must have a suicide mania. You're afraid yourself, and you use me like a piece of machinery. As if I were an extension of this shotgun. It's humiliating.

WATER HEN What a ridiculous idea! Death means nothing to me. That's the absolute truth. But I really don't want to die. Yet life means nothing to me either. What tires me most is standing here under this pole. (*The sun is setting, dusk is falling, and then it slowly turns dark.*)

EDGAR (*clutching the gun in his hands*) I can't stand this. You know what—let's stop all this and get away from here. This is a hateful place. Nothing can ever happen here.

WATER HEN (*gently*) No, Edgar, you have to make up your mind. It has to be decided today. We've already made up our minds. And that's all there is to it. I can't live the way I used to any more. Something's snapped inside me, and it will never come back again.

EDGAR (*groaning with indecision*) Hm. I hate to think what'll happen to me during the night. Boredom and suffering—a vicious circle, endless and self-contained and closed in upon itself forever. And there'll be no one to tell it to. After all, that's my only joy in life.

WATER HEN (*reproachfully*) Even at a time like this you're being small. But, honestly, you used to mean much more to me than I ever thought you could. You were my child and my father—something indefinable, something without form and without contour, filling my world with its indeterminateness. (*Changing her tone*) You're not a child, but you're so little, so hopelessly little . . .

EDGAR (*angrily*) Yes, I know. I'm not an undersecretary of state, a factory manager, a revolutionary, or a general. I'm a man without a profession and without a future. I'm not even an artist. At least artists know how to die in style.

WATER HEN Life for life's sake! Do you remember the theory of your friend the Duke of Nevermore? The so-called "creative life." Ha, ha!

EDGAR The insignificance of that concept is the cause of all my misfortunes. I waged a futile battle against myself for ten years, and after all that, you wonder why I can't make up my mind about such a trivial matter as killing you. Ha! Ha! (*He knocks the shotgun against the ground.*)

WATER HEN How stupid he is! Greatness is always irrevocable.

EDGAR There are limits to my endurance. Let's not have any contrived scenes. Even in the most idiotic plays it's definitely against the rules.

WATER HEN All right, but even you'll agree it's a vicious circle. Everything irrevocable is great, and that explains the greatness of death, first love, the loss of virginity, and so forth. Whatever one can do several times is by its very nature trivial. (*A pale gleam of moonlight shows through the clouds.*) You want to be great, and yet you don't want to do anything that can't be undone.

EDGAR (*ironically*) What about courage, self-sacrifice, suffering for someone else's sake, acts of renunciation? Aren't these forms of greatness too? But they're really not; as soon as you deny yourself something, you become so smug about your own greatness that it makes you petty. Every work of art is great because it's unique. Let's sacrifice ourselves for each other right now, or else join the circus.

WATER HEN (*ironically*) Anything that lives is unique, too, and hence great. You are great, Edgar, and so am I. If you don't shoot me this very minute, I'll despise you as an utter wet noodle.

EDGAR All this bores me. I'll shoot you like a dog. I hate you. You're my guilty conscience. It's I who despise you.

WATER HEN Let's not quarrel. I don't want to say good-bye to you in the middle of a scene. Come, kiss me on the forehead for the last time, and then shoot. We've thought it all out. Well, come on. (*After putting down the gun, Edgar approaches her hesitantly and kisses her on the forehead.*) And now go back to your place, my dear. Don't hesitate any more.

EDGAR (*goes to his former place stage left and picks up his shotgun*) Well, all right. It's all settled. I accept the inevitable. (*Examining the gun*)

WATER HEN (*clapping her hands*) Oh, how splendid!

EDGAR Stand still. (*The Hen stands still—Edgar shoulders the gun, aims for a long time, and fires from both barrels at short intervals. A pause.*)

WATER HEN (*still standing, her voice completely unchanged*) One miss. The other straight through the heart.

EDGAR (*silently ejects the cartridges from the shotgun and then slowly lays the gun on the ground and lights a cigarette*) There's one thing I've forgotten—what am I going to tell my father? Perhaps . . . (*While he is speaking, Tadzio crawls out from behind the mound, dressed in a boy's navy blue suit with a lace collar; he hides in the Hen's petticoats.*)

WATER HEN (*standing*) Go to your papa, Tadzio.

EDGAR (*turns around, notices Tadzio, and speaks with reluctance*) Oh, more surprises!

TADZIO Papa, Papa, don't be angry.

EDGAR I'm not angry, my child, I only want a little rest after all this. Where did you come from?

TADZIO I don't know. I woke up when I heard the shots. And you're my papa.

EDGAR Who knows? Maybe I'm a father, too. You see, my young man, it's all the same to me. For all I know, I might even be your father, although I can't stand children.

TADZIO But you won't beat me, Papa?

EDGAR (*somewhat dementedly*) I don't know, I don't know. (*Controlling himself*) You see, something's happened here. I can't tell you now. This woman (*pointing to the Hen*) in some way or other . . . Why am I telling you this?

TADZIO (*picking up the shotgun*) Please tell me, what were you shooting at?

EDGAR (*menacingly*) Put that down right now. (*Tadzio puts down the gun; more gently*) I was shooting because . . . How can I tell you? Well, you see I was . . .

WATER HEN (*in a weak voice*) Don't say anything . . . in just a moment . . .

EDGAR Yes, my boy, it's not as simple as you think. Assume I'm your father, if you will. But whoever your father may be, who is he really? What kind of a man will he turn out to be? These are still unanswered questions.

TADZIO But you're a grown-up, Papa, you know everything.

EDGAR Not as much as you think. (*To the Hen*) Something fatal's happened. I have so much to tell you that a whole lifetime wouldn't be long enough; then suddenly this little brat appears, and our last moments are hopelessly spoiled.

WATER HEN (*in a dying voice*) I'm dying. Remember what I told you. You must be great in one way or another.

EDGAR (*advances a few steps toward her*) Great, great, but how? At fishing or blowing soap bubbles?

WATER HEN (*weakly*) Don't come near me. This is the end. (*She slowly crumples on the mound. The moon behind the fleeting clouds occasionally lights up the stage. Now it shines rather brightly.*)

TADZIO Papa, what's the matter with that lady?

EDGAR (*signaling him to be quiet; not turning away from the Hen*) Quiet, wait. (*He gazes in silence at the Hen, who is expiring half-*

crumpled on the mound with her hands pressed to her breast. She breathes heavily and gives a death rattle. A cloud completely covers the moon. It is dark.)

TADZIO Papa, I'm afraid. It's scary here.

WATER HEN *(scarcely able to speak)* Go to him . . . I don't want . . . *(She dies. At this point the setting changes so that the field becomes the courtyard of a barracks. Two walls are slid in from the sides; a dim light appears in the center windows and at the gate below. At the same time Edgar comes up to Tadzio and silently puts his arms around him.)*

EDGAR Well, I am alone now. I can take care of you.

TADZIO I'm afraid. What happened to the lady?

EDGAR *(letting go of Tadzio)* I'll tell you the truth. She's dead.

TADZIO Dead? I don't know what dead means.

EDGAR *(surprised)* You don't know! *(Somewhat impatiently)* It's exactly as though she went to sleep, but she'll never wake up.

TADZIO Never! *(In a different tone of voice)* Never. I said I'd never steal apples, but that was different. Never—I understand now, it's the same forever and ever.

EDGAR *(impatiently)* Well, yes, that's the infinite, the eternal.

TADZIO I know God is infinite. I never could understand that. Papa, I know so much now. I understand everything. Only it's too bad about the lady. I'd like to tell her so.

EDGAR *(partly to himself, grimly)* There's a great deal I'd like to tell her, too. Much more than you.

TADZIO Papa, tell me the whole truth. Why won't you tell me? It's very important.

EDGAR *(waking up, after having been lost in his thoughts)* You're right. I have to tell you. There's no one else I can tell it to. *(Emphatically)* I killed her.

TADZIO You killed her? So you were the one who shot her. How funny! Ha, ha . . . As though you were out hunting.

EDGAR Tadzio, Tadzio, don't laugh like that. It's dreadful.

TADZIO *(becoming serious)* It's not dreadful at all, if it really happened the way you say it did. I was shooting, too, but at crows with a bird gun. You look so big, Papa. But it all seems as if some insects had eaten one another. People are like insects, and Infinity surrounds them and summons them in a mysterious voice.

EDGAR Where did you get that? Did you read it somewhere?

TADZIO Perhaps I dreamed it. I have such strange dreams. Please go on talking, Papa. I'll explain everything to you.

EDGAR *(sitting on the ground)* You see, it was like this. I should have been somebody, but I never knew what, or rather who. I don't even know whether I actually exist, although the fact that I suffer terribly is certainly real. That woman (*pointing backward with the index finger of his left hand*) wanted to help me; she was the one who asked me to kill her. Eventually all of us will die. Desperately unhappy people find consolation in that thought. (*Enter from stage right the Lamplighter; he lights the lantern. Eight concentric beams of intense green light fill the stage. Tadzio sits down next to Edgar —they talk to each other without paying any attention to the Lamplighter, who is listening to them.*) Why, why? If a man doesn't live like everybody else, if he doesn't work toward a goal, like a horse with blinders over his eyes walking around in a treadmill, then let me tell you Tadzio, quite truthfully, that he's completely in the dark. The goal is in the goal itself, as my friend Edgar, Duke of Nevermore, used to say. But I never could fathom that deep truth.

TADZIO (*nodding seriously*) Oh, I understand. I'm not satisfied with just anything, either, but right now I don't want anything at all, nothing at all—do you understand?

EDGAR (*putting his arms around him*) Oh, yes, I understand. You're starting pretty early, my young friend. What'll you be like when you're my age? (*The Lamplighter, who listened for a while, silently leaves through stage right.*)

TADZIO I'll be a robber.

EDGAR (*moving away from him in disgust*) Shut up. Don't talk that way. Sometimes I'd like to do something terrible, too.

TADZIO Ha, ha. How funny you are, Papa! There's really nothing terrible at all. Only there are certain times when it's best not to be afraid. And frightful things, really frightful things I paint in watercolors only—do you know what I mean? I have pastel colors like that, so I'm only really afraid when I'm asleep.

EDGAR (*jumping up*) Nothing happens, nothing. I thought that something would happen, but there's no change—the same silence everywhere, and the earth silently revolves on its axis. The world is a desert without meaning. (*He looks around him and notices the barracks.*) Look, Tadzio, I have the impression we're in prison. Yellow walls. (*Lights blink in the center windows of the barracks. Tadzio stands up and looks around him.*)

TADZIO I know this house. Soldiers are stationed here. The seashore is over there. (*He points to the gate of the barracks.*)

EDGAR (*disillusioned*) Oh, yes, I thought it was a prison. I feel like a dog on a chain who's been set free, but doesn't know how to run. For the rest of my life I'll walk around the kennel, and I won't have the courage to run away. Because—who knows?—I'll probably feel that perhaps it isn't true, I'm still on the chain. (*To Tadzio*) But tell me, once and for all, what were you doing here in the first place?

TADZIO (*after a moment's reflection*) I don't know, and I don't even want to remember. I was very ill in a kind of institution for boys. I didn't have a mother. And then I woke up as you were shooting, but I know this house, perhaps from my dreams.

EDGAR (*waves his hand contemptuously*) That's hardly very important. Tomorrow I'll begin your upbringing. (*At this moment Edgar's Father, wearing nautical garb, enters from stage right; he stops and listens to Edgar and Tadzio without being noticed by them.*)

TADZIO You'll never be able to bring me up, Papa. You couldn't.

EDGAR Why?

TADZIO You've had no upbringing yourself. I know that much about you at least.

FATHER (*coming up to them*) You talk very well, Sonny boy. (*To Edgar*) Where did you unearth such a precocious little imp?

EDGAR (*getting up*) I don't know. He crept out from behind that mound. (*The Father turns around and notices the Water Hen's dead body.*)

FATHER What's this? (*With a wave of his hand*) After all, it hardly matters. I don't meddle in your personal affairs. The Water Hen is dead. Since there'll be no supper at home, I trust you'll approve of our having something to eat here. I'll give orders to have the body carried out. I can't stand corpses flopping about where they have no business to be. (*He blows his whistle, which he wears on a yellow string. Edgar and Tadzio remain standing silently.*)

TADZIO This is funny. I can see myself painting it in pastels and even then . . . (*Four footmen rush in and fall in in a row.*)

FATHER (*pointing to the Hen's corpse*) Carry the lady out. There ought to be a cold cellar somewhere in this barracks. (*He uses his finger to point to one of the footmen.*) Tell the orderly that I'll send for the corpse tomorrow. Don't ask any questions, and don't go blabbing about it. And then bring a table here and serve supper.

FOOTMEN Yes, we understand. At your service. (*They immediately pounce on the Hen's corpse and carry her out stage left.*)

FATHER (*to Tadzio*) Well, young man, how do you like all this? Huh?

TADZIO It's really hilarious. Still there's something missing. I don't know what.

EDGAR Father, won't you leave him in peace? I've adopted him. I'll take care of the formalities tomorrow. I'm beginning another life. Not a new life, but another one—do you understand, Father?

FATHER You can even start at the end and go backward. You can't escape. Gauguin didn't begin to paint until he was twenty-seven, Bernard Shaw didn't begin to write plays until after he was thirty. But what's the point of giving examples? I tell you you'll be an artist, just as sure as I'm Albert Valpor, former skipper of the *Orenteso*, a vessel of ten thousand tons. Our story today is only the beginning—but a promising one. Own up to it, Ed, you killed the Water Hen.

EDGAR Yes, I did. But she asked me to.

FATHER Naturally. She preferred death to living with you. And yet she couldn't live without you. Poor silly Hen. I'm sorry about it. But what'll you do now? Who'll listen to your long, pedantic lectures justifying your downfall? Eh? Perhaps this young ward of yours. Huh?

TADZIO How wise you are, Captain! Papa has gone over everything with me. (*The Footmen bring in a table from stage left, place it before the mound, and set it for five people. A simple table, simple wicker chairs.*)

FATHER Didn't I tell you so? You've had a rendez-vous with destiny, my adopted grandson. Edgar Valpor, the great artist of the future, has taken you into his confidence. Never forget that.

EDGAR Must you joke, Father? This is hardly an appropriate time. (*He notices the table.*) Why so many place settings?

FATHER I'm expecting guests. I want to provide you with enemies disguised as friends and, vice versa, friends disguised as the bitterest enemies. You don't know how to live simply and normally, so you'll have to live your life in reverse and walk backward along wayward paths. My patience is at an end. I've had enough.

EDGAR And so Father you . . . (*Tadzio plays with the double-barreled shotgun.*)

FATHER Yes, yes, I knew what would happen. I foresaw a great deal. Not everything, of course. I didn't know you'd shoot her. Now I don't want to spoil you. Still I must admit that I'm somewhat impressed. Somewhat, I repeat, despite the fact that you've behaved like a thoroughly cheap stinker.

EDGAR You're not a man, you're a devil. So you knew all along, Father?

FATHER There's nothing remarkable about that. Don't you remember when the three of us lived in the little house on the other side of the bay at Stockfish Beach? Remember her mania for feeding lemons to my ginger cat? I was able to observe the two of you very closely then. You both thought I was only searching for buried treasure. Remember, when she gave you that purple flower and said, "A great man does not ask how to become great, he is great." I even wrote it down.

EDGAR Don't say anything more, Father. Poor Elizabeth, poor Water Hen. (*He covers his face with his hands.*)

TADZIO (*comes up to him with the shotgun in his hand*) Don't cry, Papa. These are only little pictures God paints with his magic pastels.

EDGAR (*opens his eyes and notices the gun*) Take it away! I cannot bear to look at that thing. (*He grabs the gun out of Tadzio's hands and throws it to the right. All this time the Footmen pay no attention and set the table.*)

FATHER Easy. Easy. Ham—bleeding heart—sentimental ass. (*Edgar stands still staring at the ground.*) Remember you're leading another life. Another life—as you've so aptly put it. Go live on Mars or on the star Antares if you can't get along here. My guests are about to arrive, do you understand? Don't you dare let me down with that hang-dog look! Don't you forget it! (*Nonsensical sounds from an accordion are heard from the right.*) They're coming. (*To Edgar*) Chin up. Not a whimper!

TADZIO Captain, you're wonderful! Like an evil sorcerer.

FATHER (*moved*) Call me grandfather. At last there's someone who appreciates my style. (*He strokes Tadzio's head. The accordion playing gets closer.*)

EDGAR (*explaining*) I appreciate your style, too. I just don't want you to jump to conclusions about . . .

FATHER Then don't let me jump over you as if I were a horse and you were a hurdle. Silence. The guests are coming.

(*Duchess Alice enters from stage right. She is dressed in a ball gown the color of the sea. She wears a scarf, but no hat. She is followed by Tom Hoozy* [false *Korbowa-Korbowski Richard*], *dressed in a frock coat without a hat; he enters playing the accordion. Three old men come in after them.*)

LADY How do you do, Captain? (*Father kisses her hand, playing the young man. Hoozy has stopped playing the accordion and observes the situation.*)

FATHER My dear lady—so delighted to see you. The situation here is rather snarled, but we can unsnarl it. It was hardly necessary for the Duchess to bring these gentlemen. (*Points to the old men*) However, we'll have to do the best we can.

LADY But these gentlemen are quite charming. Let me introduce them to you.

FATHER Oh, we already know one another. (*He greets the old men in a perfunctory manner.*) And now, if your Grace will allow me, I'll present to you my son, who was a great friend of your late husband. Ed, greet Her Grace. My son—Duchess Alice of Nevermore.

EDGAR Good heavens, is Edgar dead?

FATHER We'll talk about it later—behave yourself.

EDGAR (*kisses the Duchess' hand*) Please tell me what happened to Edgar.

LADY A tiger devoured him in Janjapara Jungle. He was always putting his courage to the test until finally the Supreme Being lost his patience. He died two days after the accident, and I assure you he died beautifully. His belly was torn to pieces, and he suffered terribly. But up to the last moment he was reading Russell and Whitehead's *Principia Mathematica*. You know—all those symbols.

EDGAR Yes, I know. What strength! Poor Edgar. (*To his father*) Why didn't you tell me about it before, Father? I'm buffeted by so many blows all at once. My God, did Elizabeth know about it?

LADY Has anything else happened? Tell me. I've heard so much about you from Edgar. He considered you the most interesting character on the face of our small globe.

EDGAR Yes—something strange has happened. I'm on the threshold of another life. Beyond the grave almost . . .

FATHER That's enough. As a matter of fact, today he shot the Water Hen like a dog. At her own request. Wouldn't you agree, Duchess, that's a lousy thing to do?

LADY Oh, that Elizabeth Virgeling! I've heard so much about you two from Edgar! My poor husband often received letters from her. She wrote such strange things. Afterward he was never quite himself.

FATHER I'd still like to know whether or not you think it's a lousy thing to do.

LADY But Mr. Albert—women love to sacrifice themselves: what good luck to have the chance to die for someone else. Isn't that so, Mr. . . . Edgar? It's strange to say that name again.

EDGAR Well, yes . . . I suppose so . . . I don't know. I killed her half an hour ago.

LADY What a pity. I so much wanted to meet her.

EDGAR Edgar was in love with her and worshiped her from a distance. He wrote me that she was the only woman he could really . . .

LADY (*dissatisfied, she interrupts him*) Edgar loved only me, my dear sir. (*Tadzio stands to the left and looks at everyone delightedly.*)

EDGAR But, my dear lady, I'll show you Edgar's letters.

LADY That doesn't mean anything at all. He was lying. Let's go for a stroll, and I'll explain everything to you. (*All this time the Footmen have been standing stiffly between the mound and the table. The Lady and Edgar pass to the left. The Father stands looking now at the old men and Hoozy, now at them. As she passes by*) Who's this charming little boy?

EDGAR That's my adopted son. I adopted him exactly twenty minutes ago.

LADY (*smiling*) Half an hour ago you killed her. Twenty minutes ago you adopt some boy or other. It seems to me you've really been through enough for one day. Edgar told me you were strong as Hercules. What's your name, little boy?

TADZIO My name is Tadeusz Gutzie-Virgeling. (*To the Duchess*) You're a very beautiful woman. Like the fortuneteller in the picture I drew.

EDGAR What? That too? I'll go out of my mind.

FATHER (*bursts out laughing*) Ha, ha, ha. That's a good one. (*He beats his hands rapidly up and down on his knees.*)

EDGAR Did you know about that too, father? You knew Elizabeth had a son, and you didn't tell me anything about it?

FATHER (*laughing*) As sure as I am the skipper of the *Oronteso*, I knew nothing about it. It's a surprise to me. Come here, Tadzio, let me give you a hug. (*Tadzio goes to him.*)

EDGAR What was it you wanted to tell me?

LADY I want to prove to you that it's all a mistake. (*They pass to the left and whisper. Hoozy plays the accordion impatiently.*)

EVADER Mr. Specter, this is an extraordinary affair. I think we'd better go have supper at the Astoria. Or else we'll have to face the consequences.

SPECTER Take my word for it, Mr. Evader. Nothing bad's going to happen.

FATHER (*lets go of Tadzio*) But, gentlemen, please stay to supper, they'll set the table for you right away. (*To a Footman*) Get a move on! Three more place settings and more wine; hurry up! (*The Footmen dash to the left.*) Tonight we'll drink till we all fall overboard. Isn't that right, Mr. Korbowski? You were in the navy.

KORBOWSKI (*produces a wild sob from the accordion*) All right, Mr. Valpor. But I don't like that flirtation between Alice and your only son. (*Points to the left*) She's no morsel for degenerates, my Alice isn't! Alice is mine! (*He throws down his accordion, which gives a wail. The others turn around.*)

EVADER Mr. Specter, let's go.

SPECTER I quite agree. I smell trouble.

TYPOWICZ Wait! We're invited to supper. It's an amusing situation.

EDGAR (*to the Lady*) Who's that swine? Oh, excuse me—he came with you, but after all . . .

LADY (*passing to the right*) He's my only consolation in life. Mr. Korbowski—Mr. Edgar Valpor. (*The men greet each other; the Footmen set three new places at the table.*) He's utterly primitive. If it weren't for him, I wouldn't have survived Edgar's death. We met in India. Now we go everywhere together and see the most revolting things in the world. You have no idea how beautifully he conducts himself in every situation.

KORBOWSKI Alice, darling, please don't joke. You're twisting the lion's tail. I want to be treated with respect whether we're in company or alone.

EDGAR Why is he so familiar with you? What's going on?

KORBOWSKI I'm this lady's lover. Understand? I was invited here by your father, and no uncouth only son is going to get in my way. (*The Duchess looks at both of them through her lorgnette.*)

EDGAR Don't go too far . . . or I won't be responsible for my actions. I've had enough for today. Please. (*The Footmen have set the table and stand in a row behind it.*)

KORBOWSKI I'm not going to let Alice carry on with the first ameba who happens to come along. I'm her lover, and I draw a yearly salary of forty thousand francs—with the approval of the late Duke Edgar.

EDGAR So you're just a kept man, an ordinary Alphonse . . .

KORBOWSKI (*coldly, with passion*) I'm not Alphonse, I'm Richard, and a quite extraordinary one at that. Take a good look at that. (*He shoves his fist under Edgar's nose.*)

EDGAR What? Shoving your filthy paw in my face! (*He strikes Korbowski between the eyes with his fist. A short fight.*)

KORBOWSKI You only son . . .

EDGAR Take that and that! I'll show you! (*He throws Hoozy out stage right and runs out after him.*)

LADY (*to Father*) Why, your son is an athlete! He overpowered Korbowski! And besides he's so good-looking. The photograph doesn't do him justice. It lacks expression. And what intelligence! I've read his letters to Edgar.

FATHER (*bowing*) It's only nervous energy. I never could persuade him to do his morning exercises. Nerves. Nervous energy. The way madmen in an asylum break their cell bars. Yes, nerves. We're descended from old nobility.

LADY Why, with nerves like that, who needs an athlete's muscles? What a magnificent specimen of masculinity!

FATHER I was sure your Grace would be pleased.

LADY Call me daughter, Mr. Valpor. It's all settled. (*The Father bows. Edgar comes back.*)

EDGAR (*the ruffles of his shirt are crumpled—without his hat*) Do you know what he was shouting as he ran away? That you (*pointing to the Duchess*) couldn't live without him and his evil ways, his rotten tricks, to be more precise, as he himself put it. He claims that you're an utterly depraved woman. So did Edgar.

LADY (*coquettishly*) Find out for yourself. Starting tomorrow, I'm going to be your wife. Your father's already given his consent.

EDGAR So soon? I don't really know who I am yet. Perhaps in a day or two.

FATHER Idiot, when you can get something for nothing, take it, and don't ask questions. Such a high-class woman, and yet he hesitates.

LADY (*to Father*) It's only bashfulness. (*To Edgar*) I'm sure you'll be happy with me. We've already become acquainted through all those letters and also because of what Edgar himself told me. He actually brought us together a long time ago, although he loved only me. Please believe me.

EDGAR But I do believe you, I have to. (*Takes her by the hand*) Is it really true? Can I start another life?

LADY Yes, with me. With me everything is possible.

EDGAR But that Korbowski. I'm afraid of what he's got in mind . . .

LADY Don't be afraid. With you I'm not afraid of anything. (*She takes his head in her hands and kisses him.*)

TADZIO Grandfather, will I really get such a beautiful mother?

FATHER Yes, my boy. You've won first prize. She's a genuine English Duchess. (*To everybody*) And now, gentlemen, we can sit down to supper. Please. (*He points to the table. Tadzio comes up to the Lady, who hugs him.*)

LADY My child, from now on you may call me mama.

EDGAR (*deep in thought, near the front of the stage, partly to himself*) My friend's wife—my mistress's son. At last I've created a family for myself! But won't it be too much for me? (*To his Father*) Listen to me, Father. Should I humor myself this way? Shouldn't I undergo some kind of penance first?

FATHER Sit down at the table and don't bother me.

EDGAR (*to everybody, as though justifying himself*) It's people and circumstances that have always made me what I am. I'm a manikin, a marionette. Before I can create anything, everything happens all by itself exactly the way it always has, and not because of anything I've done. What is this? Some sort of a curse?

LADY You can tell me all about it later. Now let's go eat. I'm desperately hungry. (*They sit down.*)

ACT II

A salon in Nevermore palace. To the left by the wall, a round table. Armchairs. There are no windows. Door to the left and to the right. Pictures on the walls. Everything in strawberry hues which gradually become suffused with a warm blue. In the center a wide niche and three steps which end in four thin columns made of rosy-orange marble. Behind the columns a dark cherry curtain. To the left, in the armchair, three-fourths turned toward the auditorium, the Lady sits doing embroidery. Her small son is playing on the carpet, constructing some fairly large mechanical device. His hair is cut short and looks velvety, and he is wearing a dark carmine suit. The Lady is wearing a silver-gray dress. Dusk is slowly falling. A moment of silence.

TADZIO (*without stopping his tinkering*) Mama, I forgot why He's my papa.

LADY It doesn't make any difference if you have. No one knows why things are the way they are and not some other way. You can ask such questions endlessly and never find any answers.

TADZIO I know—Infinity. I'll never forget how I first came to understand what it means. Ever since then everything's really been all right. I think everything's infinite and has to be the way it is. But there's just one thing: why exactly is He my papa and not someone else?

LADY Perhaps you'd prefer to have Mr. Korbowski as your papa, my little philosopher?

TADZIO Don't talk to me like that, Mama. I'll tell you something else: as soon as you appeared, I forgot everything that had happened before. It's like one of those dreams you can never recall. I remember only my name. Nothing else.

LADY That's a great deal. Apparently you had to forget everything else.

TADZIO I want to find out how I came to be: where I came from and where everything's going. Things keep on going all by themselves and seem to be heading somewhere. What's it all about? Where's it all rushing so fast?

LADY (*slightly disconcerted*) Ask your father. Even I don't know that.

TADZIO Mother, you're keeping something from me. But I know more than I'm letting on. Your eyes are double, like those little boxes with a secret drawer.

LADY Now it's my turn to say: don't talk to me like that. I'm very fond of you, and I don't want to have to hurt you.

TADZIO Haven't I been good? Nothing seems right. Everything's happening as if I were dreaming. (*With sudden animation*) You know, I've never been afraid of anything except in my dreams. And now that everything seems like a dream, I'm really afraid that at any moment something dreadful will happen and I'll be much more terrified than I ever was in any dream. I feel so frightened sometimes. I'm afraid of fear. (*Jan Parblichenko enters and lights the electric candelabra hanging from the ceiling.*)

LADY Jan, has the Master returned?

JAN Not yet, Your Grace.

LADY Don't forget the special liqueurs. There'll be guests for dinner.

JAN Yes, Your Grace.

TADZIO (*standing up*) So there'll be more of those repulsive characters who torment papa. (*Jan leaves stage left.*)

LADY (*somewhat venomously*) And Mr. Korbowski will be here.

TADZIO He's a man out of a bad dream. But I like him. I like to look at him. He's like a snake who eats small birds.

LADY (*ironically*) And you're a small bird, aren't you?

TADZIO Mama, why do you talk to me the way you would to a grown-up? I asked you not to talk that way.

LADY I never had any children, and I don't know how to talk to them. If you want to, go to Afrosia.

TADZIO She doesn't have double eyes. Still she bores me. I don't like good people, but bad people make me suffer.

LADY (*smiling*) Am I bad?

TADZIO I don't know. But you make me suffer, Mama, and I like to be with you because you make me suffer.

LADY (*with a smile*) What perversity!

TADZIO That's a word for a grown-up. I know. Why can't I wake up? Everything seems wrong somehow. (*Jan enters from the right.*)

JAN Mr. Korbowski, Your Grace.

LADY Ask him to come in. (*Exit Jan. Tadzio becomes silent, his gaze fixed on the door to the right. Korbowski enters wearing a frock coat.*)

KORBOWSKI Good evening. Am I late?

LADY No, dinner is late. Edgar hasn't come back yet.

KORBOWSKI (*kisses her hand and sits down next to her facing forward*) Alice, how can you call that soggy wet noodle by the same name as your husband, the late Duke? I may not be very refined, but it gives me a kind of psychological ache. (*Tadzio makes a gesture as though he wanted to throw himself on Korbowski, but he restrains himself.*)

LADY (*with a smile*) Well—as long as it's not physical, you can stand it.

KORBOWSKI Don't laugh. I wear my soul in a sling like a broken arm, like fruit stolen out of my own garden which my enemy has leased. I feel a morganatic attraction for you, strong as an American tornado. I am consumed with passion for a misalliance, transformed by a clever writer into a self-libel, with which I flog my own impotent destiny.

LADY But there's no sense at all to anything you're saying.

KORBOWSKI I know, that's why I say it. I read night and day, and my head is spinning. (*He stretches his legs out, leaning his head back behind the armchair.*)

LADY Sit up properly.

KORBOWSKI I don't have the strength. I'm like a shirt that's been embraced by a wringer. I'm afraid of time whirling past me like the wind on the pampas around the rushing antelope. I'm exhausted.

TADZIO (*seriously*) You put that very nicely. When I wake up from this dream, I'll paint it.

KORBOWSKI Listen, young aesthete, suppose you go to sleep? Really and truly, to bed, huh?

TADZIO (*leaning against the Lady's armchair*) I won't go. You're just a handsome tramp, and this is my home.

KORBOWSKI You're as much of a tramp as I am. Go to sleep, that's my advice.

LADY Mr. Korbowski is right. Both of you have an equal right to be here with me.

TADZIO That's not true. If I knew why He's my papa, I'd answer you differently. It's a mystery.

KORBOWSKI There's no mystery at all. Your so-called father is a common murderer. He may be hanged at any moment. He lives by the grace of the Duchess, like a dog on a chain. Understand?

TADZIO That's not true. If he wanted to, papa could be great, but he doesn't want to. I heard that somewhere.

KORBOWSKI (*gets up and pushes Tadzio away brutally*) You little moron, I'll give you greatness! Clear out! (*Tadzio falls down on the carpet, crawls up to the machine, and starts to operate it again, stooping over—not saying anything. Korbowski stands bending over the Lady.*) Alice! I can't take it any longer. You don't belong here. Throw that Valpor out once and for a tired wet noodle. I can't go on living like this. I can feel something new and strange, something colossally rotten growing inside me, and it'll be nasty for anyone who gets in my way. Understand? Everything I read (and I don't do anything else) I eagerly pervert into evil—odious, hairy, cruel, red-hot evil. Don't push me over the brink. Will you leave all this and come with me now? I don't want to go back to being what I was without you. I know I'm nothing. What are you paying me for? Why do I go on living? (*He clutches his head in his hands.*)

TADZIO (*turns around and looks at him ecstatically*) Blow up, Mr. Korbowski, go ahead and blow up. (*The Lady bursts out laughing.*)

KORBOWSKI (*shaking his fist at him*) Shut up! (*To the Lady*) Alice, I'm nothing at all—that's just it! That's why I used to be the happiest man in the world. Now that I have everything I've always dreamed about, it all seems worthless without you. I might as well put a bullet through my head. I'll go stark raving mad!

LADY (*coldly*) Have you been unfaithful to me?

KORBOWSKI No, no, no! Don't question me about it so casually. I can't stand it.

LADY He's suffering, too.

KORBOWSKI What's that to me? Let him go on suffering in peace and quiet. You've turned this house into a colossal torturtorium. I don't want any part of it.

LADY (*with a smile*) Then go away!

KORBOWSKI (*bending over her*) I can't. Will you leave all this and come with me now! (*Jan enters.*)

JAN Messieurs Specter, Evader, and Typowicz, Your Grace.

LADY Show them in. (*Exit Jan. Enter the three old men wearing frock coats.*)

KORBOWSKI (*bending over her embroidery, aloud*) What lovely needlework! The blues and yellows complement each other so exquisitely. (*Softly, through his teeth*) Will you leave all this and come with me now!

LADY (*gets up, passes by him, and goes to greet the old men*) Gentlemen, you'll forgive us, Edgar is late. (*The old men kiss the Lady's hand.*)

TYPOWICZ Oh, that's all right. But how are we doing with our new venture, The Theosophical Jam Company?

LADY We're putting up all our capital. We'll secure the balance with real estate as collateral. Even the name is marvelous. Edgar has gone to the Union Bank. He should be back any minute.

KORBOWSKI Alice!

LADY (*turning away, in a cold voice*) Mr. Korbowski, must I ask you to leave our house? (*Korbowski rolls up into a ball and falls into an armchair, covering his face with his hands.*)

TYPOWICZ Dear Lady, this is a great day for the corporation.

EVADER You're the only member of the aristocracy who . . .

SPECTER (*interrupts him*) Yes—you alone had the courage. Your example ought to . . .

LADY I can't talk about all this before dinner. Gentlemen, please sit down. (*Goes to the left; the old men follow her; they sit down without greeting Korbowski*) I'm in favor of a total Semitico-Aryan coalition. The Semites are the race of the future.

EVADER Yes. The spiritual rebirth of the Jews is the key to the future happiness of mankind.

SPECTER We'll show what we can do as a race. Up until now we've produced only individual geniuses.

(*The curtain in the back is drawn, and Edgar quickly runs down the stairs, dressed in a black frock coat. Tadzio flings himself toward him.*)

TADZIO Papa, I can't stand it any more! I don't know when she's telling the truth. (*He points to the Lady.*)

EDGAR (*shoving him away*) Go away. (*To everybody*) Dinner is served.

TADZIO Papa, I'm so all alone. (*Edgar talks with the old men, paying no attention to Tadzio. Korbowski sits like a mummy.*)

LADY (*rings; Afrosia, dressed entirely in green, runs in from the left side of the stage; a green scarf on her head*) Afrosia Ivanovna, take this child away. See that he drinks his herb tea and put him to bed!

(*Afrosia takes Tadzio by the hand, and they go off to the left. From the right-hand side of the stage the Water Hen enters, dressed as in Act I, but wearing silk stockings, patent leather pumps, and a cape thrown over her shoulders.*)

LADY And who is this?

EDGAR (*turning around*) It's she! You're alive?

WATER HEN That should hardly be any concern of yours.

TADZIO (*stopping at the door to the left—shouts*) Mama! (*He runs to the Hen.*)

EDGAR (*to the Hen*) Is he your son? You lied about everything.

WATER HEN (*astounded*) I have never lied. I don't know this boy at all. (*She pushes Tadzio away, and he clings to her.*)

TADZIO Mama! You don't know me?

WATER HEN Calm down, child. I never was your mother.

TADZIO So I have no one at all! (*He cries.*) And I can't wake up.

EDGAR Afrosia Ivanovna, take Tadzio out of here this very minute, see that he goes to bed immediately. (*Afrosia takes Tadzio away to the left; as he goes, he is convulsed with tears.*)

LADY (*nudging Edgar*) Tell me, who is that woman?

EDGAR It's the Water Hen—Elizabeth Virgeling.

LADY But what does this mean? You killed her.

EDGAR Apparently not, since she just walked in and is standing right there. That would appear to be fairly conclusive evidence.

KORBOWSKI (*getting up*) So she's really alive! I'm ruined. There goes my last chance of getting rid of that bad dream! (*To Edgar*) Rest assured, Mr. Valpor, the attempted blackmail didn't work.

EDGAR You and your blackmail mean nothing to me. I tolerate your presence here in this house of my own free will. I'm devoting my entire life now to penance. (*To the Hen*) Penance for what I've failed to accomplish. I failed, and I've got to suffer for it and do penance. You should be delighted—it's all your fault. Can you imagine anything worse?

WATER HEN You're still not suffering enough. Not nearly enough. And that's why everything seems so awful to you. (*Father enters from the right-hand side of the stage, in a frock coat, his beard shaved.*)

EDGAR Oh, Father, please look after the guests. I want to talk privately with this woman. It's the Water Hen—she's alive! Judging by your complete lack of surprise, I suppose you knew exactly what was going to happen.

FATHER (*cheerfully*) Well, of course.

EDGAR You monster!

FATHER Your late mother spoiled you. I've got to make up for it, so I'm bringing you up in my own way. And now, ladies and gentlemen, will you please come to the dining room. (*To the Lady*) Alice—has Mr. de Korbowa-Korbowski been invited, too?

LADY Of course. (*To the Hen*) After you've talked with my husband, please join us at the table. And after dinner you and I will have a little chat.

WATER HEN And who are you, may I ask?

LADY I am Edgar Valpor's wife and Edgar Nevermore's widow. Apparently you're the one woman my husband was in love with, from a distance of a thousand miles. Ha, ha! (*To the guests*) Please come, gentlemen. (*Korbowski offers her his arm. She motions him away and offers her arm to Typowicz. They go up the stairs. Jan draws the curtain. The two old men follow them, the Father comes next, and in the rear Korbowski drags along, completely shattered. All this while Edgar and the Hen stand still, looking at each other. All the others disappear behind the curtain, which is then drawn shut.*)

WATER HEN Do you love her?

EDGAR Don't even say that word in my presence. I hate the very sound of it.

WATER HEN Once and for all, answer my question.

EDGAR No, no, that's an entirely different matter. I'm just a marionette. I'm outside of whatever happens to me. And I watch myself like a Chinese shadow moving on a screen. I can only observe the movements, but have no control over them.

WATER HEN So nothing has happened as a result of my death?

EDGAR What's happened is that I suffer a thousand times more than I ever did. I've started another life—not a new one. I gave that up a long time ago. ANOTHER LIFE! I'm creating a new skeleton inside of what already exists. Or rather they are—my father and the Duchess.

WATER HEN And the utter void? I mean as far as feelings are concerned.

EDGAR It goes on and on.

WATER HEN What does your father expect of you? The same as always?

EDGAR Yes, he says I'll certainly become an artist.

WATER HEN But you have no talent—not for anything whatever.

EDGAR That's precisely the point. I don't have any and never will. It's as impossible as changing one's complexion. Black hair can be bleached, but can a black character?

WATER HEN Will you be angry if I ask you something: How's the greatness problem coming?

EDGAR Greatness? Monstrosity perhaps? I've already told you: I'm a buffoon, a plaything of unknown forces. I'm great—like a marionette. Ha, ha!

WATER HEN Don't laugh. What about real life?

EDGAR I manage my wife's estate; I've invested all of it in the Theosophical Jam Company. Those three men are making all the arrangements. I'm only a manikin. (*A pause*)

WATER HEN Don't get angry if I tell you something. You're not suffering enough.

EDGAR You dare say that to me? Don't you understand how absolutely ghastly my life is?

WATER HEN I understand, but it's really nothing, nothing at all. The only way to get anything out of you is to torture you. I know what I'm talking about.

EDGAR Haven't I suffered enough already? My wife keeps that Korbowski in constant tow. The slimy maggot! I hate him, I loathe him, I despise him, and yet I have to put up with him all the time. Now he'll be on the board of the new company. I don't know whether he's her lover or not; I don't ask, I don't want to find out. Isn't that enough for you? All my evenings are pinnacles of utter degradation.

WATER HEN But you don't love her.

EDGAR You're a woman, my dear. You'll never understand. For you women it's only: he loves me, he loves me not, he loves me, he loves me not. You never understand suffering any more complicated than the wrong answer to that question.

WATER HEN Go on. What else makes you suffer?

EDGAR You know how I hate reality. From early morning on I'm up to my ears in business: board meetings at banks, the stock exchange, negotiations with wholesalers and big accounts. Now it's really starting. Imagine me, Edgar, a businessman! It's the height of agony.

WATER HEN It's not enough. A propos, what about Tadzio?

EDGAR Your deathbed bequest . . .

WATER HEN I swear I never saw that boy before.

EDGAR The facts are against you. But I don't want to go over that old story again. Besides, facts don't interest me. So you're not his mother?

WATER HEN But you know I can't be a mother!

EDGAR Miracles happen. Did you know they've built a huge barracks where I once tried to kill you without much success? But no matter.

WATER HEN Tell me, what's the relationship between you?

EDGAR Between Tadzio and me? Frankly, I'm insanely attached to him, but I have a deep suspicion that he'll grow up to be a scoundrel so monstrous that Korbowski will seem a saint by comparison. Along with my insane attachment to him, I feel an unbearable physical disgust. He doesn't love me at all and doesn't want to regard me as his father. He admires Korbowski—he's his artistic ideal. Now I've listed my principal sufferings. Isn't that enough?

WATER HEN That's nothing.

JAN (appears from behind the curtain): Her Grace requests that you come to the table.

EDGAR Right away. (Jan disappears.) That's nothing? What more do you want?

WATER HEN I don't know . . . Perhaps a prison sentence or maybe physical pain will cure you. There have been cases of conversion . . .

EDGAR To what? Theosophy?

WATER HEN No—to a belief in the positive values of life.

EDGAR Wait! Physical pain. That's a new idea! (He runs over to the table and rings. The Hen watches him curiously. Four Footmen run in from the left.) Listen to me: go to the Duchess' museum immediately and bring me the Spanish instrument of torture, you know, the one with the green and yellow stripes. Hurry. (The Footmen leave quickly stage left. Edgar paces up and down nervously. The Hen goes to the left, sits down in an armchair, and follows him with her eyes.)

EDGAR Well, now I'll show you . . .

WATER HEN Just don't lie to yourself.

EDGAR Quiet! Now I'm master of my own fate. I know what I'm doing, and I'll do it myself without anyone else's help. (Stamping his foot on the floor) Quiet! I tell you . . . (The Footmen come in carrying a box eight feet long, the sides of which are latticed with yellow and

*green strips of board; at the corners there are yellow wheels which
are connected to cranks; inside there is a small bench, and thick
ropes hang from the cranks; the box looks very old.*) Set it down in
the middle of the room! (*The Footmen put the box down and stand
very stiffly by its four corners.*) And now listen to me: you'll
torture me with this machine. No matter how much I cry out and
beg for mercy, you're to stretch me till I stop screaming. Do you
understand? Tie my hands and legs and then turn the cranks.

FOOTMEN Yes sir, all right, we understand.

EDGAR Well—hurry up! (*He takes off his frock coat and throws it on
the ground; he is wearing a bluish shirt; then he quickly climbs into
the box and lies down on the bench, his head to the left.*) Hurry!
(*The Footmen tie the ropes with frantic speed and begin to turn the
cranks, at first rapidly, then slowly, with effort. Edgar starts to
groan horribly at regular intervals. The Hen laughs demonically in
her armchair. When Edgar is not groaning, her laughter can clearly
be heard.*)

EDGAR Stop—aaa! I can't stand it! Aaa! Aaa! Mercy! Enough! Aaa!
(*He croaks the last "Aaa" horribly and is suddenly silent. The
curtain is drawn, and the Lady can be seen looking in. The men
crowd behind her. The Footmen stop and look into the box, without
letting go of the cranks, which remain in the same position.*)

WATER HEN What are you gaping at? Keep on turning it. (*The company from the dining room comes slowly down into the drawing
room, with the Lady leading the way. Jan follows them. The Hen
stops laughing and sits quietly, staring madly straight ahead.*)

FOOTMAN I He's fainted.

FOOTMAN II He's had enough, poor fellow.

FATHER (*runs over to the box and looks into it*) Has he gone mad, or
what? (*To the Footmen*) Get him out of there! (*The Footmen
untie Edgar with frantic speed and pull him out, absolutely limp.*)
Put him on the couch. (*To the Hen*) Elizabeth, was this hideous
business your idea? (*At this moment, from the left side of the stage,
Tadzio, in a nightshirt and stockings, runs in with a cry. Afrosia
follows him. The Lady and her staff stay where they are, a little to
the right. The Footmen carry Edgar to a small red couch, to the
right, and stand erect to the right of it. Jan goes over to them. They
whisper.*)

TADZIO Papa, papa! Don't cry like that ever again! (*He falls on his
knees by the couch, on the far side to the rear of the stage; Edgar
opens his eyes and his face brightens.*) Papa, I love you, I woke up
from my dream. (*Edgar strokes his head.*) Papa, she's the one who's
torturing you, that strange lady who didn't want to be my mother. I

don't want her here. Take her away. (*He buries his head in Edgar's chest; Edgar hugs him.*)

KORBOWSKI (*speaks at the top of his voice in the midst of the silence*) This is barren metaphysical suffering in the fourth dimension.

FATHER Silence. (*To the Footmen*) Take that damned box out of here. Hurry up. (*The Footmen fling themselves at the box and carry it off to the left. Afrosia stands silently to the left. Edgar's black frock coat remains in the middle of the stage on the ground until the end of the act.*)

WATER HEN (*gets up and speaks to the Lady in a fiery voice*) Do you think that Edgar Nevermore loved you? He loved only me. I have his letters right here. I want you to know everything. I've always kept them with me, but now they're useless. (*She throws down a packet of letters at the Lady's feet. The packet becomes untied, and the letters scatter about. Korbowski picks them up eagerly.*)

LADY I know all that, and I've already proved to my second husband that your theory's wrong. You were only a kind of make-believe mother that certain men feel they need. Such an experiment works best at a great distance. Edgar loved only me. Korbowski knows something about it.

WATER HEN Mr. Korbowski may know a great deal, but in matters of feelings of the sort that united me with Duke Edgar, he simply isn't competent to judge.

LADY You're just a phantom. An imagined value. I'm not at all jealous of you. I prefer reality to your spiritual seductions in the fourth dimension. Edgar told me that he wrote you nonsensical letters which you took seriously. It's all ridiculous and petty.

WATER HEN That's not true.

KORBOWSKI The Duke told me so just before he died; he was reading that big fat book full of symbols and expiring at the same time.

LADY Yes, he was reading Russell and Whitehead's *Principia Mathematica* after his entrails had been torn out by a tiger. He was a hero. He was fully conscious when he said he'd duped you into a metaphysical flirtation. He called it the psychopaths' metaphysical flirtation. Yet he wasn't a madman himself.

WATER HEN (*bursts out laughing suddenly*) Ha, ha, ha! I was the one who was pulling his leg. I lie about everything. I don't exist at all. I live only by lying. Is there anything more sublime than lying for its own sake? Read those letters. That man believed in me, but he had moments of horrible despair and tried to convince himself that he was the one who was lying. In that lay the drama of his life. That's why he was so brave. I was the one who didn't want to meet him.

LADY Yes, because he would have been disillusioned. He didn't even have a photo of you; you wanted to be something in the nature of a myth. That's why you never have your picture taken. Everybody knows all about that. (*The Hen wants to say something in answer.*)

TADZIO (*jumps up*) Take that woman away. I don't want her here. She tells lies. (*He stamps his foot.*)

EDGAR (*in a weak voice*) Tadzio, don't—behave yourself!

LADY Jan, show that woman out this instant. (*Jan, who up until now has stood erect near Edgar's head, moves toward the Hen.*)

FATHER I'll escort her to the door myself. Elizabeth, give me your hand. In your own way you are great. (*They go toward the door hand in hand. Tadzio sits down at Edgar's feet.*)

EDGAR (*still lying down*) So you're against me too, Father?

FATHER (*turning around at the door*) Not against you, but with you against life. I'm waiting for you to finally become an artist.

EDGAR (*still lying down*) Alice, save me from him; save me from myself. (*He notices Korbowski standing irresolutely with the letters in his hand.*) Out, scum! Out!

KORBOWSKI (*bowing humbly; to the Lady*) And the letters?

LADY You may take them with you, Mr. Korbowski. Reading that correspondence will be good for your psyche; you'll be more mixed up than ever. Please go right ahead. (*She points to the door on the right. Afrosia sits down in the armchair to the left. Korbowski hesitates.*) Jan! (*Jan shoves Korbowski gently toward the door. Korbowski scarcely resists.*)

JAN All right, Tom, none of your tricks. (*They go off to the right.*)

TYPOWICZ (*pulls some papers out of his side pocket and goes over to Edgar*) Mr. Valpor, as guardian of your wife's estate, will you please sign here. We've drawn up the final version of the charter of the Theosophical Jam Company. (*He gives him a fountain pen. Edgar signs lying down.*)

EDGAR And now, gentlemen, forgive me, but I can't go on. (*The three old men bow, kiss Alice's hand, and leave.*) Alice, I beg you, let's start a new life.

LADY (*with a smile*) Not another one, but a new one?

EDGAR That was impossible . . . (*He looks at Tadzio as if he had not noticed him before.*) Tadzio, go to bed this minute!

TADZIO (*getting up*) But won't you believe me now? I believe in you, my dear, dear Papa. I woke up when that woman said she didn't want to be my mother. I want to be good.

LADY I want to be good, too.

EDGAR (*paying no attention to what she has said, to Tadzio*) How will wanting to be good help, if there's evil in the very depths of your soul? Besides, I must admit I've gone beyond such categories today. Ethics is only the consequence of a large number of individuals thinking the same way. A man on a desert island wouldn't have any notion of what it means. Tadzio, go to bed.

TADZIO But won't you believe me, Papa? I'm not talking about you, Mama; you have double eyes. Now I know why you're my father.

EDGAR I want to believe you, just as you want to be good. (*He kisses him on the forehead.*) (*Without saying good-bye to the Lady, Tadzio goes slowly to the left, his head lowered. Afrosia gets up and follows him.*)

LADY (*sitting down beside Edgar on the small couch*) Do you really feel as though you were on a desert island?

EDGAR Save me, Alice. I'm tired of being a superman. The temptation of penance was too much for me. Father's against me, and so is Elizabeth. Together the two of them tempt me. (*He speaks feverishly.*) There's an even worse temptation waiting for me—he inoculated me with it: the temptation to become an artist. I'm defending myself with what little strength I have left. I have no talent, I'm great in my utter nothingness. Today life has lost all meaning.

LADY Just because that liar walked out on you?

EDGAR (*still more feverishly*) No, no. This suffering . . . I don't even want to talk about it. I can't describe it. Rescue me from Art; I hate Art, and I'm afraid of it. Now that life has lost its meaning, that other temptation's becoming stronger and stronger. I won't be able to resist it unless you protect me. Alice, I hardly dare ask you; all my bones ache after those tortures. For once, kiss me as if you really loved me.

LADY (*bending over him*) I feel that I really do love you now. (*She kisses him on the lips. A long kiss.*)

EDGAR (*pushing her away*) But it's all petty, petty, petty.

LADY (*getting up and stretching*) Only in lying is there greatness.

EDGAR (*raising himself up a little*) Oh, so you're against me, too? Life awaits us in all its horror.

LADY (*slowly, emphatically*) I won't leave you. Neither you nor Tadzio.

EDGAR Like condemned prisoners we'll drag on and on until death.

ACT III

The same room as in Act II. Evening. The chandelier is lighted. Ten years have elapsed. A suite of furniture stands on the right-hand side of the stage. A small couch covered in something green on the left. On the right, by the door, a small folded card table. Tadzio, as a young man twenty years old, sits lost in thought in an armchair on the left. He is dressed in a gray suit. Suddenly he begins nervously to tap his right foot against the floor.

TADZIO When will this ghastly nightmare ever end? It's just like a life sentence. God knows what father expects of me; he's a failure himself. What a fine example! (*Gets up*) For the time being I'll listen dutifully. But as soon as it all blows up, I won't have to look up to anybody. Korbowski—there was a man. What a pity he wasn't my father! (*Walking up and down*) You forget everything—even that women exist! Mathematics, mathematics! It's a hell of a life! (*Knocking at the door to the right. Jan enters.*)

JAN Sir, the lady who was here ten years ago wishes to speak to you.

TADZIO What? (*Remembers*) Oh! Show her in. Hurry up. I behaved so badly then. (*He goes to the door. The Water Hen enters, dressed as in Act II, but she wears a black cape and a black hat, something in the style of Napoleon's "en bataille," and an orange sweater. She has not aged at all. On the contrary, she is very seductive. Her eyes seem more slanted and her lips redder. Her whole face is lighted up with sensuality, of which there was no trace in Acts I and II. Her hair is cut short and is curled.*)

WATER HEN Are you Mr. Tadeusz Valpor?

TADEUSZ (*flustered*) Yes, I am. In the old days we both had the same name.

WATER HEN I know that. A pure coincidence. That's why people suspected I was your mother. You were the one who desperately wanted me to be your mother, and you got offended when I refused. Ha, ha. What a ridiculous rumor! Don't you agree? (*Jan leaves smiling.*)

TADEUSZ (*still more flustered*) I was a child then. But please—do sit down. (*The Hen sits down in the armchair to the left where he had been sitting; Tadeusz near her, his left profile to the audience.*) But you look even younger now, as far as I can remember from the old days.

WATER HEN (*greatly flustered*) Yes . . . It's Indian yoga, plus American massage. Ludicrous, isn't it? Ha, ha! (*She conceals her embarrassment by laughing. She laughs "till her sides split," loudly. Tadeusz is grimly flustered. It is evident that the Hen is making one hell of an erotic impression on him.*)

TADEUSZ (*sullenly*) Properly speaking, why are you laughing?

WATER HEN (*pulling herself together*) Properly speaking, I'm laughing quite improperly. And what are you doing these days? (*With an ironic stress on* you.)

TADEUSZ Me? I'm not doing anything. I study. Mathematics. They torture me with mathematics, even though I don't have any talent for it.

WATER HEN That runs in your family. Your grandfather was dead set on making an artist out of your father. So far as I know, it was a complete failure.

TADEUSZ That's true, as of now. Although it's still a subject of endless controversy. (*Returning to the original topic*) You know, what I'm going to say may sound absurd: I'm so busy that I sometimes forget women exist. Yesterday as I was going to class, I caught sight of a good-looking woman, and I swear for a minute I didn't know what sort of a creature I was looking at. Then I realized that there are such things as women, and I was deliriously happy. (*He breaks off and becomes embarrassed; the Water Hen has become gloomy.*) What I'm saying is all nonsense. Maybe it seems very childish to you, but . . .

WATER HEN (*takes off her hat and puts it on the table; she tosses her cape back on the arm of the chair; her face brightens*) Well, and what else?

TADEUSZ Nothing. You said there was something that runs in our family. But you know that I'm only my father's adopted son.

WATER HEN (*flustered*) Yes, I know.

TADEUSZ But sometimes I could swear that it was you who first called him my father. I was very ill then—that's for certain.

WATER HEN (*she suddenly moves a little closer to him and asks with sudden shamelessness*): Do I appeal to you?

TADEUSZ (*he is momentarily, as they say, "thunderstruck"; suddenly he takes a deep breath and speaks in a choked voice*) I like you tremendously. I love you. (*He throws himself at her. She pushes him away, laughing.*)

WATER HEN Just like that, "I love you." And what about that woman in the street? When all of a sudden you remembered that women exist.

TADEUSZ That was nothing. I love only you. Let me kiss you . . . (*He kisses her on the lips violently. The Hen yields.*)

WATER HEN (*pushing him away*) That's enough . . . Someone's coming.

TADEUSZ (*out of his mind*) Tell me you love me. I've just kissed you for the first time. It's tremendous. Tell me you love me.

WATER HEN (*kisses him violently*) I love you—you innocent little thing. You'll be my . . .

(*Enter Father and Edgar. They stand on the threshold astounded. Tadeusz jumps away from the Hen. The Father clean-shaven, but much older. Edgar, who has aged a great deal, looks over fifty; both are dressed in the same way, like Tadeusz.*)

FATHER Here's a new development! (*He recognizes the Hen; Edgar stands by the door absorbed; Tadeusz, flustered, to the left.*) Good evening, Elizabeth. (*The Hen gets up.*) I haven't seen you for ages! You're quite the coquette now, aren't you! (*To Tadeusz*) Well, you rascal, playing footsie with her already, eh?

TADEUSZ I love this woman, and I intend to marry her. I've awakened from my dream again. Now I know what it all means and what all of you wanted from me. Nothing doing. I don't want to be that kind of person. I don't accept any of these new theories!

WATER HEN (*taking his arm*) He's mine. He's suffocating here with all of you. He's handsome. He has a beautiful soul. He'll become great through me.

EDGAR (*coming up to her, angry*) All of a sudden he's got a beautiful soul and greatness too just because you find him attractive. You don't know him. And you'll probably make him great the way you wanted to make me great. It's all petty, disgustingly petty.

FATHER Greatness has gone to your heads. In my time at least it was possible to become a great artist. But now even that doesn't work . . .

WATER HEN (*not paying attention to him*) You two want to warp his life the way I warped yours. (*She points to herself and to Edgar in a certain crude way.*)

FATHER You warped my cat's life too, Elizabeth, by feeding him lemons. But the cat died, and in this case we've got to go on living, or else we'd better blow our brains out right away.

EDGAR That's just it. I won't let you use Tadeusz for your suicidal experiments or for your artificial crimes. He'll be a scholar. The only profession in the world that hasn't already gone to the dogs or to some still worse creatures.

TADEUSZ I don't want to be a scholar at all. I love Miss Elizabeth.

EDGAR You think that'll satisfy you? You're not a woman, that won't fill your life. Look at him; he's invented a new career: being in love! A third-rate Don Juan—what am I saying?—a common Juan without the Don.

WATER HEN He knows intuitively who he is. You two can distort anything. If you won't let a criminal be a criminal, he'll become something still worse—a fake, a fraud. Father, you're the one who's contaminating everyone with your programs.

EDGAR Since when have you repudiated lying? A long time ago? Or is this a new lie especially created for the present situation?

WATER HEN There's no truth in words or in any actions or professions men devise. Truth is what is actually happening.

EDGAR Look here, what sort of real-life dadaism is that? Do as the apes do, live in trees! But I'm going to remind you once more of that other time. (*To his Father*) Father, talk with them. I'll be right back. (*He leaves, almost running, to the left.*)

FATHER Well, what do you say about that, youngsters?

TADEUSZ Nothing. Either Father lets me marry this woman, or I'll run away from home. That's final.

FATHER I have nothing more to say to you. I'll watch what happens as a spectator.

(*The Lady enters from the left side of the stage, dressed in an azure dressing gown trimmed in lace. She is very well-preserved, but slightly made up.*)

LADY Oh, it's you. New revelations about my first husband perhaps?

WATER HEN That topic doesn't concern me any more. I've destroyed the past completely.

LADY (*coming up to her and speaking with venom*) But you haven't destroyed yourself in the process, have you? You look very pretty. I realized at once that something was going on when Edgar rushed in like a lunatic racing against time and changed into his eighteenth-century outfit. Apparently he wants to entice you with the past.

WATER HEN It won't work. I love Tadeusz. He's going to marry me.

LADY So soon? (*To Tadeusz*) Tadzio, is that true?

TADEUSZ (*in a hard tone of voice*) Yes. I've finally awakened from my dream and seen through all your lies. Manufacturing artificial people, artificial crimes, artificial penance, artificial everything.

LADY This one is always waking up from some dream or other and beginning to understand everything. How many times now have you come to understand everything? What's the grand total?

TADEUSZ I've understood twice. But everything is infinite, there's no point in talking about actual quantities of anything. When I understand for the third time, it may very well be the end. (*The Hen nestles close to him in silence.*)

LADY A regular little Solomon. Watch out you don't tempt fate by talking about that third time. Watch out! (*She shakes her finger at him. Jan enters from the right.*)

JAN Tom Hoozy, Your Grace.

LADY Hoozy?

JAN *False* de Korbowa-Korbowski, Your Grace.

LADY (*amazed*) I didn't know that was his real name. Ask Mr. Hoozy to come in. (*Exit Jan.*)

FATHER Here's a new complication. Undoubtedly he knew all about it. Life holds no interest for me any more.

(*Korbowski enters, dressed in a threadbare sports coat, sports cap, a thick walking stick in his hand. His face is ravaged and aged, but handsome. He looks more noble than before.*)

LADY Mr. Korbowski, *recte* Hoozy, sit down and be a silent witness to events. (*Korbowski bows and sits in the armchair to the right. At this moment Edgar runs in, dressed in the costume he wore in Act I, with a hat.*)

WATER HEN What kind of a masquerade is this? Ham. He's changed into his old costume to create an atmosphere. Too bad you didn't dress up as a Mexican general or Julius Caesar.

TADEUSZ Really, Papa, that's too much, you're making a farce of a very serious situation.

EDGAR Silence. I forbid you to marry that person.

KORBOWSKI (*gets up*) Mr. Valpor, please wait a minute. I apologize for being here, but I've been authorized by the Duchess. I still love her. For the last five years I've been observing your life together. I spent five years in the Argentine.

EDGAR What's that to me? Get to the point.

KORBOWSKI As soon as that witch appeared, I knew that today would be the crucial day. (*Points to the Hen*) The police are on my track, but since I was a former witness, I took the chance and came to help you. Besides, there's a revolution going on, and I mean to come out on top. If everything comes crashing down today, I'll have nothing to fear.

EDGAR (*who has been listening impatiently*) That will do, you can finish later. Tadzio, today you're at the turning point of your life. If you insist on staying with that woman, you're lost.

TADEUSZ That's because you're sweet on her yourself, Father. The proof is that you've changed your clothes. You overdo everything.

EDGAR Tadzio, I'm telling you for the last time. I love you, but my patience . . .

TADEUSZ (*interrupts him brutally*) Father, you're an old ham, and besides you're not my father at all. Don't forget that while I'm talking to you, Father, I'm wide awake, not dreaming.

EDGAR (*petrified, he roars*) You scoundrel!

TADEUSZ Yes, I'm a scoundrel . . .

EDGAR Shut up! Shut up! (*Throws himself at Tadzio and tears him away from the Hen*) You won't marry her. I won't let you.

S. I. Witkiewicz. Self-Portrait, 1913. National Museum of Warsaw.
Photograph courtesy of *Poland* magazine

S. I. Witkiewicz. Self-Portrait, 1917. National Museum of Cracow.
Photograph by Z. Malinowski, courtesy of the Museum

The Madman and the Nun. Teatr Dramatyczny, Warsaw, 1959.
Director, Wanda Laskowska; designer, Józef Szajna; Walpurg, Wiesław
Gołas; Sister Anna, Lucyna Winnicka. Photograph from *Theatre in Modern
Poland* (Warsaw: Wydawnictwa Artystyczne i Filmowe, 1963)

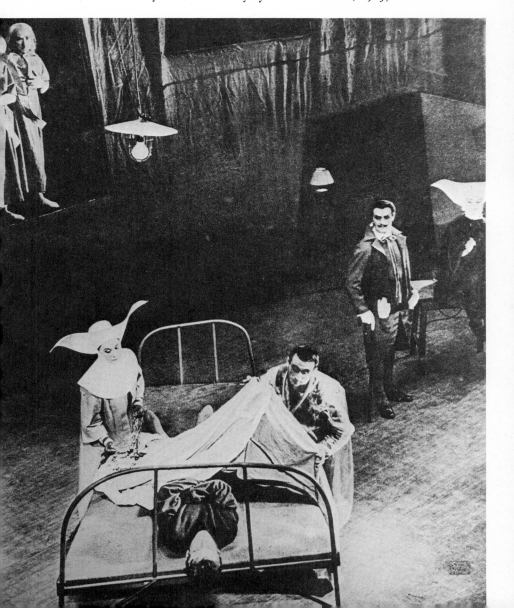

The Madman and the Nun. San Francisco State College Theater, San
Francisco, 1967. Director, Jan Kott; designer, Bill Sherman; Walpurg,
John Argue; Sister Anna, Dale Fontwit. Photograph by Joseph Diaz

The Madman and the Nun. San Francisco, 1967. Photograph by Joseph Diaz

The Water Hen. Teatr Narodowy, Warsaw, 1964. Director, Wanda Laskowska; designer, Zofia Pietrusińska; Scoundrel (Tom Hoozy), Igor Śmiałowski; Duchess, Halina Mikołajska. Photograph by Franciszek Myszkowski

The Water Hen. Warsaw, 1964. Edgar, Wieńczysław Gliński; Water Hen, Barbara Krafftówna; Lamplighter, Władysław Kaczmarski. Photograph by Franciszek Myszkowski

The Water Hen. Warsaw, 1964. Captain, Andrzej Szczepkowski.
Photograph by Franciszek Myszkowski

TADEUSZ If that's the case, I'm leaving the house right now and you'll never see me again. Understand, Father? Not another word.

KORBOWSKI (*to Edgar*) Mr. Valpor, come to your senses. First of all, we've got to kill this slut. (*Mysteriously to the Lady*) Follow my game, Alice? (*To Edgar*) It's the only way out, Mr. Valpor.

EDGAR Yes, you're right, Mr. Korbowski. I'm glad you've come. Thank you. (*Shouts*) Jan! Jan! (*Jan appears in the door to the right.*) My double-barreled shotgun, a bullet in each barrel! (*Jan disappears.*)

WATER HEN That's enough play-acting. Tadeusz, we're leaving right now. I can't stand petty lying.

EDGAR This is no lie, I'm not joking. (*The Lamplighter enters.*)

LAMPLIGHTER The lantern has been lit.

EDGAR What lantern? Who are you? (*The cherry-colored curtain is drawn back, and between the columns appears the landscape from Act I with the pole and lighted lantern. The mound is not visible behind the stairs.*)

LAMPLIGHTER Playing dumb! As though you'd just dropped in out of the blue! Look over there! (*He points out the landscape. Everybody looks in that direction.*)

EDGAR Oh, that! I'd forgotten. Thank you, my good man, you may go now. (*He gives him a tip. The Lamplighter goes away muttering something unintelligible. At the door he meets Jan carrying the gun.*)

JAN It's loaded, sir. (*Everybody turns around. Edgar takes the gun.*)

WATER HEN (*to Tadeusz*) Are you coming or not?

TADEUSZ (*he gives a start, as if awakened from a dream, and speaks in a daze*) I'm coming.

EDGAR Not one step! (*To the Hen*) Stand over there. (*He points to the stairs.*)

WATER HEN I wouldn't dream of it. I'm sick of your idiotic jokes.

EDGAR Jan, get that woman and hold her. I'm going to shoot her.

JAN Sir, I'm afraid you just might shoot me too.

EDGAR Hold that woman, I said. (*The Hen makes a movement toward the door.*)

JAN Please stop joking, sir.

EDGAR You blockhead, you know I'm an excellent shot. *Tir aux pigeons* —first prize. Take her and put her on target, or I'll shoot you dead as a dog without a moment's hesitation. (*He says the last words in a threatening tone. Jan grabs her and drags her to the left toward the stairs.*)

WATER HEN I've had enough of these idiotic jokes. Let go of me, you boor. Edgar, have you really gone mad? (*Jan drags her onto the stairs. They stand against the background of the landscape. Tadeusz has raised his hands to his head in incredulous horror. He stands petrified. Lady and Father, craning their necks this way and that, look first at Edgar and then at the group on the stairs, with horrified curiosity.*)

EDGAR (*to Jan*) Hold her still. (*He aims.*)

WATER HEN (*shouts*) Edgar, I love you, only you. I was only trying to make you jealous.

EDGAR (*coldly*) Too late!

WATER HEN He's a madman, he already shot me once. Save me! (*Edgar aims, moving the barrel to follow the Hen's movements as she struggles to tear herself away. Two shots are fired. Jan lets go of the Hen, and she falls down on the threshold between the columns.*)

JAN (*bending over her*) Her head's split wide open! (*coming down*) You sure are a whale of a madman! Damned if you're not! (*He scratches his head admiringly.*)

EDGAR (*calmly*) It all happened once before, only a little differently. (*To Jan*) Take this. (*Jan takes the shotgun and exits. At the door he passes the three detectives whom no one sees.*)

TADEUSZ Now I've finally awakened from my third dream. I know everything now. I'm an unmitigated scoundrel.

EDGAR Serves you right. I hate you. I haven't even got an adopted son. I'm all alone. (*Remembering*) What about you, Alice?

LADY (*pointing to the door*) Look over there, look over there. (*Two detectives throw themselves on Korbowski and pin his arms back. The curtain is drawn shut.*)

ORSIN My apologies, ladies and gentlemen. But we've been tipped off that Tom Hoozy, one of the most dangerous criminals in the world, just came in here.

LADY Richard, I've been the cause of your undoing. I left you for that idiot. (*She points to Edgar.*)

KORBOWSKI (*held by the detectives*) It doesn't matter. There's a revolution going on. We'll meet again. This won't last long. Perhaps today we'll all be free. Alice, I loved you and you only even in the thick of crimes so monstrous as to be four-dimensional and non-Euclidean in their swinishness. (*The Lady wants to go over to him.*)

ORSIN (*noticing the Hen's body*) Stay where you are. Who's that lying over there? (*He points to the stairs. Edgar makes a gesture, as though he wanted to say something.*)

LADY (*quickly*) I killed that woman, because she was in love with him. (*She points to Korbowski, who smiles blissfully. Tadeusz, taking advantage of the confusion, sneaks away to the left toward the door. Edgar stands still. Father, completely bewildered, is silent.*)

ORSIN Quite a cosy little nest! Madam—I mean, Duchess Nevermore—
ho, ho—*secundo voto* * Valpor—so this is how you operate? (*Tadeusz flees impetuously through the door on the right. Orsin flings
himself after him. Tadeusz escapes.*)

KORBOWSKI (*shouting after him*) Don't worry, we'll meet again. (*To
the Lady*) Don't you understand, Alice, now he's really turned into
a hopeless scoundrel. And in times like these he may be destined to
play a great role. (*Jan pulls the Hen's body to the other side of the
curtain.*)

ORSIN That's enough talk. Take them both to prison. (*Sounds like the
pounding of feet, confused singing and shouting can be heard in the
street.*)

FIRST DETECTIVE I don't know if we'll make it, things are starting to get
hot out there.

ORSIN We'd better hurry. (*Two shots are heard, followed by a burst of
machine-gun fire.*)

KORBOWSKI It's going nicely. Let's go out into the streets. I like the
atmosphere of a revolution. There's nothing more agreeable than to
swim in the black sea of a mob gone mad. (*The din offstage
continues.*)

LADY Richard, I love and admire you. Can there be any greater happiness than not to despise the man one loves?

(*The detectives lead Korbowski out. Alice follows him; Orsin
follows them.*)

LADY (*passing across the stage*) Good-bye, Father. I'm leaving the
house and the money to you. (*She leaves without looking at
Edgar.*)

FATHER Well, Sonny, now what? We've gone bankrupt. All we need
now is for Tadzio to turn out to be Korbowski's son. But we'll never
know about that. Perhaps now you'll become an artist. You could
even become an actor; after all, actors are now creative artists too,
ever since Pure Form became all the rage. (*Edgar stands silently; the
noise offstage becomes louder and louder; bursts of machine-gun
fire.*) Well, make up your mind! Surely nothing ties you to life any
more? Now you've got to become an artist.

EDGAR Death still ties me to life. That's the last thing to be disposed
of.

FATHER How?

EDGAR (*pulls a revolver out of his pocket*) Like this. (*He shows it to
his father.*)

---

* Latin, "according to vow," i.e., by marriage. [Translators' note]

FATHER You'd be an excellent actor, especially in those preposterous plays they write nowadays. But why did you use a shotgun when you had a revolver? So it would be more difficult to figure out? Huh?

EDGAR Because I wanted it to be the same as before.

FATHER I've always said you were an artist. Everything's neatly worked out in prepared speeches. You could write plays. Come here, let me give you a hug.

EDGAR Later, I don't have time now. Good-bye, Father. (*He shoots himself in the right temple and falls to the ground. Father stands goggle-eyed for a moment.*)

FATHER (*affectedly*) "Oh, thus the artist dies"—without any self-knowledge. Not like that other ham. (*He shouts*) Jan! Jan! (*Jan runs in.*) The young master has killed himself. Call the albinos, have them carry him out.

JAN I always thought it would turn out this way. (*He bends down over the corpse.*) It was a perfect shot. A tiny little hole like a nail makes. (*The noise in the street reaches its peak.*) What a shot that guy was! But he sure gave me a good scare today!

FATHER Jan, open the door, they're beating on it. The mob must be tearing everything down. (*Jan goes out.*) It's strange how old age and sea duty blunt everything in a man. I honestly don't feel anything at all—either for good or evil. Damn it all, a man isn't a ship! (*Enter Typowicz, Evader, and Specter.*) At last! (*To the old men*) My son killed himself. His nerves got the better of him. Too bad. Well, what's going on out there?

TYPOWICZ (*pale, the others frightfully dejected*) Mr. Valpor, cheer up. Everything's going to the devil. The Semites will always find a way. There are heaps of corpses out there in the street. We came on foot. Our chauffeur ran away. They took our car. We saw a strange sight. The Duchess was walking along the street in her dressing gown with Korbowski; some thugs were holding them prisoner. We couldn't get near them. (*The albinos come in and take Edgar's body out.*) Korbowski kept shouting something. Then the mob beat the thugs to a pulp, and Korbowski and the Duchess went off with the crowd to the barricade near Angry Young Man Avenue. But what am I saying? It's all a dream! Our company no longer exists. The new government has abolished all private enterprise. All we have left is what we've got abroad in foreign banks. (*During this speech, the albinos carry out Edgar's body to the left.*) And what about our homes?

EVADER They're community property too. We've lost everything.

FATHER I wonder if my adopted grandson will fight his way to the top.

(*Suddenly*) Well, gentlemen, it's our last night; the gangsters will probably butcher us tomorrow, so let's amuse ourselves for the last time. (*Shouts*) Jan! (*Jan in the doorway*) Set up the card table. (*Jan throws himself forward and with incredible speed sets up the card table in the middle of the room.*)

EVADER Have you gone out of your mind? To play cards at such a critical time?

FATHER At our age it's the only way of whiling away the time during a social upheaval. What else could we do? Whist or auction bridge? "That is the question." *

TYPOWICZ Why not whist? (*Burst of machine-gun fire*)

FATHER Oh, did you hear that? How could we do anything else except play cards? Everything's falling to pieces anyway.

SPECTER It would seem that you're right.

FATHER Of course. Jan, cold supper *extra fin* and plenty of wine for all. We'll drink like dragons. We've got to drink away three abortive generations. Maybe I'll still become a revolutionary admiral, but those others—ugh—what a comedown! (*Typowicz, Specter, and Evader sit down at the table, leaving a place facing the audience for Father. Typowicz with his back to the audience, Evader on the left, Specter to the right. Faint bursts of machine-gun fire and a distant roar of heavy artillery shells exploding.*)

FATHER (*to Jan who stands in the doorway*) Jan, one thing more. Go get those girls to keep us company at dinner, you know—the ones the young master and I used to visit.

JAN But will they want to come when all hell's breaking loose?

FATHER Certainly they'll want to, promise them anything. (*Exit Jan; Father goes over to the table and inspects the cards.*) There's no need to worry, gentlemen, perhaps we can still get jobs in the new government.

TYPOWICZ One club.

EVADER Two clubs.

FATHER (*sitting down*) Two diamonds. (*A red glare floods the stage, and the monstrous boom of a grenade exploding nearby can be heard.*) Banging away in fine style. Your bid, Mr. Specter.

SPECTER (*in a quivering, somewhat plaintive voice*) Two hearts. The world is collapsing. (*Fainter red flashes of lighting, and immediately afterward two shells exploding a little farther off*)

TYPOWICZ Pass.

---

* In English in the original. [Translators' note]

The Crazy Locomotive

INTRODUCTION

The Crazy Locomotive (*Szalona locomotywa*, 1923) is unique among Witkiewicz' dramas in that it confronts the challenge of mechanization directly. In this appropriately short, violent play, Witkiewicz puts the machine on the stage, turns it on, and lets us see where it will lead. The machine is a self-destructive machine—it blows itself up.

Witkiewicz utilizes the mechanized techniques of the enemy to subvert and destroy mechanization. The machine, simultaneously exploited and attacked, is both the locomotive engine and the movie projector. *The Crazy Locomotive* is a superparody—of the worship of the machine and of the new arts of technology: futurism and cinema. By his ironic appropriation of their ideas and devices, Witkiewicz was able to create an antifuturistic, anticinematographic play that has all the metallic brilliance and frantic speed which he is mocking.

Witkiewicz knew the futurists and their work from the Paris exhibition in February, 1912. He refers to Gino Severini in *They*, calling him "Severin." From the various manifestos published in many different languages at the time of the exhibition, Witkiewicz would have been acquainted with the principal ideas of the futurists: worship of action for its own sake; glorification of war, violence, and speed; love of physical courage and daring in the face of danger; and preference for the machine in motion as the new ideal of beauty. In the Preface to the *Initial Manifesto of Futurism*, Marinetti sees himself "alone with the black phantoms that rummage about in the red-hot bellies of the locomotives launched at furious speeds," [1] and in the Manifesto itself, he states:

> We declare that the world's splendor has been enriched by a new beauty; the beauty of speed. . . . We shall sing of the man at the steering wheel, whose ideal stem transfixes the Earth, rushing over the circuit of her orbit. . . . Why should we look behind us, when we have to break in the mysterious portals of the Impossible? Time and Space died yesterday. Already we live in the absolute, since we have already created speed, eternal and ever-present. . . . We shall sing . . . of

---

[1] Filippo Tommaso Marinetti, "Preface to the Initial Manifesto of Futurism," in Raffaele Carrieri, *Futurism* (Milan: Edizioni del Milione, 1963), p. 11.

broadchested locomotives prancing on the rails, like huge steel horses
bridled with long tubes. . . .[2]

The futurist hero was to be a mechanized superman: "the disciple of
the Engine, the enemy of books, an exponent of personal experience." [3]
He should act savagely and instinctively. "We are immoral, destroyers,
disorganizers; we want death and madness." [4] The futurists celebrated
the motorized masses who would ultimately be transformed into machines through the impact of metal and speed, "when the Animal
Kingdom comes to its end and the Mechanical Realm begins." [5]

In Act I of *The Crazy Locomotive* two social and psychological
outlaws, Tréfaldi and Travaillac, masquerading as the locomotive engineer Tenser and his fireman Slobok, embark on a desperate metaphysical adventure in search of the Absolute. The metallic beast roars
through artificial landscapes, annihilating time and space. Speed becomes the principle and criterion of all things. Through sheer acceleration the characters aboard the engine-island hope to escape from the
confines of everyday life and the boredom of existence and find a
meaning to fill the void. Traveling at breakneck speed, Tréfaldi and
Travaillac immediately experience a sense of elation and freedom denied them on firm ground. Their journey along the rails turns inward
and becomes a journey into the mind, a retreat from the world and a
return to wonderful memories of childhood. "We're on our desert
island again: Robinson Crusoe and his man Friday. We're playing the
Robinson game the way we did when we were children," Tréfaldi tells
Travaillac.

Robinson Crusoe and Friday, engineer and fireman, master and
servant, aristocrat and proletarian—the two criminals are contrasting
types with different physical traits, personalities, and social back-
grounds. Prince Tréfaldi is refined, highly educated, impractical, and
by nature philosophical; his face is long and lean, his beard and mustache elegant. Travaillac (whose name comes from the French *tra-
vailler*, "to work") is crude, uneducated, wary, and by nature a doer;
his features are coarse, his face clean-shaven. Tréfaldi has an aristocratic aloofness about him and is free from class consciousness and
sexual jealousy; Travaillac is direct in his responses and shows considerable jealousy over Julia and awareness of his social position in
relation to his boss. What unites them is the past and the future:

[2] Marinetti, "Initial Manifesto of Futurism," in Joshua C. Taylor, *Futurism*
(New York: Museum of Modern Art, 1961), p. 124.
[3] Marinetti, quoted by Rosa Trillo Clough, *Futurism* (New York: Philosophical Library, 1961), p. 33.
[4] Giulio Evola, "Notes for Friends," in *After Boccioni* (Rome: Edizioni
Mediterranee; Studio d'Arte Contemporanea "La Medusa," 1961), p. 35.
[5] Marinetti, quoted by Clough, *Futurism*, p. 41.

memories of their former criminal glories, and hopes for a new life of liberation and excitement.

Their complementary personalities and the games they play in their isolation in a self-contained world suggest the interplay between Estragon and Vladimir in Samuel Beckett's *Waiting for Godot*,[6] but the comparison only serves to show the fundamental difference between the two pairs of characters and the two plays. Witkiewicz' absurd duo are willful participants in a soul-shattering adventure. Even though the initiative rests primarily with Tréfaldi, both the engineer and his fireman are actively pursuing a goal rather than waiting passively for something to happen.

The characters abound in energy that parallels the driving force of the engine; as the locomotive speeds up, it releases the deepest and darkest forces normally hidden within the subconscious recesses of their personalities and permits them to break through into frenzied action. Minna's uncontrollable passion for Travaillac and Julia's ecstasy in being in love with both Tréfaldi and Travaillac are other manifestations of the same subliminal urges; like the frantic speed and the feverish talk, sexual attraction is an irrational, elemental plunge beyond all the bounds of society and the normal laws of conduct.

Extraordinary hopes are raised in Act I. As Tréfaldi and Travaillac reach a progressively closer intellectual rapport, the speed of the locomotive increases. They not only hope to experience a superreality; they are actually creating it themselves by their actions. Julia identifies opening the throttle all the way with her falling in love with both of them and also with the act of primeval creation. "Something's being created right here and now, the way it was in the beginning before the world began."

But in Act II the prophecy of a new birth begins to ring false. Instead of the creation of a new world, there will be only the destruction of an old one. As a machine, the locomotive must follow along the rails, and where they lead is known in advance—to a predictable, mechanized disaster. Tréfaldi is starting to become the slave of the beast which he let loose to liberate him. "I'm only an extension of this throttle," he complains, "as if my brains had been skewered and spitted on this iron lever. But it's more than that; I've become the engine." His hand on the throttle is no longer controlled by his mind; it has become part of the machine. As he wonders whether mechanized madness will eventually swallow up the whole world, he feels his personality being drained of all its energy; his head is empty, and he is powerless to stop acting as a part of a piece of machinery in which he no longer believes.

[6] Martin Esslin, *The Theater of the Absurd* (New York: Anchor Books, Doubleday and Co. 1961), p. 15.

The Epilogue shows the consequences of flight to a higher reality via a machine: death and madness. Tréfaldi—Marinetti's "man at the steering wheel"—ends up with the steering wheel twelve inches through his guts, with appropriate irony since he had wanted to live by guts alone, rather than according to his intellect. He was skewered by the instrument of control, not in his brain as he had imagined before, but in the seat of his intuition, instinct, and daring. Julia's former ecstasy has turned into madness and despair as she confronts the catastrophe in an uncomprehending state of shock. The primordial elements that were to be shaped into the great new creation have gone back to chaos and slime: the spilled guts, mushlike brains, and confused groans and cries that fill the stage. The wonderful metallic animal itself bursts into fragments; all that is left is a heap of debris.

With the introduction of the mad wife of the railway guard in the very last minutes of the play, Witkiewicz throws the whole spectral quality of the Epilogue into a new dimension of moonlight and insanity. Decked out in flowers like the mad Ophelia, Jeanne claims to have waited for such a disaster all her life. In the night a spirit with cat's eyes appeared to her in a dream, made love to her, and told her to cut the telephone wires. She points to Tréfaldi as her demon lover. Madness and dream, a collective daze and a landscape of subconscious fears and desires—this is the "black abyss" that suddenly opens before us in the Epilogue. Life is the shadow of a dream. The cold, cruel futuristic "joy ride" plunges into the void.

Jeanne's sudden, frightening appearance at the end of *The Crazy Locomotive* is an example of one of the characteristic masterstrokes of Witkiewicz' dramaturgy: his daring use of a minor character as a catalyst to open the abyss at the very denouement. The playwright is able to give strange and sinister weight to these messengers from another realm who, even though they have only a speech or two and most often are appearing on stage for the first time, act as the voice of doom. Unlike their ancestors in Greek drama, Witkiewicz' messengers do not report on the off-stage actions of the heroes and gods—they come from another world and remind the heroes of its existence and their relation to it. The ominous appearances of the Lamplighter in *The Water Hen* and of Professor Walldorff in *The Madman and the Nun* function similarly. These ghastly arrivals are unpredictable and therefore startling and theatrical, but once they have taken place they seem appropriate and inevitable—exactly the effect that Witkiewicz felt Pure Form should produce.

Dr. Marcellus Riftmaker, on the other hand, is the efficient man of science, standing outside the world of madness and coming to restore order. His prime interest is in saving Tréfaldi so that he can be punished as an example to others. "Justice first, then the wounded, and the mentally ill last of all." He is another kind of machine, the disciplinary social automationist with rigid categories and systems, and no sympathy for human weakness.

In addition to wrecking the futurist machine, *The Crazy Locomotive* collides head-on with the cinema. Witkiewicz' attitude toward the film was hostile; he saw it as a deadly challenge to the art of the theater. In *Aesthetic Sketches,* published in 1922, the year before Witkiewicz wrote *The Crazy Locomotive,* in the chapter devoted to "The Decline of Art," he poses the question of the very survival of the theater:

> With cinematography you can do absolutely anything you want, so is it worth trying to preserve idle chatter on the stage, which nobody needs anyhow, when you can have such frantic action and such violent images instead; is it worth making the effort to produce something as devilishly difficult as a real play for the theater faced with a rival as dangerous as the all-powerful cinema?

In *The Crazy Locomotive* Witkiewicz accepts the challenge and proves that the stage can present frantic action and violent images, as well as the intellectual content or "idle chatter," incorporating the film within the play and thereby deliberately calling attention to the unreal nature of this play-within-the-play. The entire play is a parody of the stereotypes of early films.

The headlong race of the crazy locomotive is itself probably inspired by famous train chases like Abel Gance's *La Roue* (1922), in which the central character is the engineer and the denouement a train wreck. The element of parody is reinforced by the actual use of film for the moving landscape and ironically commented upon by remarks such as Julia's exclamation: "I've always dreamed of something really extraordinary happening to me, like in the movies!" The double identities of Tréfaldi and Travaillac juxtapose the world of illusion and fantasy with the prosaic everyday world which they are trying to escape. Their colorful cinematographic careers as kings of the underworld are an externalization of the dreams and longings of the other passengers in the rear cars.

> TRAVAILLAC: But just think: here we are talking about all this, and back there, in one of the cars on the train, someone's reading about the very same thing, a story just like ours, in a murder mystery from the lending library.

But is the cheap fiction a parody of their lives, or are they a parody of the cheap fiction? Travaillac's speech ironically reminds the audience of the other world from which the two metaphysical adventurers think they have been freed. But there is no possibility of leaving firm ground, and soon the farcical world of cheap fiction readers—bureau-crats, thugs, and policemen—comes crawling up into the locomotive, invading the intense isolation of the questers and degrading their mission with the slapstick scuffle that follows. The fight aboard the moving train between the outlaws and the bumbling law-enforcement officials, as the passengers (representing a cross section of society) watch in outrage and horror, is cinematographic parody in another key.

The philosophical discussion between Tréfaldi and Travaillac, carried on against the ever increasing speed of the locomotive, is an attempt by men who belong to an earlier age to resolve fundamental problems through argumentation and rhetoric. It is a losing battle: philosophical dialogue versus uncontrollable movement. Cinema wins, dialogue ceases. Revolver shots, blows on the head with a shovel, a violent clang, a terrible crash finally drown out all words. The counterpoint and alternation of prolonged discussion and sudden outbursts of violence is one of Witkiewicz' basic techniques, heightened here by the cinematographic acceleration.

The Crazy Locomotive is a multisensory spectacle that holds its own against the cinema. Frightful blasts on whistles, the clanking of the cars, the flashing lights, the irrational emotions and wild philosophizing: we are bathed in a free play of vivid sense impressions, accompanying the pursuit of a superreality. Steam from the cylinder cocks obscures the stage; only voices and the rattle of the wheels can be heard. The stage ceases to be a stage in the traditional sense and becomes a playground of sound and color, confused and impenetrable as the higher reality which is sought by Tréfaldi and Travaillac but always eludes them.

The Crazy Locomotive

Motto:
"No more rum"
Billy Buns in *Treasure Island* RLS.

From the Commandments for
Locomotive Engineers:
"VI. Women should keep away
from engines; never take them
on your locomotive."
In *The Manual for Frantic
Locomotive Engineers*

Dedicated to

Miss Irena Jankowska

Siegfried Tenser

Locomotive engineer, 35 years old. Long lean, expressive face. His sharply outlined jaw and arched eyebrows clearly indicate strong will power. Dark Vandyke beard, small mustache. Dressed in a dark jacket and long black trousers with red stripes tucked into yellow leather spats. Cap with a visor.

Nicholas Slobok

Locomotive fireman, 28 years old. Completely clean-shaven. His face has coarse, strong features, but you cannot help feeling that there is a hidden streak of appalling languor that spoils his looks. Gray jacket. Green trousers, tucked into high yellow boots.

Sophia Tenser

The engineer's wife, 28 years old. Brunette, very pretty and demonic. Elegantly dressed.

Julia Tomasik

The fireman's fiancée, 18 years old. Blonde, very pretty, but with an animalistic kind of beauty.

Turbulence Guster

An elderly gentleman, dressed for traveling.

Minna, Countess de Barnhelm

A hysterical, banal young lady, but not without a certain charm characteristic of old families that have been degenerating for centuries. Dressed for traveling.

Three Third-Class Passengers

Look like thugs. One of them is a thief in handcuffs. He claims to be a locomotive engineer.

Two Gendarmes

Part of the police escort for the thug in handcuffs. Fantastic uniforms.

Miss Mira Bean

Dame de compagnie *to Minna—45 years old. Fat, wears glasses.*

Conductor

In an Austrian uniform, orange piping. A cap.

Doctor Marcellus Riftmaker

Young man with dark hair, pointed beard. White uniform. He knows his business.

Valery Bean

Mira's brother—fair-haired young man, 30 years old. A bank employee and, in his spare time, a surrealist painter.

John Cackleson	*Railway guard—reddish beard. Red-green lantern.*
His wife, the beautiful Jeanne Cackleson	*A blonde. Village fortuneteller.*
A crowd of passengers	*They all speak loudly and very distinctly.*

ACT I

The stage represents the back of the locomotive and the front of the tender. The point at which they are attached is a little to the right of the center of the stage. The locomotive can be gigantic—a model which hasn't yet been invented. The train moves to the right. In addition to directions about the right or the left side of the stage, the right and left side of the engine will be indicated according to the direction in which the train is moving. The throttle is of course on the right side. The inside of the engine is brightly lighted by two lanterns. Rods, pipes, and levers, connected with the driving mechanism, are visible, shining by the light of the lanterns. The firebox is open; light streams out of it, and fiery, blood-red flames shoot forth. The locomotive should be constructed in such a way that the empty space between the coal on the tender and the boiler is fairly large (the size of an average room) and that the roof of the locomotive does not cut off the scene of action from the view of those in the balcony. From time to time steam shoots out from the front taps and covers everything. The railroad passageway should be almost two feet high and enclosed by a railway gate, which separates the engine from the rest of the stage.

A person standing on the ground by the locomotive should be visible from the waist up. The scenery at the back of the stage should be produced by means of a movie projector which throws pictures on a screen; the projector will be placed behind the locomotive. At the beginning of the play the background scenery is motionless and represents the station. As the train begins to move, the scenery begins to move to the left (the view from the train in motion). The same sequence of pictures may be repeated occasionally. To go back: at the beginning of the play the scenery represents the railroad station, seen from the platform. The sunset is dying out on the horizon; to the left we see the engine house with its light signals and the silhouettes of locomotives. Semaphores with red and green lights, the arms raised.

Act I begins on an empty platform beyond the station buildings. In the distance, behind the semaphore, we can see the lights of the city whose glow competes with the final light of the sunset. Against this background we see the silhouettes of houses with lights here and there, towers, skyscrapers, clouds, and so on. The firebox which heats the boiler is open. Flames shoot out. The fireman Slobok is filling the firebox by throwing in large chunks of coal as he whistles "The Ideal Tango." This lull does not last long, since Julia soon appears from the left. She is elaborately, but tastelessly dressed. She is carrying a small basket. All the time the train remains standing, the normal noises of a railroad station can be heard: locomotives whistling, the clank of rail-road cars being coupled, bells ringing, and the buzz of the crowd.

JULIA Nicholas, I've brought you something to eat. You look as if you're about to explode. Here are some of those little plum cakes you like so much and a bottle of chartreuse.

NICHOLAS (*throws down his shovel and shuts the firebox; the engine begins to snort*) Thanks, Julie. (*He climbs down from the cab, picks up the basket, climbs back up again, leaves the basket in the tender, and climbs down again. He does all this with apelike agility.*)

JULIA (*while Nicholas is climbing up and down*) Where's Mr. Tenser?

NICHOLAS He and his wife have gone to the station for a beer. But you didn't come here to see him.

JULIA And what if I did? What would you know about it, you poor fool? Just look at you, you're covered with coal from head to foot.

NICHOLAS (*having come down again*) Just don't go too far, or I'll really get mad. (*Tenser and his wife approach slowly from the left; his wife is simply yet tastefully dressed. She is carrying a basket.*)

JULIA Do whatever you want. I'm not stopping you. You're always threatening to kill me, anyway.

NICHOLAS Oh . . . if I could only explain it all to you, everything would be different.

JULIA Tell me, then! I'm not afraid.

NICHOLAS (*angrily, in an undertone*) Be quiet. The Tensers are coming.

TENSER What's the steam pressure, Nicholas?

NICHOLAS Six and a half atmospheres, Mr. Tenser.

TENSER Stoke up the fire. (*Nicholas climbs up into the locomotive; feeds the fire; flames shoot out.*) Today I have a feeling I'll need enough steam for six compounds. Once it gains momentum, this beast races along at a frantic clip, but lacks pulling power. And they've gone ahead and attached a sleeping car. (*In a different tone of voice*) Julia, you look very attractive today—perfectly diabolical! But not just diabolical, nor just blonde, but diablondical. Oh . . . if it weren't for this locomotive of mine, everything would be different! It holds me back. Otherwise, I'd just blow up like a hand grenade. (*Sophia tugs at his sleeve.*) Let me alone . . .

JULIA Mr. Tenser always says such . . .

SOPHIA Yes, he's always making up some kind of nonsense. But he's really gentle as a lamb. I can't stand such docile men.

JULIA You must be joking.

SOPHIA I never joke. I was unfaithful to him yesterday with the brakeman on the Nord-Express. And he didn't even bat an eyelash.

JULIA Who? Your husband? Or the brakeman? (*Nicholas slams the firedoor with a bang and leans out of the locomotive cab.*)

TENSER Very funny! Don't pay any attention to them, Nicholas.

NICHOLAS (*angrily*) Sophia, you're corrupting my fiancée. I've asked you not to talk that way in front of her.

JULIA Don't be stupid, Nicholas. I've already been corrupted. I'm well taken care of in that department.

NICHOLAS (*about to climb down from the locomotive*) Shut up, you damned lovebird, or I'll . . . (*His words are interrupted by a toot on the horn which the conductor blows as he appears from the left to signal "All aboard."*)

TENSER We're off! (*He kisses his wife, jumps up into the locomotive, letting out a wild cry which turns into caterwauling. The women run off to the left, Nicholas leans out of the cab.*) Turn on the steam injector! Hurry up! Seven degrees on the water gauge, and . . . (*His words are drowned out by the sound of the train whistle which he has just released. Then he opens the throttle. Steam pours out of the cylinder cocks and obscures the entire stage. When the steam clears away, the landscape has started to move to the left. The wheels can be heard pounding along the tracks, and the locomotive chugs more and more loudly. The last lights of the station disappear. Then the suburbs rush by, and the outskirts of the city are lit by moonlight. A pause.*)

NICHOLAS (*looking at the pressure gauge*) Seven atmospheres. I don't think the valve will stand the pressure.

TENSER (*at the throttle*) And now let's take off our masks! We're on our desert island again: Robinson Crusoe and his man Friday. We're playing the Robinson game the way we did when we were children. (*At this moment city lights appear, and then fields, forests, valleys, and villages rush by.*)

NICHOLAS Mr. Tenser, we can't go on like this any longer! We've got to have a frank talk and settle things—once and for all. Putting aside other, more important matters, tell me: are you by any chance in love with my fiancée?

TENSER (*pushing the throttle down more vigorously*) My dear Nicholas, first throw some more coal on, and then we'll talk.

NICHOLAS Mr. Tenser—the pipes!! . . .

TENSER What do I care about pipes? (*Nicholas feeds the fire; flames shoot out.*) You see, I'm only an ordinary engineer when I want to be—the same way you're just an ordinary fireman. But it probably comes easier to you than to me. (*When Tenser pushes the throttle down, the gestures he makes are exaggerated and impressive. All the while the locomotive chugs along faster and faster.*)

NICHOLAS That remains to be seen. (*He shuts the firebox.*)

TENSER What you're saying is interesting, but right now that's not really the question. Ever since we got on the locomotive, everything's been going well. Except for the minor problem of the next station, we're alone on this iron beast, totally isolated from the rest of the world. We're not only rushing through space, we're intensely aware of it. As Lénart said, there's simply no such thing as relativity of motion for the locomotive engineer. He knows the landscape isn't moving because it's not the landscape he stokes up and oils, but his own locomotive. And the same thing applies to everything that lives and moves. Even a flea's existence disproves all the laws of physics. And that's why the scientific view of relativity can never correspond to reality!

NICHOLAS Mr. Tenser, either you're digressing, or you're joking.

TENSER Just a moment—let me think this through. If the two of us could only—and yet I'd rather do it entirely on my own—if we could construct a planet or meteor, it would be much more comfortable than breaking our necks along these rails. We know only too well where they'll lead us. A boat would be better, but I can't stand water and all the problems connected with it . . . Unfortunately, piracy's no longer possible these days.

NICHOLAS (*intrigued*) So what you're really after is solid financial gain, obtained not altogether legally?

TENSER Oh, no . . . I didn't realize quite what I was saying. Anyhow, just the two of us couldn't handle a ship—and a boat would be too small—there's no solution.

NICHOLAS (*looking at the pressure gauge*) Eight and a half, Mr. Tenser —isn't that too much?

TENSER It can go up to nine. I'm going to need more and more steam from now on, although I don't know exactly why yet. Ever since this morning a kind of vague plan has been taking shape in my mind. For a few minutes, at least, we've got to break through all normal day-to-day relationships. Then everything will become clear. And suddenly we'll reach a stage we never even dreamed of.

NICHOLAS That's strange—ever since this morning I've been thinking about strange and extraordinary things, too, but I couldn't tell you exactly what they were. As I was firing up this beast (*he hits the firebox with his fist*), something vague and formless began to stir in my brain. But for me the meaning of our existence ultimately becomes shrouded in inner darkness. Only action, not contemplation, can make it clear to us. But we have so few opportunities to do something really extraordinary—if we rule out what you like to call psychological aberrations, Mr. Tenser.

TENSER That's been my experience, too. You're right: I love Julia, but I love my wife, too, although I consider her more as a partner in my various activities, which I'd rather not talk about right now. To me Julia is the essence of all feminine charm and mystery, in spite of—or perhaps because of—her stupidity. But is any of this really very significant? It's all well and good here, but that's why it probably wouldn't mean so much out there, on relatively firm ground. But here, on this pile of metal, plunging ahead on its reckless course, things seem quite different. How can we carry this point of view of ours over into that other sphere which has grown flabby out of sheer inertia and yet at the same time observe everything from this locomotive hurtling through space? That's the problem!

NICHOLAS You know, I was thinking the very same thing myself, but I didn't have it worked out so clearly. I've read a handbook about Einstein's theory, too. The transformation of coordinates, the relativity of everything—and all that.

TENSER But here the question arises: should we be looking from the engine at the ground, or from the ground at the engine? Because on the ground everything I'm saying right now is bound to appear absurd, it's Pure Form,* that's what the FORMISTS call it—I recently read an article on the subject by one of their best essayists. But that's neither here nor there. Let me put it to you quite frankly: say it were possible to transfer life onto this locomotive, how would that be . . . ? Of course the objection could be raised: why not the sleeping car or diner instead? Still, there's a wide gulf between the locomotive and the rest of the train.

NICHOLAS (*laughing*) Yes. Even I understand the difference. After all, what is life except women, our own and other people's? The eternal rectangle of husband, wife, and engaged couple, traveling together endlessly on the locomotive? A propos, Mr. Tenser, you know, as soon as we climb aboard this engine-island, I'm not mad at you any more, not even about Julia. Here I'm the fireman, I have my own position in the world. I couldn't put up with any other boss. Everything goes along smoothly here, but it's completely two-dimensional like the surface of a painting—everything stays in its place as if it were frozen, although it's actually moving. Funny, isn't it! (*He laughs.*)

TENSER Don't make fun of it, Nicholas. It's not so silly as it seems. It's

---

* A reference to Witkiewicz' own theory of art. [Translators' note]

just that it can't really be done. But what about the idea itself? . . .
Hm . . . (*Pushes the throttle down more vigorously; the engine
chugs faster and faster*) Well, I suppose it could be done, but only
once; it could never be repeated, and it couldn't be done in reverse.
Yes, yes: I think I've got it now—that vague plan of mine.

NICHOLAS But that means death, then.

TENSER (*feverishly*) How do you know?

NICHOLAS Don't touch the throttle. Ninety-two miles an hour,* Mr.
Tenser. Another half mile and we'll reach the point of diminishing
returns. Now's the time to close the throttle.

TENSER Don't try to teach me how to drive this engine. Your job is to
stoke. More coal! Hurry up, Mr. Slobok! (*Nicholas follows the
orders; flames shoot out.*) How do you know my plan means death?
Personally, I don't picture anything as definite as that.

NICHOLAS It's there! (*He points ahead, in the direction the train is
moving.*)

TENSER Perhaps it is there. I like you because of the seismograph you
carry around in your head; you don't even know it's there, but all
the time it's recording obscure tremors on a graph inside you. (*With
admiration*) Such a dumb animal, yet so sensitive to everything. (*A
pause*) More coal. (*Nicholas follows the orders. Flames shoot out.*)

NICHOLAS (*as he's stoking*) So far we're evenly matched. Just think of
it: at the very same moment in history, Existence in all its infinity
and the two of us, alone, on this galloping monster adrift from all
mankind. Even if you tried for a thousand years, you couldn't think
up anything like that.

TENSER What do you mean "adrift from all mankind"? It's true, I
guess. But explain it a little more clearly.

NICHOLAS (*throwing down his shovel*) I already told you: close that
damn throttle and apply the brakes, so Mr. Westinghouse can go
into action, or else we'll probably be derailed at the next curve.
(*Tenser closes the throttle and applies the brakes. The knocking of
the valves on the compressed-air brakes and the clanking of the
wheels can be heard.*)

TENSER Well, go on.

NICHOLAS All you ever think about is women. You'd even like them on
the engine.

TENSER This is the second time you've told me that, Mr. Slobok. To

* In accordance with Witkiewicz' remark that the locomotive can be "a model
which hasn't yet been invented," we have increased the speed of the train to
contemporary equivalents by simply turning kilometers per hour into miles per
hour. [Translators' note]

tell the truth, for me a woman is only a symbol: visible proof of the fleeting moment. And what's more I admit I'm a professional seducer. But it's really my way of determining the principal moments of inertia of the body in relation to its axes.*

NICHOLAS But I thought you were somebody more important than that.

TENSER (*trying to distract his attention*) Well, well, well . . . no matter how much nonsense you talk, you still can never be nonsensical enough to get at the Mystery of Existence. Lunatics know that, and so do those on the verge of lunacy.

NICHOLAS Now you're getting off the subject. I'm going to take a chance and tell you the truth: I am not Slobok. Slobok has been lying in his grave for a long time. I'm living his life for him—with the aid of his papers. My name is TRAVAILLAC.

TENSER (*releases the brakes on the engine; the brakes stop clanking*) You've beaten me to it—by half a length. I was just about to introduce myself, too. So you're the great Travaillac, sought in vain by the police all over the world. I could give orders at Dumbell-Junction to have you arrested on the spot.

NICHOLAS (*trying to reach for his back pocket*) I didn't think that you . . .

TENSER Let go of that revolver, Mr. Travaillac. I was only joking. To a criminal of your stature, I too can make my introductions. I am Prince Karl Tréfaldi. I can also be arrested at any station. (*They shake hands.*)

NICHOLAS-TRAVAILLAC Yes, my intuition has never been wrong. If it had, I'd have rotted away in some prison a long time ago. It's a great pleasure for me to make the acquaintance of such a high-class colleague. You were always an inspiration to me in my work. Who knows, perhaps the two of us together can now rise above the turbulent pulp of international depravity.

TENSER-TRÉFALDI Yes—all those crimes bore me, and especially their consequences. Of course I'm not talking about prison, but about inner consequences. Nowadays crime stunts the growth of the human personality. Despite my seeming simplicity, I'm much too complicated to try to lead a normal life. And now there's Julie . . . Oh, don't be offended. Listen to me, Travaillac: we can't go on like this. We've got to do something really diabolical, not to others, but to ourselves, today, right now, without further delay. To put it bluntly, I'm in love with your fiancée, but without a really atrocious

---

* Tenser is evidently a mathematical Don Juan. In physics and engineering, "moment" is a term designating the product of a quantity and a distance to some point associated with the quantity. [Translators' note]

accident, I can't seem to get started. Here, on this engine, at least I'm racing ahead, and that calms me down a little. My wife uses blackmail to keep a hold on me.

TRAVAILLAC What? You mean Erna Abracadabra, the famous chanteuse from Beastly-Hole, New York? The partner of all your crimes?

TRÉFALDI Yes, the very same: she's the one who helped me murder my aunt, the Princess di Boscotrecase. She's dyed her hair black and wears a putty nose. I no longer find her attractive. And that's why I'm still alive today. As for me, I hardly even resemble myself . . .

TRAVAILLAC Of course, we all have to keep changing constantly. But just think: here we are talking about all this, and back there, in one of the cars on the train, someone's reading about the very same thing, a story just like ours, in a murder mystery from the lending library. Funny, isn't it!

TRÉFALDI It's possible; but such a coincidence doesn't diminish either the greatness of our thoughts or the strangeness of our meeting. And now let's get down to business: now I understand what the trouble was! It's what's been torturing me for the last three months. Ever since you became my fireman.

TRAVAILLAC You can be quite frank with me, Karl! I'm prepared for whatever happens!

TRÉFALDI We've got to take some kind of action tonight. Here we are, racing ahead nonstop at breakneck speed, and it's up to us to see it through.

TRAVAILLAC Something like a duel or God's Judgment. Good, that suits my purpose. So you're very much in love with her, in spite of your age, my dear Karl?

TRÉFALDI Yes, but it's a perfectly normal attraction—you understand —I'm not trying to lure her away from you simply because you're a subordinate in one profession and a colleague in another, higher one. We've got to settle the question in a manner befitting outmoded men who have strayed into another epoch and are hopelessly lost.

TRAVAILLAC The aristocracy never has appealed to me. I'm no snob.

TRÉFALDI That doesn't matter: two hundred years ago you certainly would have been a formidable skunk on the summits of humanity. And that's why I'm pushing the throttle down.

TRAVAILLAC All right, but what about the train? The lives of all those people?

TRÉFALDI That from you! A man, or rather a beast, on whose conscience there are at least thirty absolutely monstrous, or rather absolutely glorious murders!

TRAVAILLAC Yes, that's true—but then, in those days I had certain real goals.

TRÉFALDI And isn't our goal tonight much more real than all the other goals we've ever had? We're going to solve the essential problem: the problem of how to make sense out of the whole unsavory comedy of our existence, since our criminal period unfortunately played itself out.

TRAVAILLAC I still haven't been able to grasp the full significance of what we're planning to do—but in principle I'm satisfied with it, I know that. I've simply got to carry it out, because there's nothing else in the world which could possibly give my life any meaning.

TRÉFALDI Don't give it too much thought. Something had to happen. All the territories of crime have already been worked to death. We can't go back to our former lives. And just think how satisfying it will all be if one of us lives through this episode. The survivor will be able to burden the dead corpse with all his guilt—and feel absolutely secure.

TRAVAILLAC All right, I agree. If we pass through Dumbell-Junction without an accident, we're sure to meet No. 50; according to the timetable our paths are bound to cross. There's nothing between stations to stop the other train. I'm prepared for whatever happens, but if both of us survive, it'll be a rather awkward situation.

TRÉFALDI (*opens the throttle wide; the engine begins to snort ferociously*) I hadn't thought about the possibility of being maimed, but now it's too late for such speculation. I'm letting the engine go full steam ahead. (*They shake hands. Julia creeps along the tender by the coal pile.*)

JULIA (*gets up, staggers because the platform between the tender and the locomotive is shaking; the engine chugs faster and faster, and the landscape rushes by madly*) I planned a little surprise for you. You didn't expect it, did you? Mrs. Tenser is coming along on all fours behind me. We jumped on at the last minute. It was difficult crossing over the buffers. Why are you going so fast? It's crazy! There's a station just a little way ahead.

TRAVAILLAC You'll find out soon enough. We'll see whether you're up to the high stakes we're playing for.

JULIA High stakes? What sort of nonsense is that? Have you already drunk up all that chartreuse I gave you? You'll have to hide us till we get to the station—under the coal or somewhere.

TRÉFALDI It's happening: our dreams have come true. We've got to tell them the truth. (*Sophia Tenser*, recte * *Erna Abracadabra, creeps along the tender.*) Erna, listen to me: I love Julia. Travaillac and I are carrying out God's Judgment. I'm letting the engine rush on, full

* Latin, "rightly," to indicate Sophia's real name. [Translators' note]

steam ahead, at breakneck speed. If we come out of this alive—fine; if we're all ground into mincemeat—so much the better. I can't go on any longer constantly threatened by this blackmail. I have a feeling you'll die soon, and you're the only person my conscience wouldn't let me kill. You see—I love you in my own way—you've been a good partner and a good friend. But I think you're destined to die in an accident. You came here of your own free will. It's not my fault. (*The women listen, completely bewildered.*)

ABRACADABRA Who's Travaillac, Siegfried? Have you gone mad? You're suffering from hallucinations.

TRÉFALDI (*pointing to Travaillac*) It's Travaillac, not Slobok. The famous Travaillac. Take a good look at him. Don't you remember? We read about him in *Bulldog Magazine*. All masks are off.

ABRACADABRA Oh, my God! He's gone mad! Mr. Slobok, he's got to be put away! Oh, why did I ever let myself be talked into doing such a ridiculous thing! It's your fault, you snake! (*Throws herself on Julia*) You're the one who persuaded me to jump on the train! (*Travaillac holds Erna back.*)

JULIA Really, I didn't plan it, I didn't know anything about any of this! (*To the men*) But here I am—we're together! And I couldn't be happier! Now I know I love you both. But Mr. Tenser, what a pity that you're not a criminal too, like Nicholas.

ABRACADABRA He's even worse. (*To Travaillac*) Let go of me, you ape! Karl, save me! Close the throttle! I still have a lot to live for!

TRÉFALDI (*cuts the whistle cord in two different places*) Here, Travaillac, tie her up! That's the first time in her life she's ever forgotten her manners. (*He throws Travaillac the cord.*)

JULIE I'll help you. (*They tie up the shrieking Erna.*)

ABRACADABRA Close the throttle: Put on the brakes! I still have a great deal to live for! I've had enough of your dirty, rotten tricks! (*Travaillac gags her and throws her on the coal pile.*)

TRÉFALDI (*to Julia*) To settle the question of whether or not I'm a criminal, may I take the liberty of introducing myself: I am Karl, Prince Tréfaldi—that's quite enough, isn't it?

JULIA No . . . it's you . . . That's incredible! Tréfaldi, the most notorious criminal in the world! Oh—how perfectly marvelous! I'm so happy! I've always dreamed of something really extraordinary happening to me, like in the movies!

TRAVAILLAC Don't I count for something? And don't my crimes mean anything to you? You'd better be careful, Julia; I can kill His Highness and stop the train at any moment.

JULIA (*kissing Travaillac*) I love you both. Now I'm really in love for the first time, and with both of you. At this very moment both of you are extraordinary. Something's being created right here and now, the way it was in the beginning before the world began.

TRÉFALDI Here's a girl who's really worthy of us! We couldn't possibly abandon our plan, could we? We have to do it, Travaillac! We couldn't go on living unless we did it. Isn't that so?

TRAVAILLAC Of course it is! (*Leans out the other side of the engine*) You can already see the signals at Dumbell-Junction.

TRÉFALDI (*looking at the instruments*) Eight and a half atmospheres, 122 miles an hour. I have a feeling we're going to pass right by the station without an accident. I can just see the expression on the faces of all those imbeciles waiting for the train!

ABRACADABRA (*howling through the gag*) Ahrrmbunglohramkopr . . .

JULIA (*clasping her hands together rapturously*) Oh—it's wonderful! It's stupendous! To be with two famous criminals seconds before the crash! I love them both, and they both love me! Oh, this is really living! I'm so excited I could burst! I just can't wait till it happens! (*A frightful blast on the engine whistle interrupts her.*)

ACT II

The same setting as in Act I. The landscape rushes by incredibly fast. During the intermission the film has been changed; a lighted village should flash by for a moment, and then a railroad station with all its lights. On the right side of the engine, Tréfaldi, hanging on to the throttle and leaning out to the right. Everything is bathed in the steam coming out of the cylinder cocks.

TRÉFALDI If we have anything more to say to one another, we'd better say it quickly. In less than a minute we'll pass the first semaphore at Dumbell-Junction. We're going so fast I don't know whether we'll get past the first crossing without being derailed.

TRAVAILLAC What more is there to be said? Eleven atmospheres, 130 miles an hour. My head is hurtling into the infinite cosmic abyss, like a bullet along its trajectory.

JULIA Well, I say I feel marvelous! I've never done anything so exciting before in my whole life, and I'm supposed to be such a hysterical woman. I'd be willing to die a thousand times for a moment like this!

TRÉFALDI As for me, I've nothing more to say. I have the feeling that all my thoughts have been snuffed out of my brain. I'm only an extension of this throttle, as if my brains had been skewered and spitted on this iron lever. But it's more than that; I've become the engine. I'm the one that's racing through space like a bull, ready to impale myself on the blade of my destiny. Yes, it's really a momentous occasion. They ought to put a sign up over our heads: "Do not touch, danger, high voltage!" If a normal person, standing on firm ground, touched me, he'd fall down dead as though struck by lightning. Is this the beginning of mechanized madness?

TRAVAILLAC I'm amazed at your modesty, Karl: first you tell us you have nothing to say, then you talk your head off.

TRÉFALDI But all my talk is negative; I don't have anything positive to say. I only exist as a moving image projected on a screen in the endless void. I think if the engine stopped suddenly, I'd die.

JULIA Oh—stop psychoanalyzing yourself! Real men are always like that, unfortunately, even supermen like you. This is the only time in our lives when we can really gorge ourselves with reality. In our everyday lives we only get scraps, crumbs, and leftovers—that's all there is. But now I have everything—I'm not waiting for anything any more—because I already have it! Even a head-on collision means nothing at all to me. I've got both of you inside the kernel of death that's in me, in you, and in this crazy engine. But in that other life could I ever have had you in some ordinary room, at some ordinary hour of an ordinary night?

ABRACADABRA (*frees herself with a superhuman effort, pulls off the gag, and screams*) I see through you! You filthy slut! I know perfectly well what you want, you rotten little guttersnipe, you gluttonous hunk of vulgar horseflesh! Karl! I appeal to you for the last time! (*Travaillac holds her. They struggle. Julia bursts out laughing—a wild, crazy laugh.*)

TRÉFALDI (*in a thundering voice*) We're coming to the station! I can't let go of the throttle. Throw that trash out—it's got no soul! We're not going to let that disgusting old bag spoil these precious moments with her filthy talk! (*Travaillac and Julia throw Erna Abracadabra out from the left side.*)

TRAVAILLAC (*leans out to see if everything went successfully*) She's smashed to pieces against a pump! Here's the station! The first semaphore! The road is clear! All the crossings are clear. The second semaphore is signaling that the line is occupied. That means No. 50 is on its way to Dumbell-Junction. The crucial moment's drawing near!

TRÉFALDI (*pushes the throttle down; they all dash to the left side of the engine and lean out*) Everything's going well. If only my head didn't feel so insanely empty, I'd really be happy. (*A semaphore rushes by, then the station and its lights; the pounding of the wheels at the crossings can be heard. The crowd on the platform hoots and lets out wild cries. Another semaphore rushes by, then several fac-*

tory chimneys against a background of city lights, and the moonlit landscape starts moving again.)

TRAVAILLAC (*leans out from the left; Julia, from the center; Tréfaldi, from the right*) Someone just jumped onto the moving train! He must be crazy! He'll ruin everything . . .

JULIA (*kissing them rapturously*) Who could possibly be as crazy as we are? We're in a class by ourselves. We're absolutely unique, we're colossal. At last I understand what true greatness is! How grateful I am to you! How I love you both!

TRÉFALDI If No. 50's late, it could mean real trouble. How can we stand this suspense any longer? If our present mood deserts us, there's no guaranteeing what turn the disaster may take.

JULIA Don't talk that way. I could go on like this for hours. A whole lifetime is condensed into these moments of waiting, like a balloon filled with compressed air.

TRAVAILLAC Well, yes, women are generally hardier than men. We can take just so much and no more. If this business drags on, it won't turn out so well; in fact, it could turn out quite badly.

TRÉFALDI Look: someone's crawling along the tender toward us! (*They all look in that direction.*)

A VOICE (*coming from the part of the tender that cannot be seen*) Here they are! Up here! I told you not to give up hope! Something must have happened to the brakes. Come on! We'll help them!

TRAVAILLAC (*trying to reach for his back pocket*) Oh, hell! Now our work is cut out for us! To shoot or not to shoot—I'm not anxious to commit any more crimes! (*In despair*) Oho!—there's a whole gang crawling up here!

TRÉFALDI Don't shoot—it'll all come out all right.

JULIA Nicholas, he's backing down! He's leaving it all up to fate.

TRÉFALDI Look, I'm still doing 115 an hour, and you're complaining. Oh, you're insatiable!

(*Valery Bean, dressed in a cutaway, crawls from the tender over the hunks of coal toward the locomotive. His head is bleeding and bandaged with a bloody handkerchief. His hands are bleeding.*)

BEAN I'm Valery Bean. There's a woman here? What in God's name are you doing here? But what difference does it make? What can I do to help? Tell me quickly, because No. 50 has already left the last station; it's rushing toward us from the opposite direction. Nothing can stop it. The guard's telephone on line No. 20 is out of order. They were talking about it at the station.

JULIA (*in despair*) Nothing beautiful can exist in this world! The human animal always interferes and spoils everything!

TRÉFALDI So it's don't give up hope, is it? Damn! *Sangue del cane!* I'd forgotten about that telephone, and I work for the railroad! Ha, ha . . . We'd always counted on speed saving us. That imbecile on the freight train would never be able to back up at 130 miles an hour.

BEAN What are you talking about? She's the lunatic! Have you gone crazy, too? Can't you stop the engine? Tell me what has to be done, and I'll do it. Hurry up!

(*Minna de Barnhelm, her* dame de compagnie, *Mira Bean, Turbulence Guster, three Thugs, and two Gendarmes creep along slowly over the hunks of coal and appear on the locomotive. They are all terrified.*)

TRAVAILLAC You've come at the right time. We need two levers to stop the train: one for me and one for my boss. Lend us your rifles. (*The Gendarmes, who are frightened to death, hand over their rifles.*) Wonderful! Now beat it! (*Throws the rifles out of the train, to the left, and pulls a revolver out of his pocket*) The situation's getting more and more complicated, but we'll manage somehow. Don't move, or I'll blow your brains out!

BEAN Yes—they really are lunatics! This madness is contagious, it's becoming universal! Unless somebody does something, we're lost. I can't do anything more. I'm worn out from catching the train. I'm completely bushed.

MINNA Isn't there anyone who has enough courage to go after those murderers? In five seconds it may be too late! We'll be killed anyhow, unless someone comes to our rescue! (*Tréfaldi stands with his arms crossed. Next to him Julia, shielded by Travaillac's revolver*)

MIRA BEAN I beg and beseech you! My brother, Valery Bean, is only a bank clerk—it's true he has the reputation of being mad because at night he paints surrealistic paintings, but in spite of that he jumped on a moving train to save me, and he'll save all of us while he's at it. One hundred miles an hour—he was waiting for me at the station with a bouquet of flowers! Can you understand what that means? I was the first one in our car to pull the alarm!

GUSTER Yes, but not one of us has a gun! How could anyone have foreseen this? Such a respectable company! And now we're getting closer and closer to death every second! Death on all sides—it's enough to drive you out of your mind! (*The Conductor appears carrying a lantern.*)

CONDUCTOR Oh, my God, Mr. Guster, what's going on on this train? Nobody has any idea what's happening. The passengers think the train was supposed to pass right by the station. In the rear cars no one had tickets to Dumbell-Junction. Those two have both gone mad. And it's all due to drinking! And I don't have a gun, either!

GUSTER For God's sake, Conductor, let's not waste time arguing! We're not at the theater watching a play! You've got to help us somehow. After all, I know you personally.

CONDUCTOR I don't have any idea what to do. I don't even know where the steering wheel is! All I can do is punch tickets or check whether they've already been punched. Specialization is the great curse of our age. Wouldn't you agree?

THIRD THUG (*in handcuffs*) Mr. Guster, we're personally acquainted, too, but in a rather odd sort of way. I attacked you on the street one night, even though we've never been formally introduced. Please accept my apologies and see about getting these handcuffs taken off. I used to be an engineer.

GUSTER (*to the Gendarmes*) Take his handcuffs off.

MINNA (*to the Third Thug*) Save us, and I'll have you released from prison. My uncle is prosecutor in the appellate court. I fell in love with the fireman two minutes ago. He's my type. I've found him at last. I've got to get him away from that girl so we can live together for the rest of our lives—without any interference! I want to live! Don't you understand? Fireman, did you hear that? (*The three lunatics burst out laughing, diabolically. Meanwhile the Gendarmes unlock the handcuffs on the Third Thug.*)

TRAVAILLAC You know, that girl's a real addition to our group. It makes the situation more varied.

TRÉFALDI Seven separate destinies fatally meet at one point—it's almost mathematically inevitable. There's nothing more to be said on that subject—except the clichés second-rate dramatists use to pad out their vacuous plays. We'll just wait and see. Right now I wonder if I'll have enough courage. Julie, if we're saved, you won't be false to us, will you?

JULIA Never! I'm a superwoman, from another world. But it makes me furious they've ruined such a wonderful experience for us!

MINNA You disgusting phony! Now I see what tricks you've used to hold onto your handsome fireman!

TRAVAILLAC Karl, come here by the throttle, just in case! They're so desperate they're capable of anything!

CONDUCTOR (*holding up his lantern*) Karl? He's been Siegfried all his life!

TRÉFALDI (*edging along the boiler to the right-hand side of the engine*) Not all of it, my friend! If you live through this, there'll be even more surprises! You know, Travaillac, perhaps it's all to the good that they've come up here! It gives me the strength to go on. If it weren't for this, I admit I might have backed down in the face of death. So it's best after all to leave some odds and ends to the miserable workings of chance.

JULIA I admire your heroism in admitting your shortcomings, Karl.

GUSTER It's shocking that at this stage of civilization our lives are in the hands of such people. I just can't believe I'm here on this locomotive! (*Valery Bean faints and falls on the coal pile. All the others are extremely excited as they wait for the results of freeing the Thug.*)

TRAVAILLAC (*to Guster*) And did you think we're all lifeless manikins like you? We criminals are the only people who count for anything in this degraded world, especially those of us who are criminals, not for the sake of money or for any other motive, but for the sake of crime itself.

JULIA Yes—criminals and maybe artists, too! They're the only ones who are really alive. Of course I only know artists through their works. Maybe lunatics are, too? But I don't know any lunatics.

THIRD THUG (*the one who's been released*) Come off it! They're lunatics, aren't they? And what about you? Aren't you a lunatic?

MINNA It's all a hoax, a hideous joke! It's due to the influence of modern art!

THIRD THUG (*his hands in his pockets*) Only the biggest cowards are really brave, and that's because they're afraid; your average coward just can't make it. (*While he is saying this, Minna grabs the shovel and hits Tréfaldi on the head; he falls on the guardrail. Encouraged, the others throw themselves on Travaillac. He fires two shots from his revolver and misses both times. Travaillac is overpowered. The Third Thug closes the throttle and turns the link in the opposite direction; then he opens the throttle again to make reverse steam and says*) The link in the Heisinger von Waldeck system. A beautiful gadget—in my day we didn't have anything like it. (*A violent clang is heard inside the engine. Julia remains leaning against the boiler. She holds her head in her hands. The others utter a cry of joy.*)

GUSTER (*leaning out from the left side of the engine, shouts in despair*): Too late! No. 50's rushing toward us at top speed! We won't be able to stop! Blow the whistle, what's-your-name! Hurry! (*The Third Thug forces a forlorn whistle out of the engine. Despairing cries. In a frenzy of fear, all the characters look about wildly and let go of Travaillac.*)

TRAVAILLAC (*shouting*): Julia! Don't be afraid! Now you'll be mine! My boss got his belly split wide open, and he's kicked the bucket! He died muttering obscenities.

MINNA No, you're mine! Mine! Mine! We'll die together! There'll be nothing left of us but glue! (*She kisses Travaillac; he tears himself away. Minna's* dame de compagnie *Mira pulls her away from Travaillac. At this very moment a terrible crash and din are heard. Steam covers everything, as the engine bursts into fragments.*)*

EPILOGUE

Stationary landscape. Night, moonlight. White clouds are floating across the sky. All that remains of the wrecked engine is a heap of debris. A crowd of passengers. Groans and cries. Railway guard Cackleson, with a red lantern in his hand, is talking to the Conductor. The dead and wounded are being pulled out.

GUARD Conductor, what's happened? Were there a lot of people in the locomotive? Was there shooting? Was it a holdup?

CONDUCTOR (*holds onto his head; his shako is gone, and his coat is in shreds*): P-po-po-po-po-po-po-po . . . Oh, Oh . . . my God, my God . . .

GUARD Talk like a human being. As soon as I saw what was going on, I immediately gave the signal to stop—for both you and No. 50. You must have gone right by the station, or else my clock isn't running right. My wife's gone mad—she's been delirious all day. And then that telephone that's been out of order since five o'clock! I don't want to be held responsible for this. (*The Conductor spreads his arms, babbles incoherently, then speaks.*)

CONDUCTOR It's-s-s a m-m-mystery!!! It's a miracle that I'm still alive. My brain's like mush, and there's a hole in my head. In a minute it'll all run out through the hole. (*They pull Julia out; she runs to the front of the stage screaming.*)

JULIA (*wildly*) Nothing beautiful can exist in life! Everything's rotten! Everything beautiful has come to an end for all time! I've had enough! Kill me! I don't want anything, I don't want to see anything or know anything! I don't know whether I'm really myself or not. I don't know what'll happen next. Meaningless words are strung out through my empty brain. Everything is strange and horrible at the same time; nothing's what it really is; it's all something else. I'm so afraid! I don't know whether these people are really alive. (*Points to those present*) A black abyss, soft and impersonal, is opening up before me! (*She sits down on a heap of debris.*)

* I have seen an explosion like this and the collapse of a building in Björnson's play, Beyond Human Power (at the Cracow theater). I know that it is feasible from the technical point of view. [Author's note]

GUARD She's gone out of her mind from nervous shock. She's talking exactly like my wife. (*From under the debris they pull Tréfaldi and also the bodies of the three Thugs and the Second Gendarme.*)

FIRST GENDARME Yes, yes—those three thugs and my buddy are already nothing but a mass of pulp. (*Pointing to Tréfaldi*) That one there —he's the chief culprit. Grab him!

TRÉFALDI Don't you see, my good man, that all my guts are spilling out? I'm almost dead. The throttle went into my belly at least twelve inches. (*They pull out Travaillac and Minna, who are safe and sound.*) Besides, that young lady hit me on the head with a shovel (*he points to Minna*), and I'm still suffering from nervous shock.

MINNA We're safe and sound. Come on, Slobok; forget about that woman and all the horrible things she made you do. You'll completely regain your equilibrium with me.

TRAVAILLAC That's true, but what about my part in what happened? After all, there were witnesses. Not everything went the way it was supposed to. After what I've been through, all I want is peace and quiet.

MINNA That's easy to arrange. You'll spend six months in a lunatic asylum and get a good rest. Then I'll have you released. My uncle is the prosecutor in the appellate court. You've got to live and go free. You're my type. Even though I'm a Countess, I'd never find another man like you. (*To the Gendarme*) I'll take this fireman with me, on my own responsibility. (*The Gendarme salutes.*)

TRAVAILLAC If that's the way it's going to be, there's no point in resisting. Good-bye, Conductor. Unfortunately, it's beginning all over again for me. We have Julia and her influence to thank for all the strange things we've been through. I've had enough hysterical women to last me a lifetime! (*He and Minna go out to the left.*)

GUSTER (*crawling out from under the wreckage*) The Beans were squashed into a jelly and chopped up like cabbage. I'm all splattered with Miss Mira's guts. It seems to me it's all been a dream. (*Jeanne Cackleson enters. Disheveled hair, dressed all in white, decked out in flowers like Ophelia. She calmly observes the scene.*)

CONDUCTOR Let's go have a beer, Cackleson. We'll have time for quite a few before all this gets straightened out. The ambulance train will take care of the rest. I hope this doesn't start an epidemic among engineers throughout the whole world!

JEANNE CACKLESON (*coming up to Julia and hugging her*) I know everything, too, the way she does. Only the two of us know—all the rest of you are fools. I've always waited. I waited every time a train came by. You can't imagine what torture it is to wait and watch the trains come by and then rush away somewhere, carrying all those passengers off! Then finally I stopped waiting! Today at five o'clock I cut the telephone line. During the night, a spirit told me I had to do it. He had a dark beard, and his eyes gleamed like a cat's. He's the one I was unfaithful to my husband with while I was asleep. Ha, ha, ha!!

GUARD Jeanne, calm down and go back home. It's sickening to have to listen to you talk that way!

TRÉFALDI (*growing excited*) Jeanne! Why didn't I meet you before? I'd certainly have seduced you!

JEANNE He's the one! He's the one I dreamed about during the night! (*She falls to the ground with a wild yell. Julia kisses her. Dr. Marcellus Riftmaker and two Gendarmes run in from the left side.*)

DR. RIFTMAKER (*pointing to Tréfaldi*) First of all, let's save this one! He's the greatest criminal in the whole world, the famous Prince Tréfaldi, king of murderers. At least he's got to live so he can atone for his crimes and be an example to others. (*On his knees by Tréfaldi*) The police received a telegram. We came by handcar from Dumbell-Junction. He was to be arrested there. The public didn't suspect anything. (*Examines Tréfaldi*) Damn!—there's no getting around that! His insides are out!

TRÉFALDI Too late, Doctor! Even to please the court, I can't postpone the hour of my death. I had an inkling of it, but I swear I didn't know anything definite. I die without any regrets, so you can cheer up. Good-bye. (*He dies. They all take off their hats.*)

GUARD Doctor, forget about those murderers and, instead, please look after the women! (*Points to his wife and Julia*) They've both gone completely mad!

DR. RIFTMAKER (*getting up*) Just a minute, just a minute, my good man. Justice first, then the wounded, and the mentally ill last of all, because there's absolutely nothing we can do to help them.

CURTAIN

End of the Epilogue and of the Play

The Mother

INTRODUCTION

"THEY'VE TAKEN my anguish away! I have nothing, nothing, nothing!" Leon screams at the end of *The Mother* (*Matka*) as he crawls on his knees gathering up the straw and rag pieces of his mother's corpse. Another, living mother, twenty-three years old and pregnant with Leon, has just pressed a button in the wall, revealing a mountain landscape in spring, and stepped out through the door. Leon is strangled by six workers, and his corpse simply disappears without a trace. And nothing is left of either Leon, his mother, or their anguish.

In *The Mother* (1924) Witkiewicz presses a button in the wall of what appears to be a naturalistic drama and opens a hidden door that reveals totally new and different perspectives: the realistic characters are dummies filled with sawdust; the anguish and "wallowing in stale emotional entrail-wringing" is all false. *The Mother* is a history of modern drama, moving from Ibsen and Strindberg (the sawdust mother's favorite dramatists) to Witkiewicz and Pure Form. Acts I and II take place on the "diminished scene of rationalism" and in the "tasteless parlors" that Francis Fergusson talks about in connection with Ibsen,[1] although strange forces from outside are beating on the door. It is only in the Epilogue that Witkiewicz opens the hidden door and leads us out of the tasteless parlor into the irrational world that surrounds it.

In Acts I and II, the use of situations and motifs from Ibsen and Strindberg creates the atmosphere and milieu of the European drama at the end of the nineteenth century and the beginning of the twentieth century, but the direct references to these playwrights provide an ironic frame of reference in which to view this world and its concerns. Witkiewicz' technique of parody consists of building upon a somewhat alien and obsolescent dramatic universe and vision and then, by calling attention to this fact, of undermining its credibility and validity as a way of feeling and thinking in the modern world. Parody becomes a means of criticizing not the authors alluded to, who created what was once a viable response to life, but the delusion of trying to live in a dead world, either real or literary. It is also a form of self-criticism.

From Ibsen and Strindberg comes much of the first two acts of *The*

---

[1] Francis Fergusson, *The Idea of a Theater* (New York: Anchor Books, Doubleday and Co., 1949), pp. 159, 171.

Mother and of its portrayal of a sick bourgeois world whose most shameful and hidden secrets are mercilessly exposed. Middle-class obsessions with property and propriety dominate Mrs. Eely's tasteless parlor. Her knitting, her talks with her servant, her snobbery about her supposedly aristocratic background, her fears about her son's marrying beneath his class, and her endless talk about money and food and housekeeping establish a narrow domestic sphere in which petty social concerns are central, a world quite unlike Witkiewicz' usual international demimonde. This great interest in what people do for a living and where the money comes from leads Leon to exclaim, "But let's not have any dramas à la Ibsen, with all that tragedy business about the various professions and the shortcomings of each."

The Mother does deal with precisely the question of profession or calling, so important in Ibsen, although Witkiewicz treats it ironically. The Mother's profession is knitting and self-sacrifice; her knitting is her only creative work, once she has or will have given birth to Leon. He argues that, even if she weren't his mother, she'd be knitting socks for the poor or a chasuble for the priest. Her creative ability to help others through her knitting becomes an oppressive and destructive form of self-sacrifice. Leon's father was unsuccessful as a carpenter and as a singer; however, he found his true calling as a river bandit in Brazil, going to his death on the gallows without any remorse or regret.

Leon, like many of Witkiewicz' heroes, does not know exactly what his profession is and goes from calling to calling in search of identity. He starts as a social prophet, an artist in social thought, diagnosing the ills of Western civilization much as Witkiewicz himself did. Specialization, mechanization, and social instincts themselves threaten mankind; the individual will soon be totally subjugated by the state. His utopian ideas for collective reformation of the human race are vaguer than his incisive negative analysis. Also his profession as a social prophet is undermined by his having to live off his mother and suck her dry in order to have the time to develop his ideas without working and holding down some ordinary job. His theory of society is even able to predict this split and explain it: "But in times like ours a dissociation has taken place between the principles for which a man stands and his actual moral value as an individual. Nowadays a prophet may be a complete swine—that's sad, but it's a fact."

Leon's actions are an illustration of his theory. The great visionary social prophet is a sick, neurotic son, abnormally attached to his mother and full of childish love and hatred for her. The closed domestic circle and Leon's overdependent incestuous attachment to his mother contrast with his grandiose social dreams and create a sense of the shortcomings of his calling. Mankind needs to be born again, including the originator of the theory. But the transformation Leon and the others undergo is only degeneration: he becomes a spy and a pimp, the only professions that give him the necessary time to think and develop his schemes for saving mankind. His life is an utter contradiction and paradox.

Other professions represented in the first two acts of *The Mother* are those of Calfskin, the manager of the realistic theater, "The Illusion," whose aim is to please the audience; and of Sophia, who, having no calling, becomes a prostitute and has to please her customers: neither is a true artist. The only true workers appear in the epilogue; they do everything in unison like automatons and destroy Leon, a would-be artist of social thought who refused to work.

The vampire motif comes from Strindberg's *Ghost Sonata*, where there is talk of the Hummel family of vampires and of sucking people dry and turning them into mummies. *The Mother* opens with the Mother's description of her son: "The lowdown vampire." All the characters use one another, and give nothing back in return. Leon introduces Sophia to his family with the explanation, "We are vampires," and she soon can say, "I've turned into a vampire." The whole society is a society of bloodsuckers, who cannot even find sustenance by drinking others' blood. Using his painter's eye, Witkiewicz composes the picture entirely as a study in black and white; this is the world of the tasteless parlor full of ghosts, white as cadavers, dead while they are still alive. Vampire that he is, Leon says that he prefers the "meat-with-all-the-juices-cooked-out-of-it" tragedy à la Strindberg to the Ibsen drama of professions which makes him feel guilty toward his mother.

Ibsen's *Ghosts* is the source of other themes which Witkiewicz plays with in *The Mother:* incest, the close relationship between mother and son, the dead father who haunts the family from beyond the grave, the revelation of the shameful truth about the father, and the discovery of the hidden kinship between father and son. These items of parody are treated in no systematic way, nor are they consistent with the original; rather they are deformed fragments of Ibsen transposed into a Witkacian dimension, like pieces of a naturalistic portrait—a nose, an eye, a cheek—included within a surrealist painting. In Act I, the Mother discloses to her son and his fiancée the horrible truth about his father: "Your father died on the gallows in Parana in Brazil." In Act II, the Mother recognizes the fatal kinship between Leon and his father: "The two of you are completely alike in every way—exactly like in Ibsen's *Ghosts,*" evidently referring to Mrs. Alving's recognition of Osvald's inheritance from his father when she overhears him making advances to the maid Regina. In *Ghosts,* father and son are by no means completely alike, any more than they are in *The Mother*. Both the Mother and Witkiewicz like to misquote and misapply.

The most important use Witkiewicz makes of the ghost of the dead father is to open a skylight escape hatch in the tasteless parlor (a trapdoor appears later) and make it possible to break it completely open in the Epilogue. His technique, like that often used in the theater of the absurd, is to take what is metaphoric and symbolic in Ibsen and make it quite literal; the ghosts in *Ghosts* are figurative, but Witkiewicz makes Leon's father a real ghost whose voice from the other world is heard throughout Acts I and II, laughing at the Mother and mocking the bourgeois concerns of this world from a vantage point outside space and time. Hanged as a criminal, the father's opening "Ha, ha, ha," at the very beginning of the play puts into perspective the littleness of the tasteless parlor, and he congratulates Leon for rising above its normal, sentimental delusions at the end of Act II: "Bravo, Leon! For the first time I can see that you're my son!" Now Leon has come to accept the view from the other side: the Mystery of Existence is unfathomable, and although she is dead, the Mother "doesn't know any more about what death really means, than we do about what life is, although we're still alive."

From this outside view, people seem to be so many curious, incomprehensible insects. In order to bring both Leon and the audience to this position, Witkiewicz lets loose not only the Voice, but also a whole world of hallucinations, schizophrenia, blindness, alcoholism, madness, and drug addiction—all elements that could appear in the naturalistic theater—in speeded-up and exaggerated form. With the Voice, Mordello-Benz ("men's bordello"), La Tréfouille, and Modesta-Bladdery, the bizarre gallery of Witkacian sensualists and swindlers from the world of international crime starts to crowd into the "diminished scene of rationalism" and turn it into a surrealistic bedlam. The hilarious cocaine-sniffing party at the end of Act II wrecks the tasteless parlor and smashes all its moral and psychological furniture.

The epilogue throws us suddenly and unexpectedly into a black box. Is it a cocaine hangover? Is the room without doors or windows an inner analogue to the tasteless parlor of Acts I and II? We are in the world of Pure Form, where reality has been deformed and transposed into a new dimension; the perspective has shifted in a startling fashion, and all spatial-temporal relationships have been deranged. Leon explains directly to the audience that there is no explanation; what is happening must be accepted as such:

Please take the present situation for what it is and nothing more. Despite all its seeming complexity, it's something immediate, like the color red, for example, or the musical note A. Some people might consider it a hoax, a dream, a symbol, or God knows what. I leave them complete freedom of interpretation. . . .

When Leon claps his hands, a black curtain is drawn at the back of the stage, and the characters from the preceding two acts, plus several unknown ones, are revealed sitting on red chairs. Leon exclaims: "Oh —what a surprise! All of us here together in a room without doors or windows." Nobody knows how they got there or how they will ever get out. Leon's mother as a young woman of twenty-three is among those sitting on the red chairs. She is pregnant with Leon, and the grown Leon talks to his mother at the same time that he is in her rounded stomach and her corpse is lying on a black six-sided pedestal in the middle of the stage. Two different dimensions of time and space exist simultaneously. We know that there was a two-year interval between Acts I and II, but it is impossible to say how much time has elapsed between the cocaine-sniffing party and the epilogue. Leon refuses to disclose anything on this subject: "There are just a few things I won't go into, the spatial-temporal relationships in particular. I don't know, for instance, how much time has elapsed since that other evening, and I don't want to know." There is movement in depth, rather than progression in time.

The Epilogue to *The Mother* is one of the greatest pieces of virtuoso writing in Witkiewicz and in the twentieth-century experimental theater. To attempt to explain its incalculable effect of the mystery of existence through a network of heavy-handed symbols would be to go contrary to Witkiewicz' theory and Leon's specific instructions to the audience. Instead the Epilogue can best be approached as a painting or musical composition in which we see and hear recurrent motifs and parallels. It has a weird design, as in a dream in which images both within the dream and from waking life are repeated. Doubleness is the key.

A black tube appears in the black box. A young mother rips apart an old mother as a fraud. A grown Leon confronts an embryo Leon folded in his mother's womb. The characters do not know how they got into the black room without doors or windows any more than Leon knows how he got into his mother's womb or how or why he finally disappears forever from the room. It is nothingness from which he comes and nothingness into which he goes. The tube that spews out workers is like a factory chimney, or a womb, or a tube of heroin.

The tube is also a staged metaphor. The bewildered manager of the realistic theater "The Illusion" says, "I'll tell you what it is—it's a machine for sucking dry what's left of mothers' corpses that haven't been completely sucked dry by their only sons." Leon's earlier obsessive phrase is given mechanical concreteness; it is a mechanism that can suck everyone dry.

The Epilogue is a play within a play. "The whole thing—all of us *y compris*—has been brilliantly put on, although no one knows by whom." The theater manager comes out of the tube as part of this theatrical event; Calfskin has become a participant in experimental theater and takes his part in the happening that occurs. When his lines prove to be stale old jokes, he gets a sock in the jaw and ends muttering on the stage unconsciously; he has not been able to adapt well to the new kind of spectacle.

Leon's social views have, for him, been destroyed by his personal life. At last, when his ideas begin to triumph, he no longer cares. All he wants is to hang on desperately to his remorse and pangs of conscience, which he clutches with the rags and straw that were his mother. Leon tried to plan a creative society; he ends up with nothing—even his anguish has been taken from him. There is no place for him in the society of the future in which the six automated workers pass judgment on those who never did any "honest work." Leon was split as a man and as a prophet. Only if the society he wanted to bring about had already existed could he have survived. His old world is torn apart and scattered into pieces, like his mother—and there is absolutely nothing left of him.

The Mother

AN UNSAVORY PLAY
IN TWO ACTS
AND AN EPILOGUE

Dedicated to
Mieczysław Szpakiewicz

Janina Eely — *A matron, 54 years old. Tall, thin. Gray hair. She speaks in two different ways: down-to-earth and direct—and more refined and mannered. (1) indicates the first, (2) indicates the second.*

Leon Eely — *Her son. Good-looking, dark hair, 30 years old. Clean-shaven.*

Sophia Stonybroke — *Unmarried, 24 years old. A very pretty brunette.*

Josephine, Baroness Oates — *Janina's sister. A thin old maid. 65 years old.*

Joachim Calfskin — *Theater director. Gray. Fat and red-faced. Beard and mustache. 60 years old.*

Apollinaire Stonybroke — *Sophia's father. Gray. Sweeping mustache. 75 years old.*

Anthony Mordello-Benz — *A suspicious individual. Small mustache. No beard. Dark-haired, 35 years old.*

Lucina Beer — *Very tall and beautiful lady, about 24 years old. Semitic type.*

Unknown Young Woman — *23 years old. Very beautiful and strikingly similar to Janina.*

Unknown Young Man — *Dark hair, very good-looking, with a dark mustache. Has a very beautiful baritone voice.*

Off-stage Voice — *Similar to the voice of the Unknown Young Man.*

Alfred, Count de la Tréfouille — *An aristocratic partyboy. 30 years old.*

Albert de Modesta-Bladdery — *A playboy type of rich landowner. 32 years old.*

Six Workers — *Ugly customers, some with beards and some clean-shaven.*

Dorothy — *The maid, 40 years old.*

In Act I all the characters are an absolutely cadaverous white without the slightest trace of color. Black lips, darkly flushed cheeks. Costumes and sets only in blacks and whites. The only colored thing is the Mother's knitting—here the colors can be: blue, pink, yellow, and pale orange. When-ever any other colors are to appear, a separate explanation will be given.

ACT I

The stage represents a small living room with a dining area. Rather shabby furniture. A cheap imitation leather sofa up against the wall. Next to the sofa a table covered with a decorated oilcloth. The Mother sits alone at the table and knits with wool of various colors: blue, pink, yellow, and pale orange. To the left a window, to the right a door.

MOTHER *(laying aside her knitting for a moment and looking straight ahead. Slowly, with venom)* [1] The lowdown vampire. He takes after his father. But maybe I'm being unfair to both of them—maybe it's my fault he's the way he is? How have I deserved a different kind of life from the one I'm leading? Have I done anything very unusual? No, nothing . . . I'm just a mother hen, that's all. But what have I done to have to suffer so frightfully? Oh, God! I have two lives; my other true existence which has died and this one floating by me like a nightmare. I've got to try to understand it all. Maybe it will give me the strength to endure still worse things that are in store for me. *(She suddenly begins to wail the following song in a wild voice.)*

> When I was beautiful and young
> I had a body and a soul.
> But happiness was not my goal,
> Now nothing's left, my song is sung.
> What a pity!
> What a pity!

(She is figuring.) One hundred and fifty to the bookstore, fifty for overdue library books, two hundred for the room. And all of it for the sake of what passes for an education. How will I ever be able to afford all this just by my knitting? The idiot! The fool! The daydreamer! If only he'd do something more worthwhile! He'll never write anything that amounts to anything. And what about me? I used to paint, I had great talent for music, I wrote stories that weren't at all bad . . . I'm not saying this from any need to show off —there's nobody here—I'm sure of that. Oh—this eternal loneliness. And not one word of comfort.

VOICE Ha, ha, ha, ha! *(The Mother pays no attention to the voice.)*

MOTHER I don't know what reminded me of his laugh. Leon has a similar laugh, but more unpleasant. What was at least out-and-out crime in him, is petty meanness in Leon, something disgusting that gets trampled on by a shiny boot—all you can see is its tail, but that's enough for me . . . oh—what a good-for-nothing that son of mine

[1] Down-to-earth and direct. [Author's note]

121

is! Why didn't I bring him up on alcohol from childhood on? At least he'd be small, like those Japanese dogs that guzzle alcohol from the time they're puppies—he wouldn't be the repulsive full-grown nonentity he is. If he'd been a midget or an imbecile I would have been able to love him, I'm sure. I've grown completely coarse—I, the Baroness von Oates. Josie's grown coarse, too. Maybe it's all a delusion about the Oates spelled with an "e"—maybe we're just ordinary oats, spelled with a small "o" and no "e." But they say that good families don't grow coarse even under the most adverse circumstances. (*She wails again.*)

> The most beautiful mask hangs over my head,
> A spiritual devil lures me to bed,
> Although I've had lovers, one, two, three—
> My bones still crack with lechery.

Should I tell him? or not? (*Enter Dorothy*) [2]—Dorothy, dear, would you please put the macaroni on in cold water, Italian style, the way my son likes it. It's so nice to be a mother and be able to pamper your little boy. Isn't that right?

DOROTHY Yes, ma'am. I was a mother once, too. But I'm lucky—my son was killed in the war.

MOTHER [2] Come on, now! Get going! Put the macaroni on! I kept my son out of the war, since he's going to save the entire human race. He's a great thinker, but a physical weakling. Men like that shouldn't be allowed to die—there ought to be a special board . . .

DOROTHY (*interrupts her*) You've been drinking too much again, ma'am, and most likely on an empty stomach. Couldn't you at least have waited until supper time, ma'am?

MOTHER [1] Oh . . . (*Makes a gesture of disapproval*)

DOROTHY I'm not saying anything against Mr. Leon. But sometimes it's better to have happy memories about your son than to have him alive and healthy, but not the way you'd have wanted him to be. How do I know what kind of a man my Freddy would've been today—the way people get pushed around nowadays. He was a horrible little brat, and at least now I have the satisfaction of knowing he's a hero, and that's the end of it.

MOTHER [2] (*imploring*) Dorothy dear, can't you see I'm suffering, can't you tell I'm really suffering horribly? I can't go on working like this any more, and then just look at him—he's busy all the time and so distant from me, so above everything, I can't even make him understand that I just can't go on any longer . . . with this endless knitting—oh, God! The whole house . . . oh, my eyes . . . I've

[2] Refined and mannered. [Author's note]

already started to go blind, the doctor's forbidden me to ever knit again . . . oh, Dorothy, Dorothy . . .

DOROTHY You ought to have spanked him when he was little. Nowadays, in hard times like these, someone like him will turn into such a liar, will lie so wildly about everything under the sun, will lie his head off to himself and even to his own mother, and then he'll stick so stubbornly to the lies he's told absolutely everyone including himself, that no one on earth and no force in the world will ever be able to pry him loose from his lying. He's got to go right on lying to the very end. Until he becomes a living lie—that can happen.

VOICE That's just like me. But I was consistent—I wasn't afraid of the noose. (*He sings.*)

    Eely to a criminal has an almost sacred fame,
    And juvenile delinquents daydream only of that name.

MOTHER [2] Something reminded me of my husband again. It was simply a dreadful misalliance. And God has punished me for it. God doesn't like misalliances. Dorothy, did you know that my husband died on the gallows in Castel del Assucar, in Brazil, as a river bandit? He undertook extremely dangerous expeditions . . . but that's another story. I'd have to say this for him: he was a magnificent baritone, he was handsome and daring, and he had imagination. And what's more, he never had any feelings of remorse. He was a real soldier of fortune—*un vrai chevalier de fortune.*

DOROTHY Well, I'll be off to the kitchen now; later on you're going to regret telling me all these things. But please: couldn't you stop drinking so much?

MOTHER [2] No—I'm going to go right on drinking—it's the only thing I've still got left. But he doesn't know anything about it. He takes morphine himself, but not too often. There's a percentage of my wages that I've been keeping back for myself. Dorothy, what I just told you is in the strictest confidence. And actually, somewhere deep down, this completely senseless life of mine sends me into raptures—I adore wallowing in my own self-sacrifice and sinking into the common slime. I love every crack and cranny, every speck of dust, every scrap of thread. But it's myself I love in all these things, Dorothy dear. I'm chasing myself through flowerbeds of mignonettes and heliotrope as if I were my own little sister—this isn't a normal love of the world—it's a horrible perverted form of egotism. He's egotistical, too, but not in that perverted way. In his innermost soul he hates everything, including me. I've tried to fatten him up, the poor little thing was about to die from starvation. Until he was seven—he was thin as a rail. Oh—his neck was no bigger than this. (*She demonstrates by making a circle with her thumb and index finger.*) I love myself in him, and perhaps I love him all the more because he's such a little stinker—that makes me feel so sorry for him that my heart is ready to break. Such contradictory feelings are beyond belief, and beyond human endurance. He feels the same way—I know him. But the only thing worse than the contradictory feelings themselves is the weight of them on your conscience—when you burden others with your own feelings and make them feel guilty, and ultimately crush them. This is the form of torture my son has to endure. I understand it all, but there's absolutely nothing I can do to relieve his pain—on the contrary, despite all my good intentions, everything I do just makes it harder for him. And I know he won't be able to survive my death. But maybe it only seems that way to me? Maybe that ungrateful child has no such feelings and I'm torturing myself for nothing? But who cares? All that learning of his is a big hoax, real "phoniness," as you call it. No one understands it, maybe he doesn't even himself. He's just a cipher with a streak of sneakiness . . . but maybe I don't understand him. Maybe he's a great intellect. Almighty God! How beautifully You have arranged the lives of even the most lowly, how Your concern for Your own glory is apparent in everything! (*She weeps.*)

DOROTHY Whew—you really got smashed today, ma'am. (*The doorbell rings; Dorothy goes to open the door. Leon enters.*)

LEON What's this? Mama's crying? Another attack of nerves? (*He sits down next to her and puts his arm around her.*) Darling, today I was especially hoping that you'd be completely calm and reasonable, and not be so overly sensitive.

MOTHER (*whimpers, but controls herself*) All right, Lenny, all right. I'll be all right in a minute. Don't you know that everything I've done, I've done just for you . . . if it weren't for you I wouldn't go on living for another second . . . my strength has already run out . . .

LEON I know, I know. But why do you have to instantly overwhelm me with the whole weight of your self-sacrifice? Why not ask yourself what you'd actually be doing if you weren't my mother, if you didn't have to do all that endless knitting, if you could do exactly what you wanted all day long. Wouldn't you be doing just the same kind of thing, and just as doggedly? Instead of selling the things you knit, you'd have been embroidering a chasuble for the priest, or stockings for the poor—and I don't know what all. Well, isn't that so?

MOTHER That's right, that's right, my dearest. Now tell me, why did you particularly want me to be calm today? Are you trying to prepare me for some bad news?

LEON I wouldn't exactly call it that. You know what a terribly distracting influence all "my women," as they're called, have on my mind. So I've decided to break off my last five love affairs, which have become much too complicated for me, and marry someone from an entirely different psychic sphere. As an Eely, son of an unsuccessful carpenter and singer, I can indulge in a little misalliance—at least a psychic one. Anyhow, it would be difficult for me to enter into any other kind of misalliance. And even—if we take into account the so-called distaff side, and not only the spear side—well, even then from the point of view of the Almanach de Gotha, it's still . . .

MOTHER Lenny!

LEON But I was just joking. I don't know whether the Oates spelled with an "e" are recorded there or not, and I couldn't care less . . .

MOTHER But of course they are. It's a shame I sold that wonderful book when you were still a child. Respect for one's forebears . . .

LEON (*ironically*) Yes—my father in particular is respected in this house. Still, it doesn't matter: I hope you won't create needless difficulties. Why shouldn't tin be joined to an alloy of tin and gold? She's here waiting downstairs, in that little coffee shop next door. Well, what do you say, Mother?

MOTHER (*after a short pause*) You're acting in poor taste, Leon. Is she . . . is she rich?

LEON (*hesitating*) First, let's admit that we're all acting in poor taste, and that includes you too, Mama. No, she's not rich—she literally doesn't have a thing. She's been very badly brought up, she has dreadful manners, and she has no desire to do anything. She's not even my type. Remember what my late uncle used to say: "Never marry your own type—the first pretty girl of that kind you run into on the street will outdo your wife." But Sophie is beautiful, and I'm madly attracted to her even though I shouldn't be. Apparently it's daring combinations like these that are the most productive.

MOTHER And the most dangerous . . .

LEON Whew—let's not talk about that kind of danger—there are far worse ones looming on the horizon. And then, she suffers from complete alienation from life—it's surprising in such a primitive person. I've pooled our individual resources most ingeniously—don't you think? They'll pay off in another sphere. It's a perfect antidote to intellectual fatigue. You don't think I do anything at all, do you? Well, I'm overworked—my work's at a stage now where I'm reaching my final conclusions. And my fiancée has one real virtue: she understands everything, no matter what I say or read to her. We've only known each other for a few days—so far I haven't had a chance to give her a full explication of my basic ideas.

MOTHER That's just it: what's basic is that I don't understand what you're talking about—that's all I know. So one more burden falls on my shoulders. Can't you see that I really can't go on like this—with the little strength I have left . . .

LEON Just one more year, or two at the most. Mama, you know I'm abnormally proud when it comes to money. There's one thing I could never do, that's marry into money. If I ever did that I'd be quite capable of walking out on my wife forever over some stupid, insignificant trifle.

MOTHER Yes—it's only in your dealings with me that you don't have any such pride. You won't walk out on me over some insignificant trifle.

LEON But you're my mother, aren't you?

MOTHER There are times when I don't really know who I am any more: I'm a mother when I'm in the kitchen, or when I'm knitting, or dusting and mending the linen, but . . .

LEON Oh! Just for once I so wanted to avoid all those unpleasant subjects of conversation—just for one evening . . . in this house you have to have the patience of a saint not to go stark raving mad!

MOTHER For you it's just an unpleasant subject of conversation, but for me it's my whole life, the burdens of which are . . .

LEON Oh, that's enough, for God's sake! Just one evening, just one evening of peace and quiet! (*Trying another tack*) In a year, maybe even in nine months, I expect to be teaching in my own school which I'm planning to open . . .

MOTHER What, without a doctor's degree, without academic rank, and especially without any connections? Don't you think you're exaggerating a little, my dear?

LEON There you go running me down again, the way you did when I discovered the basic principles for the logicizing not only of the fundamentals of mathematics, but also of all the other sciences. And now it would be hard to keep track of all the people who are writing about that very subject and using my method. And when I was a child things like that happened over and over again so many times.

MOTHER I know—I spoil everything. And in exchange for having run down everything you've ever done, all I give you in return is your room and board—which isn't very much. And I know about how much that means to you.

LEON Mama, would you really rather that I go out right now and become a pimp or a spy? Those professions don't require any special training and aren't intellectually fatiguing.

MOTHER And now aren't you just being needlessly unpleasant? Can't you understand that I'm simply trying to open your eyes to the way the world actually is? Have you ever given any thought to what'll happen to you when I'm suddenly taken away from you?

LEON I've thought about it. And Sophie's the only one who can keep me from committing suicide when that happens. But there's one thing you don't understand, and that's that I really do love you and up till now I couldn't conceive of going on living without you. Even my great ideas about . . .

MOTHER Forget about your great ideas for a moment. You think you have feelings—but you're only sentimental. At the thought of my possible death there's only one thing that comes into your mind: your own suicide, which won't ever happen anyhow, since basically you're a coward.

LEON If that's the way I am, it's your fault, since you brought me up that way.

MOTHER You always were such a weakling . . . Oh, what am I saying? The way we talk to each other all the time now—it's just dreadful.

LEON That's just it, we're caught in a vicious circle. Wouldn't it be better to stop all these endless discussions and accept our lives for what they are?

MOTHER Oh, yes—I know, that means sucking your poor old mother dry till she drops dead like a worn-out beast of burden. I know, I know—you call this the tragedizing of life. Logicizing—tragedizing. You logicize knowledge about the future of the human race, and I tragedize knowledge about myself and you.

LEON And what's the result of a discussion like this? There's only one conclusion to be drawn: I should give up my life's work and take any old job just to make money.

MOTHER Oh, Lenny, do you think it's really me talking to you now?

LEON (taking her in his arms) I know, I know just what you mean— I'm not as much of a stinker as you think, either. And everything will still come out all right!

MOTHER There's only one thing I want: for you to get over your delusions about yourself. Maybe I don't understand this work of yours, but I don't believe in it. You don't understand anything about life. I've been protecting you from it like a suit of armor. And I'm afraid of what'll finally happen when you realize that I'm your whole life and that you don't have anyone else or anything else.

LEON Do you think I wasn't aware of that? That's why I was talking about suicide.

MOTHER If you were aware of it, then, not only wouldn't you have talked to me about suicide—it wouldn't even have occurred to you.

LEON Yes—and in that case you wouldn't have told me the horrible truth about myself, that I'm a coward—if that really is the truth.

MOTHER No—you'll climb up onto some high peak or other—you might even fight a duel—just to cause me anxiety—but that's not the point, that's not it . . .

LEON I know: I don't have the courage to become a factory worker or a post office employee—that's what it is. This is how our conversations go—not even their frankness can make them tragic. Should I call Sophie now?

MOTHER I'm so afraid, I'm so terribly afraid that I'm not going to be able to help hating her.

LEON And I'm afraid of something quite different—and it's that you'll completely stop paying any attention to me, and even stop loving me, once you get to know her. Apart from the fact that she's utterly lazy and inconsiderate, she's a marvelous creature. I'll go get her now. (*Exit*)

MOTHER (*to herself*) Almighty God! The same thing all over again. I swore to myself that I'd never say any of that to him ever again—and yet it didn't help at all: I had to, I had to . . . Oh, what horrible torture it is to be driven to act by unknown inner forces! Our stupid, would-be human veneer cracks in horror—that miserable little mask we wear at the masked ball for cattle which society has become ever since the French Revolution. Still, that monster's right. (*Dorothy enters and sets the table.*) Where are my manners and breeding, where's all my supposedly aristocratic finesse? And yet you have to brace yourself for the final struggle and be yourself once more. (*In a different tone*) Dorothy, will you please hand me my black cap. (*Dorothy hands it to her. The Mother makes eyes at herself in the mirror to the right. The bell rings. The Mother sits down inertly. Dorothy goes and opens the door. Enter Sophia and Leon.*)

LEON Mother dear, this is my fiancée, Miss Sophia Stonybroke—the only girl we could take into our home without any fear of upsetting its subtle inner harmonies. (*Dorothy continues to set the table.*)

MOTHER Into my home, you mean. (*Gets up*) Good evening. (*Sophia tries to kiss her.*) That's not necessary; we'll get to know each other in good time—without forcing it.

LEON Sometimes mother likes to appear worse than she is. Don't be put off by that, Miss Stonybroke. Starting today, you and your father will be eating with us regularly. (*To his Mother*) Her father used to be a carpenter, just like mine.

MOTHER But Lenny, your father wasn't just a carpenter, he was a singer, too. (*To Sophia*) Since you and your whole family are planning to take your meals with us, you might just as well learn right away everything there is to know about us.

LEON But let's not have any dramas à la Ibsen, with all that tragedy
business about the various professions and the shortcomings of each.
I'd rather have a cold-soup tragedy or a meat-with-all-the-juices-
cooked-out-of-it tragedy à la Strindberg.

MOTHER Nothing's sacred to you. You treat Ibsen and Strindberg just
the same way you treat me. Is there any greater work of genius in
the whole world than Strindberg's *The Ghost Sonata?* But that's
beside the point. Well, Sophia dear—tell me, may I call you that?

SOPHIA (*shyly*) Your son and I are still calling each other Mr. and
Miss. We only got engaged a half hour ago.

LEON (*suggestively*) Hell—we've got all eternity ahead of us. We'll
get on a first-name basis right away.

MOTHER (*to Leon*) Don't be vulgar. What you call each other isn't the
important thing. (*To Sophia*) Are you in love with each other? (*A
pause. Dorothy leaves quietly.*) You're not?—so it's just the same as
with him and me. He doesn't love me—he doesn't love anybody. He
claims to be attached only to his great ideas, but even that isn't
certain.

SOPHIA And do you love him? (*A painful pause*)

MOTHER (*somberly*) I don't know. All I know is that if he died, I
wouldn't be able to . . .

LEON Why all these big words and big problems? Don't get into a
sweat over it.

MOTHER You're a boor. Aren't you ashamed of yourself in her presence?

LEON Oh, all this bores me to death. There are things a hundred times
more important than the question of whether we love each other or
not. You can create a new life for yourself without ever resolving
those apparently great, but in reality petty bourgeois issues . . .
(*They all sit down.*)

MOTHER But still, in practical terms . . .

LEON Couldn't we stay entirely in the purely psychic sphere?

MOTHER No, no—it's all tied up together into a single whole. Cold soup
and sweeping the room—I have a maid now, but my eyes . . .

LEON (*jumping up*) My God, my God! I'll go right out of my mind!

MOTHER You might—that would be very typical of you.

SOPHIA (*stands up and puts her hand on Leon's head*) Calm down,
Leon darling. (*Leon goes limp as a wet noodle and sits down. Sophia
also sits down.*)

LEON Yes—we've reached the stage where we don't know any
more whether we love each other or not, but we couldn't live
without each other. Could there be anything worse than that? And
I'll tell you quite frankly: she says I'm a vampire—now another

vampire has joined us—that's Sophie, and her father makes the third; let's have more vampires so I can go on living, since I justify the existence of all of you.

SOPHIE I can't understand any of this. Don't get angry, Leon.

MOTHER What he's saying is monstrous.

LEON Not at all. It was a real stroke of genius on my part. You didn't know that I could have been an artist in three different branches of art, did you? I played the piano, I painted, and I wrote. I could also have been an ordinary conventional craftsman in these same trades: a realistic paint slinger, copying inimitable nature, or a fashionable dispenser of new sentimental thrills in music for the benefit of hysterical women, or a literary critic—that is to say, some one who can write about everything under the sun, and I could have made money. I could have been a real artist, too, in those branches of art, I mean, someone who creates a sense of formal perfection through the deformation of reality. I might have gained recognition or I might not—that's another question—or else I could have been a fake taking advantage of the general decline of art, a jackal licking up what's left on other men's plates, and I'd have unquestionably made a lot of money that way—but I didn't want to. My ambitions go further than all that.

MOTHER You've always been a dilettante, and dilettantes lack real ambition.

LEON You're wrong, Mama; to be a dilettante nowadays means more sometimes—I say sometimes—than to be a specialist going around and around in a treadmill with blinders on your eyes. Now we've got specialists in art, as well as in science—but there's no genius of the caliber of Leonardo da Vinci, and it's impossible there ever could be one. What's responsible for all this is the growth of all these different spheres and the impossibility of ever grasping the whole. But that's not all—the power of the individual really has diminished; it doesn't just seem so in the light of the way society has grown in recent times. And do you know where you can still be a good dilettante?—in history and in the conclusions which can be drawn from it about the future. You'll say that I'm using this to my own advantage, in order to make myself seem more important. I agree: my life is unique and exceptional like everybody else's, and I'm the one who's living it, not anyone else, especially not any collective group . . .

SOPHIA You're spouting nonsense, Leon—what you're saying is obvious.

LEON Wait a minute, maybe it just seems so to you. To the nonspecialist, the fundamentals of logic might also seem to be the wildest nonsense, repeating over and over that A equals A. I'm not going to give in passively and follow the line of least resistance—I'm trying to live my life on the highest possible level assigned to me by my destiny which I have to fulfill. Someone finally had to sacrifice himself in order to do precisely what I'm doing—just as Judas had to sacrifice himself in order to betray Christ—otherwise there wouldn't have been any salvation.

SOPHIA But what exactly is this utopian scheme of yours, Len? Explain it to us clearly once and for all.

MOTHER He's explained it to me a thousand times already. I don't understand a word of it. Let him explain it to you, Sophie dear. I'm going to prepare supper. (*Exit*)

LEON I gave my first public lecture today, although I didn't tell you anything about it. But I ran away before the discussion began. I've made a start, and if it doesn't come off, I'm washed up for years and years, and I'll have to go on sucking my mother dry, as the saying goes, and live off her work.

SOPHIA Leave your mother out of it for once in your life. You're sucking yourself dry most of all with your pangs of conscience.

LEON (*speaks with mounting enthusiasm*) You're right; well, it's all crystal clear. It's a fact that the human race is degenerating faster and faster. Art has declined, and may it die a peaceful death—we can get along without it quite nicely. Religion has run its course; philosophy is eating its own guts out and will also come to a suicidal end. The individual is coming to an end; society's killing him—that already sounds hackneyed now. How is it possible to reverse what's apparently an absolutely irreversible process of socialization, in which everything that is great, everything that has any connection with Infinity or the Mystery of Existence dies?

SOPHIA It can't be reversed.

LEON Oh yes, it can! But not through the rebirth of a race of supermen —that's a bad joke dreamed up by that abominable intellectual impotent, Nietzsche—and not through daydreams about universal happiness, when all good men will have time for everything—maybe they'll have the time, but they'll be a different kind of men, or rather they'll be mechanized cattle, our naïve dreamers can't understand that; and not through the artificial renovation of religion with the aid of newly fabricated myths—that's double-talk invented by the historically innocent babes in arms of our epoch. All of this is simply closing your eyes to the horrible fact that we're dying! That's loathsome. What the hell, if we really possess the intellect which Spengler says is a symptom of the decline, we must have it for some purpose, and not just be conscious of the decline and nothing else.

This same intellect can become something creative and avert the final catastrophe.

SOPHIA Those are just hollow promises. You don't have any idea of how to go about it.

LEON I know how to begin. First of all, not hide our heads in the sand, but look the truth straight in the face, and with the help of precisely this intellect which is so scorned nowadays, resist the historical truth that is rushing at us: universal grayness, mechanization, a foul swamp of social perfection. Just because the intellect has turned out to be a symptom of decadence, why become an anti-intellectual, a synthetic simpleton, a practical joker à la Bergson? Oh, no. Just the reverse: all the more reason to become aware of all this oneself, to the highest possible degree, and not only yourself, but to make others aware of it, too. A damn difficult assignment: to make the broad masses aware that spontaneous, natural social development threatens us with annihilation. Special institutions will have to be created to disseminate this knowledge, and various steps taken to make it popular. It must be a collective action on a huge scale. And if a billion people deliberately resist this deterioration, it won't take place. If only we could bring about a general consciousness on the part of all classes and all society, there'd simply be no place for degeneration, except among the ants, perhaps.

SOPHIA I just can't see that your idea has any relation with reality.

LEON Don't you see, our social instincts are killing us—what if we could direct them against themselves—that's why we have a collective organization, so as not to allow ourselves to be crushed, but to kill what's harmful to the individual in it. Instead of feeding the masses on utopias of state socialism and the ghastly reality of industrial unionism and cooperatives—why not utilize the social organization that's already been worked out to make everyone aware of the dangers if it goes on developing any further. If everyone started thinking the way I do, then by its very nature society wouldn't outgrow the individual. That's what we have educational organizations for, and social discipline, to do just that, and then, perhaps, when mankind has reached such a collective stage of development, new, unforeseen perspectives will open up. In any case, there are no new possibilities in the concept of universal happiness dreamed up by our wretched idealistic cowards—there's only the dusk of mechanized grayness. Yes—the individual, as such, has had it. Maybe I'm the very last individual left of the species who can make possible a bold new step forward, really forward, instead of simply continuing what we have now, a decline into the abyss of cattlelike misery masquerading as the highest ideals. This has got to be a collective act

of making people aware on a fantastic scale. We've got to create a
state of mutual antisocial diversity among ourselves that exceeds the
force of social conformity, and then we'll see.

SOPHIA Oh, if only we could live to see that! If that idea could ever be
realized, we'd have something truly great.

LEON But you've got to realize that no one man nor any group of
individuals can possibly do the job. Only the entire human race,
alerted to the danger, can create the sort of social atmosphere in
which individuals of a new type can arise, because this atmosphere
will be new—something that has never existed before since
the creation of the world. This won't be any sickeningly democratic
organization composed of the self-styled "intelligentsia" like the
kind we've had up till now—that sort of mealy-mouthed democracy
is nothing but a big lie—it doesn't permit us to look squarely at the
truth, and only what I was arguing for earlier, this collective act
performed by the masses, can create the new collective state I'm
talking about.

SOPHIA And what if it doesn't work? What then?

LEON We have nothing to lose. It may be claptrap, too, but it's the only
kind still worth trying. In any case, where we're headed now, where
blind social forces are dragging us, that is, toward total mechanization and imbecility, there's absolutely nothing in store for us.
There's a fantastic amount of work to be done—out of nothing we
must forge the foundations of infinite new possibilities. That's the
most diabolical transformation imaginable. And that's why to start
with, socialism must be dematerialized, as a first step—it won't ever
be completely possible, but it's still a necessity. Not to destroy
society and create clowns à la Nietzsche, but to utilize social forces
and create for once social, not individual, possibilities for the formation of a new humanity. And besides that, all the other physical
means of regeneration should be still further intensified. But we're
moving in the other direction, toward the production of healthy
automatons, a hundred times more tragic in their automatism than
the insects—because we had everything and lost it all. (*Sinks exhausted into a chair*)

SOPHIA Yes—I understand. You've really worn me out. That's a great
idea, there's no doubt about it. But I want to say just one thing to
you: are you doing this out of love of humanity?

LEON No—I hate mankind. I'm ashamed to be a human being. But in
times like ours a dissociation has taken place between the principles
for which a man stands and his actual moral value as an individual.
Nowadays a prophet may be a perfect swine—that's sad, but it's a
fact. Anyhow, I'm not a perfect swine so far, despite all my loathing

for human beings—I really hate the race of men alive today. And yet please understand, despite that, I don't know if I'd even like to have been an Egyptian Pharaoh; as far as I'm concerned, given the grotesque tragedy of the way society's been developing, the Pharaoh himself is just as ridiculous as a petty Papuan chieftain—the Pharaoh's archaic fossil on a smaller social scale; or as the Wilhelm II's and Ludendorff's of today—Nietzschean men all of them. And I also find everything about this lying, half-hearted democracy of ours just as repulsive as the deliberate reduction of human beings into cattle which is the basis of communism and fascism. And the result's only too well-known in this case—only an imbecile can't see that—but on the other hand what I'm talking about contains possibilities for opening new horizons, is unpredictable, therefore worth doing. And I base my belief on the fact that the Mystery of Existence hasn't been fathomed and that all of it can't be contained in any one system of ideas.

SOPHIA And where do you come in, in all this?

LEON I can be the starting point in a wave of universal events. That's all I ask for. Besides, perhaps I'm not the only one, there may be many others who think the same way I do. But they find it hard to start it on a large scale and especially to formulate it clearly in their own minds—they prefer to go on deceiving themselves.

SOPHIA But to put this into practice will require tremendous ruthlessness toward all existing ideals; everyone will have to be as farsighted as you are, or rather they'll have to be as mad as you are—in other words, what's needed is an organized group of such madmen.

LEON You're right—I can see you understand me. You'll help me in the campaign—a woman can be very useful in such a venture.

SOPHIA You know, a new expanse of inner space just opened up before me. I think I'm in love with you after all. Just now, when you were talking I found you very attractive. But perhaps we're taking the same drug; it helps you to live your life as a would-be artist and me to live my life as a would-be third-class tart—since I don't know whether I could have been a first-class mistress.

LEON What of it? You're not saying anything new.

SOPHIA It's just possible that if I hadn't met you yesterday, I'd sell myself today to the first person who came along. I don't know how to do ordinary work, and I don't want to. This isn't work, though, it's a kind of artistic improvisation.

LEON We're vampires! For the time being we'll live off Mother. She'll make ends meet with her knitting—it's monstrous. But I have no time for anything else. What I've worked out has required extraor-

dinary preparation, solitude, intense outward laziness, and thought
—endless concentrated thought. Until now, at last, everything has
ripened and is ready to explode. I'm like a high explosive shell, lying
quietly in a meadow. But there isn't any cannon as yet, and there's
no one to fire me. And I can't do it all myself—I have to have
others.

SOPHIA I want to be set off, along with you.

LEON I thought that at first you'd begin by helping Mother with her
work.

SOPHIA Never—you won't get me to do that. I'd rather leave you and
promote your idea as a streetwalker.

LEON All right, all right—maybe we can work it out somehow. (*The
Mother and Dorothy enter; supper is served.*)

MOTHER What do you think now, Sophie? You can see it's all a baseless
illusion. Isn't that so? It would be better if he just got a job. Both of
you could get jobs.

LEON (*to Sophia*) You see?

SOPHIA No, Mother—may I call you "Mother"?

MOTHER But of course, my dear child. I am his mother in the physical
sense. Spiritually, Leon is exactly like his father. Only he hasn't
become a criminal yet.

SOPHIA and LEON What's that?

MOTHER Aha—so that revelation's making some impression on you.

LEON Mother, tell me what this is all about.

MOTHER Your father died on the gallows in Parana in Brazil. I fled from
there and brought you here, only to experience great unhappiness.
I've had three lovers since then.

LEON This is priceless! And you saved it as your last trump for the day
I got engaged! What for? It's extraordinary! What's your reaction
to this, Sophia? Perhaps you'd like to break everything off?

SOPHIA You know—I'll be quite frank with you—if I'd heard about this
before you explained your philosophic views, I'd have broken off
the engagement. But now I won't. (*To the Mother*) You know
what, Mother, I think I do love Leon, but I won't work for him—I'll
work with him. I've turned into a vampire. For the first time in my
life I'll be myself.

MOTHER Yes—poor child. He's got you in his power now. I don't blame
you in the least. Maybe it will be different someday. In the meantime
let's sit down to supper.

SOPHIA Oh—things aren't the way I thought—I thought . . .

LEON Oh, don't say anything more. Let's sit down and have supper, and
after all that's happened, let's try and enjoy it. There's one more

thing, do you understand—the thought just came to me for the first time—I'm utterly disillusioned; you're a frightening woman, Sophie . . .

MOTHER Leon. She's a poor demented . . .

LEON Listen to me. Can't you understand that I'm the one who gives your life a higher meaning? Only me. Mother can never get this through her head. If it weren't for me both of you would only be ordinary by-products of dull lower-middle-class life, tragic only in its infinite pettiness and vapidness. I throw a different light of a brighter sort on all this and create a background that exalts this cold-soup tragedy, mother's failing eyesight, and her hands worn to the bone from knitting. I'm the one who gives it real significance. Oh, she's never been able to understand this. Even if my great idea is nonsense, I'm still great as a vampire—but are they? Perhaps Sophie is great, too, in her own way, as a baby vampire that's attached itself and is sucking away from the side. If it weren't for me, we'd be just one of hundreds of thousands of ruined families: you know, a misalliance, a son with a criminal for a father, a baroness (*to Sophia*) —you ought to be told that mother's maiden name was von Oates, spelled with an "e," and not just ordinary "oats," as you might think —in the eleventh century the family was already established along the Rhine. Ha, ha. I'm something of a snob, too, but at the same time I'm delighted my father was hanged—I'm a snob of the highest order. I'm deliberately talking like a rotten low-down lousy bastard.

SOPHIA (*embarrassed but delighted*) I had no idea . . . I'm amazed . . . (*She doesn't know what to say.*)

LEON You see, Mother: Sophie is delighted to have a baroness as her mother-in-law and also to learn that I'm from the nobility, or at least half of me is. (*Doorbell. A pause. Dorothy goes out and comes back immediately.*)

DOROTHY There's a man here who wants to talk to Mr. Leon.

LEON Invite him to supper. Dorothy, will you please serve the vodka. (*Exit Dorothy*)

MOTHER Leon!

LEON Don't worry—there'll be enough for everybody. I feel it's simply my duty to suck my mother dry—this way, once I've sucked her absolutely dry, she'll become a part of history. (*Enter Mr. Calfskin, manager of a theater.*) Oh—it's you, Mr. Calfskin. Mr. Calfskin's the manager of the Illusion Theater; he rented me the auditorium for my lecture this afternoon. Mother will have to make up the difference—barely half the seats were sold. I haven't said anything about

it yet, but I gave my first lecture today. This is my mother and my
fiancée, Miss Stonybroke.

CALFSKIN (*greets the ladies*) Listen, my friend, it was worse than you
can imagine. There was a discussion after the lecture. You skipped
out. But all hell broke loose.

LEON So much the better for publicity.

CALFSKIN No, my friend, this has finished you. The police are looking
for you. Half the seats were broken, the lights smashed, everything's
a wreck. Someone's going to have to pay, my friend—someone's
going to have to pay.

MOTHER (*ironically*) Don't worry about that. I'll pay for it with what
I get from my knitting. Oh—I'm just finishing a beautiful jumper.
Please sit down. You and Leon can share what's on his plate. I can
get along without any food; besides, it's not good for me to eat
before going to bed.

CALFSKIN Oh, thank you—I can't stay more than a couple of minutes.
(*To Leon*) You know, I felt there was something in what you were
saying, but still I don't completely understand you. But no one in
the auditorium understood you: the biggest intellectuals in town
were there—they all had complimentary tickets—they almost had to
be dragged in. No one understood a single word: they thought you
were talking double-talk. Now, of course, I'm not saying . . . But
everyone's furious with you. They're saying that you're out to
undermine all our ideals, with your morbid pessimism and complete
intellectual anarchy—and even worse: your degenerate bourgeois
nihilism. Others are saying it's even worse than communism. Now,
of course, I don't know anything about it myself.

LEON So there wasn't a serious duscussion?

CALFSKIN No. There was a serious fist fight. You had two supporters
there—real tough guys, let me tell you, a couple of ugly customers
—with friends like that who needs enemies? They got beaten to a
pulp. It's just as well you skipped out right after your speech.
Otherwise you'd have got knocked around a bit yourself.

MOTHER Yes—Lenny has such a weak nervous system, it's better for
him not to run any risks . . .

LEON Mother, please don't . . . so they're all idiots? Those famous
moguls of yours that are the cream of the intellectual community?
After all, you can be against an idea and still try to understand it,
you can combat it reasonably and factually. But those great minds
are afraid to.

CALFSKIN You'll have to forgive me, but I don't quite understand what
you're talking about either . . .

LEON So you were just pretending that you understood before the lecture? Is that right?

CALFSKIN I don't want to go on talking with you any more as long as you're so edgy. Here's the bill, if you'll be so kind: two thousand marks. Good-bye. Good-bye. (*Exit, bowing. A pause*)

MOTHER Well—let's not take this too seriously. No man is a prophet in his own country. Let's drink to this first success. The more a person is unrecognized, the greater he is. Sophie, dear, will you have a glass of vodka with me?

LEON Mother! Have you been drinking again?

MOTHER I've been drinking for the last two years. Do you think I would have been able to stand all this otherwise? I'm a chronic alcoholic.

LEON Ha—that's another blow. But we'll have to put up with that, too. I'll be ruined for the next two years or so, but I won't give up.

MOTHER I won't, either—I'll go on bearing it to the very end. But suppose I die inopportunely before you complete your great work?

LEON Mother, for once let's eat our supper in peace. (*He pours himself a glass of vodka and drinks it.*)

MOTHER Leon!

LEON I've taken to drinking, too. If you like, you can turn it into a horrifying drama. Sophie, why don't you drink, too—our engagement night should be fun! (*The women drink out of small glasses. Leon downs a second large glass.*)

SOPHIA There's just one thing I can't figure out: since he hates mankind in general, and all individuals in particular, and since he's so cruel toward those nearest to him—but, I might add, I can understand this perfectly—why does he still want to do all this? What's the psychological mechanism that keeps driving him on?

LEON (*drunk; ironically*) You don't understand great men at all; you're just a child. But you'll learn in time. I won't give up.

MOTHER It's easy for you to say that. Sophie, won't you have some more macaroni? Don't be bashful. I've been very thoughtless and rude because of all this.

SOPHIA Oh, by the way, I completely forgot—in fact, Leon and I both forgot that my father is waiting in the pastry shop on the corner. I think I'd better go bring him here.

LEON By all means. I can't, I'm too drunk. Anyhow, Calfskin was going to stay to supper, so now there's an extra place. Hurry up, Sophie, and apologize to your father for having kept him waiting so long. (*Exit Sophia*) Mother, you know how much I appreciate all this—if it weren't for you, I wouldn't have accomplished anything.

The Mother. Stary Teatr, Cracow, 1964. Director, Jerzy Jarocki; designer, Krystyna Zachwatowicz; Leon, Antoni Pszoniak; Sophia, Romana Próchnicka; Stonybroke, Wojciech Ruszkowski. Photograph by Wojciech Plewiński, courtesy of the Polish Centre of the International Theatre Institute

They. Teatr Polski (Scena Kameralna), Warsaw, 1966.
Director, Witold Skaruch; designer, Franciszek Starowieyski.
Photograph by Franciszek Myszkowski

They. Warsaw, 1966. Spika, Renata Kossobudzka; Tefuan, Krysztof Kowalewski;
Rosika, Jolanta Czaplińska. Photograph by Franciszek Myszkowski

They. Warsaw, 1966. Photograph by Franciszek Myszkowski

They. Stary Teatr, Cracow, 1967. Director and designer, Józef Szajna; Callisto, Marek Walczewski; Spika, Izabela Olszewska; Marianna, Halina Kuźniakówna. Photograph by Wojciech Plewiński, courtesy of the Polish Centre of the International Theatre Institute

The Shoemakers. Kalambur Student Theater of Wrocław, Wrocław
(International Festival of Student Theater Groups), 1965. Director,
Włodzimierz Herman; Sajetan, Janusz Hejnowicz. Photograph by Tadeusz
Szwed, courtesy of the Polish Centre of the International Theatre Institute

The Shoemakers. Wrocław, 1965. Scurvy, Ryszard Wojtyłło; Duchess,
Krystyna Kutz. Photograph by Tadeusz Szwed, courtesy of the Polish
Centre of the International Theatre Institute

S. I. Witkiewicz. Self-Portrait, 1939. National Museum of Cracow.
Photograph by Z. Malinowski, courtesy of the Museum

MOTHER Yes—you've accomplished a great deal: a bill for two thousand marks.

LEON Mother, don't you see that in order to keep on going, you have to have diabolical energy, too?

MOTHER Let's not start that all over again. You'd better eat something—you've had too much to drink.

LEON (*trying to hug her*) Mother, you must know, I swear I'm totally . . . you know, without you I couldn't . . .

MOTHER (*pulling away from him*) Yes, yes—without your mother. You hang onto my apron strings to keep from falling. You're disgusting.

LEON Mother, I'm not sure I'll even be able to say it . . . but I'd be so happy if we could . . . if we could—love each other . . . (*Throws his arms around her*)

MOTHER You vampire! You vampire! Get away from me! Never touch me again! We'll only greet one another from a distance. You have a new victim: that poor Sophia. (*Enter Sophia and her old buzzard of a father. The Mother controls herself. Leon stands petrified.*)

LEON (*frantically; with concentration*) This is the worst of all, not to know how much of it's the truth and how much a swindle, a rotten swindle. There's only one thing certain in this world, the suffering that . . . (*Stands still*)

MOTHER You're most welcome to our house. I'm so glad to meet the father of my prospective daughter-in-law. Please sit down at the table. It's just a simple supper. Would you like some vodka? Don't pay any attention to him—he's had too much to drink because of the engagement.

SOPHIA Ha! Ha! Ha! Ha!

ACT II

A salon in a rather luxurious apartment. Doors straight ahead and to the right. Evening. The lamps are lit. The only colors: black and white, as in Act I. The color of the costumes and of the characters' faces also the same as in Act I, until further directions are given in the course of the act. The Mother, dressed as before, sits on an ordinary kitchen stool in the middle of the salon and knits with light-brown wool in a wild frenzy. Next to her on a small table, a large siphon bottle and a bottle of liquor. From time to time the Mother fixes herself a whisky and soda and sips it. From the adjoining room, to the right, probably the dining

room, the noise of dishes being put away in the cupboard can be heard.
A pause.

MOTHER Dorothy! Dorothy! (*Enter Dorothy, dressed in black and white, but much more chic than in Act I.*)

DOROTHY Yes, ma'am.

MOTHER It was so nice out there in the kitchen with all of you, Dorothy dear. I felt so at home there. But in here, even when I sit on this stool, everything's so strange and frightening, like something from another world.

DOROTHY You're just imagining it, ma'am: actually everything here is new, and attractive, and not in the least frightening. Mr. Leon's been so nice lately . . .

MOTHER He wouldn't let me sit out there in the kitchen with all of you. But I feel so very odd in here, so ghastly, as if I were being strangled in a horrible nightmare. Something sticky, without arms or legs, is lying on top of me. And I don't know whether it's a dismembered torso or a wild beast. But I feel immense. And I wander around, tall as a tower, through those other rooms, and watch my second, other self as it runs through them like a tiny mouse. And then "klk"—the mouse gets caught in the mousetrap, and I wake up. This happens to me several times a day.

DOROTHY And you're not just dreaming all that?

MOTHER No—I'm doing my knitting, everything's the way it always is, and still that other thing's happening in what seems to be another world, yet one that's right here all the time. Maybe that's the Plurality of Realities Chwistek talks about; he's the philosopher Mr. Leon spends all his time reading nowadays—he's got a pet idea about logicizing social changes so as to break the chain of cyclic phenomena—my son, that is, not Chwistek.

DOROTHY I don't understand that.

MOTHER You don't think I do, do you, Dorothy? I don't understand a word of it. And he travels all the time now. My son's become the representative for a business firm—not a traveling salesman, but something higher up. What are you laughing at, Dorothy? Don't you believe me?

DOROTHY I wasn't laughing at all. You only imagined it, the way you imagined that mouse. You shouldn't drink so much. (*The Mother fixes herself a whisky and soda, sips it, and then offers Dorothy a drink.*) Well—I guess I'll take mine straight. (*Pours herself a liqueur glass full and tosses it off*) Oh, a little like that does you good.

MOTHER Unless I have a little, I can't see a thing—everything I look at is covered with flickering spots. Since this morning I haven't been able to see anything at all.

DOROTHY What do you keep on knitting for, ma'am? After all, Mr. Leon's earning quite a bit these days, and Miss Sophie's making quite a bit too doing that night nursing.

MOTHER Three thousand marks a week. But my son doesn't always get paid regularly—it depends on how the sales go. Oh—as soon as I have a drink, I start to see things again, but without liquor, I'd be totally blind. But why did you talk so strangely about the children's work? As though there were something about it you didn't like—is that it?

DOROTHY But—I wasn't thinking anything about it at all. Why should I find anything wrong with it? One job's as good as another—the pay's what counts. But you haven't told me yet, ma'am, why you keep wearing yourself out with that eternal knitting. You could take it easy now that the young people have settled down to work in earnest. Otherwise you're going to ruin what's left of your eyesight.

MOTHER Oh, be quiet, Dorothy. Everything's beginning to go round and round in circles before my eyes. I can't see anything. I've got to have a drink. (*Takes a drink*) But I'm still doing a little work—it brings in something all the same, even though compared to what they make it amounts to practically nothing. Still, my son's after me all the time to give up doing even that much work. I've almost got to hide it from him and pretend I'm doing it just for fun. But, after all, what else could I do? It's all so strange and frightening—I think I'd probably go mad if I had to sit around all day long doing nothing. For me taking it easy is the worst possible torture. And it's worst of all at night. Lying alone in that luxurious bed—it seems to me I'm a little girl again, when I was still living at home, with my father, the baron—you do know, don't you, Dorothy, that I come from a very distinguished . . .

DOROTHY (*impatiently*) Oh—you already told me all about it a long time ago, ma'am. But you know Mr. Leon has ordered me not to call him "sir"—and the young lady doesn't want me calling her "ma'am," either.

MOTHER What can you do?—Leon's father was a carpenter and a singer and was hanged for his great crimes. Still, he made me so happy during those three years that it keeps me from having any regrets whatever happens in my life now, even though it is so horrible, so horrible—worse than being tortured to death. I'm probably going mad, Dorothy dear. I'll tell you a secret, Dorothy—even though I'm afraid to talk about it, for fear something'll burst in my head—I've got to hold on to myself every minute so as not to go mad. I can't sleep at all without morphine. And I have to drink more and more, and my whole body is covered with needle marks.

DOROTHY Now just calm down, ma'am. I'm beginning to feel sick myself. You've got to pull yourself together, stop drinking or drink less, and quit taking that filthy poison.

MOTHER But it's my son who's buying it all for me. And I don't know whether he's doing it so I'll die off sooner, or simply out of kindness since he knows I couldn't go on living otherwise. (*She weeps.*)

DOROTHY I'm going now—I can't stand talking like this. I know it's hard for you all alone, too, ma'am, but I just can't go on this way any more. (*Exit*)

MOTHER (*alone*) My God! My God! Those spots are getting worse and worse. (*She takes a drink.*) I don't know whether I'm alive any more or whether this is a nightmare from the other world. And perhaps I don't even know that I'm dead and that this is punishment in hell, or in purgatory, for bringing him up this way and for pushing his father into a life of crime. Maybe—I didn't really want that—I only wanted to be a little better off. It's all my fault—if only I hadn't constantly hounded him with it, he would have developed into a famous singer and wouldn't have died with a noose around his neck. He stole and murdered for my sake, the poor thing, and he made me so very happy. (*Weeps*) Oh—I'll have to drink a great deal to get through this. (*She begins drinking again. She tries to get a grip on herself. Old Stonybroke, very elegantly dressed in a black frock coat, enters through the center door, coughing.*)

STONYBROKE (*deferentially*) Everything going well, Madam Mother? Working away at your knitting as usual, I see? Heh, heh!

MOTHER Ah, Mr. Apollinaire—do sit down. I'm very tired.

STONYBROKE From doing what, Madam Mother, from doing what? (*He sits down.*)

MOTHER Ah—let's not talk about it, let's not talk about anything. Can't you see that your being here is a perfect nightmare to me?

STONYBROKE Well, really, Baroness . . .

MOTHER I've already told you a hundred times, I'm not a baroness.

STONYBROKE Yes, yes, I know—you're the daughter of a baron. Well then, My Lady . . .

MOTHER Oh, even the most external forms of this ghastly thing called life are nothing but frightful misery! . . .

STONYBROKE Well, now—we can't complain about suffering any misery, can we? The children are working like horses. Your son's away a lot of the time on business. But what I like far less are all those

things that Sophie has to do all night long, her duties as a night
nurse, plus her night course in bookbinding and her night recrea-
tional modern dancing.

MOTHER (*begins to speak in a refined manner*) Is there really anything
inappropriate about it? I have the feeling that their love for each
other has in some strange way been under a strain. He's completely
stopped talking about his great ideas, although some kind of meetings are taking place and something's getting started as a result of all
this. It's impossible to know anything for sure in these matters, do
you understand? Our times are full of such strange contrasts, and
who people are and what they believe are so mixed up—I can't get
my bearings myself . . .

STONYBROKE (*he begins to feel ill at ease; he tries to get over it by being
frank*) I'm not implying anything—all I wanted to say was that I
haven't liked the way my daughter's looked for the past year. She's
dressing strangely, and can't sit still a minute—it must be a result of
trying to put his great ideas into operation, plus the fact that he's
away so much of the time. A couple of times I saw her out riding
with some men—from the upper crust—that is, what I'm trying to
say is, from the aristocracy—when quite by accident I happened to
get stuck on the wrong side of town, where as a matter of fact I
never go . . .

MOTHER (*as if waking from a dream*) What are you saying, Mr.
Stonybroke? (*Not in the form of a question, but really: "how dare
you etc.?"*)

STONYBROKE I'm just saying what I think, madam, that my daughter
looks and behaves like a common, ordinary—I mean, like a girl of
the streets.

MOTHER And you dare say that to me?

STONYBROKE Haven't you noticed it yourself?

MOTHER Perhaps I have: she seems more animated, she dresses differently . . . But she's working now, and on the whole marriage has
had quite a good effect on her.

STONYBROKE You think so? You're quite an optimist, My Lady.

MOTHER That's enough of those titles! Do you understand? Don't
make fun of me! My God! I can't see anything! (*Takes a drink*) Oh
—I feel terribly dizzy. You've touched on my innermost doubts.

STONYBROKE I'll tell you something else: in town they're saying that
your son—from idealistic motives, of course—has been forced to
move in circles which are quite improper for a young husband and
for the son of a woman as eminently respectable as you.

MOTHER What do you mean by that? For God's sake, Mr. Stonybroke,
don't torture me!

STONYBROKE I'll tell you everything quite frankly if it'll make you feel any better; they say he's in cahoots with certain individuals who are seen a bit too often hanging around the embassies of countries not in the least friendly to us. It's impossible to prove anything against them, but there are certain people it's best to avoid. I've been hearing about a really scandalous club, run by, let's say . . . men with very bad reputations. To top it all, begging your pardon, my dear Madam Mother, how can a young husband make a public spectacle of himself with that dreadful millionairess Lucina Beer who poisoned her husband and went scot-free, and now runs around with a cheap crowd of spongers and amuses herself corrupting the young? Yesterday he was seen with her at the Illusion or the Excelsior or someplace like that. That's where our children's earnings . . .

MOTHER (*jumping up*) Shut up, you boor! Get out of my house!! Go out in the kitchen and beg for leftovers. You're not allowed in here . . . Shut up! Or I'll have the police after you, you scum . . . Get out!!! (*Stonybroke runs out to the right, coughing. The Mother sinks into an armchair.*) So that's how they . . . Oh, this is ghastly. But it's strange how normal I feel now. I really feel quite sane. (*She remembers again what Stonybroke has just told her.*) Oh, it's frightful! (*Suddenly, in a different tone of voice*) No—it's not possible, it's not possible!

THE VOICE But you'd thought of it yourself not long ago. You even talked to Dorothy about it. Ha, ha, ha!

MOTHER (*without hearing the Voice*) Was it I who drove them to it? Oh—that's not possible . . . But I thought of it myself, I even talked to Dorothy about it myself. No, no, no—that's absolutely impossible. They'll be here any minute now, they'll have to deny it. I never wanted to have things turn out like this. After all, I'm not getting anything out of this luxury. I've gotten along very nicely on what I earn from my knitting. Addiction to work—that's what Leon called it. Oh, how despicable! I've been working for him for the past twenty-seven years!

THE VOICE And you drove me—yes, you virtually drove me to a life of crime, because you wanted to live in luxury. Ha, ha—that's a riot!

MOTHER (*answering, but as if to herself*) No, no—I didn't drive anyone to do anything—not my husband or the children. I wanted Leon to earn an honest living. And he is earning an honest living—my son is. After all, I love him. I'm proud of him. His ideas are starting to catch on, there are meetings held to discuss them. I was unfair. Leon, I apologize for everything. I never wanted things to turn out this way—I never wanted them to, I never wanted them to! (*Enter Leon. The Mother buries her face in her knitting.*)

LEON What's this? Hunched over your knitting again, Mama? Have you really gone out of your mind? Please stop immediately! You'll completely ruin what's left of your eyesight.

MOTHER (*calmly*) Just a minute, Lenny—I don't want to see anything. I've got to get a little rest.

LEON What are you doing this for then? Alcohol, morphine, and that damned knitting. No—up till now I've put up with it, but this is going too far. Will you please get rid of that and promise me it'll never happen again.

MOTHER (*with her knitting still held over her eyes, until further notice*) But I couldn't live without working. I've been working for twenty-seven years. I've become addicted to it, like liquor.

LEON Stop it. I can't stand it another second. I'm not coming near you, because you remember what you said to me on that terrible evening when I got engaged: that I should never come near you, or touch you, or kiss you again. Will you please get rid of that immediately.

MOTHER I beg you, it's my only consolation.

LEON Ah, what a hell of a note! I give you everything, Mama. (*In a different tone of voice—weakly and uncertainly*) I'm working so you'll have all that—Sophie and I are both working . . .

THE VOICE Yes—they're working, but at what?

LEON Have I got the heebie-jeebies—or am I hearing things? (*He shakes it off.*) I'm just overtired—I had the impression my father was talking to me. But I don't even know him.

MOTHER Oh—he worked like that for me too—that's what he used to tell me all the time . . .

LEON Who, in the name of hell! . . .

MOTHER Your father. The two of you are completely alike in every way—just like in Ibsen's *Ghosts* . . .

LEON Maybe you're the one who's always the same, and you produce similar reactions in people, no matter how unalike they may be. Well, that's enough of that—will you get rid of that knitting?

MOTHER I beg you . . .

LEON All right, I'll show you who's the master of this household. No mother sucked dry by vampires is going to maintain this household by knitting. (*He tears the knitting out of the Mother's hands, throws it on the floor, kicks it, and tramples on it. The Mother covers her face with her hands and remains seated. She does all this in such a way that when Leon pulls the knitting away, it slips out from between her face and her hands. She doesn't see anything while he does it.*) Aaah—at last. And let that be the end of it.

MOTHER (*without uncovering her eyes*) Oh, you're so cruel . . .

LEON (*with a sudden burst of affection*) Mother, darling! I'm only doing it for your own good, can't you see? (*He draws close to her.*) May I kiss you the way I used to? (*In a different tone of voice*) Oh —I don't know whether I still have the right to. And yet you're the only one I really love.

MOTHER (*her eyes still covered*) What are you saying? What sort of right do you need? I only love you, too. Put your arms around me. There's been some horrible misunderstanding. Sons and mothers and fathers and brothers are only people, and they've got to love one another despite differences between them—they've got to. They should smooth over these differences so they can stand one another. Otherwise life simply becomes hell, when those who should love one another—not because society says so, but because they're fated to—hate one another instead. Come, put your arms around me the way you used to. I have the feeling we're back there again, in our old apartment. We were happy there.

LEON Don't talk like that, **don't talk** like that. Neither of us knew how to be happy in a simple way. Yes—we both did everything we could to spoil it.

MOTHER (*her eyes covered*) Let's not blame ourselves. Everything will still be all right. Somehow I feel strangely at peace. Either I've sobered up, or I'm very, very drunk. It's all gone away: all that madness of mine. (*In fear*) But maybe I've really gone mad already? (*Leon hugs her in a wild embrace. A pause*) Yes—it's really you. You're no longer that other, strange person. We're not in this horrible place any more. But tell me now: this is what's torturing me so awfully. Sophie's father, that disgusting boor, was telling me such frightful things—answer me: yes or no. Just answer in one word— I'll believe you. You know—there's some gossip about you, and Sophie, and some suspicious characters, and money . . . (*Anxiously*) Where's all this luxury coming from? Tell me, Leon, tell me! (*Leon stands up. The Mother does not uncover her eyes. Leon struggles with himself.*)

LEON (*in a hard tone of voice*) No—it's all vicious slander. Neither Sophie or I are doing anything of the sort.

MOTHER (*suddenly uncovers her eyes, stands up, and throws herself at him, then suddenly staggers and sits on the floor*) What's happened? I can't see anything at all. Just red spots. Leon, I've gone totally blind. Give me some liquor—a whole glass—straight, without any water. Quickly! I'm so happy—I don't want to go blind. How are we going to make ends meet now? I've got to finish those things I'm knitting . . . Leon! Leon!! (*Leon pours out the liquor like an automaton. The Mother drinks it all at one gulp.*) It's nothing, it'll

pass—although it was never as bad as this before. (*A pause*) Oh—it's
not going away. So it's finally happened—I'm going blind. What
does it matter? At least I know it's not true—all that other business.
Whatever happens, I'll always be happy. I won't ever see you again.
But you've got your work now, you're somebody. (*Leon hugs her.*)
I'm very drunk. When I sober up, I may go mad, but I can't drink
any more. Do we have any bromide or chloral hydrate in the house?
Now I don't want to go mad.

LEON Mama, Mama! It's that damned knitting and drugs—morphine
along with your liquor! Why didn't I have enough strength to keep
you away from it?! I even helped you get it myself, since I hadn't
the heart to say no. My God, my God—you have to pay a terrible
price for everything in this life.

(*The doorbell rings. The door is opened, and someone enters;
sounds of a scuffle are heard. Lucina Beer rushes into the salon.*)

LUCINA Leon, Leon! I couldn't stand it any longer! You haven't been
to see me for a week. I finally got hold of your address. Ah—this
must be your mother. I apologize for this intrusion. I'm going to
marry you. I love only you. You know, he's my perfect, my only
love. I can't live without him. Madam, why are you sitting on the
floor?

LEON Get out of here, will you. My mother's just gone blind. Absolutely everything's collapsed.

MOTHER (*still sitting on the floor*) What's going on here? Who's that
woman?

LEON (*coldly*) This is Mrs. Beer—she's in love with me, but it's not
mutual.

LUCINA Not mutual? Oh, no—you love me all right. Don't be cruel,
Leon.

LEON (*trying to have some effect on her*) Can't you see there are more
important things in the world, more important even than love? Why
don't you leave now? Can't you see there's been a tragedy in this
house? (*The Mother stands up and remains standing very straight,
leaning against a chair.*)

LUCINA When I appear, tragedy disappears. I'll save you both. You
must be on the verge of disaster. He has to fulfill his destiny. His
great ideas must be universally accepted. I know I came at the
wrong time, but you'll have to forgive me. Now, after not having
seen you for a whole week, I realize that you're the only thing that
counts in my life. Let's be unhappy together. He never even wanted
to give me his address. I couldn't find it anywhere. Are you still
ashamed of me? (*To the Mother*) We've only appeared in public
together once. (*To Leon*) Even the police don't know where you

live. I got it from that—you know? (*To the Mother*) Mrs. Pipewicker, why don't you say something—For you I'll do just
anything . . .

MOTHER (*in a strangely composed way*) Now just pull yourself together, please! My name is not Pipewicker, but Eely, and my maiden
name was von Oates spelled with an "e." My son is a married man.

LUCINA That's not true! You may be right about the name, but he's not
married.

LEON Unfortunately, Mama's right. My name is Eely, and I am married. (*He makes a signal to her with his eyes. Then he remembers
something and whispers in her ear.*)

LUCINA You'll get a divorce? Now I don't believe anything any more.
So you're really married? That was despicable. (*Ironically*) He
didn't want to lose me so he kept it a secret from me. (*To the
Mother*) You can't imagine how much he's cost me in the past year.
He's wheedled me out of thousands. I've already lost count. But it's
not the amount that gets me. He was always talking about how to
put his great ideas into practice and about how poor you all were at
home. But you seem to live pretty well—I can see that now for the
first time. (*She looks around.*) I couldn't see the rest of the world
because of him; through him I became a different person. But what
about him? Your son's a pimp, an ordinary pimp. Do you understand, you blind old witch? You've brought up your son to be a
pimp. That's how this monster makes his living. Yes—you won't
have to get a divorce! And I was in love with him! My God, what
an abomination! How many emotions, how many beautiful emotions
I've wasted on him! (*The Mother stands perfectly still, holding onto
the arm of the chair.*)

LEON Please leave. I'm capable of just about anything today. Do you
understand? All of this has worn me out too, both physically and
emotionally (*he says this ironically*). All the techniques for exciting
what's known as love are harmful, Mrs. Beer. Fortunately, it didn't
have any bad aftereffects on my mind. Maybe what I've just said
will finally make you get out.

LUCINA What cynicism. This is my house. I have no legal right to
throw you out, but you're thieves all the same.

LEON You'll get your money back, just as soon as my ideas start to be
generally accepted.

LUCINA His ideas. Rubbish that no sensible person believes in, rubbish
dreamed up by a pimp. (*Leon rushes at her and tries to throw her
out. But at the door [new arrivals come in without ringing the
doorbell] he runs into Sophia, dressed in a black ball gown. Sophia's*

*face is colored, but unnaturally—she gives the impression of being
excessively made up, even when seen from the auditorium. After her
come two men in black and white [faces y compris], in tail coats,
unbuttoned sealskin coats, and top hats.*)

SOPHIA (*abnormally excited to the highest degree*) So the slut who's
keeping you has moved right into the house? How nice! I took
cocaine for the first time today. All the prostitutes take it, so why
shouldn't I? I say anything that comes into my head, I go wherever I
please, I float above life, I don't have any worries. I'm a streetwalker.
Do you all understand?—The young Mrs. Eely. And so Mama's
finally gone blind from all that knitting—great—as if it mattered—
I've got the money. Allow me to introduce: Count de la Tréfouille
and Mr. de Modesta-Bladdery. Mr. de Modesta-Bladdery doesn't use
his title as a duke, even though he's descended from Timur-Chan.
My mother-in-law: nee Baroness von und zu Oates, in a previous
incarnation an eleventh-century Freifrau, spelled with an "e." I feel
so wonderful and light, and somehow the whole universe seems
strangely harmonious even though everything is really rotten. How
beautiful everything is! People are like wonderful memories of
themselves, but they're alive, they're real. (*She goes numb with bliss,
in a state of perfect ecstasy. Lucina sits down on a chair by the
door.*)

LUCINA Pardon me, gentlemen. (*To Sophia*) Give me some cocaine,
too. Maybe that way I'll be able to stand all this; my head's already
going round and round in circles.

SOPHIA These gentlemen can give you some. I got it from them. Leon,
you have no idea how wonderful it is. I've started to live a completely new life.

DE MODESTA (*offering Leon cocaine in a glass tube*) You must be Miss
Sophia's brother?

LEON (*taking a large dose; gets sprinkled with white powder*) No—
her husband. But this lady's keeping me. Mrs. Lucina Beer.

DE LA TREFOUILLE Oh, we like things that are somewhat unusual.

LEON (*sniffs*) You're right, Sophie—cocaine's a wonderful thing. My
mind's so clear, and nothing bothers me any more. You'll stay to
supper, won't you, gentlemen? Mama, try some—it's phenomenal.
Everything seems different now. It isn't like your disgusting morphine and alcohol.

MOTHER Give me some. I already feel I'm in another world. Maybe I've
gone mad. (*Leon takes the cocaine Modesta gave him and pours it
into her nose.*)

SOPHIA Well, boys, make yourselves right at home. Now I'll go see about supper. (*To Lucina*) You can stay too, you slut. (*She goes out to the right.*)

DE MODESTA (*to Leon*) I don't know whether you know that both Tréfouille and I are your wife's lovers.

LEON (*sniffs*) That's great. Oh, what a wonderful feeling! Right now I'm completely at peace with myself.

MOTHER (*sitting down; sniffing*) You know, Leon, my mind's perfectly lucid now, and it seems to me everything has to be the way it is and couldn't be any other way—it's even beautiful. Oh—it's getting more and more beautiful all the time . . . (*She goes numb with ecstasy.*)

LUCINA (*getting up*) Give me some, too. Today I lost all my illusions. I'm finished. Up till now I never dared try it.

DE MODESTA (*giving her cocaine*) Well, young lady, all your troubles will vanish in a minute. New horizons will open up before your very eyes. Mrs. Eely senior is really feeling it, since she's already been drinking. (*Lucina takes some, then drinks some liquor.*)

LEON Gentlemen, you understand that I have the right to die any way I want. My normal life was simply torture to me. I can see that now that I'm under the influence of cocaine. It's wonderful—life isn't at all tragic. And my great ideas, which you're not yet acquainted with, are already set in motion. "*Les idées-forces,*" as Fouillet said, or was it Guyot or somebody like that? My mind is really working beautifully now! The whole world is surging through the icy logic of my system.

DE MODESTA Yes, but later on a terrible depression sets in. Everything's dazzling and beautiful right now, but later on it's going to be just that much more—oh, God! it's as hideous as—I'm at a loss for words. Tréfouille and I are just moderate cocaine sniffers—we're not addicts.

DE LA TREFOUILLE Well—let's face it, that's really just double talk; you can't take cocaine without becoming an addict. So you think you can grasp your ideas with perfect clarity. Cocaine doesn't offer anything new except a sense of ecstasy. An absolutely uncreative drug. But it's good enough for us.

LUCINA (*sniffs*) Oh, I feel so good, so good . . .

LEON Oh, I won't be moderate. My life's come to an end. (*He sniffs. They all sniff as a group and go into raptures.*)

SOPHIA (*entering*) There'll be some refreshments now, just some cold snacks. Come on, boys. The liquor and hors d'oeuvres are ready. Let's all go into the dining room. We're going to have a good time and behave like a pack of wild animals. An evening of pure fun.

MOTHER We're not part of any great drama—what you said was quite true, Lenny. I'm completely sober, but in a different dimension: not down below, but up above—beyond alcohol. It's phenomenal. Could one of you gentlemen give me his arm. I'm blind.

DE LA TREFOUILLE (*offers her his arm; both he and De Modesta have already thrown off their fur coats and removed their top hats*) Yes, yes, after you've had some liquor, cocaine works infinitely better. And it's much better for your health too. Ha, ha, ha—that's funny. (*De Modesta offers his arm to Sophia. They all move toward the dining room on the right. Leon is the last. The doorbell rings, some-one opens the door. Enter Mordello-Benz.*)

BENZ Leon, I'd like to have a word with you.

LEON Ah—good evening, Anthony. Wait a second. Go ahead, I'll be right with you. (*All the others go into the dining room. Leon and Benz stand with their backs to the dining-room door. The Mother comes back silently and gropingly, and listens to their conversation without their seeing her.*) Well, you're brave to come here. And without even taking cocaine first.

BENZ (*in black and white, like everybody else*) Who's got time for cocaine? I had to get hold of you immediately. I've got to have the number of that mobilization plan. They don't believe the docu-ment's authentic. They've got to check it. I'll give it back to you right away. (*Leon takes a small memorandum book out of his billfold, and a little card out of the small memorandum book.*)

LEON Here you are. (*Benz takes the little card and hides it. Leon writes down something in his small memorandum book.*)

BENZ Thanks. You know what? I didn't believe it myself. We'll make a bundle out of this. Good for a year of good clean living. Heh, heh.

MOTHER (*the two men turn in her direction*) What sort of a number is that you're talking about, Lenny? Is that man someone connected with your business affairs—it is business, isn't it?

LEON No, mother—let's be frank. The whole Lucina affair was only good for pocket money. The main source of our income is military espionage. Those are the only two professions I didn't find intellec-tually exhausting—you know all about them now. In the first place, I'm a very sophisticated sex maniac; and in the second place—I like secretive and dangerous things, even if sometimes I act like a cow-ard. It's all due to the movies—as far as I can see. Even I have to relax sometimes. The number is from stolen military documents. It's a proof of my services, a receipt I can present in order to get paid—now you know it all.

BENZ What are you saying, Leon? After all, this is a highly secret matter. Have you gone out of your mind? You've got such a wild look in your eyes.

LEON Look—this is my mother. She went blind today and lost her mind—she's quite harmless. And besides, I've already sucked her dry like a vampire. It's perfectly hilarious: I sucked her dry through needlework. (*The Mother goes gradually stiff as the conversation continues.*)

BENZ What's the matter with you? I'm afraid of you.

LEON But there's nothing to be afraid of, my friend. I just took a little cocaine for the first time in my life. Well—why don't you go now? (*Exit Benz, bowing to the Mother, as Leon pushes him out.*)

MOTHER Even cocaine doesn't make it bearable. I'm almost dead. My heart's beating for the last time. It's beating so fast. I don't know who I am any more. Leon a spy!!! (*She falls over backward dead. Leon throws himself toward her.*)

LEON Mother, Mother!!! (*Examines her and gets up*) It wasn't moral suffering that killed her. Nothing moral can kill anyone. My poor dear old mother simply took too large a dose of cocaine. (*They all squeeze through the door leading to the dining room, including Dorothy.*) Dorothy, the old lady's dead. After all, it would have to happen sooner or later. I don't know who I am either. Mother said the same thing about herself just before she died. And what about all of you, do you know who you are? No one knows. We don't even know what it means to be alive. The Mystery of Existence is unfathomable—that's the basis for my whole system of organizing the fight against automation. Someone had to be sacrificed in order to work it out. It was my destiny. I can go ahead and die some way or other, the whole thing's already started on its prescribed course. It can't be stopped. They say cocaine destroys your memory and intelligence, and usually turns people into walking zombies. But what's that to me?

DOROTHY What are you ranting about? We've got to try to save her.

LEON Ah, that's right, Dorothy, you're the only person in the group who didn't take cocaine. We'll carry the old lady to the sofa—that's the way. (*Dorothy helps them carry the Mother to the sofa on the left.*) And now let's go drink some more and take that wonderful stuff that lets us escape real-life dramas or else to postpone them indefinitely. (*He rushes everybody into the dining room and goes there himself. Dorothy kneels by the Mother's corpse. Suddenly the corpse's right arm, which was placed on her breast, falls to the floor. Dorothy jumps up with a cry. They all rush in again from the next room, with glasses and sandwiches in their hands. Some of them are chewing.*)

LEON What's going on here now?

DOROTHY Nothing; her arm fell down, and it frightened me so!

LEON All right, but don't scare us any more with that kind of nonsense. Your mistress is dead, no doubt about that; all the same, she doesn't know any more about what death really means than we do about what life is, although we're still alive. Being under the influence of cocaine, it seems to me I've said something very profound. It's probably all nonsense. Let's get out of here. (*He rushes everybody into the dining room.*)

THE VOICE Bravo, Leon! For the first time I can see that you're my son.

ACT III, in the Form of an Epilogue

A room done all in black; there are no doors, or windows. The wall facing the audience consists of a black curtain which can be drawn to either side. In the center of the stage (the floor is covered with a black carpet) there is a black six-sided pedestal, on which the Mother's dead body lies, with her feet toward the audience, her head considerably raised, and her arms folded on her breast. Leon, dressed in a tailcoat, stands in front of the pedestal. Then he starts talking and pacing about. He holds his mother's light-brown knitting which he had kicked repeatedly in Act II. This is the only color on stage until further notice.

LEON (*to the audience*) Please accept the present situation for what it is and nothing more. Despite all its seeming complexity, it's something immediate, like the color red, for example, or the musical note A. Some people might think it's a hoax, a dream, a symbol, or God knows what. I leave them complete freedom of interpretation, since even if I didn't, they'd all act the same way anyhow. "You can't cut glass with your finger," as the old Russian proverb says. I am even reconciled to my lot—despite all I've been through. And please don't any of you think that I've been taking cocaine again as on that memorable night when my mother died. (*Pointing at the corpse, without turning around to look at it*) Cocaine is fine at the time, but afterward you have to pay a terrible price. I took more and more and, toward the end, all of reality, heightened to the utmost, and swelling to the bursting point, sprang up snarling against me, and everything that had been beautiful before, now became equally incomprehensible and frightening. I was in a kind of hell on a different planet, I was the one and only being of my own kind, completely alone and feeling terribly estranged from everything, and other people—even my own dead mother—became like so many curious, incomprehensible insects. Yes—I can tell you, I was in a spiritual hell, and I don't even know what its hellishness consisted of. No, oh no—not all our problems can be solved that way. I don't want to moralize, but I wouldn't advise anyone to take that filthy stuff, unless he really doesn't have anything more to lose. Of course I could do it now, but I don't want to for reasons I'll never disclose. I have no idea what's behind that curtain. This room, so they say—oh, I'll never say who—has neither doors nor windows. Why I'm here with the corpse of my late mother is a complete mystery to me. All I can remember is that that last night I kept on drinking and taking cocaine and drinking and taking cocaine until finally: "bang"—and here I am. Now I've got a terrible hangover and headache, and that unbearable feeling of alienation which they say is the special reaction to cocaine. Please note that the whole situation is quite real, I mean, I'm really me and not some double, I didn't kill myself, I feel quite sane and in good mental health, and so on and so forth. There are just some things I won't go into, the spatial-temporal relationships in particular. I don't know, for instance, how much time has elapsed since that other evening, and I don't want to know.

THE VOICE Have you finally finished?

LEON I've finished. (*He claps his hands; the curtain is drawn, and the entire cast of characters from the preceding acts are revealed sitting on red chairs against the background of a black wall, and in addition the following characters: the Aunt, Baroness von Oates spelled with an "e"; and an Unknown Woman whose face is a normal color [all the others are entirely black-and-white, with the exception of Sophia who is wearing make-up], dressed in red, green, and violet—her face, figure, and gestures are strikingly similar to those of the Mother. In addition to these characters, there is also an Unknown Man in a dark suit.*) Oh—what a surprise. All of us here together in a room without doors or windows. I swear I didn't know anything about it. I'm not counting that empty space which opens out directly onto the interplanetary abyss. (*He points to the auditorium*) I can see many familiar faces—where did they come from?—it's not my concern. But what seems strange to me is the presence of people I don't know and I can't tell exactly why it seems strange to me. (*The Woman with natural color and the Unknown Man get up and go over to him.*)

UNKNOWN WOMAN I'm sure you don't know who I am, Lenny, I'm
your mother at the age of twenty-three—before you were even
born. (*The Aunt gets up and comes over to them.*)

LEON My mother's lying over there dead. First I sucked her completely
dry, and then I used her own weaknesses to finish her off. I'll come
to that in just a second . . .

AUNT Yes—this woman's trying to pretend she can perform miracles.
Physical doubling plus displacement in time—no, that's going too
far. We've been raised on Einstein, but we can't take a hoax like that
seriously, even as an intellectual experiment. There are some intellectual experiments that shouldn't be allowed: like those that contradict
the fundamental laws of General Ontology. And then what's the use
of talking about reality, even if you accept the plurality of realities,
as expounded by Leon Chwistek. Reality can't be made logical
without falsifying it. I'm the sister of the deceased: Baroness von
Oates, spelled with an "e."

LEON I almost succeeded in making sociology logical, so I know something about that. You're right, Auntie.

AUNT I don't have to be told I'm right by unfortunate products of
misalliances like you, Lenny; I mean, like you, Mr. Eely.

UNKNOWN WOMAN I'm not at all surprised that you think that way. But
Lenny, how could you, you're such an intelligent boy—it's just that
I am with you, that is: I'm expecting to be with you—that's not
quite it—I'm spending lots of time in your company inwardly, in a
delicate condition.

AUNT Please refrain from making unseemly jokes in my presence.

UNKNOWN WOMAN (*menacingly*) And I'd advise you to calm down,
since you may turn out to be much less real than you imagine. Do
you know how you got in here?

AUNT (*awfully confused*) I didn't mean anything . . . I only wanted
. . . I don't know anything . . . I'm afraid.

UNKNOWN WOMAN So why don't you go back to your seat and sit
there quietly. (*To Leon*) Lenny, your intellectual denseness appalls
me, particularly after that speech you gave at the beginning which
we listened to behind the curtain.

LEON As a matter of fact, I was just thinking about that. I'm surprised
myself at how conventional my ideas are. That's what cocaine does to
you. Oh, I'll never take another grain of that filthy stuff again. Yes,
you are my mother in her youth. That's a basic fact which cannot be
analyzed any further. Existence is so strange . . .

UNKNOWN WOMAN Stop. You show a tendency to give long speeches,
and this bores the audience, particularly those not adequately quali-
fied to understand your ideas. I should tell you that your ideas are

those of a man of genius—your social concepts, I mean. If they'd proved successful earlier, everything would have worked out differently.

LEON You're consoling me, Mother. But this doesn't in the least change the fact that my mother's corpse is lying over there, and that I killed her.

UNKNOWN WOMAN That's enough of that—I want to introduce you to your father—you hardly even knew him. He was hanged when you were three years old. You certainly won't remember him. Albert (*she pronounces his name in the French manner*)—your son, Leon.

UNKNOWN MAN (ALBERT EELY) You're quite a boy, Leon. I like you, and I've always liked you, even when you were a little kid. I always knew you'd be a success.

LEON But Father, I've really been a colossal failure. I brought about my mother's death, and my ideas are too—how can I put it without exaggerating . . .

ALBERT (*speaking with a French accent*) Now, now—no false modesty. You're a greater genius than many artists, inventors, engineers, and prophets, and founders of new religions.

LEON Yes, but nothing ever comes of anything I do, nothing ever . . .

ALBERT On the contrary. You've been misinformed. I've taken charge of all your mail which has been accumulating for some time now. Right here in our own country there are already at least thirty societies representing the new intellectuals, not in the old faint-hearted liberal democratic tradition with everyone reduced to the level of sheep, but right along the lines you set forth in your monograph—not to speak of what's going on abroad.

LEON Yes—that's my only work. Thirty-six pages.

ALBERT That's the whole brilliance of it. In just thirty-six pages to stir up the greatest fuss in the history of the world since the French Revolution. Just look at the papers: Uruguay, Paraguay, Honduras, the Philippines, Japan—you name it, and you've got it. You're world-famous. The name Eely has eclipsed all others, not in the useless arts and sciences or in crime, but because you've solved the basic problem confronting the entire human race. That's something great. Leon, I'm proud of you. (*He slaps him on the shoulder. Leon glances through the papers and letters. Suddenly he throws all of it on the floor and kicks it, and pulls the knitting out from under his arm.*)

LEON And it's all happening now, now that Mother's not alive any more. Goddamn it—what a cruel stroke of bad luck. But suppose I

died some time ago, then I wouldn't even have had this much
satisfaction. What an obscene mess it all is. At least you two can
move about freely in time—I can't even do that.

UNKNOWN WOMAN You're forgetting that I'm your mother. I'm tremendously pleased about all this. I forgive you everything.

LEON Yes, but there's a corpse lying over there that won't ever be able
to forgive me anything. Oh my God, my God. Just look, here's her
knitting; the poor thing lost her eyesight working on it. And everything she ever said during her whole life was well calculated—I
know: she couldn't help it—to make it impossible for me to bear her
death. And I can't. I remember every word, and every word pains
me like a million brain tumors and I don't know what I wouldn't
give this instant: every scrap of fame, every bit of pride in seeing my
great plan become a reality—I'd give I don't know what, there's
nothing big enough—if I could only take back just one harsh word I
said to her or just one evil thought I had about her. (*He weeps.*)
You don't know how terrible such pangs of conscience can be. I
won't be able to live through it.

UNKNOWN WOMAN If you don't want to believe me, there's nothing I
can do about it. There's no remedy for stubbornness. (*Leon goes
over to the corpse, places the knitting in its hands, and falls on his
knees, sobbing.*)

LEON Boo-hoo-hooo boo-hoo . . .

UNKNOWN WOMAN Lenny, if you'll only let me, I'll prove to you that
that corpse is a fraud. It's only a manikin. In fact, the whole
thing—all of us *y compris*—has been brilliantly put on, although no
one knows by whom. But it's nothing more than the pure form of
certain events, congealed in the infinity of Existence. (*She tries to
lift the corpse. Leon jumps up and speaks, sobbing.*)

LEON Mother, don't you dare touch her. That would be a frightful
sacrilege. Go away. Leave me alone with her.

ALBERT Leave her alone, Nina. And leave him alone, too. Let him cry
to his heart's content. Have a good cry, my boy—it'll make you feel
better.

UNKNOWN WOMAN You're right, Albert. Maybe he'll get over it if we
let him go through it all in his own way.

LEON (*weeping in despair*) I don't understand a thing, not a thing. But
still: would I be the same person, if I hadn't gone through it all? I
had to. I guess I preferred to earn my living by having jobs where I
could relax intellectually and gather strength for future thought. But
if I'd had any real will power, I could have done honest work and
still achieved my other goal. She supported me for twenty-seven
years with her knitting, and then I supported her for two, getting

involved in one obscene mess after another in my attempt to find some peace. Oh my God, my God, what a horrible punishment has been inflicted on me. Oh, if only she'd be just like Mother (*he points to the Unknown Woman*), everything would be different.

UNKNOWN WOMAN Don't be too demanding. She was old—and I'm still young. I haven't been through anything yet.

LEON My poor old unhappy mother. Now there's nothing that can help her any more. Oh, how despicable I've been, how thoroughly despicable! (*He weeps.*)

ALBERT I'm a little disappointed in him. He acts as if he's grieving for his mother, but deep down he really feels sorry for himself. It's a sticky situation. I'd thought—judging by his great ideas and his conduct that night—I saw everything through a certain little chink in the wall—that he had a strong character. And yet, when you try to beat it into his head that he shouldn't have any regrets, all this slop gets slung around just because of a few stupid pangs of conscience. Leon, I'm telling you for the last time: pull yourself together, go ahead and suffer, but make something out of this suffering and forge new strength for yourself. Now then, Leon! Chin up. You can't turn the clock back. It would please your dead mother most of all, if you stopped crying over spilt milk and began your life completely anew.

LEON I know—you're right, Father. But how should I begin?

ALBERT You've got to go on fighting. It hasn't all been done yet. You've got to complete your work. Trips throughout the entire world, lectures, conferences, and organizational work—the whole business of putting your scheme into operation. Your great work is only just beginning. The whole human race is eagerly awaiting it.

LEON Father, do you think that the whole human race means anything to me? I'd gladly give it all up if I could add one more minute to poor Mother's life and if I could take back all those rotten things I did.

ALBERT Oh—his condition is serious. Let's wait and see what happens. (*Old Stonybroke comes up to them.*)

STONYBROKE Aah—Leon, good to see you. Aah! But they're saying that you deliberately got your mother drunk and gave her morphine so she'd die quicker. Maybe it was all subconscious—I don't know. There are a lot of theories like that nowadays . . .

LEON (*promptly pulls out a revolver and fires at Stonybroke*) That's a lie, you slob! It was just that I was too kind to her. I knew it was her only consolation. (*Stonybroke falls to the floor.*)

ALBERT Bravo, Leon. You're beginning to regain your equilibrium a little.

LEON And you're beginning to drive me out of my mind, Father. All these delightful tendencies I get from you. A gallows-bird, goddamn it, a Brazilian pickpocket and cutthroat. It's thanks to my father that I turned into a spy and a pimp.

ALBERT Uuuh—I'm beginning to take a strong dislike to you, Len. You're being quite rude. It's a little bit in your late mother's style to blame me for all your own shortcomings. That's a fault you get from your mother.

LEON But in sheer nastiness I take after my father. If you breathe another word, I'll shoot you like a dog.

UNKNOWN WOMAN Leave him alone, Albert, he's a nervous wreck, and I can't tolerate all this bickering in my delicate condition.

(*Lucina and Benz come up to them.*)

BENZ As for the spying, you don't have to have any pangs about that. It was never found out, and nothing's ever going to come of it. We made a few cents out of it, and it didn't do our country any harm either since we were taking the other side for a ride, too. They've got morons as agents. It's their own fault.

LEON Good old Benz. You know, you've cheered me up more than anyone. (*He slaps him on the shoulder.*)

LUCINA Leon, I don't have the slightest grudge against you either. I suffered a lot on your account. You taught me what love is—ultimate, true love. And above all, you taught me that you shouldn't defile it. And you'll be able to pay all the money back to me, since you're going to be rich now.

LEON (*kissing her hand*) I really don't know how to thank you, Lucina. Yes, of course—I'll pay you back everything. But the amounts are large. It'll take several years in installments . . . (*He kisses her hand once again, and she kisses him on the forehead. Sophia comes up to him—followed by her lovers.*)

SOPHIA Well—since you're becoming reconciled to everyone this way, maybe you'll make up with me too, Len. If you want, we can forget about sex, and just be friends who share the same ideals. I'll continue to help you. After all, you believe in my integrity in intellectual matters, and you really pushed me into that other thing yourself. But I haven't stopped loving you, not even for a second.

LEON Well, yes—I pushed you into it with the aid of your own natural tendencies. Otherwise I couldn't have swung it. All right—we're all made up, but I still have to settle my accounts with those guys. My act will be symbolic—by killing them I symbolically kill all your other lovers. I'm sure you can't remember how many you've had. (*He shoots at de la Tréfouille and de Modesta. They both fall to the floor.*)

ALBERT (*to the Unknown Woman*) Listen, Nina—let's get out of here. Once he gets going, he'll shoot us down like ducks.

DOROTHY (*drawing near*) It's easy to say: "Let's get out of here"—but how? There are no doors or windows, and nobody—I've asked everybody—nobody knows how we got here in the first place.

(*From the ceiling, a little to the right, a huge, black, shiny pipe comes sliding down; it's three feet wide and has iron rungs on the side for climbing, like a factory chimney. A small door at the back of the pipe opens, and out of it comes Calfskin followed by six workers dressed in black. The pipe comes right down over the trap, and the others crawl up out of it.*)

CALFSKIN Good evening, friends.

ALBERT At last we're in communication with the world. Where did all of you come from? Is there a way out?

CALFSKIN What way out? We've been sitting in this pipe from the beginning, and we don't know how we got stuffed into it either. I'm Calfskin the theater director. There are various gadgets up in there. It's a very complicated machine, but it's really a toy. I'll tell you what it is—it's a machine for sucking dry what's left of mothers' corpses that haven't been completely sucked dry by their only sons. Right now we're going to take the late Mrs. Eely, Senior, into the apparatus. There's an engineer and twenty of his men still sitting up there, and they apparently don't know how they got in here either. We heard them talking through the wall, but they couldn't hear anything we were saying to them.

LEON You know—your jokes are in poor taste. That's all right, but just don't go too far. (*The pipe goes up. The workers stand in a row to the right.*)

CALFSKIN Well, I'll be damned! Now we'll never get out of here. And there are corpses all over the place already. Like father, like son, Mr. Albert (*pronounced in the French style*) Eely. A chip off the old block.

LEON Here's a chip off your old block for your stupid yakking. (*He punches Calfskin so hard that he falls down flat on his face and lies there as if dead.*) Oh! What am I doing all this for? How's this going to help my poor old mother even a little? And that swine dared to make jokes like that here! The scum! My God, my God! Now I've got nothing ahead of me but anguish.

UNKNOWN WOMAN And I've had just about enough of all this: enough of your murders, and all this shooting, and yakking, all this double-talk, punching people in the jaw, this spiritual poverty, all this wallowing in stale emotional entrail-twisting. I want to live. Look here, Leon. All of this is just one big phony. (*She goes over to the corpse, grabs hold of it by the hair, and yanks off the wooden head and the old rags attached to it, stuffed with straw.*) This isn't a corpse, it's just a manikin. The head is made out of wood. (*She throws the head on the floor; a dull wooden thud*) And anyhow it was made by some famous sculptor. It seems to me it was either Zamoyski or Archipenko—despite the fact that it's naturalistic and quite a remarkable likeness. And the hands are plaster of Paris—some sort of old cast from the woodcraft school. And the rest—it's just oakum. (*She scatters the whole corpse along the ground; straw, rags, etc. She tears off the black pall with which all of it had been covered and throws it on the ground too.*)

LEON (*frightened*) Aah! Aaah! This is horrible! How can I go on living now? This is the worst, this is the worst—how can I even die now? You've destroyed everything. Aaah! Aaah! Aaah!

UNKNOWN WOMAN Let's get out of here, Albert—let's all get out of here. If he can live through this he'll be strong. If not—let him rot in hell—he's accomplished his purpose anyhow. His ideas are already in circulation, and nothing can stop them now. It's just sheer nonsense that there's no way out of this room. I'm certain there's a door behind those chairs over there. (*She goes straight ahead, pushing the chairs out of her way. The Aunt stands up. All of them—with the exception of the immobile workers and the corpses—follow the Unknown Woman. She feels the wall.*) Oh—there's a hidden door, here's the button.

(*She presses the button. A door* à deux battants *comes open. A mountain landscape in spring, flooded with sunshine, becomes visible. The light in the room grows dim and turns reddish. They all leave through the door. Just as the last one is leaving, the black curtain is drawn shut. During all this time Leon remains standing with his hands thrust into his hair and his eyes popping out. As soon as the curtain is drawn, Leon falls down on his knees, gathers up the scattered fragments of the manikin of his Mother, and presses them to his breast, crawling on his knees on the floor.*)

LEON Aaah! Now I don't have anything left any more. They've even taken my pangs of conscience away from me! They've taken my anguish away! I have nothing, nothing, nothing! Only these tragic souvenirs! Aaah!

THE ONE ON THE RIGHT SIDE IN THE ROW OF WORKERS: Well, and now, my friends, a little kangaroo court in the name of mealy-mouthed democracy. (*They all throw themselves on Leon, tearing him away from the fragments of the manikin, and begin to strangle him, dragging him in the direction of the trapdoor into which the pipe was lowered. They suffocate him there, hiding him completely from the audience, and push him into the trap.*)

WORKERS Oh, that's how, that's how, that's how, that's how, oh, that's ho-o-o-w-w-w! (*They stand up and pant. There is no trace left of Leon. The pipe comes down quickly. The workers stand in a line in front of the door in it and begin to enter one at a time. Calfskin tosses about a bit, muttering unconsciously. Meanwhile the curtain comes down slowly.*)

CURTAIN

December 13, 1924

They

They (*Oni*, 1920) opens on a note of characteristic Witkacian ambiguity and threat. Has the director of Spika's theater gone mad, or is he perhaps in the pay of the secret government, working for the secret committee to bring about the total collapse of art? Is that why he is putting on nonsensical Pure Form plays? And does the secret committee or secret government really exist at all? Then, too, all the lights are suddenly on in the previously unoccupied house next door. "You can see shadows moving behind the curtains," Balandash's cook reports, "They have moved in"; "They are running everything, but no one knows who They actually are."

Who are They? What are They planning to do to Callisto Balandash, elegant aesthete and art collector, secure in his country house, surrounded by his period furniture in dark plum, his Japanese wood carvings, his cubist Picasso, his nudes, and immersed in the aroma of quince mingled with "Chevalier d'Orsay" and in voluptuous discussions of Pure Form with his beautiful actress-mistress Spika, Countess Tremendosa?

When he was asked what the two people in his play *The Room* were afraid of, Harold Pinter replied: "Obviously they are scared of what is outside the room. Outside the room there is a world bearing upon them which is frightening. I am sure it is frightening to you and me as well." [1] Out of this fear of who will open the door and come into the room, Pinter has created his theater of menace.

Like Pinter, Witkiewicz uses uncertainty to create a feeling of dread and menace; unknown forces are lurking in the house next door, even right outside the room, behind the walls and curtains "in the murky depths of the hall." A "sinister intruder" in red pants is waiting out there, threatening to burst into the combination art gallery, gourmet restaurant, and love nest where Balandash hopes to slake his insatiable thirst for new artistic and sensual pleasures. He had planned to assuage his metaphysical feeling of emptiness with a "unique evening of love," while looking at his Giorgione, Picasso, and Wang Wei, and savoring mushrooms, vermouth, and pâté made out of black-haired new-born baby goats' legs.

[1] Harold Pinter, quoted in Martin Esslin, *The Theatre of the Absurd* (New York: Anchor Books, Doubleday and Co., 1961), p. 199.

Now suddenly They have come to examine Balandash's gallery. His individuality and neuroses, his boredom and connoisseurship are under attack from a grotesque collection of fanatics—more bizarre than his collection of paintings—who are out to change the world into a constructive place where automatons can live happily without art, without split personalities, without metaphysical longings. They are all the organized and mechanized forces in the world out to crush the individual, his eccentricity and creativity. Above all, They are intent on destroying art. And They are everywhere; it is impossible to tell who They are or where They will turn up next.

By the vastness and vagueness of the conspiracy, Witkiewicz creates a feeling of uneasy fear. Nothing is what it seems, no one is who he appears to be. In this world of shifting appearances, reality becomes utterly problematic. The author of the most extreme avant-garde plays turns out to be Seraskier (a Turkish title for generals and potentates) Banga Tefuan, head of the secret committee for destroying art, who is also revealed to be Richard Tremendosa, Spika's husband.

The "pure nonsense" play in which Spika is to appear—*The Independence of Triangles*—was therefore written by Banga Tefuan as part of his campaign to undermine the theater by pushing it to ludicrous extremes, but it is also the title of the play Witkiewicz was writing at this time dealing with the same theme as *They:* the crushing of an individual by a mechanized totalitarian society. In *The Independence of Triangles* the painter and aesthete Pembroke goes to the South Sea Islands to create a new kind of art that will bring formal perfection out of perversion and distortion, but he is plunged into despair much of the time because of difficulties not only with art, but also with his beautiful red-haired mistress Seraphombix. At the same time, two vast navies, headed by Vice Admiral Bageloff-Moltocockroachin and Marine General Viviani fight for domination of the entire world. The outcome of the power struggle is the formation of a superstate that regiments and overpowers the individual through agencies like the Commissariat of Sexual Nonsense and the Department of Metaphysical Absurdity.

Pembroke moves from one form of enslavement to another—from personal bondage to aesthetic ideals and sexual and psychological drives to subjugation by a ruthless yet bizarre political system. At the end of the play, when he is falsely accused of rebellion and high treason, Pembroke goes off to prison willingly; he hopes to be able to devote himself to art and escape from the nightmare of power politics by means of a life sentence. *The Independence of Triangles* has the same dramatic structure as *They* and a number of Witkiewicz' other plays. Politics forcibly brings to an end the would-be artist's leisurely pursuit of artistic and sensual complexities. Art and the art of life submit to social pressures for uniformity and mechanization, generated by the formation of a totalitarian state.

In construction, *They* is a play in "two and a half acts"; the half act poses the threat to Balandash; Acts I and II carry it out and could be called the degradation and destruction of Balandash. In part, it is a process of self-degradation and self-destruction, since the League of Absolute Automationism is able to destroy him only because he is so vulnerable. The secret forces that crush him are really inside him as well as outside him. "They" can be taken to be all the forces hostile to man, both within and without. Witkiewicz does not oversimplify the issues by making Balandash a noble artist battling evil philistines; both sides are sick and mad.

Balandash is an aesthete without being an artist. He is an eclectic dilettante and decadent anarchist who cherishes the freedom to dabble in food, women, and painting. Although he himself is not able to create, he tries to battle against boredom and chaos ("our very life is the continuous collapse of something or other") by his enjoyment of the creations of others. As his ideal, he envisages a totally permissive society in which he can indulge his individualistic tastes: "Any society is good only to the extent that even though you're a member of it you don't really feel that you are."

In his personal life, Balandash is divided against himself and incapable of emotional fulfillment. His life and his art are at odds; his feelings and intellect do not work together. His quest for satisfaction is hopeless; he is sterile, uncreative, and doomed to frustration. "You never look at my body the way you look at Giorgione's Venus," Spika accuses him; "you're an automaton, an inhuman sex machine." Spika, too, is incapable of being herself in life and can only find satisfaction in playing roles on the stage.

Balandash seeks repose in art and looks to it for beauty and stability. However, his life of art and art of life are menaced from all sides, from within and from without—by those artists pushing art to extremes of madness and perversion and by those reformers out to suppress it. It is hard to tell which is which; the secret committee for promoting the total collapse of art is promoting Pure Form. Balandash lives in an unpredictable world in which "isms" have gone berserk and all extremes not only are possible, but meet.

Even the past with its seeming repose offers no consolation to Balandash's imagination. Spika points out to him that, with his origins and name, he would have been winnowing chaff in a mill by the road, and the great would have stepped on his subservient mug. There is no home or refuge for Balandash in the past, present, or future, neither in art, where he is at best a noncreative appreciator, or in society, where he can only serve as an automated cog in the machinery.

Blow by blow we follow Balandash's growing frustration and defeat. His gallery is taken away from him and destroyed for his own good, just as in *The Madman and the Nun* Walpurg is put into a straitjacket out of benevolence. We witness Balandash's grotesque degradation from his absurd exclamation of horror at the destruction of his paintings: "Why did I create the theory of Pure Form? If there isn't going to be any new art, why have a theory?" to his dark forebodings about Spika and his overwhelming weakness in needing a dark woman while the rest of his life is collapsing about him. As a final blow, the old family servant Marianna, who had kept Balandash informed about what They were doing, is revealed to be a government spy, informing against her master.

By the end of the play, Balandash has nothing left; everything has been stripped away from him until he is left naked in an empty world. Here is where They come in and provide an answer to the question ironically posed by Sajetan in *The Shoemakers:*

> Oh, when will the individual lose himself in a mechanically perfect society? Oh, when will the end come at last to the suffering caused by the individual's own personality, eternally stuck out and left hanging on its own in the void like a transcendental rear end . . .

Tefuan, the visionary intellectual leader of the secret committee, perceives that man is a transcendental rear end in the void who must lose himself in a mechanically perfect society, and he proposes regimentation and regulation so that people like Balandash will no longer have the leisure to wallow in their own frustrations and sense of emptiness: "A truly automated man should be in bed by nine o'clock in the evening and not haunting various fleabags that pretend to be theaters. Think of all the social energy that's wasted in such distractions." Above all, Tefuan is an enemy of art, because art is the enemy of social progress, order, and morality. He particularly hates the theater: "Art is social lawlessness. It confirms and affirms, and even reaffirms the value of individual experience . . . In five years' time we will convert all the theaters into orphanages for idiot foundlings."

If Tefuan wants to fill the metaphysical void, it is because he has known it himself. He tells Balandash that he once collected women with the same desperation that Callisto collects paintings. If he hates the theater, it is because he knows it well and is, in fact, a gifted playwright. His knowledge and intellect are astounding. To console the distraught Balandash, he quotes from *Henry VI, Part II* Jack Cade's

paradox: "But then are we in order when we are most out of order."
With irony both on his part and on Witkiewicz', Tefuan, the great
opponent of the theater, gives a citation from a rarely performed play
of Shakespeare's about Cade's insane egalitarian revolution which attempted to turn the whole world upside down by reverse logic.

By Cade's orders, those who can read and write will be killed; all
that man's reason has created will be destroyed—he wants to burn all
the records of the realm and set London Bridge on fire. This senseless
self-destructive principle gains momentum as disorder and chaos spread
throughout the country. Cade's absurd utopian schemes and wild leveling of society in which talent and intellect will be annihilated must
have interested both authors of *The Independence of Triangles*, Tefuan and Witkiewicz.

If Tefuan is a metaphysical and surrealistic Jack Cade, a demented
genius out to force happiness on everyone by taking all their freedom
away, his followers are a bizarre crew composed of playboys, corpulent bankers, society matrons, retired colonels, crackpots, and sexpots.
Seemingly a recognizable right-wing fascist group in favor of authori-
tarian moral reform and suppression of artistic freedom, its program of
social progress veers suddenly and unexpectedly toward the left. Its
basic premises are as weird and self-contradictory as the group itself
and as its leader, Tefuan, who may in fact be acting primarily out of
jealousy and vengeance because of his love for Spika.

Spika's death is the hideous denouement to the farcical games, shattering both Balandash and Tefuan. Man has nothing and is nothing; he
is utterly impermanent and insubstantial. Death rips off the masks and
postures. Neither Balandash's collecting mania for art nor Tefuan's
lunatic social schemes can dispel man's fundamental boredom and hopelessness. The characters are ultimately confronted with an ineradicable
nausea in the face of life. The more extravagant the games they play
for or against art, the more extreme the hangover and subsequent
feeling of emptiness and despair.

Tefuan, who throughout the play feverishly organized and preached
automated happiness for the world of the future, is suddenly struck by
the futility of all his schemes. Before he is led off to prison, Balandash
has ceased to believe in art. The metaphysical condition of man, against
which both of them have been struggling, is ineluctable. In his final
speech Tefuan abandons his role as social prophet for future happiness
and peers longingly backward at an earlier time in man's history when
life was still wild and beautiful: "Our god is an automaton. God used to
be an autocratic, spiteful, pleasure-loving tyrant who loved life, our
human life. Today no one loves it. No one loves life, not even the
gods."

The founder of the religion of Absolute Automation expresses his utter nihilism, but his second in command, Colonel Fondoloff, is troubled by no such philosophical problems. He is by nature good-hearted and good-natured, concerned with practical matters like hacking up the Picasso that got overlooked and staying in power, regardless of whether life has any meaning or not. The colonel in his hearty, bluff way tries to win Balandash over to accepting his views by a combination of threats and bribery. After the destruction of Balandash's gallery, the good colonel puts his arms around his victim and cajoles him: "He's laughing already. He's agreed to it voluntarily—that's the important thing—he's agreed to it voluntarily." The awful process of degradation continues as the colonel offers him substitutes: "You've got a woman, you've got money—you'll find consolation."

When Spika's murder is announced, it is the colonel who decides to make Balandash the scapegoat to hide the identities of those who committed the crime. This is the last stage in Balandash's brainwashing. As he is led off to prison, having confessed to a crime he did not commit, the battle between the aesthete with the split personality and the new automated state comes to an end. Only Spika and Balandash had any humanity or decency. She is dead; he has been subjugated and defeated. But in another, more fundamental way, in his last speech Balandash achieves a greater sense of identity than anywhere else in the play. He is on his way to being as healed internally as he could ever be.

> I don't even hope for death, only life imprisonment, only a prison cell. I want to be alone. I don't want to be a member of any society or any gang of thieves; I don't even want to be an artist, which I longed to be throughout all my miserable life. I want to be myself. That's all.

They

A DRAMA IN
TWO AND A HALF ACTS

CHARACTERS

Mr. Callisto Balandash	*Very good-looking, dark blond hair. Medium height, slender, 36 years old. In the Half Act, at the beginning of the play, dressed in a dark suit. In Act I, in striped trousers and a cutaway; in Act II, in a frock coat. Very rich, a so-called connoisseur of the "visual arts." Usually shy, but given to occasional fits of really mulish stubborness. Clean-shaven, his hair parted in the middle.*
Spika, Countess Tremendosa	*An actress. She is living with Balandash and is going to marry him. She is in the process of obtaining a divorce from her husband, Count Tremendosa, whom she has not laid eyes on for years. Light blonde, her hair combed high with a curl coming forward on each side. Prominent pale eyes. Her entire face is permeated with hidden suffering. Very beautiful. 28 years old.*
Marianna Splendorek	*The cook. She has chestnut hair, dresses quite tastefully in violet. Very beautiful. 39 years old. She has a black lace mantilla which she is constantly putting over her head and then taking off.*
Fitty	*The maid. An attractive dizzy young girl, 18 years old. Dressed in black with a white apron and dickey.*
The Director of the Theater (Pandarsome Vigor)	*A gentleman wearing a frock coat with an elegant fur coat thrown over his shoulders. A shock of blond hair and a blond beard cut straight across the bottom. The perfect gentleman.*
Two Footmen	*In frock coats. They serve refreshing alcoholic beverages.*

Next "They"

Melchior Fondoloff	*A colonel, 55 years old. Bushy graying mustache and black, grizzled crop of hair. In Act I, in civvies. Tobacco-colored overcoat. Trousers with tiny checks. Patent*

leather shoes. White tie and shirt front. Broad nose. A good-hearted man: ready to establish a heaven on earth for absolutely everyone. In Act II, in the full-dress uniform worn by the red hussars in the President's Guard: red uniform trimmed with gold, white trousers, patent leather boots with spurs. He holds his black fur shako with a white plume in his hand. He speaks in a droning-through-mustache-and-beard tone of voice, although he has only a mustache and no beard at all. His accent indicates that he comes from the eastern part of the country, near the Russian border.

Fermen Puberstoop

A lieutenant in the gendarmerie. A pleasant boy, 28 years old. Rather delicate, fair-haired. He displays very good manners, but beneath these external forms he conceals an inflexible character and an iron will. In Act I, in civvies. In Act II, in the uniform of the soldiers in the Police Force described below.

Protruda Ballafresco

A lady 69 years old. A matronlike toad. Gray, toadlike. Dressed in décolletage, black and violet in Act II; a similar dress in Act I but without décolletage. She speaks with great authority. She is the wife of the leader of the automationist party.

Halucina Bleichertowa

A thin old lady, 66 years old. She is tall and speaks softly, but firmly. She is the President's wife. And, by his own admission, his most horrible aberration.

Solomon Pillory

A financier. A stocky bull with square shoulders. An incredible tyrant. 46 years old. Reddish-brown hair. Crewcut. Closely trimmed mustache. In Act I, a light-gray suit and loud yellow American shoes; in Act II, a frock coat.

Rosika Pillory

His wife. A brunette of the Rumanian type. A former chansoniste. 22 years old. Very pretty and attractive, a high-class doll. In Act I, she is dressed in black and red; in Act II, in a red ballgown with corresponding accessories.

Three Secretaries
a. Count Peter Snorbray   *Dark-haired, with a mustache.*
b. Baron Ruprecht   *Fair-haired, clean-shaven.*
   Baehrenklotz
c. Marquis Fibroma da   *Dark-haired, with a Vandyke beard.*
   Mijoma   *They are all refined young men to the nth degree. In Act I, dressed in striped trousers and cutaways; in Act II, in frock coats.*

Seraskier Banga Tefuan   *The founder of the new religion of Absolute Automation. A great friend of Colonel Fondoloff. In Act I and in the Half Act, dressed in wide red galligaskins and a yellow blouse tied with a red belt with tassels. He wears bast shoes. Yataghan saber in his belt. In Act II, in a frock coat. Huge head of black hair. Aquiline nose, black mustache. Thin, tall. His face is blackened by powder burns. An enemy of art.*

Soldiers in the Police Force   *Dressed like Puberstoop in Act II, that is, in black uniforms and black pants with green stripes. They wear steel helmets. There are at least eight of them. Carbines with fixed bayonets.*

Three Beautiful Ladies   *In ball gowns, for the ball at Balandash's house. The first, in a green dress. The second, in a violet-blue dress. The third, in a rose-colored dress.*

HALF ACT

The stage represents a small drawing room in Balandash's country house, about three miles from the center of the capital. In the background, a little to the right, a door hung with a blue curtain, leading to the ballroom. To the left of the door, a suite of furniture in the style of Louis XVI: table, sofa, armchairs. The colors are dark plum. On the right and the left walls there are doors also hung with blue curtains. A little to the left, closer to the audience, there is a blue sofa, the head to the left, the feet toward the audience. There is a whatnot adorned with knicknacks by the door on the left near the audience. Between it and the door, there is a window. To the right, a table and three armchairs placed at random. On the floor, a dark red and blue carpet. Pictures on the walls: straight ahead, a large painting of nude figures (a copy of some old master). To the left of it, futurist and cubist "blobs." On the left wall, a Chinese portrait and Japanese wood carvings; on the right wall, a huge cubist painting by Picasso. Evening. A pale milky light from above. One side of the curtain on the center door is drawn. Through the opening the murky depths of the hall can be seen. Mr. Balandash is sitting on the sofa. Spika sits beside him on his left, with a script in her hand. She is wearing a pearl-gray dress, with a touch of orange and yellow in it.

SPIKA *(thumbing through her part)* Has the director gone mad, or what? This makes absolutely no sense whatsoever. He says to me— listen to this, Callisto: "Neurodendrons thrust the life force through my infinity so I can watch myself play the eternal fool. Is this how you want me?" And then I say: "I know, you're only yourself as an inverse ratio which Nothingness fills with the voice of . . ." *(She reads the passages in quotation marks in a drawn-out, monotonous fashion.)*

BALANDASH I know, I know! We've already discussed it a hundred times. Pure Form in the theater! It's the latest joke the riffraff have thought up to vulgarize art for the masses; they're insatiable. But it won't ever really work, and it's bound to lead to complete decadence. A dream is a purely private affair; you can't create a collective dream on the stage. They're aware of this in the secret committee for promoting the total collapse of art—provided of course that the committee really exists, which I strongly doubt—and that's why they're backing that sort of thing so enthusiastically. If it's true, then that director of yours is nothing but a hired assassin.

SPIKA The art of the theater must not be destroyed. We—the actors— will save the theater. Our union . . .

BALANDASH (*interrupting her*) What can your union do against forces
   organized by the state or a secret committee working to undermine
   everything? To create something is difficult enough. But to organize
   its collapse—is that any easier? Our very existence is the continuous
   collapse of something or other. I'm racking my brains, but I can't
   figure out what it actually is. It's easy to rant and rave à la
   Bergson.

SPIKA You and your philosophizing. I have to memorize all this gibber-
   ish by tomorrow. Oh! how boring it all is. (*She reads in an absolutely monotonous tone of voice.*) "I know, you're only yourself as
   an inverse ratio which Nothingness fills with the voice of the phantoms of the past, murdered in the back alleys of a cadaverous,
   passionless night. Shut up! You'll come to know cruel love, full of
   inertia and ecstatic pain. [*She tempts him.*]" Oh, how am I supposed to tempt him? Show me how, Balandash. (*Mrs. Splendorek
   appears in the door leading to the ballroom.*)

BALANDASH (*turning around*) We'd better speak to Marianna about
   tomorrow's dinner. (*He rubs his hands.*) It's just great: sometimes I
   feel everything's just great, really just great. And I feel like crying,
   everything seems so full of impersonal happiness. (*To Marianna*) Sit
   down, my wonderful, my darling little cook. (*To Spika*) Why
   don't you sit in the armchair and let me enjoy the company of our
   good angel, our incomparable Mrs. Splendorek. (*Without a word
   Spika moves to the right and sits in an armchair where she watches
   the scene that is enacted between Balandash and Marianna.*)

MARIANNA (*sitting down in Spika's former place*) I'm completely
   bushed. But here's what I brought: two pounds of carrots and peas,
   one strictly fresh cucumber, and a pound of biscuits for the stuffing.
   (*Balandash tries to snuggle right into her lap.*) And what's most
   important and best of all: raisins from Mindanao, big as a new-born
   baby's fist.

BALANDASH (*rubbing up against her like a cat*) Oh, what a marvelous
   smell of quince you have, my adorable cook. To be able to look at
   all those different masterpieces indiscriminately hanging together on
   one small wall: Giorgione alongside Wang Wei, Picasso's cubist
   forms going raving mad because they're right next to Thaulow's
   naturalistic brooks and streams, and at the same time to look forward
   to one of your dinners, as I inhale the aroma of quince mingled with
   "Chevalier d'Orsay." Oh, it's really great, really great!

MARIANNA (*moving away slightly*) But you know, in town everybody's saying the committee of the secret government for combating modern art has ordered all the theaters, except the worst fleabags, to perform *commedia dell'arte* in Pure Form.

SPIKA (*appalled*) What are you talking about? *Commedia dell'arte?* How's that possible? After all, tomorrow I'm acting in a "pure nonsense" play called *The Independence of Triangles.*

BALANDASH (*without moving*) Marianna, you're going to ruin my evening for me! Remember, there's no way of salvaging a ruined evening. You'd better serve those mushrooms in cabbage kvass, and we'll make inroads into that bottle of vermouth. There are times when I don't even believe that the secret committee really exists.

SPIKA (*to Balandash*) Be quiet! (*To Marianna*) Go on. This is absolutely crucial for me. There isn't enough nonsense for them as it is. They had to dream up some new angle.

MARIANNA *Na, hören Sie mal, Frau Gräfin:* they're planning to let you loose on stage. You can all dress any way you like and be as drunk or sober as you please. And then all you have to do is make up a play and say whatever comes into your head: first somebody says one thing, then somebody else says something else, and so on, one after the other improvising the worst drivel right down to the last gasp. And that's supposed to be free Pure Form, and it's to replace the older ceremonies in honor of Cybele, Attis, and Adonis, the legends you've already written up in your book, my dear Mr. Balandash.

BALANDASH (*jumping up*) Now you've done it—you've ruined my evening, my little cook! Why don't you serve those mushrooms; they might cheer me up. She certainly doesn't give me any peace or comfort. (*He points to Spika.*)

SPIKA (*getting up*) But you don't understand at all. You men can play any parts you want. You don't have to play yourselves. But I can only act out my life within certain definite bounds; the director's got to keep me in check like a dog on a leash, and I've got to know who I'm playing, damn it all.

BALANDASH Yes, yes, you can play yourself at home, outside all the bounds, and make scenes with me or with Fitty or even Jack or Bitsie. Bitsie is still running around with a bandaged tail.

SPIKA You're horrible. You don't understand me at all as an actress. You're only an egotistical male, a rarefied aesthete in the visual arts . . .

BALANDASH No more scenes! For God's sake, no more scenes! (*To Marianna*) Serve the mushrooms, my little cook! Oh, here! (*He points to the right.*) The little table, some mushrooms, and a small bottle of vermouth. But hurry up. Perhaps I can still recapture that feeling of the infinite goodness of everything, that vision of the eternally satisfied smile of uninterrupted delight.

MARIANNA All right, all right. Just don't fight, children. (*She leaves by the door to the right.*)

SPIKA Callisto! I love you. You believe me, don't you? But sometimes I feel so frightfully sad with you, so sad that I'd like to do something dreadful or have someone torture me to death, if only I could get rid of this unbearable sadness.

BALANDASH (*clutching his head*) That's enough, please! Tonight's been our only good evening in the last few months. It was just great, just great! And of course you want to spoil it.

SPIKA You don't have any feelings at all, Balandash, with all your aesthetics of the visual arts. Sometimes you're just detestable with your eternal: "It's great, great, it's just great." (*She parodies him.*) Just think how many people there are in the world who are in pain right now. Just think how much anguish, suffering, and hideousness there is in our whole supposedly enlightened society.

BALANDASH (*in a wise tone of voice*) Any society is good only to the extent that even though you're a member of it you don't really feel that you are. It's like a woman's dress when it's well made—the woman seems naked in it. Just like your dress, like all the dresses I've designed for you: they drive the public wild. (*More and more passionately*) It's as if you're naked in them—do you understand? Naked and dressed at the same time—oh! how perverse! (*He draws nearer to her; Spika retreats behind the table, into a narrow passage between the table and the wall.*) Why are you running away, Spika my dear? My one and only . . . (*He pronounces the last words in a voice trembling with passion.*)

SPIKA (*speaks with contempt, leaning against the wall and drawing herself up*) You're nothing but a horrible sex maniac—you have no feelings at all.

BALANDASH (*without paying any attention to what she is saying*) But you'll be good to me later on, won't you, Spika? Remember, I don't want to have to force you. Be good now and don't run away from me. Tomorrow you'll be acting it out as Pure Form, but today be just a nice little homebody.

SPIKA (*drawn up, speaks with tears in her voice, controlling herself*) Be quiet! Unless you want to drive me mad. (*Frightened, Balandash runs away to the sofa and sits there, covering his face with his hands. Spika gradually goes limp as a wet noodle, takes her hand away from the table, and slowly comes out from behind it, crossing over the rear of the stage. She sits down in an armchair and nervously begins to read her part; she becomes engrossed in reading.*) "I know, you're only yourself as an inverse ratio which Nothingness fills with the voice of . . ." (*Balandash bursts out laughing for a moment and jumps up from the sofa. Marianna enters from the right, carrying a small table in her left hand, forks and a plate of mushrooms in her right hand, and a bottle of vermouth under her arm.)*

BALANDASH No, nothing can spoil my high spirits today. Everything's great, and that's that. I'm elated by the wild perfection of the entire universe. *(Marianna puts the table down, sets it, and fills the glasses.)*

SPIKA *(grimly)* Today I have an awful feeling that . . .

BALANDASH *(interrupting her)* Tell me, haven't you always had awful feelings? Did any of them ever come true? You use your awful feelings to protect yourself from misfortunes which will never happen. But in the process you're poisoning my life as well as your own.

SPIKA That's enough, oh, that's enough! Don't tempt fate! *(She clenches her fists.)*

MARIANNA It's all ready. Why don't you calm down and eat some mushrooms. And if there's anything more you want, don't be shy, just call me. *(She leaves. Spika and Balandash sit down in the armchairs with their profiles to the audience: Balandash with his right profile, Spika with her left profile. Balandash drinks and gazes with admiration at Spika.)*

SPIKA *(eating mushrooms)* Do you think it's very pleasant for me to receive anonymous letters which you must admit contain some truth, whether you want to or not. *(She takes a piece of paper out of the front of her dress and reads it.)*

> Callisto B. and Spika T.
> Shacked up in his gallery.
> Although he was an awful swine
> His dumplings simply were divine.
> She gobbles them up—one, two, three—
> Who needs the visual arts, says she.
> With all her soul she may rebel,
> But food sustains her stomach well.
> Without ever having to break her bond,
> (This Callisto couldn't stand)
> She'll escape to the world beyond.

BALANDASH *(helping himself to the mushrooms)* The idea's bad, and the execution's even worse. So I'm a pig, and you're threatening to kill yourself outright.

SPIKA *(hiding the piece of paper)* I'm not threatening. I can live alone again the way I used to. I can't stand the theater and its atmosphere of supposed "theatricality." If I wanted to, I could have thousands of lovers. But I don't want to. All I'd like is a little real feeling. You're everything I want. I love you like my own child, and in return I get only ingratitude. You have diabolical erotic thoughts without any feelings—that's hideous. You split into two utterly different people.

BALANDASH (*calmly*) Be glad it isn't three.

SPIKA It's no joking matter. The one who makes love to me is a kind of automated monster, a sex machine.

BALANDASH The rubber goods store at Piccadilly Circus, London Central. I know.

SPIKA All your ideas are disgusting, and after you make love to me I'm still so unsatisfied, and so tired, too, that I'm completely blank. And yet I love you all the same, like a poor little boy I'd like to rock to sleep and give candy to. But that's just when you start to look at your pictures and you go cold again once you've submerged yourself in their lines and colors.

BALANDASH (*who has abandoned the idea of having a serious conversation*) Don't you think it's torture for me, too? There really are two separate people inside me. It's not just something you're imagining—it's a fact. I could just as well be a pirate or even a common house thief, and not someone satiated with the beauty others create. But I don't know anything, and I'm not able to create. Believe me, I'm undergoing awful tortures. In fact, you're the only one, Spika dear, who's able to assuage a little my feeling of emptiness. Without you there are times when I'd go mad. That's why I've got to take advantage of these rare moments when I feel relaxed. Sometimes I'd like to rest in a soft case like a jewel. But what obsesses me is whether I'm not really just an ordinary piece of cut glass, and whether my case is not worth more than its content.

SPIKA (*drinking vermouth*) Stop it. You get too tangled up in your own doubts. *I* don't want an artist. I know what they're like, those creative spirits! (*She pronounces the last words with infinite contempt. Then all of a sudden, leaning her elbows on the table, she says passionately*) Oh, if only you could kiss me just once, not like an expert automaton, but like a lover. Callisto, take pity on me!

BALANDASH (*moving his hand across his forehead*) I know. I'll do all I can. After all, I love you too, Spika. But is it the fault of the picket in the fence that it's just a picket and not a live liana, devouring mango trees?

SPIKA Why can't you accept things as they are? There's so much real suffering as it is. Like my relationship to you. You don't see real suffering at all, but instead you invent your own.

BALANDASH And what about you, do you take everything as it really is?
Why don't you want to accept me for what I am, and, even worse,
for what I have been since the very beginning?

SPIKA (*getting up*) I want to! (*In despair*) I want to, but I can't. If
only I could get just a spark out of you, oh, what happiness that
would be! If only just once you'd look at me the way you sometimes look at those damned blobs. (*She points to the pictures.*)
You're in love with them. You're unfaithful to me with those
rectangular monsters, with those cubist sluts. And then all you leave
me is your body, to scorch me with its agonizing icy sensuality.
(*She comes up to him with her arms outspread and then suddenly
comes to a stop, pulling her arms back; Balandash gets up.*) Oh no! I
won't! The same thing will happen all over again. To be grasped
again by that cold, inhuman machine. (*She covers her face with her
hands.*)

BALANDASH (*he doesn't dare come up to her*) But Spika, my dear!
You've got to distinguish between Pure Form and life. They don't
have anything to do with each other. I believe in Pure Form in
painting, but I don't believe in it in the theater, any more than you
do. Nothing separates us, except these wild hallucinations of yours.
(*Heatedly, almost with real feeling*) Spika! My dearest Spika! I'm
yours and yours alone. Be good to me, don't deny me anything.

SPIKA (*uncovering her face and suddenly throwing herself toward him
with her entire body*) I love you, my poor little boy, my little son,
how I love you! I often think that if my poor Alfred were alive,
he'd be just like you, and there's nothing I wouldn't do for him.

BALANDASH (*strokes her head, speaks quite calmly again*) Oh! Now I
feel great again. Why can't you always be like this? I'll try too.

SPIKA (*pulling him onto the sofa*) Don't say a word. Or you'll spoil
everything again. I know you don't really mean the things you say,
you only do it out of a bad, vicious habit. You're essentially good!
(*They sit on the sofa: Balandash nearer, Spika farther away from the
audience. At this moment Marianna enters quickly through the door
on the right.*)

MARIANNA Children, do you know what's happened? You know the
villa next door, the one on the right, with the large garden—no one
knows who it really belongs to—well, the janitor told me just now
that somebody has moved in there. The whole house is lighted up,
and there's lots of commotion. You can see shadows moving behind
the curtains. He says They have moved in there.

BALANDASH What do you mean—They? (*They all pronounce the
word "They" in a special tone and with a special stress.*)

MARIANNA Well, you know—They, the committee of the main secret
    government. Everybody knows they're the ones who govern us, and
    not those other puppets.
BALANDASH What sort of nonsense are you talking, Marianna? I don't
    believe in any They or the Others. It's all stories the newspapers
    make up against the government. (*Becomes lost in thought*) Al-
    though sometimes I even believe in It, our ways of thinking have
    changed so much, the whole idea of what our country is has been
    turned inside out. And that's not all! The whole concept of govern-
    ment has been . . .
SPIKA I believe They exist. That's the only thing that makes life worth
    living. Didn't we believe in the Freemasons, didn't we believe in the
    Jews, spelled with a capital J? Now we believe in Them. We've got
    to have faith in something, no matter what it is.
MARIANNA Good God, Countess! What's faith got to do with it?
    There's some truth at the bottom of all those stories. We know who
    the Jews are, we know who the Union Leaders are. But who They
    really are—we don't know. A secret government—that's all we
    know, and that's enough—it's secret. They are running everything,
    but no one knows who They actually are.
BALANDASH You're mixing everything up, Marianna, you're confusing
    two different things. Either they exist or they don't—that's what it
    all boils down to. But if they do exist, then they actually have to
    exist in some real way. Please don't just make up stories as you go
    along.
MARIANNA Times are changing, times are changing—that's all there is
    to it. You won't be able to ogle your picture gallery much longer.
    I'll always be able to fix a good dinner. But are those blobs going to
    survive in the light of what's going to happen? That's the question,
    that's the question.
BALANDASH (*to Spika*) You set a fine example! Instead of her usual
    chatter, now that witch Marianna's posing questions which only
    history can answer. You're contributing to the general downfall,
    Spika. I always said so! And the reason is you let yourself be swayed
    by current fads—you're a true actress. When they fiddle, you have
    to dance, or rather, when they scribble, you have to prance.
SPIKA For heaven's sake, Callisto, stop it!
BALANDASH I won't, so help me God, I won't. I've always been true to
    myself, despite my whole split personality. You know that, don't
    you? I've always been an objective piece of equipment capable of
    appreciating not only Rembrandt and Rubens, but also Picasso and
    Matisse, and even Derain and Severin. I'm versatile. Everybody
    hangs on my walls, everybody without exception, as long as they're

everybody that's anybody. I'm the ballot box for the ages, the alpha and omega of objectivity. My theories exclude no one, not even Czyżewski. I'm like the spirit that hovered above the waters before creation when all was chaos.

SPIKA But you're not suffering. You're watching from the sidelines. You're not in the theater. If you had to . . .

BALANDASH Down with your theater. There's no Pure Form in the theater. That's for sure. You don't know all of French literature, you haven't the faintest idea about Greece: you're a perfect idiot. If you knew it all, if you could enter into every unfinished phase of the historical development of ideas and feelings, but especially feelings, above all else feelings, then you'd know what it's all about, what's really happening. But you're only a "poor benighted goat," as Miciński put it in his *Basilissa Teophan*, when Nikefor describes Basilissa herself.*

SPIKA I know. I played that part a hundred and thirty-six times in front of a bunch of morons who didn't understand a thing. It was all clear to me. I understood it perfectly when Basilissa, Mistress of the Cosmos, went off to the convent dressed like a leper after deflowering the King of Arabia and murdering the virtue of unvanquished Nikefor. You don't understand anything, my beloved aesthete, Balandash. You never look at my body the way you look at Giorgione's Venus. You're an automaton, an inhuman sex machine.

BALANDASH (*coldly*) No, I don't want to hear any more about it. At this moment, here, in my picture gallery, where there reigns the cold, still, unattainable and soundless construction of Form, you spew out all the hysterical pent-up venom of a cheap little pick-up from the tenderloin. You'd better stop, or I'll lose my self-control.

SPIKA (*getting up*) Oh, if only you *would* lose your self-control just once. To have to actually be someone in real life, different from what I am on stage, is really the worst thing that could possibly happen to me. On stage I'm really myself. Covered from head to foot with dust from rotten boards and faded rags, sweating from trying to create nonexistent emotions—that's when I'm really myself, and not when I'm with you, my beloved, my one and only, my cruel, hateful Balandash! (*She sits down again.*)

BALANDASH And yet I feel great today, in spite of being at odds with my loved one, whom I can't do without. I love you, you're the ultimate in feminine hypocrisy. I love you, you even play being Bamblioni's mistress like a ham. And he's a great theatrical genius,

* Tadeusz Miciński's *Basilissa Teophan* (1909) was staged in Poznań in the fall of 1967 as a pre-Witkiewicz play. [Translators' note]

he's the only really creative actor there is. He's banished all illusion from the stage forever. Bamblioni is a true creator. He illustrates my theory that, unlikely as it would seem, an actor or director, say one of Reinhardt's Semitic pupils, may turn out to be just as creative as that colossus who constructed those abstractions in space. (*He points to Picasso's paintings.*) Bamblioni's a true creator—but not in the world of Pure Form. The theater's not allowed in there and never will be.

SPIKA (*with dogged persistence*) I've got to get you away from those blobs, or your hideous sensuality will be the death of me if you keep on making love to me so coldly. Listen, I'll be good to you, I'll perform your wildest fantasies, if only you'll love me for one moment, if only for a second you'll be those thousands of lovers I refused for your sake.

BALANDASH (*embracing her*) Yes, I'll really make love to you. For once in my life. It's a psychic rape not yet known to the species of creatures called man. But what am I saying all these things for, since according to my own theories I can't go beyond the limits set by the very essence of the concept itself. I can't do away with duality, conceived in terms of sign and meaning, with its irreducibility to the concept—oh, those concepts!—of the semantic complex.

SPIKA (*reluctantly*) So you're planning to spoil our unique evening of love with that sterile drivel? That's what you want to do, isn't it? (*Balandash keeps on kissing her on the lips without saying a word.*)

MARIANNA (*who so far has been watching them with her arms crossed*) Oh, children, children! Maybe you'd like some pâté made out of black-haired new-born baby goats' legs? Maybe you'll come to your senses for a moment or two? If They are setting up shop here, it's curtains for you.

BALANDASH (*lets go of Spika and shouts*) Serve away, my little cook! Bring us whatever you have. Serve the pâté even if it's made out of young demons' legs, or young white dwarfs, or even marinated young green vipers. Just as long as it's quick. Today I'm really myself, and there's only one woman in my life. Oh, that's happiness! To be able to love only one, and look at all the other girls in the world as if they were so many penguins or inhabitants of another planet.

SPIKA So you really do love me?

BALANDASH But of course I do, of course I do. I've told you so a thousand times only in another way. Oh, I feel great! The hell with others' sufferings. Not every Tom, Dick, or Harry has the right to call his own sufferings the sufferings of man, and certainly not the sufferings of all humanity. Humanity doesn't even exist in the way certain gentlemen would have us believe—and certain ladies, too, in recent times! There are a number of sterile consumers of the treasures created by the unhappy slaves of certain manias, slaves who grow like mold on the species of beings unjustly called man. Oh, I feel great in my absolute barrenness, in my wonderful jewel case of absolute idleness.

SPIKA Shut up! With a barrage of words like that, you'll kill the only chance you have to really love me. (*Fitty runs in through the door to the ballroom with her hair disheveled.*)

FITTY (*out of breath, speaks in a loud whisper*) There's a gentleman in red pants waiting in the hall. He came in the front door himself. Shall I show him in? (*She hands Balandash the visiting card.*) The whole house is lighted up. The janitor says They have already moved in.

BALANDASH (*reads*) "Seraskier Banga Tefuan, Chairman of the League of Absolute Automationism." (*To Fitty*) Well, show him in, by all means, show him in. (*Fitty runs out to the right.*)

SPIKA (*drawing nearer to Balandash*) And what about our unique evening of love? (*Reproachfully*) You always have to have a third person around. You always use someone else to detach yourself from me at the very last minute, when you could forget everything.

BALANDASH (*moving her away somewhat*) There'll be time enough for all that. I won't dissipate any of my natural energy by seeing that man.

MARIANNA (*calming Spika down*) He always has time for everything. No one's ever seen him sleeping. (*With compassion*) Our poor Mr. Callisto. The greatest connoisseur of the visual arts, the great Balandash. (*Seraskier Banga Tefuan comes through the door leading to the ballroom. Spika screams and collapses on the sofa.*)

BALANDASH Now you, sir, in the crimson pants with the strange name which almost matches them—Mr. Chairman of a League I've never heard of before—with whom do I have the pleasure of speaking? I'd appreciate some clarification even if it is a bit late in the day. (*Marianna moves the table with the food to the back of the stage.*)

TEFUAN (*in a thundering voice*) I am a close friend of Colonel Melchior Fondoloff, commanding officer of the President's entire mounted guard.

BALANDASH (*ironically*) And a friend, too, of the minister of war in the Secret De Facto Government. I've heard the rumors, Mr.— (*looks at the card*) Tefuan Seraskier plus Banga. Ha! ha! ha! (*He laughs wildly and uncontrollably.*) In that government the idiot rabble dreamed up. You're a delusion as a man and a delusion as a digit in the grand total of all those who have lived, are living, or are yet to be born.

TEFUAN You've forgotten the dead martyrs. They make up a part of that total, too.

BALANDASH (*stubbornly*) Your values are all delusions, and I sneer at them. The only true value in our times is over there—(*he points to the pictures*) my pictures, the works of the great martyrs, the true martyrs to the metaphysical navel, wretched maniacs and not the victims of a few petty social ideas, whether Christian, Buddhist, or Trade Union—what's the difference? Do you understand, Mr. Tefuan?

TEFUAN Shut up, you punk! I'm an enemy of the arts and chairman of an association for combating art in all its aspects, except those which further the future development of a new and better humanity. Tomorrow we'll have your picture gallery registered and evaluated by competent authorities. I can assure you, I'll pass judgment on everything.

SPIKA (*jumping up from the sofa*) It's he! That's my husband! Tremendosa! (*To Tefuan*) Richard! Why did you have to come here and ruin the most remarkable evening of my life?

TEFUAN (*coldly*) You're mistaken. It's strange how people sometimes look like one another. I am Seraskier Banga Tefuan, and I have never been anybody else. So your husband looked like me, did he? Things like that happen, they happen all the time.

BALANDASH (*to Spika*) You're only imagining it, Spika! Calm down. Our evening isn't over yet. (*To Tefuan*) And now listen to me, you sinister intruder: You're a phantom, and I'm going to treat you like a phantom. (*He shouts.*) Get out of here, damn it, or else I'll shoot you like a dog, you and your chairmanship and your hatred of art!!! Understand? (*Spika stands as if turned to stone; a moment of silence.*)

SPIKA Well, perhaps I only imagined it. Bamblioni sometimes seemed to look like him, too. Anyhow Richard didn't have an ugly face all pockmarked with black dots like this monster.

MARIANNA (*cautioning*) This is no time to joke, Mr. Callisto.

BALANDASH (*coldly to Tefuan*) Did you understand, or didn't you?

TEFUAN But my dear sir . . .

BALANDASH No excuses. Get out, or all that'll be left of you is a corpse. (*A pause. They size up one another with glances like fighting cocks; suddenly Balandash throws himself at Tefuan and hurls him out the door to the right. A thud is heard behind the door. The blue curtain falls down. As Balandash disengages himself from its folds, he shouts*

toward the door) Joseph! Michael! Throw him down the stairs! But
be careful not to break any of his ribs. Understand? (*A great racket
is heard backstage; Balandash listens attentively, then walks over to
Spika, who looks frightened to death.*) Well, now our great night of
true love can begin. (*He takes her in his arms.*)

SPIKA (*yielding to him passively*) I like knowing you can protect
me.

MARIANNA May all the gods of eternal darkness watch over us. Be
careful about analyzing your innermost feelings, Mr. Callisto. (*She
runs out through the door leading to the ballroom. Balandash gives
Spika long, insatiable kisses.*)

ACT I

*The same room and the same arrangement of furniture as at the
beginning of the Half Act. The sun is shining through the window on
the left. The next day, three o'clock in the afternoon. Spika is sitting on
the sofa learning her part. She is wearing a cream-colored dressing
gown with yellow ribbons.*

SPIKA (*reads*) "With a bronze twist of your serpent muscles you have
pressed my soul into a medallion made of unknown matter. You are
the center of the Nothingness of the Universe, into which the urge
for existence makes its way—impersonal and barren—so as to create
something that was never meant to be. You are that thing—I love
you!" (*As she speaks the last words, Balandash enters from the left
wearing a cutaway and striped trousers.*)

BALANDASH So you really love me, Spika?

SPIKA I've been waiting for you to wake up for such a long time. Was
it really true love or only pretending that made you so tired out?
You prematurely shriveled spine of the promising young man you
used to be.

BALANDASH You're talking like a character in one of those trashy plays
written according to what they call the "pure nonsense theory."
Let's be completely frank: tell me how you really feel, Spika my
dearest.

SPIKA Always stay just the way you are now. Stop analyzing everything, stop thinking, and I'll love you forever, even after you're
dead.

BALANDASH Stop thinking, and then what happens—you're nothing but
a wild animal with automatic reflexes. For a man to stop thinking is
almost the same as to stop living. Damned women—won't They ever

understand? Why are there so many of them? Why are there red-heads and brunettes, why are there golden-blondes and ash-blondes? Since I can't love only one girl, I want millions, in all possible colors and hues. The infinity of existence which any slob of a painter can transfer into reality on some damned canvas or piece of drawing paper. (*He points to the pictures.*) How I envy artists! No doubt about it, I'm nothing but a sex fiend. And I envy them their gift of finding complete satisfaction in an accidental light-blonde or red-haired encounter in the trolley, or at some nameless street corner, without any demands, without any desire to capture the essence, without wishing for the eternal peace that comes from deep feeling, without longing for death. Oh, how I envy them, Spika!

SPIKA Don't be cruel. So for you nothing can take the place of a flock of fluttering multicolored females? With you, a woman has to be as cruel as the ruler of Hades was with Tyndall, who was covered by an avalanche of snow; she has to be deaf when you cry out for pity, the way the Fates were, when they cut the thread Ariadne gave Theseus to tie the Farnese bull.

BALANDASH That's enough! The ignorance of actresses nowadays depresses me and makes me profoundly ashamed. How many times have I tried to teach you? And I'm the creator of a new theory of Oriental myths myself! But you don't remember anything, you don't understand anything. You're a lazy good-for-nothing and a dunce. I won't teach you anything more, I won't coach you for any future roles. *Débrouillez-vous vous-même autant que vous pouvrez.* You've disgraced me long enough. Later on people are going to say I was the one who taught Spika Tremendosa. This is what happens when you try to forcibly cram knowledge into the small feminine mind, unaccustomed to intellectual work for centuries. It's pure nonsense as far as life is concerned, but not in art. To put it bluntly, nobody could live with you women. It's the result of modern social changes. Real men are bound to go under in this mess, too. Men of genius will become mere automated eunuchs of the mind. I'm not blaming you women in the least. We men are simply reaping the fruit of our own high-minded social aims.

SPIKA Remember how a petty aristocrat had his flunkies teach Voltaire a lesson during the reign of whoever was the king of France then. Given your origins and the name Balandash, do you think you'd have been who you are now? You'd be winnowing chaff in a mill by the road, and the great would tread on your subservient mug with their red heels—why, you're just something that got accidentally thrown out when all the scum was slopping about in the bucket.

BALANDASH I like the way women who live with intellectuals of some standing know how to exploit their victims. You peck our brains out and then try to impress us or, what's worse, to impress your admirers who succeed us. A woman's soul, if it can be called that, is something incredibly rotten. Lies, lies, and more lies—from the smallest to the largest issues. One gigantic falsehood, so big that the most famous literary men in the world couldn't possibly describe it. The woman problem—what a filthy mess. I'd like to spit on any artist who would devote his energies for even two seconds to this most infinitesimal of all problems.

SPIKA (*with pity*) Just imagine a connoisseur of beauty like you uttering such banalities and spouting such nonsense! Shame on you!

BALANDASH There's always the same old confusion between the two concepts of the beautiful: the realistic and the formal. No matter how banal this may seem to you, I repeat, I do not even recognize the existence of women.

SPIKA That's enough, Callisto. Don't you realize that you're going to see this in an entirely different light this evening? And I may not even have to wait for it to get dark; any time from five o'clock on, you might change your mind—if only I had the courage right now, at least in principle, to deny you what you men call feminine swinishness when you're feeling morally superior to us—for you it narrows down to one thing and one thing only.

BALANDASH But, Spika, when all is said and done, I love you. Haven't I tried to prove it to you today? Wasn't I a good lover?

SPIKA (*jumping up from the sofa*) No—you've got to be treated just like any old Tom, Dick, or Harry: a woman's got to keep her man down and give him just so much of herself, that once he's experienced wild sexual ecstasy and glutted his desires hopelessly and grimly, like serving time in prison, he'll howl in despair later on during long days and nights when he remembers the treasures he's lost. And then in impotent frenzy he'll call it swinishness and trample on his own puffed-up masculine pride. This is what you need, and this is what you'll get, and you'll go on loving me. You've had enough for now, but in a week's time you'll sing a different tune, you impotent crab insolently promising extraordinary suffering and pleasure.

BALANDASH (*anxiously*) Oh, so you really think the highest form of love is the degradation men undergo because of the charms of the flesh? But my dear: you know I'm not in need of any demonic plays to be reasonably good company for you. You have to admit yourself that the times are long since past when anything had any value.

You're an ephemeral type, and perhaps that's why I'm so deeply attached to you.

SPIKA You're backing down already. That does credit to you, as an animal fit for vivisection. I can promise you, today you'll gauge your own depths and find out what your lack of feelings has done to you. Up till now you haven't known any demonic women. You'll find out what demonism is, before the sun descends in its zodiac to the last degree of the azimuth from the side of the excessive pressures of the spectral analysis in its yearly perihelium.

BALANDASH So you've really been boning up on astronomy? Oh, how mixed up everything has become in the poor little female brain, that pitiful tool for the blind urges of nature! (*With affection*) Oh, how I pity you, Spika dear!

SPIKA (*pulling away from him*) Why don't you wait till this evening, or better still the third day after my death. I'm going to act in a *commedia dell'arte* with Bamblioni and other demons. It won't be difficult for me to incite them to a little homicide . . .

FITTY (*runs in through the door on the right*) Mr. Callisto! They're at the door. The one in the red pants is the most high and mighty; he's demanding to be let in, even over our dead bodies. Should I let them in?

BALANDASH Let them in, Fitty, let them in. Let me take care of that pack of hams once and for all. (*Fitty runs out; to Spika*) Well, this is the end. Now we're in agreement. We'll act together like one big block of porphyry, like the double gut of some monstrous organism. That's all I'm asking you. Will you promise me? Frankly speaking, I don't consider this meeting really important. They're a gang of criminals taking advantage of the reputation of the Secret De Facto Government. In any case, so be it. Right?

SPIKA We'll soon see. It'll depend on whether we've really suffered a defeat or not. I'm concerned about who's really won the battle, not about future consequences. (*Tefuan enters through the door on the right.*)

TEFUAN Yes, that's right. What's at stake, first and foremost, is whether we've won the battle; further consequences will be the business of my close friend Colonel Melchior Fondoloff. Well, what next, Mr. Balandash?

BALANDASH (*with his hands on his hips*) Well, what next, Mr. Seraskier Banga? Well, what next?

TEFUAN Just this—we're going to appraise your picture gallery right down to the last impressionist, take an inventory, and condemn it all to be destroyed. That's all for the time being. Later on we're going to make finer distinctions. You love all these new movements, I know that. But for the good of humanity, you're going to have to renounce them.

BALANDASH Humanity doesn't need lunatics to help it, Mr. Tefuan. Humanity will choose its own prophets, and not buffoons who try to utilize partisan politics and the imbecile quarrels of petty party bosses.

TEFUAN So you don't believe that the secret government exists? And yet yesterday you threw me out of your house. You'll pay for that, you'll have to pay for that. (*During this speech the Footmen lift the curtain in the doorway leading to the ballroom, and Protruda Ballafresco and Halucina Bleichertowa enter the small salon. The three secretaries follow them. Then comes Solomon Pillory with his wife on his arm; he holds her tightly under his arm as though she were a bundle. He has a chewed-on cigar butt between his teeth. Colonel Fondoloff comes after them. Simultaneously Fermen Puberstoop enters through the door on the left with two militia men. Fermen is dressed in civilian clothes.*)

FITZMORON (*shouts*) Ready arms! Aim! (*The soldiers standing in the doorway aim at Balandash.*)

BALANDASH (*looking around*) Tell those peasants to lower their guns. (*To the entire company*) Whoever you are: criminals or representatives of some legalized gang, we're going to talk *à l'aimable*. "I'm a reasonable man, and I don't like to quarrel," said Israel Hands, and with one well-aimed shot in the ear he felled O'Brien on the spot.

FONDOLOFF (*as Fermen pushes out the soldiers who are still aiming at Balandash, since Fermen never gave the command "as you were"; Fondoloff watches the scene.*) Well, of course what can you expect —desk soldiers. No idea of what military discipline is. (*To Balandash*) But to get back to business: I am Colonel Fondoloff, commander of our President's guard. (*He shakes Balandash's hand with boundless enthusiasm, then looks him directly in the eye for a moment and kisses him on both cheeks.*)

PROTRUDA (*looking through her* face-à-main *at Spika, very close up*) So this is the person, notorious for her promiscuous conduct, whose dresses I've admired so many times on the stage at the Great Theater. (*Balandash, who has been led off to the right by Fondoloff and Tefuan, confers with them just in front of the doors.*)

SPIKA (*straightens herself up angrily*) What kind of a thing is that to say? I'm not an insect under a microscope!

ROSIKA (*after a short struggle she tears herself away from under Pillory's arm and flings herself at Spika*) My dear, we're colleagues! I appeared on the stage at Osz-Buda-War in Pest. I also appeared in Tivoli and Monika-Bar in Temeszwar. I was even at Manolescu-

Tingel in Bucharest itself. I've been wanting to meet you for such a long time.

SPIKA (*turning slowly to the left*) But, my dear, I'm an actress. And that doesn't make me friends with every questionable person in all of southeast Europe.

PILLORY (*yells threateningly*) Don't insult my wife, you vile little praying mantis.

BALANDASH (*suddenly breaks off his conversation with Fondoloff, who is almost holding him in his arms, flings himself toward Spika, and gets between her and Pillory*) Spika, my dear! Have a heart! *À l'aimable!* It's really They. They actually exist, and what's even stranger, they're all here in my house, in full force, and I didn't believe in their activities or even in their existence.

SPIKA But why did you deceive me by saying they didn't exist? Now I'm even ready to believe in that diabolical *commedia dell'arte*. (*Marianna enters through the door on the right.*)

MARIANNA I told you so, I told you so. Don't say I didn't tell you! And now you'll see, children. You'll see what they'll do with your blobs, Mr. Callisto. It'll be just like what happened with the Florentine painters and the monks: they'll throw everything in a pile and burn it—that's what they're going to do.

TEFUAN Yes. It's taken a cook to call us back to our duty. Now listen to me, Mr. Balandash: our aim is to purify the visual arts as they have heretofore existed, and then to cut off all future production, since it would mean nothing but further decline and fall, a complete *dégringolade*.

FONDOLOFF That's it—it's a *dégringolade*. You've put it very nicely, my friend. Go on.

TEFUAN We're going to begin with the most magnificent private gallery and with the greatest connoisseur. For the sake of appearances, we'd like it all to be voluntary. We've got to destroy cubism while it's still in its embryonic stage, and in general all the potential forms of artistic perversion, such as clumso and neoclumsoism, selfeating-navelism, and pseudoinfantilism . . . The only things that will be allowed to remain are those which uplift the spirit, promote social discipline, and serve in utilizing national values, as a kind of compost or manure . . .

FONDOLOFF Oh, yes, yes—manure. That's wonderful! Mr. Balandash: we're going to do all this together, just the way it ought to be done. And later on we'll be the best of friends. Right? (*He laughs delightedly.*)

TEFUAN (*finishing his sentence*) . . . manure for the creation of a new, transformed, and more truly human human nature, far less akin to the animals, as it were, but instead imbued with the highest patriotic sentiments. We have no intention of abolishing private property or individual initiative and capital—these elements have proved to be essential. We want to destroy the very source of evil—and that source is Art. Art is the only stick in the spokes of the carriage wheel bearing mankind forward to complete automation. Once we have destroyed the embryo, we'll be able to sleep soundly.

FONDOLOFF Yes. We'll sleep like tops, Mr. Balandash. Without even dreaming, like supertops.

TEFUAN Let me finish, Melchior. Art is social lawlessness. It confirms and affirms and even reaffirms the value of individual experience, in other words, the personal, unpredictable, and therefore pernicious . . .

SNORBRAY Come to the point, Mr. Chairman.

PROTRUDA Yes, come to the point, you old blockhead.

TEFUAN (*bowing respectfully toward Protruda*) Certainly, Your Excellency. I count on your backing up my words against those empty manikins who are only façades.

FIBROMA Don't worry about the President, Mr. Chairman. The President's wife keeps her husband in her clutches by using the most terrible blackmail. Even all the time that I was in Australia, and it's a democratic country par excellence, I could never bring myself to do anything like that.

BAEHRENKLOTZ I couldn't ever do that either when I was a military attaché overseas in Matabelesa.

SPIKA Fine, but what about the theater? Why do you want to destroy Pure Form in painting, but keep it in the theater where it's impossible and neither Balandash nor I believe in it? Well, why?

TEFUAN (*confused*) In the theater? Do we really want to keep it there? Do we? (*Getting control of himself*) That's something entirely different. That's pure phoniness masquerading as Pure Form. That's really, really—(*he gets confused again*) that's life itself, that's life utterly deformed. First we have to destroy, then we create. The theater must also be an agent for automation. In five years' time we will convert all the theaters into orphanages for idiot foundlings.

PROTRUDA You fool, why do you answer that clown? You don't have to explain yourself. It's got to be that way, and that's that. There's no time now.

TEFUAN Well, I'll be as brief as possible. (*To Spika*) By order of the President, the performance of the play called *The Independence of Triangles* is canceled. Today you're to appear in a diabolical farce *dell'arte* without any title. Once the play is over, the title will be announced to the audience. Ha! Ha! Ha! Who could tell the title of *commedia dell'arte* in Pure Form before it ends? Ha! Ha! Ha!

HALUCINA (*severely*) Stop laughing in that childish way, you old fogey. Go on.

TEFUAN (*getting control of himself*) The President himself will be present, wearing the white uniform of the Federated Brotherhood of Footmen and Barbers. I'm trying to be as brief as possible. All beings, in other words, animals and so on, are also made up of other beings. Another step ahead in the direction of total mechanization, and now we're going to create a hyperorganism, a new society, a new Individual Being, whose multiplicity will create new fusions with other beings, perhaps from another planet . . .

FONDOLOFF (*interrupting him*) Yes. The devil only knows what will happen. Take me, I've always said that when you get right down to it no one knows anything at all.

TEFUAN If you'll allow me, my friend. In this fashion, moving toward Infinity, we come to the concept of the Supreme Being, which must be the embodiment of mechanization, the apex of automation, the most automatic of automatons. This is our deity, as real as we ourselves—lost beings that we are, not yet automated. Not Beings —but their surrogates. We're heading toward this, and nothing can stop us. That's the theory, and now the practice! (*He bows to the colonel.*)

FONDOLOFF And now we're going to examine your gallery. Mr. Balandash, and destroy every trace of the human personality and in general all individuality, whether in man or elsewhere.

BALANDASH All right. But why destroy? Can't you cut off all further creativity without destroying what's already been done?

FONDOLOFF It's not possible, my good friend, it's not possible. We've got to destroy the seeds, that's what! The seeds are the starting point. Later on you can spread around whatever manure you like. It won't grow without seeds, a barren field's a bare knee, let me tell you. Well, cheer up and show us the way. You've got a woman, you've got money—you'll find consolation.

SPIKA Maybe then you'll start to love me, Callisto. I've always detested all the recent trends in modern art.

BALANDASH (*quite stupefied*) Maybe so. Do you think so? I don't know. It seems to me that not only won't my gallery exist, but neither will I, or you, or any of our feelings. Oh, God, oh, God, when was yesterday evening? It seems to me years have passed and at least ten geological ages have rolled over me between yesterday and this unbelievable and horrible today.

PILLORY (*biting his cigar with frantic force*) That's enough! Forward march to the gallery! First the President's wife, then me. Follow me, forward march. Lead the way, connoisseur of art. (*Protruda is the first one to go to the door on the left. Balandash runs up to her, walks backward, bowing, and leads her to the door. Pillory, Halucina, and the three secretaries follow her, and Fermen takes Tefuan and Fondoloff by the arm and comes after the others. Rosika is the last to leave; at the door she turns around and stands in front of Spika, who is looking to the left. A moment of silence*)

SPIKA Are you in love with him?

ROSIKA Who? Solomon Pillory? I detest him. He's crushing me with his power, he's ruining me, he's killing me . . .

SPIKA Stop acting. You're in love with my fiancé.

ROSIKA I'm so unhappy. Don't torture me. I want to be friends with you.

SPIKA I have no intention of making friends with cabaret singers.

ROSIKA You'd better not start a fight with me. I'm bound to win. My husband is top man in the secret government. Even though he's killing me slowly, I have a certain power over him. I'm an expert at perversions in the Hungaro-Rumanian style, the abnormal, spiderlike, psychosomatic kinds. I give my titan unbearable sensual pleasures, and then for a while he becomes soft as a baby's spittle.

SPIKA And so that's how you plan to catch him? My beloved Balandash? Oh, there are no depths of depravity to which women won't sink. (*She falls onto the sofa.*)

ROSIKA (*in a conciliatory tone of voice*) You're a woman, too, aren't you? Don't you use the same techniques? (*Sneeringly*) And if you can't win him that way, it's just because you don't know how. But you'd like to learn. I can see that by the look in your eyes. (*Beseechingly*) Give him to me. No matter what you do, you won't succeed. I know everything. We have our police everywhere. Marianna tells me everything. He doesn't love you. (*She pronounces the last words coldly and cruelly, with special emphasis.*) Try to deny that! Do you dare lie to me? Remember I'm a woman just like you, only superior; I don't go looking for nonexistent feelings where there are none to be found, not even fake ones. (*Beseechingly*) No matter what you do, you can't have everything. It isn't his fault. You can't arouse in him that something that unites two souls, even when the bodies are suffering from cold, hideous desire without passion. Disembodied desire. Can you understand that? (*Threateningly*) Answer me! He'll be mine no matter what happens. I'm already the secret mistress of your leading man Bamblioni. With me he actually experiences what with you is just artificially created for him by someone else—by that eternally damned Seraskier Banga Tefuan. You know, he's the one who writes all those "pure nonsense" plays, under the pseudonyms of various useless young dilettantes; as a creative artist you find absolutely no satisfaction in those plays, and that's why you poison the only happy moments poor Balandash has.

SPIKA (*jumping up from the sofa*) I don't care who writes those plays. I love Balandash like a son. I could give up his body, I could live with him through all eternity without even touching his lips, but he has to be mine, mine! Do you understand, you whore?

ROSIKA Then do without his body for my sake. What does it matter who gets the cheap slipcover of his soul that you regard as your private property? (*She says the last words with venomous irony.*)

SPIKA Never. For you, never. For many others, for all the girls I don't know about, maybe, but not for you. You love him. Oh, I know you do—in your own way. And you'll be able to ensnare him with your tricks, so that he'll believe in love. I won't let you do that—not until after I'm dead.

ROSIKA You're forgetting that you're not on stage now. Sometimes a corpse turns up in real life, they even find them in baskets, and we read about it in the newspapers. Now mightn't a corpse just turn up in your life, you vestal burning with an impure flame?

SPIKA I suppose you're pure, with all your disgusting tricks? He taught me everything I know. I was a virgin when that damned husband of mine let me slip out of his hands. I'd never experienced sensual pleasure.

ROSIKA You're lying. You knew everything! But you can't put it into practice. We women know everything almost from the very moment we're born, only we don't know how to put it into practice. They teach us how to do that—those vile, strong, cruel, arrogant creatures! You can be sure that every hump-backed, half-witted old maid knows all about it; she just can't put it into action.

SPIKA (*frightened, aware of Rosika's overpowering strength*) Well? Tell me quickly, what do you want?

ROSIKA I want him. All of him, just as he is. I really love him. I know everything from Marianna, about how you torture him with your insatiable spiritual desires. With you he's a man split in two, a man whose existence is a lie. I'm a whole person, and in me alone he can heal his split personality.

SPIKA You mean: in a certain part of your physical being. Let's drop all this talk about the soul.

ROSIKA You're the one who started it. He's poisoned your soul with that horrible masculine split personality of his. Body and soul don't exist separately. They're one and the same thing, and it all runs together at the moment of intensest sensual pleasure.

SPIKA Oh, what a revolting pig you are, Mrs. Pillory. I've never met such a cynical woman before.

ROSIKA You're the one who's a pig, a pig in disguise. In southeastern Europe we still tell you the truth right to your face. You not only lie to him, you lie to yourself, and that's the worst thing a woman can do. You disgust me, the way a reptile does. (*Tefuan enters from the left.*)

SPIKA (*throwing herself toward him ecstatically*) How lucky that you've come, Mr. Tefuan. Change the subject, please—as the English say. You've no idea how my conversation with Mrs. Pillory has worn me out.

TEFUAN Yes, I know exactly what you mean—she's the biggest bore in our society. Rosika, sit down over there (*he points to the suite of furniture at the back of the stage*) and look at those photographs. In the meantime, I'll calm down the poor victim of our idealistic ventures, the unfortunate Balandash. (*Rosika goes obediently to the small table and looks through the albums. To Spika*) You can't imagine how that man suffers when we point out to him the necessity of destroying this or that picture in his collection. An excellent example of the collector's mania. The theory of Pure Form is only his way of trying to keep from facing the inevitable results of social progress. It's both comic and tragic at the same time.

SPIKA That's all very well and good, but what's going to happen to the theater? We haven't finished talking about that yet. Oh, sometimes you remind me so much of my husband—Richard Count Tremendosa.

TEFUAN (*with sudden resolution*) Well, if you really must know—I'll tell you the truth, Spika! I am your unhappy Richard of former days, whom you pushed down to the very bottom of where a woman can push a man. I am Count Tremendosa.

SPIKA (*she staggers and falls on the sofa, covering her face with her hands*) Richard! You won't try to take him away from me, will you? (*She uncovers her face.*) Have pity on me! He's all I have left in the world. The theater and him—I don't have anything else. You haven't changed your previous plans, have you?

TEFUAN Be quiet, don't cry. I'll explain it all to you now. (*In the meantime, Rosika jumps up from the albums.*)

ROSIKA Don't give her a divorce. She wants to take my only love away from me and destroy him: poor Callisto Balandash.

TEFUAN (*to Rosika*) What? So you're here, too, meddling in something that isn't any of your business? Why don't you go right out and rummage through garbage cans instead, you cheap slut from a third-rate chorus line!

ROSIKA Don't forget who my husband is!

TEFUAN To me, your husband is simply a financial firm. Do you understand? He's a pawn that I push about wherever I want. Do you understand? I lead him around. Like a dog on a leash, wherever I need him. Sit down. (*Rosika sits down again at the table to the left; Tefuan speaks quietly to Spika.*) I'll explain it to you in a minute. (*To Rosika*) Now, you listen to me, too, you star in the Balkan nightclub circuit. (*Rosika lifts up her head; Tefuan speaks with rapidly growing enthusiasm.*) In short, here's the situation: I've come to the conviction that theater and poetry are the arts that hold sway throughout absolutely all of existence. The qualities that go to make up the temporal dimensions of various Individual Beings may vary. Perhaps on Mars there are no colors, but there are qualities X_1. But if any given species of Being has already attained a position in the hierarchy of Beings sufficiently high so that it is capable of creating concepts and can move and act, then it doesn't matter whether there are sounds, or colors, or qualities X_1 or X_2 or even X_{n-1}, because that species of Being is still bound to have poetry utilizing the meanings of concepts, in other words, utilizing artistic elements, and it's bound to have theater, because the theater is a construction of the acts of Separate Beings capable of progressive movement in space. It's clear, then, that painting and music may not exist somewhere else, and arts X_1 and X_2 may take their place. But poetry and the theater must exist everywhere where there are Beings who have reached a certain level in the hierarchy.*

SPIKA I understand. It's a wonderful idea. I'm proud to be an actress in the theater. But in that case, why do you have to destroy the theater, Richard?

TEFUAN Since you already know what the last open secret of the secret government is—oh, there are spies everywhere, Marianna will be hanged tomorrow—I'll tell you: it's because of you and through you.

ROSIKA Because of that foolish marionnette?

TEFUAN (*to Rosika*) Shut up! (*To Spika*) It's connected with the theory of automation I created to keep myself from loving you. I'm free now, and what's more, by losing you I discovered the great truth that hyperorganisms may be possible, and that the Supreme

---

* In the event of the play's being performed, not a single word can be cut from this monologue—the author's last will. December 12, 1920 [Author's note]

Being—if it exists, and let me stress that it's impossible not to be ultimately skeptical—is an absolute automaton. Art, then, is the negation of the Supreme Being, which is simply an infinite hyperorganism.

SPIKA Fine. I understand all that even though Balandash thinks I'm an idiot. But I still don't understand why you're going to destroy me . . .

TEFUAN By destroying the theater, I'll destroy you completely. You once told me that you really exist only in two ways: in sexual ecstasy, which I never gave you, and on the stage. The former you'll never experience again, and I'll destroy the theater. You might as well know that I'm the one who wrote all those "pure nonsense" plays in order to prepare the ground for *commedia dell'arte* in Pure Form which will mean the end of the theater and of actors. We can't simply close down all those fleabags. And this isn't painting, which no one really cares about. People are too accustomed to the theater. We have to kill it slowly. A truly automated man should be in bed by nine o'clock in the evening, and not haunting various fleabags that claim to be theaters. Think of all the social energy that's wasted in such distractions. Your unions won't help you at all. We automationists are the rulers of this small globe which everyone living here thinks of as the earth, but which is only a planet subordinate to the laws of Existence. And I'm the only one who knows those laws. Those laws are known to me, and only to me! (*Silent pause*) I'm going to destroy you because I love you, and I can't live without you! Damn you! (*Exhausted, he sits down in an armchair.*)

SPIKA Oh, Callisto, why couldn't you hear this! Maybe it would have struck a spark of feeling from him—I want it so much, I desire it so hopelessly.

TEFUAN Don't even mention your desires, or I'll kill you on the spot! I want you to die a slow death and suffer horrible mental anguish: you'll lose the possibility of living emotionally on the stage. Then your energy will have no outlet, and you'll consume first Balandash, and then yourself. Do you remember your unlucky lover, Edward Nefas, who died because of you at the age of twenty-four? Do you remember what he wrote about you?

> "When she's not acting on the stage
> She's sending lovers to the grave."

ROSIKA And yet, Spika, it's we women who are responsible for everything that happens in the world. I'll be noble and forgive you for being demonic—you can't help it. We create men—they don't create us. Everything they say on that subject is a joke, a rotten joke.

SPIKA I'd rather be a hermaphrodite, I'd rather not be loved by Callisto at all, I'd even rather die than identify with other women for one single moment and become part of that miserable group of pigs. Bound together by a repulsive instinct they can't rise above, they hate and mutually fear one another. Oh, how I envy men who can be friends with each other without any feelings of superiority or inferiority.

TEFUAN *(sadly)* You're mistaken. In friendship between men, there's always both the male and the female. Even among us there are problems of gender. From a certain point of view, Fondoloff is my psychic mistress. There are no friends—this is the awful truth you learn only through the ghastly experience of living. *(The entire company, with the exception of two of the secretaries and Balandash, comes in through the door leading to the ballroom. First Protruda, then Halucina, Pillory, Fondoloff, and Snorbray.)*

FONDOLOFF *(officially)* The total destruction of all modern art was decreed only this morning, and I am happy to report that this afternoon the first step will be taken toward the realization of our truly splendid goal. Further artistic production is forbidden, on pain of death, to be preceded by two years by blinding with sulphuric acid dropped into the eyes through special tubes. As concerns musicians, in the same event both hands will be cut off and the eardrums drilled out, etcetera, likewise two years before the death sentence. We are proud to initiate this great work. The idea is spreading to all parts of the Old and the New World. Long live Automation! Hurrah! Hurrah! *(In an ordinary tone of voice)* Balandash is desperate; he's in there fighting with the secretaries, but it won't do him any good. He'll understand it all soon enough. He's a good man, down deep he's a decent sort, he's got a kind heart. *(Suddenly severe, in a military tone to Spika)* As for you, honored Artist and Leading Lady, you will lend your glory to the first neo-farce *dell'arte* which the president has discovered, or rather recreated, and whose title the audience will learn for the first time only at twelve midnight sharp. Bamblioni is playing the principal role. We've given him complete freedom. For three hours tonight state censorship will be lifted. Everything is supposed to happen spontaneously and freely. *(Spika curtsies humbly to Fondoloff.)* As for us, ladies and gentlemen, to honor this great occasion, we're going to inaugurate the evening with a gala ball in the grand ballroom. *(He points toward the door leading to the ballroom.)* And we'll dance with the firm conviction that, following our example, all of mankind will rise up purified, no longer weighted down by all that is shameful, depressing, and, so to speak, indigestible in modern art. Three cheers for Balandash, the most dedicated connoisseur we've ever had! Hurrah! Hurrah! (*Balandash runs in from the ballroom, followed by Fibroma and Baehrenklotz.*)

BALANDASH (*beside himself*) Colonel! My best Derain and my one and only Czyżewski! They've smashed all of Zamoyski and Archipenko's sculpture! In the name of God! What am I going to do? I won't be able to live through this. (*He stands helplessly.*)

SPIKA (*suddenly stands beside him and embraces him*) I'll take their place: I'll be your Picasso, Derain, and Czyżewski. I'm Spika, your Spika. Calm down, Callisto.

BALANDASH I won't, I don't want to calm down. Damn it all to hell! Oh! Why did I create the theory of Pure Form? If there isn't going to be any new art, why have a theory?

FONDOLOFF (*embracing him from the other side*) Mr. Callisto. Sure as God's in heaven, I won't be able to stand it either, in a minute we'll both be in tears. It's inevitable. You can't prevent the inevitable. I'll help you bear it. Tonight we'll inaugurate the ball, we'll have a good time, we'll drink, we'll eat, and that'll be it. To the new life, to the new world. Something always has to die, so something new can be born. (*Looks him in the face very close up*) Yoohoo, see the birdie? You're not crying any more. You're laughing already. Mr. Balandash, Mr. Balandash! (*Balandash is laughing like a child who has been forced to laugh while he's crying.*) Just look, he's laughing already. He agreed to it of his own free will—that's the important thing—he agreed to it of his own free will. All the rest will go smoothly, "*et ça ira comme un gant,*" as the French say. Eh? (*He throws his arms around Balandash and hugs him. Fibroma and Baehrenklotz go out to the left.*)

PROTRUDA That's enough show of affection.

PILLORY That's right—that's enough. Rosika! We're going! (*Rosika gets up from the table, crying.*)

ROSIKA I don't want to, I can't. After all, he's a human being. He's got his own tastes and preferences. Oh, how you're torturing him!

HALUCINA All right, all right, but no sentimentality. We're going to change and then go to the ball. We're going to forget all about this. (*Fibroma and Baehrenklotz enter through the door on the left.*) Oh! Our boys have finally finished their work. We'll see you at nine, good-bye for now. (*She goes into the ballroom, followed by the three secretaries. Pillory grabs his wife and drags her out weeping into the ballroom. Last of all, Fondoloff and Protruda follow the others.*)

TEFUAN Good-bye, until nine this evening. And I'll see you, my dear wife, at twelve. After the performance, I'll wait for you here in the drawing room so we can have a serious talk. (*Exit to the right*)

SPIKA (*drawing nearer to Balandash*) Callisto, is this a dream? We're alone at last. Oh, what I've been through, what I've been through! Did you know that that Seraskier Banga is really my husband? He's willing to grant me a divorce, but he wants to destroy me through the theater, with that diabolical *commedia dell'arte*. Did you know that he's the one who writes all those "pure nonsense" plays?

BALANDASH (*wildly*) Leave me alone. They've robbed me of everything that had any value. Tomorrow they want to burn it all officially in the presence of the legal government and the president himself. THEY want to, do you understand? They! They exist, and they're capable of anything.

SPIKA You're forgetting that they'll crush me, too. Now the theater's bound to collapse. I can see that clearly. What will become of me after tonight doesn't interest you at all!

BALANDASH You can be whatever you want. You've never understood me, and you never will. Now when it's something crucial, all she ever says is: but I, but I . . . You can go straight to hell, you and your love, your theater, your husband, and all the rest. (*He collapses on the sofa and sobs convulsively.*)

SPIKA (*stands for a moment, as though struggling with herself. She wants to go over to him, but moves away again.*) Ah, you're evil, evil to the core. Even when things are going badly for you, you push me away brutally, in a most abominable way. Now I'm going to get dressed. I have an awful feeling that something's going to happen. If you suffer from pangs of conscience later on, it won't be my fault.

BALANDASH (*without uncovering his face*) You can go wherever you want. Just leave me alone for a little while.

SPIKA I'm going to change, and then I'm going to the theater. Remember what I've said, or later on you may suffer from pangs of conscience, Callisto. (*She goes slowly toward the door on the left. At the door she turns around and looks at him, then she leaves suddenly. Balandash remains lying down without moving, his face buried in his hands.*)

ACT II

The same room. Dim red light from above. The same lamp covered all around with a red scarf. Half of the curtain on the door leading to the ballroom is drawn. A small portion of the ballroom can be seen flooded with bright light. Dancing couples move through this small area. Music plays quietly, but uninterruptedly until further notice; the following are heard: cakewalks, maxixes, two- and one-steps, très moutarde, homobocco, "The Farewell" of Robert Lee, and other rousing tunes. It is rather dark in the drawing room, in contrast to the lighting in the ballroom. The futuristic paintings have been taken down, except for the huge Picasso which has been forgotten and still hangs on the right. Balandash runs in from the left, dressed in a frock coat, and comes to a halt in the middle of the drawing room, wringing his hands.

BALANDASH (*to himself*) That damn telephone! It would have to stop working just now. It's already after twelve, and she's not here. Thundering herds of buffalo! I didn't even say good-bye to her.

PROTRUDA (*enters from the ballroom*) Well, what's going on here, Balandash: Why are you baring your soul here in the middle of the drawing room?

BALANDASH I'm in a dreadful state about Spika, damn it! She left without even saying good-bye. We even quarreled a little.

PROTRUDA Aha—you're bothered by pangs of conscience. How repulsive the younger generation is today. Everybody can have pangs of conscience—they can afford to now. But to act so they won't have them—that they can't do. You're all weak, weak trash. Our age can't even produce high-class scum. (*Snorbray enters from the ballroom; Balandash runs off to the right.*)

SNORBRAY Mrs. Bleichertowa's dancing so hard I'm sure she's going to drop dead. The poor president. She's his only support and creates his most sinister plots. (*Fitty runs in.*)

FITTY Mrs. Halucina is acting like a crazy woman! From the back you could take her for a young girl, if it weren't for her white hair.

PROTRUDA Why are you all paying attention to her while I'm here? Aren't I interesting enough for you? Have I lost all my charm just because that old bat has drunk too much champagne and cognac?

BAEHRENKLOTZ (*runs in*) What madness! Halucina really has gone crazy!

FIBROMA (*to Protruda*) But Your Excellency! You know that you're the real center around which our lives revolve. You have almost as much vitality as Catherine the Great. Only times have changed. There aren't any suitable partners for you.

BAEHRENKLOTZ We're always prepared for anything. I always have several apotransformine pills with me. After all, you're a baroness, and you come from a princely line. I'll bet you were a wonderful girl in your day.

PROTRUDA You all think I'm old, do you? Even now I have more spirit than any of your girls. Take that famous Tremendosa, for instance. She's an alley cat, not a woman.

BALANDASH (*runs in, dragging Marianna after him*) Come here, my little cook! I know you're a wretched little spy. Still it doesn't really matter. Come and cheer me up.

MARIANNA Not me, sir. I serve whoever is in power, nothing more. I'm more devoted to the state than to the Balandash family. Nothing more.

PROTRUDA That's the way it should be. Down with the unions. Without the state, humanity can't be properly automated. (*The Footmen serve drinks.*) Isn't that right, gentlemen? (*Everybody drinks.*)

THE SECRETARIES Yes, of course. Certainly. Naturally. It couldn't be otherwise. That's obvious. (*They flock around Protruda and go into the ballroom. The Footmen follow them.*)

BALANDASH What could possibly be the matter with her? Oh! my nerves are on edge. Marianna, tell me what could have happened to the mistress?

MARIANNA She'll come back safe and sound, and you'll still be able to quarrel to your heart's content. It's clear as daylight; they've been cooking up a *commedia dell'arte,* and it's lasted a little longer than usual.

FONDOLOFF (*comes out of the ballroom in full uniform; shako under his arm; cavalry saber at his side*) I've heard you're worried about the countess. Nonsense! She'll come back alive, safe and sound, roaring in here like a steam rhinoceros! * You two will still lead a full life together. Nothing's ever lost. Even suffering and painful, delirious raving, looked at from the right perspective, have some meaning—a secret one, certainly, I agree with you there, but in any event a meaning. Did you know I'm a philosopher, too—after a fashion—a self-taught one? There's nothing that doesn't make some sense, even those plays and poems that our chairman writes in order to wipe out the theater and amateur theatricals. Take it from me, Mr. Callisto, even if you invent things like that, it makes sense, too: your own made-up meaning, and not someone else's. There you have it! Right, Callisto! Let's be brothers. Let's call each other by our first names without any more ado. (*Marianna stands next to them adjusting her scarf.*)

BALANDASH I appreciate that, Colonel. Melchior? Is that right? (*Ges-*

* We call the reader's attention to the fact that the concept of the steam animal in general (not only the horse) and of actual individuals (for example, the steam Napoleon) is our personal invention, dating back to the years 1906–7. [Author's note]

ture of confirmation from Fondoloff) Melchior! For pity's sake, why hasn't she come back? I'll go out of my mind! I'm suffering from a rash of horrible guilt feelings; I won't be able to stand it much longer.

FONDOLOFF If you're suffering from a rash of guilt feelings, why don't you go to a dermatologist: a little brownish ointment, and you'll be cured in a week's time. Now when it comes to a spiritual rash, simply clear your throat and spit it out, that's all there is to it! You look like a little boy who's lost his mama. Come now, Callisto! Chin up! The main thing is not to lose your nerve—not to "chicken out," as they say in our regiment. I'm going to dance a little; I haven't danced yet this evening. And you might like to drink a little more —that's right. (*He heads toward the ballroom; suddenly he notices the Picasso on the right wall.*) What's that? Picasso? How did they ever miss that? (*Reproachfully to Balandash*) Oh, that wasn't fair, Callisto. (*Turning around*) No, I won't be able to stand it. I'll have to slash it right through with my saber. Instead of smashing a mirror. That's what they're always doing in our regiment. It's just like one of those announcements in the newspaper: instead of a funeral wreath on the grave of shop clerk so-and-so, buy milk for his idiot son. (*He pulls his saber out of its sheath with a swish and strikes it against the picture with all his strength: the painting breaks into small fragments.*) It's smashed into a hundred pieces. (*He quickly unbuckles his sword belt and throws it on the sofa.*) Don't be offended, Callisto. We military men—we're frank and open. And that's why you can trust us as you would your own wife. Ha! ha! ha! (*He leaves.*)

BALANDASH (*who has been standing as if petrified, shouts in wild despair*) My last Picasso! I thought I could at least save that one from those barbarians!

MARIANNA (*who has not flinched during the last scene*) Oh pooh! One blob more or less. Calm down, Mr. Callisto. True masterpieces are the only ones worth keeping, After all, sir, you don't know for sure if all of that wasn't just a joke.

BALANDASH (*suddenly*) Oh! Picasso can go to hell, if only she'd come back. And on top of all my other frustrations and awful forebodings, as the crowning blow, now I want a dark woman. Dark as pitch, her eyes shining with dark Oriental falsehood. Where have I seen her before? Did I dream there was such a woman?

MARIANNA In there, in the ballroom, there's someone like that. The wife of Mr. Pillory, the secret minister of finance.

BALANDASH My dear cook! I'm going to ask you one last favor. Go into the ballroom and ask that woman to come here—discreetly, so her husband won't see. Tell her Mr. Balandash has something very important to tell her.

MARIANNA All right, I'll go. I've always brought you girls—I'll go even now. But there's going to be trouble, yes, there's going to be trouble. (*She goes out to the right. Balandash falls onto the sofa and covers his face with his hands; the music and dancing reach a climax.*)

TEFUAN (*enters from the ballroom*) Well, what's this? You still can't snap out of that depression over losing your blobs, can you? Surely you're intelligent enough to realize how important my theories are? If you'd understood it, you'd have stopped worrying a long time ago, and if you haven't, then, in my opinion, you're a complete moron.

BALANDASH (*getting up*) Oh, I have much worse worries. Your wife, or rather my fiancée, hasn't come back. I'm as anxious as a weasel in a cage. I have sinister forebodings. And on top of it all, I've developed a craving for a really dark woman, I desire her so madly I could gnaw on old tree trunks. I'm simply howling on the inside from lust. You know those sudden, violent urges, don't you? No one knows where they come from, but all of a sudden, man, a reasonable creature, becomes the tool of a spit-out peach stone, of a lever without any hand guiding it, of a hunk of dried-out meat, of some old creampuff or other. How do I know of what? Oh, it's horrible!

TEFUAN There's nothing horrible about it. Don't ramble on so. Things like that happen all the time and there's no need to blow them up to metaphysical dimensions. You want a dark woman—all right, have a dark woman. What's stopping you? Why can't you allow yourself a little pleasure? Maybe you're going through the agony all collectors suffer? Know what that's like? A dozen Chinese cups—there goes one—bang! There's the saucer all by itself, here are the pieces on the floor, and endless heartache. You've got to find compensation in another dimension. I know. I once collected women, the way you collected paintings—when I was a young man, of course. If some specimen escaped me—I was in despair. Not any more, though. I know all of these things *au fond*. No one's going to take me in. You remember in Shakespeare what that foul traitor Jack Cade says: "But then are we in order when we are most out of order." *

BALANDASH You're consoling me. I'm starting to feel all right again, almost, but not quite. Oh, I'm so consumed with anxiety and guilt feelings about my fiancée! And now I want a dark woman, dark as velvet. I tell you: my brain is pouring out like red-hot lava. But at least you saved me from having to analyze myself. Sometimes a

---

* *II Henry VI*, IV. ii. 199–200. [Translators' note]

good quotation from one of the old boys means much more than all our present experience. That's what the old masters are for, so we can quote them—at just the right moment. We're no longer capable of experiencing anything for ourselves. (*Mrs. Pillory enters from the ballroom. She speaks with an effort and with many pauses.*)

ROSIKA You—wanted to speak to me—Mr. Callisto?

BALANDASH Yes. That's right, or rather I didn't, but some demon inside me did—someone I don't know. Do you understand?

TEFUAN I don't want to be indiscreet. I'm leaving. I understand these matters. Oh, how well I understand them. (*He goes back to the ballroom.*)

ROSIKA Please go ahead. I understand perfectly.

BALANDASH I'm undergoing a crisis. I'm up to my neck in contradictions. But it seems to me you're the only one—please don't think I've gone mad, but I really don't want to lie. But doesn't love come down to just this: a couple of animals lusting for each other to the point of madness?

ROSIKA (*coming up to him*) Don't say anything more. I know. There are only moments of desire and of sudden unexpected satiation. Sometimes it happens (*in a voice trembling with lust*), but not very often—in a streetcar—in a train or hotel, two people come together who have to, do you understand?—who have to belong to each other, who have to be one another's mutual property—I don't like that word "ego"—it's both too big and too small. But you understand me, don't you? That's all there is, there's nothing else, and happiness, infinite happiness. I'm just a woman, I'm yours . . .

BALANDASH (*throwing himself toward her*) That's right, that's right! I said the same thing to myself, word for word. Am I dreaming all this? I love you, I love you! (*He reflects upon all this for the last time.*) What I'm saying is the absolute truth: street, streetcar, hotel —it doesn't matter where. That's all it is, and nothing more. Not those long, painful romances, those endless complications! And now, I have a craving for a woman dark as Nothingness!

ROSIKA (*embracing him*) You have me. I'm dark, I belong to no one. I don't exist. I'm a phantom whose body is on fire. Don't say anything more. Take me away from here. I'm yours. There's nothing in the world but you. (*Balandash drags her off to the left where they disappear through the doorway leading to the gallery.*)

TEFUAN (*comes out of the ballroom and looks around the room; to himself*) Everything's going nicely—that pair of sexual degenerates has disappeared. (*To those in the ballroom*) Please, you may come in now. We can talk quite freely. (*Enter Protruda, Halucina, and Fondoloff.*) And now we can talk openly, to our heart's content—

we, old men standing on the edge of the grave, and you, mummies
burnt out with the heat of the past.

PROTRUDA (*sitting on the sofa*) Well, I'll put it quite frankly: we've
had enough of this secret power. I'd like to reign on a real throne,
and not on some chair in the vestibule of the person everyone thinks
is the great man. I want open power.

FONDOLOFF Your Excellency, that will come, that has to come. Just be
patient. You women never know how to be patient.

TEFUAN It just amuses me. I go into a restaurant—everybody knows me
as just Tefuan, and who the hell knows who he is? And I think to
myself: just wait, you scum, you don't know that I'm the one who's
running your lives, that I'm the one who's automating you without
your even knowing it, and that if someday you'll achieve happiness
by identifying with the Supreme Being—I'm the one who'll do it for
you, I alone and no one else. I beg your pardon, I appreciate the
value of your contribution, ladies and gentlemen, but when all is said
and done the idea is mine.

HALUCINA But say you dropped dead today, Count? All your work
would go to waste.

FONDOLOFF Posthumous fame instead! We great men, we creators of
new things, only really live after death. Artists or men of action: it's
the same for all of us.

HALUCINA We can't accept that; we're women. And, what's more,
older women. We won't be around much longer, and we want
everything put right in front of us, on a platter. Give us everything
you've got right away or else go to hell. Apropos: after the last
one-step, Fibroma and I went into one of the rooms to cool off a bit,
and we almost stepped on a nest of madly writhing snakes that were
all knotted up together. Our host and someone else—hmm—still,
youth is a beautiful thing.

FONDOLOFF (*out-talking her*) Shame on you! Stop talking that way! I
understand what you want, and you'll even get that, my fine ladies.
But not today. Thank God, if not today, at least tomorrow everything will be cleared up. I'm a specialist in military revolutions,
"*pronunciamentos*," as they're called in South America. If we can't
get anywhere by peaceful means, I'll call up the army and then we'll
settle everything once and for all.

TEFUAN Don't do it yet, Melchior. *Pronunciamentos* don't produce
lasting effects. As for me, I start from the kernel itself, destroy it,
and then I work my way up to the surface; there's nothing under it
any more, the kernel's gone, and I reign and reign without any
hindrance or check. I've achieved this in the theater already. Now I
can devote myself entirely to you, since I'll have more time once

commedia dell'arte has caught on in the theater as Pure Form. There'll be no more need for me to write all those plays and go on making up "pure nonsense," if that's what it is.

FITTY (*runs in from the right*) Help! They've brought my mistress home dead. (*She jumps up and down for a moment and then runs out.*)

FONDOLOFF That's a bolt from the blue! Our poor friend Callisto will be very unhappy. That Spika was such a nice girl. (*They all stand petrified, as a strange thundering voice is heard from the ballroom.*)

VIGOR'S VOICE Stop the dancing. Stop the music. There's a corpse in the house. (*The director, Pandarsome Vigor, enters from the ballroom, wearing a fur coat draped over his shoulders on top of his frock coat; Balandash bursts in from the door on the left and hurls himself toward the door on the right, as though he's gone out of his mind; the whole company gathers by the door leading to the salon; the music stops.*)

VIGOR Ladies and gentlemen, a tragedy has occurred. I've brought my prima donna, Countess Spika Tremendosa, here—dead. We're all friends here, and I can speak frankly. Although I am not one of you (*he bows*), I am with you. (*Slowly and emphatically*) Bamblioni killed his leading lady in a fit of madness by plunging her own knife into her heart; this happened in connection with certain intrigues which affect you all most intimately. The finance minister's wife isn't entirely guiltless in all this, but let's not talk about that. I know the title of the play now. It was a diabolical superfarce *dell'arte;* it's called—it's escaped me for the moment—aha: *Metaphysics of a Two-headed Calf.* The audience doesn't know anything about the murder. They think it was part of the play. We'll have to make use of that. I'm afraid there may be a revolution; the guests at my palace of art have scattered all over the city in a state of wild, simply hysterical excitement. The President's suffered a slight stroke, but we saved him. He's now at the Footmen and Barbers' Club.

TEFUAN Poor Spika. I wanted her to suffer a little longer. Yes, we have to conceal what's happened. Our whole idea will collapse if the wretched mob find out that there are already corpses. Later on, after some time has elapsed, they can kill each other to their hearts' content, but right now at the start, it might produce a reaction and bring about a rebirth of the old, antisocial theater.

FONDOLOFF (*in a voice as though he has made a great discovery*) Listen! Listen! We'll say that Balandash is guilty. He killed the Countess, just a few minutes ago, right here. It's the Mexican method of putting the guilt on the innocent, who are worthless anyway. It's like performing physiological experiments on those condemned to death. In any case, Balandash reached the end of his tether today. For him, it doesn't matter, but for us—no, it's not the same. And so we're sacrificing him. Sacrifice a part to save the whole, as Napoleon I used to say. Fermen! Lieutenant Puberstoop! From this moment on, you are on duty. Get your men ready. (*Fermen puts on his cap and salutes.*)

VIGOR You can do whatever you want. I've got to have clean hands to show the official government. The rest is no concern of mine. (*Two Footmen carry in Spika's body through the half-opened door on the right. She is dressed as a sylph—a green dress, blue wings, green slippers with turned-up toes. She is wearing thick make-up—extra thick make-up—which can be seen by the audience. She is incredibly beautiful and looks as though she were sleeping. Fondoloff throws his saber off the sofa, and he and Tefuan move the sofa so it stands sideways with its feet toward the audience, just the opposite of the way it was before. They take Spika out of the Footmen's hands and put her down so that she can be seen from the left side, with her face toward the audience. Her head hangs down in the same direction as her left hand, which touches the floor. Balandash, supported by Fitty and Marianna, walks behind Spika's body.*)

BALANDASH It was I, it was I who killed her. No one else is guilty. I threw her out of my house like a poor homeless dog. (*He falls on his knees by the sofa, kissing Spika's left hand almost at the level of the floor.*)

FONDOLOFF You see? Balandash is decent—he acknowledges his guilt.

BALANDASH (*getting up violently*) I confess to what I did. I don't admit to the physical murder. (*He falls down again.*) Spika, Spika dear, you're the only one I've ever loved in my whole life, in all my miserable, uncreative life; I wanted to create, but instead I collected what others created. Oh, my God! I can't bear it: a collector and a theorist. Oh! what a come-down! I'll die, killed by my own poison. I was unfaithful to you at the very moment when you were dying, murdered by that ham Bamblioni. I won't be able to bear it, I'll die here and now.

FONDOLOFF Instead of dying, just confess it was you who killed her. It doesn't matter to you, but it does to us. It certainly does.

BALANDASH (*who has straightened himself up while still kneeling*) All right. I confess. I was the one who killed Miss Tremendosa. So be it. (*He falls on his face again.*)

TEFUAN (*falling on his knees on the other side of the sofa*) And yet she was a demon, that Spika. Ladies and gentlemen, I was her husband —I know all about her. She was and still is a demon. Even now that she's dead, she's a demon. (*He falls upon her body and kisses her feet, her beautiful feet in the green slippers with turned-up toes. Meanwhile, Rosika rushes in through the door on the left, hair disheveled, like a charged-up hyena.*)

ROSIKA I won't let him go. He belongs to me. He gave himself to me, to me alone, when he needed to express his most basic desires. What he felt toward me—that's love. Everything else is a swindle. If you're going to put him in prison—I'll go with him. I want to be locked up in the same cell with him. (*The three ladies laugh.*)

PILLORY My wife! Oh, this is going too far. Perhaps I drank too much champagne today? (*In a terrible voice*) Rosika! Come to your senses!

ROSIKA I want to be locked up in the same cell with him. (*Silence*)

FONDOLOFF If they're going to lock all us criminals up with women like that—wait a minute, what am I saying? But it doesn't really matter —what I wanted to say was that I'd like to spend the rest of my life there.

PILLORY Rosika! I'm telling you for the last time: come to your senses!

BALANDASH (*rising*) I don't want her. Take your wife, Mr. Pillory. It was only a whim. I suddenly had a craving for a dark woman—that's all. I seduced your wife, well, so what? If I hadn't, somebody else would have. Doesn't it all come out the same?

ROSIKA Oh, the cheap coward! Just like a man! He seduced me, and now he doesn't want to have anything to do with me.

BALANDASH (*coldly*) What's happened to your theory of the casual life? A streetcar, a hotel, a train, a boat—it was all supposed to come out the same. I'm finished as a man. The only thing left for me is physical pain. I'm completely unfit for moral suffering or sensual pleasure. I loved her, and I still love her and only her. (*He points to Spika.*)

TEFUAN (*gets up and runs over to him*) You, too? And I thought you were an overrefined aesthete? We're brothers. I swear I'll be your friend from now on. I also loved her and only her. (*He hugs him and lifts him up off the ground.*)

ROSIKA Lock me up in the same cell with him, with that monster, Balandash. I want to die from sensual pleasure, I don't want anything else. He'll die, too—I'll make him gasp contentedly there on the prison mattress! (*Pillory throws himself at her and drags her off to the ballroom.*)

BALANDASH (*tearing himself away from Tefuan's embraces*) I don't want any kind of love or even friendship. I'm completely alone, and I don't know, first of all, who I am, second, why I exist, third . . . Oh, there's no third point. I just imagined there was. Who and why —these are the two questions confronting man! How! There's one more question: how? Here's my answer to that question: if there aren't any answers to the first two, what does it matter about how? Do you have any idea what these words mean, you slaves of a society which is nothing but a bunch of gangsters, you rapists in broad daylight, you parasites? Oh! There are so many useless beings! I am one of them, and it's quite enough for me: artists lie, men of action lie. I'm the only one that really exists. I belong to the third category of beings, those who exist and at the same time do not exist. You can do whatever you want with me. I, Callisto Balandash, killed that woman. (*He points to Spika.*) Not any old Bamblioni. Let's forget about that despicable ham! It was I who killed her! I did! Why? I don't know! How did I do it, you ask? My ghost did it, embodied in a whole infernal chain of cause and effect, or rather functional relationships. I am the murderer!

PROTRUDA You've said quite enough, young man. We don't need to hear any more. Calm down and go straight to prison.

BALANDASH (*suddenly quite calm*) All right, all right. I don't hope for anything else. I don't even hope for death, only life imprisonment, only a prison cell. I want to be alone. I don't want to be a member of any society or any gang of thieves; I don't even want to be an artist, which I longed to be throughout all of my miserable life. I want to be myself. That's all.

FONDOLOFF It all fits together very nicely! We've killed several birds with one stone. Lieutenant Puberstoop! (*Fermen stands at attention in front of him.*) Guard all the exits and other ways out.

TEFUAN That's right, that's right. Guard all the ways out. I beg you! Don't let me go mad today. I'm still in control of myself, but I can't guarantee what will happen the next minute. (*Fondoloff takes hold of him. Fermen blows his whistle. Soldiers appear at all the entrances.*)

FERMEN Take Mr. Balandash to the dungeons of the secret government. Keep in step! Forward, march! (*The soldiers surround Balandash and lead him into the ballroom, followed by Fermen, and then by the two matrons, the three young women, and the secretaries.*)

FONDOLOFF (*to Tefuan, as he fastens on his saber*) Well, what next, my friend? Life is hard, but with the help of the Black One, we'll bear it somehow.

TEFUAN (*staggering as Fondoloff holds him*) It was I who killed her. I did. A little earlier, three centuries ago, I'd have done it differently, all by myself, with my own stiletto or with poison, and I'd have no pangs of conscience. Today I'm doing it like a coward, using that loathsome ham actor, after having previously written two dozen plays that make no sense whatsoever. Oh, how disgraceful! Oh, how shameful! I did it all for her. (*Points to Spika*) Now my life has no meaning, like the plays I wrote.

FONDOLOFF Cheer up, my friend! Times have changed, and people, too. Besides, there are no longer any people in this world. You know that yourself, don't you?

TEFUAN Yes, I know it, I know it. Our god is an automaton. God used to be an autocratic, spiteful, pleasure-loving tyrant who loved life, our human life. Today no one loves it. No one loves life, not even the gods. That's how it is. You see, I don't believe in anything myself—not even in automationism. Damn it!—I don't believe in anything, and that's that. I loved only her, and now a ham actor has killed her for that stupid aesthete! By his prayers to Baphomet, one of them has obtained a pleasant old age for the other. Ah! They're all black—heart and soul! Life doesn't exist! There's nothing! Do you understand that, Melchior?

FONDOLOFF (*leading him toward the ballroom*) Nothing exists, but we remain. We've got to go on playing the secret government and the rest of our comedy to the very end. Just as you have to drink all night long when you're invited out to a party whether you want to or not, so we've got to play out our secret government and all that. Maybe we'll make a small *pronunciamento;* maybe life will take on some meaning. Richard! Our little revolution is hanging by just a hair. We'll come to the surface yet! We'll turn life into *commedia dell'arte* in Pure Form, pure as crystal. (*Exit They*)

MARIANNA (*kneeling at Spika's feet, from the left side*) Our poor mistress. Where is her soul, if there is no other world? Where is she thinking about the menu for her next dinner or her new clothes now? She doesn't exist, she doesn't exist at all. They've taken the other world away from us, and they haven't put a new one in its place.

FITTY (*kneeling, from the right side*) There is no other world. I don't believe in anything myself. And yet it's so hard to live, so terribly hard. (*The Footmen stand stiffly by the door leading into the ballroom.*)

FONDOLOFF (*offstage*) Michael! Joseph! Get our fur coats, you striped devils! (*The Footmen throw themselves toward the door.*)

CURTAIN

End of the second and last act

May 3, 1920

The Shoemakers

INTRODUCTION

AT THE END of *The Shoemakers* (*Szewcy*, 1931–34) we hear the frightful footsteps of someone walking with lead soles on his shoes; the Duchess's footman comes running in terrified, announcing that a super-revolutionary Hyperworkoid is coming, brandishing a huge bomb with which he's going to blow up everyone. The dreadful Hyperworkoid appears and throws his bomb, causing all the others to fling themselves to the ground in terror—but nothing happens. The Hyperworkoid then unscrews the top of the bomb and pours himself a cup of coffee. The bomb is a thermos, so that he can have a coffee break and then go on working harder. Only in wartime does it turn into a bomb for use against the enemy.

The Hyperworkoid is a new breed: the live, mechanical corpse in the service of the state. Unlike the old master shoemaker Sajetan, who stands for the revolutionary workers of the world who will unite and overthrow the state and abolish nationalism and imperialistic wars, the Hyperworkoid is a dud, his bomb is a dud. There will be no more revolution, no further explosion. Instead of the sense of release that even Witkiewicz' most disastrous and destructive denouements produced in the early plays, in *The Shoemakers*, written some ten years later, we are confronted with frustration, boredom, and despair that has no outlet.

Both in its vision and technique, *The Shoemakers* is a departure from Witkiewicz' earlier dramas. He has abandoned Pure Form and the distance that went with it. *The Shoemakers* has a different relation to life than *The Water Hen* does; it reflects the political and social reality of its time and the views of its author more directly—sometimes in undigested form. We recognize the expiration of a rotten capitalist system, the conflict of fascism with a peasant brand of socialism, and the rise of a totalitarian state, all in Polish terms and against a recognizably Polish background. At the same time, as in his novels, Witkiewicz pours into the play an astonishing variety of digressions, polemics, philosophical discussions, personal invective, gags, literary criticism, references to his own friends, invented obscenities, and ironic parodies.

The Shoemakers is a monstrous, frightening play—a grotesque vision of Europe at the time of Hitler, heading toward the Second World War, and a black prophecy about the world of the future. At times it seems less a play than the chaotic outpourings of a man's obsessions and sense of horror in the face of a ghastly world. However, it is far less a portrayal of Witkiewicz' own life than many of the Pure Form plays with artist-heroes. *The Shoemakers* records the historical experiences of a country and an epoch; as such, it is an incredible document, infinitely richer in historic insight and depth than any realistic play could ever be.

As a play for the stage, the long speeches and interminable discussions may sometimes make *The Shoemakers* appear undramatic in the reading. In the theater, however, its intense theatricality comes to life. The Student Theater of Wrocław achieved a stunning success with *The Shoemakers* at the International Student Theater Festival in Warsaw in 1965 and revealed the tremendous dramatic power behind the words. Sexual and political tensions mount within a closed circle of characters constantly together in something approximating a cage until the pressure becomes unbearable.

Here Witkiewicz pushes to extremes his technique of alternating philosophical discussion and violent action. The characters wait endlessly for something to happen—for work to stop or to start, for a revolution to take place, for a life of anguish to come to an end. When they can stand it no longer, there is an outburst of violence. Sajetan suddenly "belts the Duchess one in the mouth"; she falls to her knees, her face smeared with blood. Violence is a consequence of deep antagonisms and endlessly frustrating verbal attempts to find solutions to the dilemma of existence. Metaphysical speculations lead inevitably to reaching for one's revolver. The endless flow of words does not change anything or satisfy anyone; suddenly it is interrupted by blows and gunfire. Things break down and blow up; fights and corpses are corollaries of feverish talk.

The sign with BOREDOM written on it is not only a piece of characteristic self-irony on the author's part; it is symptomatic of the self-defeating stagnation of words and concepts which invites violent counteraction. "Vigilant Youth," the secret government, and the Shoemakers' rebellion are all attempts to substitute action for words. The welter of words from old liberal days proves futile; violent techniques and tough guys will liquidate talk and establish a ruthless new order. Anger and frustration give *The Shoemakers* a powerful dramatic subtext, lending excitement to what may seem at first to be the most irrelevant and abstruse theorizing and mental gymnastics. No matter what is said, everyone wants to rape the Duchess.

The Shoemakers is also a play that assaults the spectator with a barrage of sense impressions extremely rich, dense, and unpleasant. In Act I, the constant hammering creates an oppressive rhythm, punctuated by Sajetan's "heying," Scurvy's "hee-heeing," and the Duchess's "tch-tching." Visually the Duchess's gray suit and yellow flowers and Scurvy's top hat, umbrella, and cutaway contrast with the Shoemakers' leather aprons. The fox terrier pulls on the leash and sniffs at Scurvy obscenely. The salty, visceral language creates a series of repulsive images of smell and touch.

The end of the last act is a perfect illustration of the theater Artaud would propose "in which violent physical images crush and hypnotize the sensibility of the spectator seized by the theater as by a whirlwind of higher forces." [1] The Duchess, dressed in a short green petticoat with red drawers, green bat wings, décolletage to the navel, and plumed three-cornered hat, dances to the tango coming from the Savoy Hotel in London, as Scurvy in a dog's skin with a pink woolen cap and bell howls and jerks on the chain that holds him to a dead stump, all the time smoking cigarettes. The Duchess rushes up onto a pedestal and spreads her bat wings, fireworks go off, and a bird cage is lowered over her, as the Apprentices, Pugnatsy Jawbloatski, and the dying Sajetan all crawl on their bellies toward her. Scurvy goes mad, Sajetan stammers incoherently, and the Duchess raves—it is a terrifying orgy of lust, madness, and cruelty, the final hysterical end of Western civilization.

Wyspiański's Mulch plays an important part in this apocalypse, and a word should be said about Wyspiański, whose play *The Wedding* is the basis for an extended parody in Act III of *The Shoemakers*. Less international and universal than Witkiewicz' other plays, *The Shoemakers* is full of satiric and ironic allusions to Polish culture and literature which would immediately strike a responsive chord in a Polish audience, but which would have to be cut or adapted for performance outside Poland. Witkiewicz' attitude toward his country's romantic and patriotic literary folklore is somewhat in the spirit of Joyce's treatment of the Irish Revival in *Ulysses*, but more violent and bitter. Like Joyce and Eliot, Witkiewicz uses national myths and symbols ironically to expose the degradation and emptiness of life in the twentieth century.

Stanisław Wyspiański (1869–1907), who, like Witkiewicz, was also a painter, created the modern Polish theater in a number of antirealistic plays that utilize all the elements of spectacle for a total theatrical experience. Witkiewicz admired his work on a purely formal level and called him "a writer for the theater in the sphere of Pure Form." [2] *The Wedding*, performed in 1901 in Cracow with great success, dealt in

---

[1] Antonin Artaud, *The Theater and Its Double*, trans. M. C. Richards (New York: Grove Press, 1958), pp. 82–83.

[2] Witkiewicz, "Pure Form in the Theatre of Wyspiański," quoted by Konstanty Puzyna, *Preface* to S. I. Witkiewicz, *Plays* (Warsaw, 1962), I, 9.

symbolic and fantastic terms with the wedding of an intellectual and a peasant girl. The crucial issue is the relationship between the intelligentsia and the peasants; national unity can be achieved only through closer cooperation between these two classes.

In Act II, at the stroke of midnight, the Mulch (a straw covering for rosebushes in winter, looking something like a packing cover for a giant wine bottle) enters and prophetically announces that extraordinary things will happen. Various historical, legendary, and symbolic figures appear to talk of the fate of Poland; all await the great miracle that never happens.

In *The Shoemakers*, Witkiewicz unexpectedly introduces the two peasants and barefoot girl, bringing along the famous Mulch with them, at a time when everyone was expecting the chorus girls from the "Euphorion." The peasants are ridiculed as pompous fools with their obsolete notion that they have some sort of historic "mission" to perform in the world of power politics. The Mulch, used in Wyspiański's play as a voice of prophecy, is exposed in *The Shoemakers* as a fraud. When his straw falls off, he turns out to be a Mulch-about-Town. In a world of the insane and dying, a grotesque modern dance of death, the Mulch-on-the-Make sidles up to the new sex goddess with bat wings and invites her to dance the tango, the cosmopolitan song for the fast set of the 1930's, the real culture of the mulches of the period.

The parody of national symbols and myths in *The Shoemakers* is designed to show that the traditional view of Polish culture is a delusion that has lost all meaning in the synthetic world of the twentieth century. It is the most pessimistic of Witkiewicz' plays, full of tough-minded despair about the state of Western civilization.

> Mankind is suffocating, squashed under the body of the rotting, malignant tumor of capitalism, on which fascist governments swell and burst like putrefying blisters, discharging foul-smelling gases from the faceless mass of humanity gone rotten from stewing in its own juice.

Despite the intellectual and linguistic complexity of the speeches, the structure of *The Shoemakers* is relatively simple. Act I presents the rotten, dying world of capitalism in the interrelations of workers, bourgeois establishment, and aristocracy. At the end of the act, the first revolution takes place; it is a fascist coup executed by Scurvy. The change is not drastic, since the bourgeois regime had fostered fascism and crumbled away through its own falsity.

Act II presents the oppressive conditions of this system, leading to the Shoemakers' rebellion at the end of the act. Act III shows the consequences of this revolution, the last uprising possible. Now as the members of the old generation of the oppressors and the oppressed go mad or are killed as obsolete, two technocrats in well-tailored business suits arrive, look indifferently at the hysterical death throes of the decadent past, and step over the corpses. They have come to automate all of life. There will be total annihilation of freedom and individuality.

Three central characters represent the antagonistic forces ceaselessly at war with one another. They are Sajetan, the worker; Scurvy, the bourgeois; and the Duchess, the aristocrat—a garrulous old idealistic dreamer, a cowardly political opportunist, and a sadistic nymphomaniac. Their follies and neuroses embody the sickness of liberal democracy in the throes of disintegration and doomed to violent extinction.

Sajetan is the self-made, self-educated socialist of the old school, a dupe of his own ideals, rambling on about a better world to come. He advocates world government, opposes nationalism and war, and triumphantly challenges the idle rich with the anarchist's eternal hope: "But when the real socialists abolish the state altogether, there'll be no need for men like you." Ironically, when the revolution finally comes, he is the one for whom there is no need. His ideas now become dangerous and bourgeois. His followers cut him down as a menace to the revolution in order to make a myth out of him, once he is dead, that will be much more socially beneficial than his living reality could ever be. Sajetan is utterly expendable in the world of the Hyperworkoid, the inhuman servant of the totalitarian regime who has been brutalized and sterilized by years of imprisonment and torture under Scurvy and the capitalist system.

Sajetan is a moving figure in a play of great gloom and terror; there is a personal note of heartbreak to many of his speeches of frustration and failure:

> I don't even hate anyone—I only hate myself—oh, horror, horror: to the edge of what precipices and overhanging cliffs of the soul have I been dragged by my vile ambitions to be somebody on this round little earth of ours, holy but incomprehensible!

Scurvy, who has gleefully watched the deaths of so many others, is totally responsible for his own downfall and does not elicit the sympathy we feel for Sajetan; we feel only a repulsive pity for the anguished writhings of this poisonous insect. A social climber, a man utterly divided within and against himself, unsatisfied sexually, insecure socially, perverted psychologically, Scurvy (whose name in Polish means "son of a whore," another of Witkiewicz' international puns) is the eager tool of any government in power. Victim of his own sick sensuality, he is ready to do anything to get "jellied plenckus," the Duchess, and other such delicacies. Scurvy's longing to have been born a nobleman drives him on to seek power, but instead of becoming a count he is transformed into a dog on a chain and howls himself to death out of frustrated desire.

The Duchess is the pivotal figure in *The Shoemakers* and a powerful force for destruction in a world bent on disintegration. She is the object of desire for almost all the characters—Scurvy, Sajetan, the Apprentices, even the head of "Vigilant Youth" and the Mulch—with the sole exception of the sexless Hyperworkoid. The physical desire to get her and either rape her or beat her up or both is a driving force in the action of the play and a major source of dramatic tension. She is a whore in every sense of the word, challenging all social values and political ideologies with her sexuality. Perverse and sadistic, she hates men and wants to enslave them. She welcomes the impending cataclysm which will destroy civilization and sees women as emerging from the chaos as the governing race of the future.

Sex and politics are intertwined themes in *The Shoemakers*, and Witkiewicz reveals how sexual and political frustrations and aggressions are inseparably interrelated. For Witkiewicz, the three great creative passions and urges are the sexual, the social, and the artistic, but in each, creation is closely allied to destructiveness and can at any moment revert to chaos. When slightly warped, the creative instinct turns self-destructive.

In *The Shoemakers*, the sexual urge and the social urge have both turned negative; lust and revolution do not bring liberation, but only more frustration and repression. Only the artistic impulse to create retains any constructive purpose and dignity in man's life, but now Witkiewicz no longer associates this kind of creativity with the fine arts, in which he has apparently lost belief, but with the work a man can do with his hands—in this case the art of shoemaking, an art that will soon be obsolete in a mechanized world.

The most creative moment in the play is the Shoemakers' rebellion at the end of Act II, led by Sajetan, where the desire for making something, sexual release, and social revolution join forces. The language of shoemaking and the language of sexual intercourse merge in the frenzy of creation. When the Shoemakers and the Vigilant Youthers pound, sew, and hammer together spontaneously, in wild sexual rhythms, they assert for the last time the value of an individual act, carried out on a collective scale, untrammeled by government restrictions and regulations. In Sajetan's motto, "The boot as the ab-so-lute," shoemaking becomes an act of defiance against all authority. A future in which a man can work and love freely as an individual momentarily seems possible, as though Leon's plans for social utopia in *The Mother* were coming true. The frantic boot race and unexpected revolutionary conversion of "Vigilant Youth" to the Shoemakers' side are the last signs of creative effort.

Unfortunately, the political world of the play is dominated by forces that do not permit freedom and individuality. The exact nature of the secret government, to which Scurvy, "Vigilant Youth," the Hyperworkoid, and the two Comrades belong, is merely hinted at. The Hyperworkoid announces that he belongs to "THEM," and just before the very end the TERRIBLE VOICE announces over the "hypersuper-megaphonopump" that "THEY HAVE ABSOLUTE POWER NOW."

In *The Shoemakers,* as in *They,* the sinister new regime is never clearly defined—we only know that it is secret, all-powerful, and totalitarian. Witkiewicz' technique is to create a sense of fear and foreboding by making the presence of this totalitarian regime felt everywhere without ever revealing its seat of power, tactics, or true character. Its power is therefore in large part psychological; people submit to it because they believe in it. The secret government is a force for repression and mechanization to the extent that we join it or fear it, but do nothing to resist it. When Joe Tempe comes with "Vigilant Youth" and arrests his own father, Sajetan, he says: "the individual is making a last-ditch stand against a future in which there'll only be lice." The sinister force of the secret government can be felt everywhere around us, in any country, under any political system, no matter what it claims to be.

The Shoemakers

A THEORETICAL PLAY
WITH "SONGS" IN THREE ACTS

Dedicated to Stefan Szuman

Sajetan Tempe	*Master shoemaker; thin "wild" beard and mustache. Blond hair going gray. Wearing an ordinary shoemaker's clothes with an apron. About 60 years old.*
Apprentices I (Joe) and II (Andy)	*Very good-looking, ordinary young shoe-makers. Wearing ordinary shoemakers' clothes with aprons. About 20 years old.*
Duchess Irina Nikitovna Provokskaya-Debochkova	*With chestnut hair, extraordinarily beauti-ful, unusually charming and attractive. 27–28 years old.*
Prosecuting Attorney Robert Scurvy	*A broad face, as if made out of red head-cheese, in which are incrusted eyes pale blue as the buttons on underpants. Wide jaws—they'd grind a piece of granite to a fine powder (that's how it seems). Wear-ing a cutaway and a Derby. A walking stick with a gold knob (très démodé). A folded white ascot with a huge pearl in it.*
The Duchess's Footman, Fidgeons	*Made to look a little like a manikin. Red costume with gold trimmings. Short red cape. Matching hat.*
Hyperworkoid	*Dressed in overalls and a cap. Clean-shaven, wide jaws. Carries a huge copper thermos bottle.*
Two Dignitaries: Comrade Abramowski and Comrade X	*Elegantly dressed civilians, of high intel-ligence and first-rate in all other respects. X clean-shaven; Abramowski with beard and mustache.*
Joseph Tempe	*Sajetan's son, 20 years old.*
Peasants	*An old peasant, a young peasant, and a country girl. Cracow peasant costumes.*
The Woman Guard	*A pretty young girl. Wearing an apron over her uniform.*
The Mulch *	*From Wyspiański's* The Wedding.
The Guard	*An ordinary young fellow, green uniform.*

* A straw covering put on rosebushes in winter. [Translators' note]

ACT I

The stage represents a shoemaker's workshop (it can be set up in a thoroughly fantastic fashion) in a small semicircular space. To the left, a triangular opening hung with a cherry-colored curtain. In the center, a triangular gray wall with a small round window. To the right, a dried-up, twisted tree—between it and the wall, a triangular sky. Further to the right, a distant landscape with villages on a plain. The workshop is situated high above a valley in the background, as if placed on high mountains. The shoemakers are working in the workshop, Sajetan in the middle, the two apprentices on either side, Apprentice I on the left, Apprentice II on the right. In the distance is heard the roar of automobiles and heaven knows what else and the shrieking of factory sirens.

SAJETAN (*banging on some shoes with his hammer*) Let's not talk about unimportant things. Hey! Hey! Hammer the soles! Hammer the soles! Bend the tough leather, break your fingers! Oh, what the hell—let's not talk about unimportant things! The Prince's shoes! But being an eternal wanderer, I wander so much I'm always nailed to the same spot. Hey! Hammer the soles for those dirty bastards. Let's not talk about unimportant things—ever!

FIRST APPRENTICE (*interrupting him*) You got the guts to kill her? (*Second Apprentice stops hammering the soles and listens attentively.*)

SAJETAN Once I would've, but not now! Hey! (*Brandishing his hammer*)

SECOND APPRENTICE Quit saying "hey" all the time, it bugs me.

SAJETAN It bugs me more to have to make shoes for them. I could have been President, king of the whole shebang—at least for a while, at least for a little while. Lanterns, garlands, and words, dancing about the lamplights, and here I am, a poor filthy louse, with the sun on my breast, shining like the gold shield of Heliodorus, like a hundred Aldebarans and Vegas—I can't go on. Hey! (*Brandishing his hammer*)

FIRST APPRENTICE Why can't you?

SAJETAN They wouldn't let me. Hey! They were scared.

SECOND APPRENTICE Say "hey" once more, and I'll quit. You can't imagine how it bugs me. Incidentally, who's Heliodorus?

SAJETAN Some fictitious character—maybe I made it up—I'm not sure any more. That's the way it always is. Wait a minute . . . I don't believe in revolutions any more . . . The very word is revolting, like "cockroach" or "spider" or "louse." Everything's going against us.

227

We're manure, like former kings and intellectuals in relation to the totem clan—manure.

SECOND APPRENTICE At least you didn't say "hey"—I'd have killed you if you had. Manure or not, they sure lived well. Their broads didn't stink like ours do, son of a sucking prunt, the stupid, lousy, crock-picking skonkies! Oh, Jesus!

SAJETAN Everything's grown so ugly in the world, there's no use talking about anything at all. Mankind is suffocating, squashed under the body of the rotting, malignant tumor of capital, on which fascist governments swell and burst, like putrefying blisters, discharging foul-smelling gases from the faceless mass of humanity gone rotten from stewing in its own juice. There's no need to say anything any more. Everything's already been said over and over again. We've got to wait till it happens and do what we can. Aren't we human, too? Maybe they're the only humans—and, merciful Jesus, we're just the sweepings from the slaughterhouse floor, with the side effect that we suffer all the more and howl enviously while they enjoy themselves. Hey! Hey! (*He hits everything at hand with his hammer.*) Those cigar-smoking fatguts certainly think that way, soaking in their slimy cocktail made out of their sensuality and our stench, hopeless in its misery. Hey! Hey!

SECOND APPRENTICE That was put so astutely that even that repulsive "hey" of yours didn't offend me. I forgive you this time. But God help you if you ever do it again.

SAJETAN (*not paying any attention*) And what's worse, there'll never be an end to work, the damned social machinery can't go backward. There'll only be one consolation—absolutely everybody will be slaving away with a vengeance, like one great big sweaty peasant, and there won't even be any loafers like . . .

FIRST APPRENTICE (*shrewdly*) Like those in the top positions of authority?

SAJETAN So you've given it some thought too, man? Hey! But how can two brains be compared? Not compared—that's hard enough—but pared down to the same level. Well, they'll all be working the same way—the point is it won't be pleasant. Those bastards are having too much fun now—there's still the possibility of creating something— hey! I could think up a new style, but it won't be the same. No. It won't! It won't!

FIRST APPRENTICE The poor boss! He wants work to be automated and at the same time to animate this mechanism with a soul, the way those musicians and painters of the past did their outpourings by giving them the unique stamp of their own personalities. Am I talking nonsense?

SECOND APPRENTICE No—only a little peculiar. I'll put it in a more down-to-earth way. Maybe it's not worth it? (*A pause; no one gives him any encouragement. He speaks just the same.*) An awkward pause. No one's giving me any encouragement. I'll say something anyhow. I've got to: I can't hold it back. The Duchess is coming here today with her prosecuting attorney dog, and she'll talk a lot too and drill holes in our metaphysical navels, which those rich people regard as the after-dinner mints of their inner life—but for us they're itching sores and always will be. They can only express it by contradictions which no one else can get at all—these are the things, I mean, which that high-class trash call their metaphysical experiences, the holy sons of bitches. They tickle their fat bellies with them, and every tickle of a glutted hog means a pain in our guts. I wanted to talk, you know, and I'm talking: live and die; contract into the eye of a needle and spread oneself out over the entire world; grow elated and wallow in the dust . . . (*A sudden emptiness in the head makes it impossible for him to go on talking.*) I won't say anything more, because my mind's gone suddenly blank, like a cow in a barn or on the way to the stockyards.

FIRST APPRENTICE Yes—you really didn't make much of an effort in your speech, with an *s*, and a *p*, and an *eech*. Listen, Andy, I know all about Kretschmer's theory of the different physical and psychological types. I took a course with that intellectual slut Zahorska at our Free Workers College. Oh, it's free all right, so free it's come loose. They get a solid education for themselves, but they see to it that we only get a good case of mental diarrhea, so they can swindle us even more than all the religious authorities put together did in the past, when they were the paid tools of heavy industry and the feudal powers. Andy, I'm telling you, that's the psychology of the schizoid. But not everyone's like that. It's a dying race. There are more and more endomorphs in the world all the time. Got a radio, got a fountain pen, got the movies, got a typewriter, got a belly and ears that don't stink or drip, got enough of everything—so what else do you want? But deep down you're just a common piece of dirt, a fine little specimen of repulsive guano. That's the endomorph, you know? But that other kind's never satisfied with himself, always trying to raise himself up in his own eyes and appear to himself better than he really is—not so as to be better, but to appear that way, and not better even, but cleverer and sharper. That's the kind that thinks he's real sharp. (*After a pause*) I don't know which kind I am myself: endomorph or schizoid.

SAJETAN (*harshly. He hammers on a last, or something similar.*) Hey! Hey! You'll talk your life away. I'd have liked to deflower their broads, have real orgies, get some real thrills out of them, perform the *jus primae noctis* with them, sink down into their soft feather beds, shovel down their food until I puked my guts out, and then gag ecstatically on their souls from the great beyond—but not copy them—no—create something higher: new religions—just for laughs, and new paintings and symphonies and poems and machines and a new, completely ethereal woman, beautiful like my Cynthia . . . (*He breaks off.*) Oh, I shouldn't even mention that name here—in their terms that's blasphemy. (*Vehemently*) What do I really have? What's left for me in life?

SECOND APPRENTICE Take it easy . . . !

SAJETAN I won't be quiet—you jerk! Hey! Hey! Hey! Hey—Hey! (*He hammers.*) That son of mine—he's joined that group with the revolting name, "Vigilant Youth." Sort of an organization of those that want to get their hands on everything right away. They want to get rid of the intellectuals, but they don't want to kill anybody, unless there's no other way. Hey!

   (*Enter from the right the prosecuting attorney Scurvy. Top hat. Umbrella. Cutaway. In his brightly gloved hands, yellow flowers.*)

SCURVY What do you mean: don't want to kill "unless there's no other way." There's never any other way, and it's always necessary— that's how it is. Hee-hee.

SECOND APPRENTICE There he goes "hee-heeing" again. One says "hey," and the other "hee"—I can't stand it. (*He works furiously on a gigantic, unnaturally large officer's boot which he pulled out from a pile of rubbish in the corner to the left. After a moment—Scurvy looks at him with an expectant smile—he cries out in despair*) I don't want to work for that kind of dough! I won't! Let me out of here!

SCURVY (*coldly. His smile has vanished as though blown out.*) Hee, hee. No one's stopping you. Why don't you go crawl into a hole and die? True freedom comes only through work.

SAJETAN But you work in an easy chair, smoking fancy cigarettes, stuffed up to here with whatever you want. "Intellectual work." Ya' bastard! And interlecherous too—hey! (*He laughs wildly.*)

SCURVY Sajetan, do you think it'll be any different in the future? Do you really think that all of us can be mechanized and standardized in the ranks of manual labor? No—there'll always be directors and high officials who'll have to eat something different even from what foremen in factories eat. Intellectual work requires different suste- nance for the brain—for the brain and for the stomach. (*Second Apprentice weeps.*)

SAJETAN Hey!—but the future directors and high officials will be eating scientifically predigested meals without any taste, not langouste and jellied plenckus, the way you do, Mr. Prosecuting Attorney for the Supreme Court in charge of arbitrating the differences between capital and labor. You elitistical eunuch! In times like these when there are fascist youth organizations like my son's, you can still go on living like a tapeworm in the rotten gut of a disintegrating society. But when the real socialists abolish the state altogether, there'll be no need for men like you. There'll be an honest-to-God comrade-director keeping himself going on revolting little pills . . . (*He weeps.*)

SCURVY Your trouble is you have a langouste complex—you and your kind. No, Sajetan, that'll never happen. Our species can't degenerate to the point where the digestive organs will shrink and be satisfied with only a few pills. In that case everything else would also degenerate to such an extent that there wouldn't be any problems left at all: there'd be just a bunch of almost extinct protozoans, instead of a society incurably ill in the interrelationship of its parts.

SECOND APPRENTICE I'll tell you something: we'd go along with any of those propositions, if our private lives weren't what they are. Mr. Prosecuting Attorney, when you knock off work, you can mull over abstract issues quite independent of your stomach and other intesticles . . .

SCURVY Well, now—that's an exaggeration . . .

SECOND APPRENTICE But not a gross one. (*In despair*) I want good-looking women and lots of beer. But all I get is two large glasses and always the same girl, always the same old Gertie—screw it! . . .

SCURVY (*distastefully*) That's enough . . .

FIRST APPRENTICE (*coming up to him with clenched fists, ironically*) That's enough, is it? Mr. Prosecuting Attorney of the Supreme Court's turning up his nose at the thought that Andy always has to have the same girl. As for him, he's a theosophist. He has some pretty snooty ideas. And he has as many broads as he wants. But he'd really like it with only one certain person, but there's no getting it from her, heh, heh—everywhere the same old problems, the relations simply transposed along parallel lines, or laid out horizontally—heh, heh.

SCURVY (*coldly*) Shut up, you son of a guttersnatch, shut up, you twisted gut pipe.

FIRST APPRENTICE Ha, ha! Hey! Honest to God, I hit the nail on the head. She'll be here any minute, that angel-faced sadist, that high-principled poisoneress—thinks she's Lucrezia Borgia. For her, the Prosecuting Attorney's agonies, when he has to do it with other broads and can only dream about her "unattainable" pudy—now there's nothing wrong with pudy—for her these sufferings are just like taking a look in the workshops where we sweat and croak from stinking hard work, or like taking a peek at prisons where the toughest men rot and disintegrate spiritually and physically in a state of sexual, or maybe transsexual despair . . .

SCURVY He's gone crazy, it was too much for him, and his lunacy's affecting me like locoweed. I'm going mad! (*He falls on the shoemakers' stool.*) I understand her so perfectly, even in the depths of her feminine spiritual depravity . . . and it would be so wonderful . . . But what can I do when she doesn't even want to at all? Oh, oh! My anguish gives her more satisfaction than the wildest superrape I could commit.

SAJETAN Oh—you see—he's broken down into his basic elements—he doesn't even stink any more. Why not make a pair of boots—it'll do you good—better than watching condemned men at dawn.

SCURVY (*sobbing*) So you know even that, Sajetan? Sajetan! It's so horrible . . .

(*Enter the Duchess, dressed in a gray suit, with a magnificent bouquet of yellow flowers. She gives flowers from it to everyone in turn, not excluding Scurvy who, without getting up from the stool, accepts them in a dignified manner but is secretly hurt [how to show that on the stage, eh?]. Then she puts the bouquet into a huge multicolored vase, which the footman [in gala] Fidgeons carries behind her. At the same time Fidgeons leads in on a leash a fox terrier, named Terrell.*)

DUCHESS Good morning, Sajetan, good morning. How do you do, how do you do? Good morning, apprentices. Ho, ho—I can see you're working away here zealously, as the spiritual forefathers of our writers used to put it in the eighteenth century. Zealously—a beautiful word. Could you love zealously, Mr. Prosecuting Attorney? (*Terrell sniffs at Scurvy.*) Terrell, tch-tch!

SCURVY (*groaning on the stool*) I want to make a pair of boots—just one pair of boots! Then I'll be worthy of you, only then. Then I'll be able to do what I want, and make people into what I want. Even make you into a good, loving homebody—dearest monster, my one and only. . . . (*All choked up*)

SAJETAN (*with superstitious awe*) Look at him! He's getting all choked up—hey!

DUCHESS Dr. Scurvy, your utter helplessness excites me to perfect madness. I'd like you to have watched me while I was—you know? —doing it—but I'm not going to say with whom—but there's a really divine lieutenant in the blue hussars, someone from my own class or social sphere, too, and there's a certain actor, too . . . Your doubts are a reservoir for me of the choicest, sexual, female, straight-from-the-guts-insect-style sensuality—I'd like to be like the female praying mantis—near the climax they devour their partners from the head down, who, despite that, keep on doing it—you know, hee-hee!

SECOND APPRENTICE (*pronounces the French words dreadfully, like Mrs. Jones. He's holding the gigantic officer's boot.*) *Quelle expression grotesque!* (*Unusual excitement can be felt among the shoemakers.*)

SAJETAN Give him the officer's boot, the cuirassier's, the son of a shint! Let him finish it for you. He needs boots like that, him and the rulers for whom he puts the future heroes of humanity into his palaces—palaces of his soul. Lead the mob by the nose—that's their highest motto. Hey! Hey! Hey!

FIRST APPRENTICE And you know, comrade-boss, there's something else, you know, that makes him suffer: he's in love with our perverted angel only because she's a duchess, and he's an ordinary bourgeois from the third estate, and not a count. Only two hundred years ago counts used to crack guys like him right in the face with complete impunity. So he's suffering and wallowing in his own suffering still more—without it, the son of a pussycat wouldn't enjoy himself half so much, as Zeleński-Boy so aptly put it.

SCURVY (*jumping up. At the same time the Second Apprentice thrusts the gigantic officer's boot into Scurvy's arms. Scurvy hugs it and roars impressively*.) Not that—don't take that one last thing away from me: I'm a true, liberal democrat—in money matters.

SAJETAN You hit him where it hurts. Yes—he's sorry he didn't smack his lips over the mangiest existence possible, living in the false illusion a count is still somebody in the last half of the twentieth century. He'd give I don't know what to be able to be a suffering count and adopt, toward our existence, you know, a pose of subtle superiority, son of a bitch—and I don't know what all. It isn't enough for him that he'll be making boots in his capacity as doctor of law and chief prosecuting attorney for what's practically the court of the last judgment—to which this little angel here (*he points to the Duchess*) will call him, playing on her cute little internal organs.

DUCHESS (*to the fox terrier, which Fidgeons is trying to quiet down*) Terrell, tch-tch! And you too, Sajetan, tch-tch! This won't do—"Heaven forfend," as the Slavophile wits used to say with their love of meaningless words. It's in bad taste, and that's all there is to it. You've always showed so much tact, but what's happened to you now?

SAJETAN I want to be in bad taste—I want to! There's been enough good taste. I'll blast everything to the final stench and filth. Let it all stink, let this world stink itself out of existence and let it stink itself down to the last drop, then maybe at last it'll smell sweet; because you really can't live in this world the way it is. The poor people don't smell how the democratic lie stinks, but a pair of dogs can smell the stink of the outhouse, hey! And that's the truth: he'd give anything to be a real count for just a moment. But he can't, he's out of luck, poor guy, hey.

scurvy Have pity on me! I'll make a confession to you. This morning I watched them hang Count Cocoblinski, who was condemned to death because of me. It was Bertrand, not Edward, who murdered the streetwalker Ripsy Goldfinch and embezzled public funds at the State Insurance Bureau, office number 18. I confess: I was so envious that a true aristocrat was being hanged! Of course, if it came right down to it, I wouldn't care to be hanged for nine heraldic emblems —but all the same, I was envious! He was talking, and at the same time vomiting from fear, like a mutt with worms: "See how a real count throws up for the last time." Oh—to be able to say that just once and then die.

duchess (*to the fox terrier*) Terrell, tch-tch! I'm just melting away with ferocious sensual desires! (*She sings—the first song*)
> My maiden name was "von und zu."
> He's impressed and grovels too.
> I can fly like an antelope "gnu,"
> Over the earth, and up in the blue!

That's my first song for the day. Tornado Babel-burg is my maiden name, Mr. Robert. You have no idea what bliss it is to have such a name.

scurvy (*fainting*) Oh—she was a virgin once! It never occurred to me before. She was a baby girl—someone's little girl—a poor tiny little tyke! That song of hers was in such perfectly execrable taste that it brought tears to my eyes. Things like that have much more effect on me than actual suffering. It's the little embarrassing things that happen to people that drive me out of my mind, but I can look at spilled guts without batting an eyelash. My precious jewel! How infinitely I love you. It's horrible how demonic lust and the greatest tenderness can go hand in hand. Then the male is ready—*rédi*, as they say in France. (*He lunges off the stool with the boot in his arms. The shoemakers hold him up, without letting go of the yellow flowers which they received from the Duchess. They wink at one another knowingly, sucking in diseased reality by the very bucket-ful.*)

SECOND APPRENTICE (*sniffing the bouquet. They have put Scurvy on the stool in a very uncomfortable position—with his head hanging down.*) A martyr! I'm sucking up reality from a dirty slop pail. Unhealthy as Campagna Romana. I'm drinking frozen hogwash through a straw like iced coffee. What terrible suffering! My guts are scalded as if I'd been given an enema of concentrated acid.

DUCHESS (*rhetorically*) You're exaggerating.

SECOND APPRENTICE (*stubbornly*) No. Just think about it: why am I who I am, and not someone else? It's not true that I couldn't think of somebody else as "I." I could just as well be that pile of garbage there (*points to Scurvy*), but instead I'm a frigid superlouse, or something close to it—I'm just speaking in general—it's the height of pure nonsense: my personality and body are all mixed up. I don't understand myself, you know . . . (*Embarrassed, falls silent*)

SAJETAN Don't be apologetic, Andy! It's not true: the author of this play says something quite different with his biological materialism; it's a synthesis of Cornelius' revised psychologism and Leibniz' improved monadology. For billions of years cells have been fusing and dividing so that such a despicable piece of stockyard refuse, like me, could say "I" about himself! The Duchess is a metaphysical prostitute—why mince words?—to hell with her, she's a bitch, she comes from a long line of high-class bitches . . .

DUCHESS (*reproachfully*) Sajetan . . .

SAJETAN (*feverishly*) Irina Nikitovna—Chwistek has denied you a place in Polish literature. And that's why you have to wander in and out of nonsensical plays which are not even literature, and which no one will put on. He can't bear Russian duchesses, he can't stand them, the poor guy. The only thing he'd like is seamstresses, secretaries—and what have you. But that's way beyond me! For me, for us, there are only stinking broads and still stinkier gutter matrons and barn sows: our grandmothers, our aunts, our uncles' wives . . . hey!

SECOND APPRENTICE Boss: that's real self-flagellation of our own class. It's a good thing you didn't mention mothers, or I'd let you have it.

SCURVY (*with a wild, lunatic smile*) Classes within classes! Haha! Logistics of class warfare. The class of classes at war with itself. I despise myself for this wretched "witticism," but I couldn't come up with anything better.

DUCHESS (*coldly*) Why indulge in "witticisms" anyway?

SCURVY It's the bad example set by our literary wits: wit turned rancid long ago, and now the riffraff are constantly making "witticisms." Ha—that's enough: to escape those pitfalls, you've got to be somebody; you've got to take a stand somewhere. Because of my fear of responsibility, I'm about to lose the choicest morsel destined for me in my life here on earth. As a count I could be merely an observer.

DUCHESS It's only in Poland that the count problem, as such, is posed so dramatically. From this moment on no one's allowed to talk about it —*schluss, finito,* my wonderful boys! (*She kisses the apprentices.*)

SCURVY How can you call them "wonderful boys"—ugh . . . (*He shudders with disgust and goes numb.*) It's the pinnacle of bad taste and *mauvais genre!* I'm trembling with shame and going completely numb. (*He does so.*)

SECOND APPRENTICE (*wiping the sweat away*) I don't want any dough for the duchess' shoes, just ten passionate kisses, like Mrs. de Korponay gave Csikos in Jókai's * novel I read when I was a kid.

DUCHESS (*pointing a small silver Browning at him*) I know: I read *The White Lady* too—you'll get ten bullets too, the way Csikos did.

FIRST APPRENTICE (*greatly astounded*) That's the way those ignorant hacks write—those masters of intellectual confusion, those unclean monists, crap all over them: "life is art, and art is life." Well, we've got that right here, you know, here on our small shoemakers' stage —that's what those knuckleheads are always gassing about.

SCURVY (*suddenly gets a grip on himself and gets up*) Hee, hee!

SAJETAN Look at him: he's heeheeing again. He sure must have devised something new to raise himself above us still higher. He's a seesaw, not a man. But he hasn't had his fill yet either and isn't so satisfied himself. I can tell you: the poor bastard's suffering all the tortures of hell, as Karol Szymanowski † often used to say. Incidentally, he was recently buried at Wawel, and not at Skalka as some people wanted. Skalka is for local celebrities, and not for true geniuses.

SCURVY (*through his teeth, coldly, tearing up the flowers*) I want to and I will. I'll become their leader and show you the castle of my soul owned by the greatest man in my social class, the poor, democratic bourgeoisie that's still not reached the point of extinction yet. I've got to! I'll overcome the stomach problem and put your issues on a higher spiritual plane. The time will come when you'll kiss my hands, you, my brothers in spiritual poverty.

SAJETAN No one's begging you, you Robert Fraternité! We no longer need the intelligentsia—your time is past. We've risen up out of the vibrio—we'll turn back into vibrio again. I love animals. I really feel

---

* Maurus Jókai (1825–1904), Hungarian novelist and playwright. [Translators' note]

† Karol Szymanowski (1882–1937), Polish composer and pianist. [Translators' note]

I'm a cousin of the Jurassic reptiles and the Silurian trilobites, and of
pigs and lemurs too—I feel I'm intimately linked with all of creation
—it's one of those rare moments of truth! Hey, hey! (*He falls into a
state of ecstasy.*)

DUCHESS (*rapturously*) Oh, how I love you for that, Sajetan. I love
you as you are, a stinking louse, warmed by the sun of universal love
for all crawling things, which fills the heart of the old shoemaker
who made our planet. I'll probably give myself to you one of these
days just for the sake of doing it, because it's stylish, because it will
look well—it's got to happen once at least.

SAJETAN (*sings to the tune of a mazurka*)
> A little variety doesn't hurt,
> Just don't rub your nose in the dirt,
> We don't care, if you don't smell,
> So strictly speaking, what the Hell?

DUCHESS (*strewing flowers on him*) I care—I really do! But stop versifying, when you do it's in such poor taste it's the living end. I
positively feel embarrassed for you. Now take me, I can afford to
because you know, to put it in simple everyday language, a duchess
is a duchess—take it or leave it. (*Shouts*) Hey! Hey! Long live
vulgarity! I'll come down to your level and let myself go after all
my sufferings, mine and my forebears' and their bare rears, too.
Even poor old Scurvy doesn't look so puny today.

SECOND APPRENTICE There's something in this ancestor business! Parents
count for something, too—they're not just incubators—and therefore distant forebears count for something, too, what the hell! But
you mustn't push it to absurd lengths, the way those aristocrats and
semiaristocrats do. That's the heart of the matter: in this one thing
I'd suggest going easy. For the worst thing in the world is a Polish
aristocrat—the only thing worse is a Polish half-aristocrat, all puffed
up with no reason to be. The genes, you know. It's the Dobermans
and the airdale-terriers all over again . . .

FIRST APPRENTICE (*interrupting him*) Man, just try to find something
in this world that isn't being pushed to absurd lengths since all of
existence, both sacred and profane, is one great absurdity—a struggle among monsters, that's all . . .

DUCHESS (*fervently*) And that's why fervent belief in God is no
longer . . . (*Sajetan belts her in the mouth, and she becomes all
smeared with blood [a small balloon filled with fuchsin]. She falls on
her knees.*) He's knocked my teeth out—my pearly white teeth!
He's a real . . . (*Sajetan hits her again; then she becomes silent and
remains kneeling and sobs.*)

SCURVY Rena! Rena! Now I'll never be able to extricate myself from the influence of your lunar soul. (*Recites*)

> Through silver fields I'd like to follow you
> And dream away my life the whole night through—
> To dream about another life in peace,
> To share with you, then solitude will cease.

FIRST APPRENTICE And at dawn watch the live corpses you condemned to death vomit from fear. That's what you feed on, scum: even before they die, you vampirize them, as the Americans say. You rascal! I was in Ohio.

SCURVY What you're saying can't hurt me any more. What you want to do in a hideous, stinking, mangy way, I'll perform in a most beautiful dream about myself and about all of you—in heavenly colors, with me dressed in tails from New Bond Street and scented with California poppy, like the most fashionable man-about-town, I'll save the world with a single magic word, but not in the way you'd like: everything equalized—exit culture. The magical value of words hasn't died out yet; our old bards used to believe in it, and logicians and Husserlites still do today. I've already said something on that subject—look, here are my monographs—which, *nota bene*, no one ever read—even before the crash.

DUCHESS (*on her knees*) Dear God, how he does go on!

SCURVY The aristocracy has had it, they're not human beings any more —they're ghosts! For too long now mankind has been going around with those phantom lice on its body. Capitalism is a malignant tumor which has begun to rot, devour, and gangrene the organism that produced it—that's the social structure today. We must reform capitalism, not destroy private enterprise.

SAJETAN Garbage!

SCURVY (*feverishly*) Either the entire earth will voluntarily transform itself into one single mass of people capable of governing themselves on an elite basis, which is most unlikely unless there's an ultimate catastrophe—and this must be avoided at all costs—or the level of culture will have to be set back. The chaos in my mind is really inconceivable! It isn't possible to create an objective apparatus by forming an elite of all mankind, because development of intellect takes away the courage to act: the most intelligent man won't dare follow his own thoughts to their logical conclusion if he's afraid of himself and of going mad, and anyway he'll be too weak to face reality. Being afraid of oneself is not a fantasy, it's a fact—mankind is afraid of itself, too—mankind is going collectively mad—individuals know that but are helpless—black thoughts from the abyss—if I could come off my liberal tone and temporarily enter into them, so as to take them apart and see what makes them tick! (*He falls into deep thought with his finger in his mouth.*)

DUCHESS (*gets up, wipes her bloody mouth with a handkerchief, and says*) You bore me, Robert. You're just mouthing the platitudes of a socially impotent drone who lacks any real convictions.

SCURVY (*coldly*) Oh, really? Well, then, good-bye. (*He leaves without looking back.*)

SECOND APPRENTICE All the same that prosecuting attorney mutt has a wonderful sense of style: he left just at the right time. But still he's too intelligent to be somebody nowadays: to accomplish anything nowadays, you have to be something of an ass.

DUCHESS So now we'll go back to our ordinary daily business. Go on working—the time hasn't come yet. Someday I'll turn into a vampire and let all the monsters in the world out of their cages. But, as for him, in order to carry out his program as a bolshevik intellectual, he first has to annihilate all free and spontaneous social activity. He'll clamp down hard on everything, but in addition to clamping down, he'll wring the necks of half of you to cut you down to size. He's the only one who has any influence on the commandant of "Vigilant Youth," Pugnatsy Jawbloatski, but he refuses to use it because of a firm belief in absolute social laisser faire, laisser aller, and lesbianism. (*She sits down on a stool and begins her lecture.*) And so, Dearest Shoemakers: you're even closer to me in spirit than the factory workers, who, thanks to Taylor, have been thoroughly automated; because you representatives of the handicrafts still have hidden in you the special nostalgia of a primitive animal that once lived in the woods and lakes. We aristocrats have lost it completely along with our intellect and even the most basic peasant common sense. Somehow I'm not doing very well today, but maybe it'll pass. (*She clears her throat for a long time and in a very significant manner.*)

SAJETAN (*deliberately, insincerely*) Hey! Hey! Only don't try to put anything over on us with your prolonged and significant throat-clearings—it won't work! Hey!

APPRENTICES Ha, ha! Hm, hm. Go on—keep it up! It's getting good! Huh, huh!

DUCHESS (*continuing in her lecture tone*) These flowers I brought you today are jonquils. Just look—see!—they have pistils and stamens; that's how they get fertilized. Now when the insect goes into the . . .

FIRST APPRENTICE Holy Christ, I studied all that while I was still in grade school! But I get so excited when you explain it, Duchess . . .

SAJETAN Hey! Hey! Hey!

SECOND APPRENTICE I can't tear myself away. Such black sexual boredom and sexual hopelessness is dreadful, like serving a life sentence. If, God forbid, I was to experience anything now, it would make me feel so good I'd go whining after it regretfully to the end of my days.

FIRST APPRENTICE I'll say the Duchess knows how to titillate the most sensitive nerves of refined sexuality even in a simple man like me . . . Ah! I almost feel dizzy just thinking about such agonizing, ecstatic torture . . . Cruelty is the essence . . .

SAJETAN Hey! Take it easy! Let the strange moment of our stink-filled life continue, let it be sanctified and pass, let it kill us poor lice with murderous, tragic lust. I'd like to live a short time only, like an ephemerid, and live to the full, but here this shit sausage stretches out endlessly, as far as the gray monotonous horizon of the hopeless, fruitless day—eternal as juniper—where death awaits us, moldy and lice-covered. Drippings into a gravedigger's bucket—that's all it is, isn't it—nothing more.

DUCHESS (*covers her eyes in delight*) My dream is coming true! I've discovered the proper medium for my second incarnation on this earth. (*To the Shoemakers*) I'd like to ennoble your hatred and change your envy, jealousy, frenzy, and insatiability into wild creative energy for the superconstruction—that's the word for it—of a new social life, whose seeds must be embedded in your souls which certainly have nothing in common with your sweating, stinking, overworked bodies. I'd like to drink the agony your work causes you through a straw, the way a gnat sucks a hippopotamus' blood—to the extent that that's possible—and transmute your pain into my pet schemes for the future; they're such beauties, delicate butterflies that'll one day turn into oxen. Institutions don't make the man, man makes the institutions.

FIRST APPRENTICE Just don't try to put one over on us, lady. Institutions are the expression of our highest aspirations, they only come into being because of them—and if they don't perform their function, do away with them—understand, superbitch?

SECOND APPRENTICE Quiet—let her have her say.

DUCHESS Yes—for once let me bare my soul, moldy and tired as it is. Now, just where were we? Aha—change your hatred and anger into bursts of creative energy. Hm, I don't know how to do it myself, but my feminine intuition will tell me what to do—it comes from within . . .

SAJETAN (*in pain*) Ooouch! . . . And there are certain things on the outside, too . . . Ouch!

DUCHESS But how can I calm you down? It's a well-known fact that people sometimes try to calm a person down just to make him all the more angry. Now you're furious at me, Sajetan, but at the same time you're forced to admire me as something completely above you; I know: that's torture! If I were to stroke your hand—like this—(*she strokes his hand*) you'd get still more furious—you'd jump out of your skin . . .

SAJETAN (*pulls or, rather, tears his hand away, as if burned*) Oh, you slut! (*To the Apprentices*) Did you see that? That's classy willful perversion for you! I'd like the chance to be as class-conscious as that bitch-box is in her perversely feminine way.

DUCHESS (*laughing*) What I like in all of you is your higher conscious-ness of your own misery and of the pain that tickles you and licks you into a paste of squashed lice. Just think: if I were to do this to Scurvy, who lusts after me madly and already is like a glass filled to the brim which the slightest touch would shatter, just think, Sajetan, how wild and furious he'd be if I stroked him tenderly and compas-sionately and he could be all three of you at the same time. (*A menacing movement of the three Shoemakers toward her*)

SAJETAN (*threateningly*) Hands off, boys!!

FIRST APPRENTICE Hands off yourself, boss!

SECOND APPRENTICE Just one good one!

DUCHESS And then fifteen years in jail! Scurvy wouldn't show you any mercy. No—get away! Terrell, tch-tch! Fidgeons, bring me the English smelling salts at once. (*Fidgeons hands her the English smelling salts in a green phial. She smells them and gives them to the Shoemakers to smell, which unfortunately calms them down for a short time only.*) There, you see: the only thing that your getting so excited accomplished is that the others are starting to quarrel among themselves. If Scurvy, as the highest representative of justice, with its unhealthy tendency toward independence, ever succeeds in cur-rying enough favor with the "Vigilant Youth" organization . . .

SAJETAN (*in pain, unmatched by anyone*) And my son's one of them —for that lousy money—my own son—my own son in that "Vigi-lant Youth"; I hope they choke on their own vigilance, the brave bullies! Oh—if only I'd burst from all this pain—I have no guts left. The ruptured screctum-scrapers—I don't even know how to swear any more—I can't even do that now.

FIRST APPRENTICE Take it easy—let that pig have her say once and for all, and may her grandmother be covered with batshit.

SECOND APPRENTICE Once and for all, once and for all! (*Writhing wildly*)

DUCHESS (*as if nothing were happening*) The truth of the matter is simply that you don't know how to organize yourselves because you're afraid you might create a managerial aristocracy and hierarchy although you're the ones now leading a stinking life—ha, ha!

FIRST APPRENTICE Son of a winking prunt! Belt her in her bitch pot!

SAJETAN The way you're swearing your tongue must have already turned into a pork sausage—simmer down. I want someone to clear up this business point by point once and for all, but that guy there just goes on swearing without any wit whatsoever, no light French touch. You'd better read Boy's *Little Words* if you want to improve your vocabulary, you gazoony, you bahooley, you dejuiced soaksocker, you gutreamed pukeslurper, you lousy bum . . .

DUCHESS (*coldly, hurt*) Are you listening, or aren't you? If you're going to continue to swear at one another, I'm leaving this instant for five o'clock tea, a time-honored custom among the aristocracy. As for your swearing directed at me, it only makes me laugh, you snotswallowers, you twimpicks, you unwiped fatasses running around on spindly legs . . .

SAJETAN (*grimly*) We're listening! We'll shut up now.

DUCHESS Now then, the ones "against" you—I'll put this in simple down-to-earth language so even you'll finally be able to understand (*with a Russian accent*) "in what the matter is"—they're diverse—that's the most important thing. We, that is, the aristocracy, are multicolored butterflies hovering above the excrement of this world —you've noticed how a butterfly sometimes alights on a little pile of shit. In the good old days we were like iron worms in the bowels of life's infinity, obeying transcendental laws or something: I'm no expert on the subject; I'm just a simple countess, let it go at that— but that's another story. Now then, it's this diversity that's causing our downfall, since for us, *pour les aristos*, "Vigilant Youth" is just that: too democratically vigilant, and no one knows what they might turn into. Scurvy's already sniffed out national socialism of an earlier vintage, but for his Supreme Vigilance, Pugnatsy Jawbloatski, even Scurvy's too much like you—oh, all social viewpoints are utterly relative! See how twisted this chain of relativity gets. What stinks in someone's nostrils smells sweet to somebody else, and vice versa. Personally I can't stand this kind of drama of ideas, as you well know: with the mayor, the blacksmith, twelve aldermen, woman spelled with a capital W, as the symbol of ur-lust, "he"—evidently the most important character—no one knows what his name is—workers both male and female, a mysterious stranger, and high above in the clouds, Christ and Karl Marx—not Karl Szymanowski —walking hand in hand; you can't kid me that way; I have to have a stake run through my body and then get whacked in the mouth. I like reality, and not obscure symbolism, derived from the half-baked political and economic theories of cheap newspapers, and turned into greeting-card jingles by Wyspiański's epigones.

FIRST APPRENTICE She's talking through her hat again, the bigmouth squawking bitch. Belt her one in the mouth, in that angelic puss of hers, and then let the chips fall where they may.

SECOND APPRENTICE I'm afraid if I let her have it, there's going to be a little crime-and-passion next—I won't be able to stop. Oh—the boss's got a real funny look on his face, he's already clobbered her. We'll tear her to pieces, boys, that spiritual, corncob madrona . . . (*He savors it in advance, making gestures in the air with his hands and smacking his lips.*)

SAJETAN (*drawing near, he clears his throat threateningly. The fox terrier springs at him.*) Hmr, hmr, hmr . . .

THE DUCHESS Terrell! Tch-tch!

(*The wall with the small window tumbles down; the rotten stump collapses; suddenly the view in the background darkens, with only the small lights glimmering in the distance and the lamp hanging from the ceiling gleaming weakly. Scurvy comes out from behind the curtain, dressed in a red hussar's uniform à la Lassalle. "Vigilant Youth" come rushing in behind him, dressed in red sweatshirts trimmed with gold galloon, and led by Sajetan's son, Joe.*)

SCURVY Here comes "Vigilant Youth"—here comes Joe Tempe, son of our Sajetan here. Now we're going to have one of those "abridged symbolic scenes" as they're called—we don't have time for a long process of development in the natural way. Round them all up. This is a hotbed of the most abominable anti-elite revolutionaries in the world. They're trying to paralyze all activity from the top down— and it's being hatched right here by a perverse woman, an insatiable female, a traitor to her own class, and her ultimate goal is an old-bag matriarchy whose sole purpose is to degrade virile, masculine force —society's a woman—it's got to have a male to rape it—black thoughts from the abyss—right?

SAJETAN You ought to be ashamed of yourself—that's absolute garbage.

SCURVY Quiet, Sajetan, quite, for God's sake. You're president of the secret society for lowering the level of culture; we're going to do it, without any loss of power; your son has the say here, you're nothing but an old fool, to put it simply—I won't use stronger language. A telephone call has just made me both Attorney General and Secretary of the Plurality of Realities, straight out of Chwistek's philosophy. I'm having everyone sent to jail in order to maintain an elite of superior minds.

SAJETAN (*in despair*) Or rather an elite of a few potbellies and maniacs —slaves to the power of money for its own sake—*als solches*—damn it all.

SCURVY Shut up, for Christ's sake . . .

DUCHESS You don't have any right to . . . (*They seize her, but then let her go.*)

SCURVY (*finishing his sentence*) . . . you old idiot, and don't talk in clichés; today I'd be capable of anything, and I don't want to begin my new career as the chief prosecuting attorney for the state with a crime of passion, although as a last resort, I could get away with it. I'll sign all the papers tomorrow at the office; I don't have a rubber stamp yet.

SAJETAN What a stupid, petty, small-minded thing to think of at a time like this!!

SCURVY (*to the Duchess, who is quietly smelling a flower*) You see, that's how I subdue man's purely animal desires: I want nothing for myself; I give everything to society.

DUCHESS (*her servant Fidgeons hands her her riding crop; she aims a blow with it at the lower part of Scurvy's belly.*) And are you going to give that, too?

SCURVY (*parrying the blow from the riding crop, he shouts in a mad frenzy*) Take them away, take them away, all four of them! This may seem very funny to you, but none of you realize what a giant web of depraved forces were mixed up in this. They could have blown up our whole future life and plunged the world into anarchy. I'll settle my accounts with you later, Duchess, now that at last we've got all the time in the world.

SAJETAN (*presenting his hands to be handcuffed*) Well—Joey: hurry up. I never thought that from my loins there'd spring such a . . .

JOSEPH TEMPE (*in a very theatrical manner*) All right, all right, father —none of your flowery language. There aren't any loins here, only hard facts, facts about society, and our petty personal gripes don't count: the individual is making a last-ditch stand against a future in which there'll be only lice.

SAJETAN Now, unfortunately, we really won't be saying unnecessary things any more—hey!!! (*The "Vigilant Youth" slowly start leading off all those present. Silence. Boredom. The curtain falls slowly, rises and falls once more. Still worse boredom.*)

The End of Act I

ACT II

The prison. The hall of compulsory unemployment divided into two parts by what are known as "balusters": on the left there's nothing—on the right a magnificently equipped shoemaker's workshop. In the middle, on a podium, a lectern for the prosecuting attorney, which is fenced off from the rest of the hall by ornate bars, behind it a door, and over it a stained-glass window, representing "the blessedness of working for one's living"—it can be completely unintelligible cubist rubbish —it's made clear to the audience by an inscription written in huge letters. In the left part of the hall the Shoemakers from Act I wander about aimlessly like hungry hyenas. From time to time they lie down or sit down on the ground—their movements reveal how monstrously worn out they are from boredom and lack of work. They often scratch themselves or scratch one another on the back. To the left by the door stands a Guard, a perfectly normal young man in a green uniform, obviously strong as an ox. Every moment or so he throws himself at one of the Shoemakers and despite any resistance drags him out through the door, and then almost immediately hauls him back again.

GUARD (*pointing to the back of the stage*) That's the hall for programed unemployment, devised to torment inmates who want to work. Simply out of spite that stained-glass window (*he points to the back of the stage*) represents the beatitudes of working for one's living. I have nothing more to say, and no one can force me to say anything. Prostitutes of Charity are strictly forbidden here. Mankind has become depraved—if we don't get anywhere this way, we'll officially go back to torture.

SAJETAN (*clutching his head*) Work, work, work! No matter what kind, as long as it's work. Oh, God—ah, I don't know anything any more. I've such pains in my innards from this compulsory idleness, as though burning lust for work were eating me up. Maybe I didn't say that so good. But what can I do? What can I do?

FIRST APPRENTICE I've never wanted a good piece the way I want to get my hands on workbenches and tools. I think I'll go mad. It's stupid, goddamn it! Prison sure can change a guy. I've been changed, like Wilde and Verlaine were, but without undergoing any conversion the way they did—oh, oh!

SECOND APPRENTICE Now it's my turn: give me work or I'll go mad, and then what'll happen? Give me anything: dolls' slippers, hoofs for artificial animals, imaginary sandals for nonexistent Cinderellas!

Oh—to make something—what happiness that would be! And we didn't appreciate it when we were up to our necks in it. Oh—for God's triple jewel—we've got too much suffering now, and before we didn't have much to call our own. Gertie, where are you now? Never again!

SAJETAN Take it easy, boys. I have a very strong feeling that their regime can't last long: something has to happen, and when it does . . . (*The Guard throws himself at the First Apprentice and drags him out to the left despite his cries and protests. Sajetan finishes his speech as if nothing had happened.*) I can't believe a force as tremendous as ours will simply rot away impotently without accomplishing anything.

SECOND APPRENTICE Quite a few have thought that way, and rotted away all the same. Life is terrible.

SAJETAN You're talking in clichés, baby.

SECOND APPRENTICE Clichés, clichés. The greatest truths are clichés, too. We can't make anything decent for ourselves out of our own guts any more. To be bored to death by a planned program of idleness, while being fed enough to keep forty bulls alive. It's hideous! You're old, but I feel like howling, and it won't be long before I howl myself to death. And yet life could be so beautiful, so really great: after a whole day of inhuman work, Gertie and I'd toss off a couple of large beers! (*Scurvy enters through the upper door on the left and comes to the lectern.*)

SCURVY (*dressed in a red robe and red biretta, sings*)
>   Mahatma downed a glass of beer,
>   It filled him with the greatest cheer,
>   He'll feel just grand for half a year,
>   If it's not there, perhaps it's here.

(*He points at the ground with his finger. The Guard throws the First Apprentice in. A very young and pretty female Guard wearing an apron over her uniform brings Scurvy's breakfast to the lectern. Scurvy drinks beer out of a large mug.*)

SECOND APPRENTICE There he is, our only consolation, our tormentor, our benemalefactor. If it weren't for him, you could really go mad. Poor humanity, can you understand that your best sons have sunk so low that now looking at one's executioner is the only cultural distraction left and one of the noblest? And besides, I mean, the two of us—but not the boss—hee, hee—I loathe my own laughter which sounds like an abandoned snotnose kid crying over a garbage can full of half-eaten scraps, cigarette butts, matted hair from combs, melon rinds, and tin cans—a pretty collection.

SAJETAN Shut up—don't bare your disgusting wounds in front of our master-executioner—he gets all puffed up when you do that and grows spiritually fat. (*The Guard looks at his watch—throws himself on the Second Apprentice and drags him out, despite his moans and all his resistance.*)

SECOND APPRENTICE (*during a short pause while he is being dragged out*) Oh, what agony, what agony—not to be able to do what you want for even a moment! What's compulsory work in comparison to that . . . (*Exit*)

SCURVY Hee, hee. I suffer more, because I haven't had any idea who I am ever since I gained political power. True justice under law has existed only in the most insipid, democratic, petit-bourgeois republics, when nothing socially important was happening, when there were no actual changes, when (*with despair in his voice*) all there was was a stagnant, fetid bog! Oh—if we could only arrange to have a Soviet-style Cheka and let the Secret Police run everything openly, without having to have anything to do with the courts.

SAJETAN Only great social ideas can justify such institutions and a double standard of justice. For the sake of the fat stomachs and ruined digestion of a few maniacs who've concentrated all the capital in their own hands, this would be just plain swinishness.

SCURVY (*deep in thought*) I don't know whether I'm the type of coward that dictatorship creates or a true adherent of fascism of the "Vigilant Youth" variety. Strength and manliness for their own sake! Who am I? My God! What have I made of myself! Liberalism is batshit—it's the biggest lie there is. God, oh, God! I'm made entirely of rubber which is being stretched over something indescribable. When will I finally burst? You can't live this way, it's not possible, but yet I'm living—it's horrible.

SAJETAN He's deliberately parading his sufferings in front of us, to show us it's possible to suffer in style, because of supposedly vital issues, out there, in the world of the free, where there's plenty of work, where there's sunshine and broads. Hey, hey: Mr. Prosecuting Attorney, I think someone will be using your head for a plough very soon. Maybe it'll be me—hee, hee!

SCURVY I've had enough of that—and of those jingles, in the post-Wyspiański prophetic style, produced by his wretched epigones. The race of bards has died out, and you won't ever be able to resurrect them or give birth to them again, even if you were to marry Wyspiański's celebrated, quote, "barefoot girl" . . .

FIRST APPRENTICE (*interrupts him*) Merciful God, don't even mention barefoot girls; just thinking about them here in this prison chokes me up.

SCURVY (*finishing his sentence kindly and calmly*) . . . and settle down here for life, which you'll probably do anyway, considering what our legal system is today. And your revolution may come, maybe just twenty-four hours after your richly deserved death. You'll all rot on a heap of damp hay: *"sur la paille humide,"* as the French say—(*he hums.*) Oh, the French, could we ever be so brilliant if we couldn't use our French words? (*The others grow conspicuously pale, gape, and fall on their knees.*) Ha—you're turning distinctly pale, my kittens, and your mouths are gaping in such a funny way that I taste both pleasure and pain. For some people there's no better emotional cocktail: it gives you in concentrated form the deepest, never-to-be-repeated miracle of existence, and at the same time its hopelessness. (*The Second Apprentice rushes in, pushed by the Guard, and also falls on his knees.*) Revolutions are never in a hurry—they take their time, the impersonal monsters.

SAJETAN (*on his knees*) Oh—such half-baked profundities: doesn't know himself what he's blabbing about, but everybody else thinks he's some kind of Socrates.

FIRST APPRENTICE (*with blanched lips*) I'm cringing in fear, and my lips have gone all white. And settle down here for life! (*He pronounces the first syllables distinctly—the last he crows wildly.*)

SAJETAN (*controlling himself by a superhuman effort and getting up off his knees*) I'm making a really superhuman effort to control myself. And I know I'll live to see our revolution. I've got good intuition and a sense of tempo: *tempo di pempo,* as someone once said, the slobbering pig drool. I know times are changing—in the past nationalism was something actually holy, especially for the subjugated and the conquered, but nowadays it's a plague, and I'll keep on saying so, even if you double my life sentence and give me a daily beauty treatment with a billy club every time I open my mouth.

SCURVY How's that again?

SAJETAN He's still asking questions, the shallow-naveled wretch: his one great pseudo-accomplishment has been to develop a way for getting all the capital in the hands of a few international bastards.

SCURVY I've had enough of your tiresome swearing and, worse still, your hackneyed ideology; stop it or I'll have you flogged.

SECOND APPRENTICE (*to Sajetan*) Take it easy—you're old: you can afford to say whatever you want, even to act heroic. But me—yes, me, well I'm still young—yeah, yeah: young and that's what. I want broads, nice hot juicy broads! (*He howls dismally.*)

SCURVY (*officially*) Mention a broad once more, and off you go to solitary confinement, so help me God. Prison is sacred, it's a place of duly constituted and legal punishment, and the prisoners are forbidden to sully it with such a dirty word!

SAJETAN As I was saying: nationalism won't produce a new civilization, it's all petered out. And yet in every country it's high treason to deliberately stir up antinationalism—despite the fact that nationalism is the cause of wars, international armament concerns, customs barriers, poverty, unemployment, and depressions. And yet this nightmare goes on and on to the eternal shame of mankind, and it will, I say, engulf wretched humanity, unworthy of itself, and suicidal in its stupidity.

SCURVY You know, I once . . .

SAJETAN (*ironically*) Once! Everybody did something once—what counts is what's being done now: if only there were a league, not for resolving official business of those nationalistic states, which by the very nature of the, if you'll excuse the expression, capitalistic structure is impossible, but instead a league for combating nationalistic egotism and for doing this from the top down, beginning with the enlightened intellectuals among the elite. But one thing is certain: whoever owns something won't passively give it up—it has to be torn out of his flesh and guts. Individual volunteers are rare as radium, a group of volunteers all the more so—and a whole class the rarest. A class is a class and will remain one till it's exterminated right down to the last bedbug—ha!

SCURVY (*actually in terrible pain*) Sajetan, Sajetan!

SAJETAN After all, no one wants to rip out someone else's tongue. New synthetic peoples who have lost their national characteristics in a natural way might still be able to come up with something, which they never will as things are now because they're rotting away, hey! From the top down! Please understand, Mr. Scurvy: this wouldn't be high treason then—it would be a beautiful humanitarian ideal, no matter how you look at it—I ask you, isn't that so?

SCURVY You've got a head on your shoulders, Sajetan—I don't deny you that. The whole world would be organized under one single authority, and universal prosperity would become established quite naturally through the increase in knowhow about the distribution of wealth; wars would be utterly unimaginable . . .

SAJETAN (*reaching out his arms toward him—the first time that he is facing him—up till now he has been facing the son-of-a-bitch of an audience*) Well, why don't you start it yourself? Do you all think that we have to begin the revolution from the bottom, even if it could be started from the top without making any compromises? Everybody continues to occupy the same jobs. Those who don't

want to work for the new regime—shoot them, and you immediately knock the weapons out of the hands of the opposition by
depriving them of their subordinates. What's a battalion commander
without his battalion—a scarecrow in a uniform, that's all.

SCURVY *(perplexed)* Hm, hm . . .

SAJETAN All you'd have to do is issue orders—one, two, three, and
schluss, finito! I repeat, why don't you start it yourself, since you
have the power and it's rotting away into shit in your hands, you son
of a whore, when it could be a fistfull of creative thunderbolts? If
you know all this, why don't you have the courage to do it? Are
you so concerned about giving up your petty little creature com-
forts, which are of no damn importance to anyone? Or is it out of
consideration for that cheap little son-of-a-bitch of an audience, for
popularity's sake, or what? Oh—if higher powers existed, I'd pray to
them to instruct this high-explosive F-bomb how to explode of its
own free will. If there's a planned parenthood association, why isn't
there an institute for instructing statesmen what the basic meaning
of the word "humanity" is, and the true nature of decisive moments
in history! Why are they always narrow-minded pawns of some
provincial scheme or conspiracy at the back of which, or rather at
the bottom of which, sits the hideous, sterile, sexless octopus of
international finance and of bastardism and crookedness in Pure
Form, and so forth and so on? Why won't you do it, since you have
the power? Why not?

SCURVY It's not as simple as that, *mon cher* Sayetang!

SAJETAN You got your power from them, and you're afraid to use it
against them—you're too honest. But look, sir, this would be mach-
iavellianism of the highest sort in the name of the highest ideals:
for all humanity. Don't be a fool, like a second Alfonso XIII, or
some old Louis, and wait till they forcibly drive you out of this
palace and off this lectern.

SCURVY *(sadly, with irony)* So as to leave you something to do, Sajetan. If I were to step down of my own free will, you'd lose your
heroic place in the history of the world: you'd be as completely out
of work as all the national bards and messianic prophets after what
came to be officially known as "Poland's bursting forth on the
scene." There's no such thing as humanity—there's only worms in
the cheese, which is a heap of worms itself.

SAJETAN What stupid jokes: they're not worth the left half-toenail on
Pugnatsy Jawbloatski's right foot.

SCURVY *(calmly)* Since you're in here for life, I can't punish you any
further. You have the right to insult me with impunity, but it's the
height of poor taste, and not in the aristocratic sense of the word, to

take advantage of this right. I won't have you flogged—I only said
that to frighten you—I'm a humanitarian.

SAJETAN (*ashamed*) Mr. Scurvy, I beg you to forgive me! I won't ever
do it again.

SCURVY Never mind, never mind—go on. I'm talking to you this way
to bridge the gap between us.

SAJETAN When you talk to children and simple people, you shouldn't
ever talk down to them. They can see right away that that's what
you're doing, and it offends them.

SCURVY (*with a certain impatience, he looks at his watch at the same
time*) All right, all right—go on.

SAJETAN Look, Mr. Scurvy, this moment is unique, as lovers used to
say to each other in erotic novels—fortunately that tribe's already
become extinct. The representatives of the two fundamental powers,
typifying the two movements dominant in each class: the individual
and the group, have never spoken to each other before face to face.
It's a diabolically complicated matter: for the individual must stand
for the group, and at times for only a small part of it, until the time
comes when that small part has the task of representing the whole
class, in whose name the Revolution must be undertaken—is that
clear?

SCURVY There's historical metaphysics for you! But, Sajetan: that mission—as you put it—will be carried out by the "small part of the
group," as it's called, which is the worst off materially. But authority
comes from the totem—remember, without authority, mankind as
we know it today wouldn't even exist, and you wouldn't be able to
raise such a ruckus about your freedom (*with a frenzied
insistence*) and—I say this most emphatically—find your greatest
fulfillment as an individual in it. That's the crucial point, that's
where the nobility has a little bit of truth on its side, the sons-of-
bitches. But in order to accomplish anything, you have to be somewhat stupid and have a one-track mind. A really clever character
won't do anything: he'll contemplate his own navel and that's all. I
don't want to rob you of your spiritual goods. I can see the innermost lining of life and of human souls, too.

SAJETAN You're a scab, you're a prosecuting attorney, in the worst
sense of the word—stop that flopping around like a fish. You're no
expert on life, you're just an expert at considering everyone, even
yourself, as so many different kinds of pigs. Anyhow, maybe there's
some truth in it, but it's like that trite maxim that altruism is only
egotism—here we touch on something fundamental: existence without individuality and without a plurality of individuals is un-i-mag-
i-na-ble. But let's go back to the previous subject, even though the

idiot public of today vomits when you give them long involved
speeches. Well, why don't you give this some serious thought: you
can go straight to the front and tear down all barriers between
nations, a golden age for mankind will begin, even if that's a cliché.
Whatever national culture had to offer, it's already given us—why
live burdened by its rotting carcass? Why? After all, you don't
believe that the future of mankind lies in this particular form of
society, do you?

SCURVY Sajetan, Sajetan! Was the cortex of certain salamanders in the
Jurassic and Triassic periods necessary to create something both as
radiant and as repulsive as the human species?

SAJETAN Quit trying to get out of answering! What's holding you
back? Now you're lying, and you know it. I can see clearly, it's a
matter of intuition: that you're no bigoted fanatical nationalist, out
for aggression, to put it ultrapolitely.

SCURVY (*evasively, but in a towering state of despair*) You have no
idea what a tragedy . . .

SAJETAN Now he'll pester me with his imaginary little tragedies! Mine
—is a real tragedy! I see the ultimate truth for all mankind because
I'm really seeing it, my personal life is flowing away like the blackest
nightmare out of a sewer, while you bathe in girls and mayonnaise.

BOTH APPRENTICES (*shouting*) Haaa! Haaaaa!!

SCURVY A girl in mayonnaise! What won't the poor think of next! I'll
have to give it a try!

SAJETAN Answer me, you son of a sucking prunt, or else I'll paralyze
the nerve centers of your conscience with my special concentrated
extract: will power of the masses.

SCURVY An inspired old man—a rarity these days.

SAJETAN Hey, hey, Mr. Prosecuting Attorney; talk's cheap—I have a
feeling you'll regret those words before long!

SCURVY (*more serious and growing disconcerted*) Sajetan, can't you
see that I'm hiding from the monstrous tragedy of my real situation
and my really frightful inner emptiness? Apart from my Duchess
problem, there's literally nothing inside me—I'm the eaten-out shell
of a crab that never existed. Witkacy, that slop-artist from Zakopane, tried to persuade me to take up philosophy—I couldn't even
do that. When she stops torturing me, I'll stop existing and simply
go on living out of habit . . .

SAJETAN And stuff yourself with jellied plenckus in quasi-astral sauces,
while we catch six lice a minute here, have insomnia because of
constant itching, freeze in winter, suffocate in summer, in the transcendental stink and continual, all-pervasive irritation of all our
senses, leading to madness, with hatred, envy, and jealousy so violent

it simply can't be expressed by words, but only by a good shove
. . . (*makes the gesture*)

SCURVY Stop that, or else I'll smother like a baby duck—I know what
I'm talking about—I'm *à bout de mes forces vitales.* You'd like to
know, wouldn't you, you mule, why I won't step down? Because I
have to eat what I have to eat and what I've been brought up to eat;
I have to wash myself properly, have my fingernails manicured,
sleep on a soft bed, and not stink like you; go to the theater and have
a nice girl as an antidote for that pearl of all the hells on earth, that
. . . (*He shakes both his fists, first to the right, and then to the
left.*) Even my authority and power to torture can't crush her,
because she likes it, the cunning hunk of cut-up slut really likes it,
but I don't feel anything myself—I'm as horrified of rape as a
corporal is of cockroaches in the barracks—whatever I do only gives
her more pleasure . . . (*He sings the words from "only" on, in
what is virtually a baritone.*)

SAJETAN So these are the essential problems, the really important problems facing the men who run our lives. It's such an abomination that
words literally cannot express it. Everything a man like you does is
supposed to be for the good of the state, for all sorts of high ideals,
for the good of mankind—but what really counts is what goes on
after "office hours"—I say that in quotation marks—that's when a
man shows his true character.

SCURVY Shut up—you can't possibly grasp the terrible conflict of contradictory forces going on inside me. As minister of justice I lie
intentionally and deliberately, have people hanged without any conviction, just so I can go on gorging myself on jellied plenckus and
cuttlefish from the Gulf of Mexico which are so damned delicious
—yes: I have to lie, and I assure you that nowadays 98 per cent—
these are the latest figures from the Central Bureau of Statistics—and
nowadays statistics are everything, not only in physics but what's
most significant in monadological metaphysics, too, with its stress on
living matter—well, 98 per cent of our entire gang is doing just the
same thing without any belief in what they're doing, solely to prop
up the remnants of a dying class—made up of what kind of individuals, you'd like to know?—of ordinary crooks masquerading behind a
few supposed ideals, all of which are more or less fraudulent. Now
the only real people left are you—everybody knows that. But that's
only because you're on the other side—when you once cross the
line, you'll become just as bad as we are.

SAJETAN (*emphatically*) Never—never in a thousand years! (*Scurvy
laughs ironically.*) We're going to create a new, uncorruptible type
of man. Soviet Russia is just a heroic attempt—good as far as it

goes, like a small island in the midst of a hostile sea. But right from the very start we're going to create a new form of humanity which will endure until the final setting of the sun, until the shit-covered extinction of our reptiles on the frozen earth, so dear and holy to us.

SCURVY He always has to butt in with something in poor taste: the rabble will never learn tact and a sense of moderation. (*Shouts*) Off to the *pissoir* with him! (*They drag the First Apprentice out to the pissoir.*)

SAJETAN And where's your sense of moderation when you think about her?—you pig?! (*The Prosecuting Attorney bristles and snorts angrily.*)

SCURVY I've bristled, I've snorted angrily, and I feel better already. (*Rings a hand bell; guards rush in from both sides behind the balusters.*) Bring in Irina Moltocockroachin to be cross-examined! I don't know why I'm talking like this. It's no joke—even when we're free to act, there's a strange surrealistic compulsion that makes us do what we do.

SAJETAN What's this monster getting all involved in?—idiotic hair-splitting—that's what they call their intellectual life, once they've finished their official duties in offices and bedrooms pushing others around.

SCURVY You don't understand what a delight it is for an impotent drone like me to gain self-knowledge—what an abyss of ecstasy to try to justify my own existence—by rummaging around in myself . . .

SAJETAN For God's sake, calm down, Mr. Scurvy. Oh, God, my God— I'm talking like a machine. How can I ever fill the emptiness of these days? Talking with this personification of falsehood (*he points to the Prosecuting Attorney*) was like paradise in comparison with the loneliness and compulsory idleness I felt in my cell. Everything is relative! Don't let me change so much that I won't even know who I am any more! Who will I be in three days, in two weeks, in three years . . . years . . . years . . . (*He falls on his knees and weeps. The Guards bring the Duchess into the compartment on the right, throw her down next to the stools, and go out again. In a convict's uniform the Duchess looks charming, like a schoolgirl.*)

SCURVY (*coldly*) Get on with your work. (*The Duchess, glumly silent, sets to work making boots very ineptly, with grim abhorrence.*) All right, all right—no crying or hysterics—don't interrupt me. It was interesting talking with you—that's a fact. (*The Guards throw the First Apprentice back in.*)

DUCHESS I loathe and abhor stitching these boots, but it gives me a thrill all the same. I can get a thrill out of anything, I'm so weird. (*In a haughty tone*) For you, everything's grist for your pure dialectics mill. You think it's no more necessary for ideas to have counterparts in reality than it is for a goat to wear a monocle, as the Poles say. You're only interested in the interrelationship of ideas among themselves. (*She weeps.*)

SCURVY For example, the interrelationship between the idea of your body, or more precisely: the idea of its dilating itself and the idea of a similar swelling in mine—Hee, hee, haha! (*He laughs hysterically, sobs a little, and speaks to Sajetan, who has just stopped crying—so there was a moment when all three of them were crying at once—even the Apprentices were blubbering a little, too.*) What gets me about everything you've all been saying is that you've unashamedly been doing it all solely to fill your belly—oh, how unoriginal! We still have ideals.

SAJETAN I feel like throwing up, this conversation is trite as the thoughts of a corpulent corporal on the isle of Capri—this witless witticism expresses how absolutely hideous this life is. You have principles because your belly's stuffed and you got the time, too.

DUCHESS (*making shoes*) Yes—oh, yes—oh, yes . . .

SCURVY Your materialism's flat as a tapeworm, it frightens me. What's going to happen later on, later on, later on . . . I desperately envy you your ability to speak the truth, and what's even more important, to feel it. A vision of mankind, eating itself up tail first, frightens me like a vision of the future.

SAJETAN As for you, pussycat, you're only defending your own belly and other bellies just like yours—that cliché gives me a pain, like a red-hot poker up my ass. We'll create a new life once we conquer the belly—is that a profound belief, or a meaningless platitude? Put culture back where it belongs without losing spiritual values—that's our aim. But you can't begin until you've knocked down all the national toll gates and boundary posts.

SCURVY I don't believe in that—you'll forgive me, Sajetan, although I may have said the same thing a moment ago. But . . . after having thought it over—yes, I admit: we simply can't renounce our standard of living voluntarily—that's the most difficult thing. A few saints have done it, but no one knows exactly what pleasure they derived from it on some other level.

SAJETAN There must be some compensation. But on the other hand, how many saints have suffered inhumanly to the end of their lives because of ambition, a sense of honor, and public pressure . . .

SCURVY Wait—let me think—as the critic Emil Breiter used to say, if no one aimed at a higher standard of living, nothing at all would ever happen: no culture, no science, no art—just a communistic, totemistic, primitive tribe would go on and on without "potlatch," that ridiculous struggle for power which is the origin of authority . . .

SAJETAN I know: you catch six hundred fish, say, your opponent catches three hundred, and you throw two hundred back into the sea.

SCURVY You're quite the know-it-all, aren't you, Sajetan. So that clan of yours would last till the end of the world—then what? It would be formless, astructural, without any possibility of transcending itself or moving into the higher regions of a new social organization. My ordinary little life is mine—I'm a small-town boy, I snatched my existence out of the great void by studying law, by long years of legalized murder, by spending all my waking moments, not amusing myself, but boning up on everything I could lay my hands on. My ordinary little life is mine, it belongs to me, and I'll never give it up. And I don't believe in this new life you're going to create—and that's my tragedy, pure and simple.

SAJETAN I spit on your tragedy; I crap on it! There are endless possibilities once the barriers between nations are abolished. With our imperfect knowledge of legal history and the wretched mess our ideas are in today, we can't even envisage what new ideas will be born then.

SCURVY I don't like your venturing into speculations above your intellectual capacity. Your ideas are inadequate to express what you want to say. Now I have the necessary mental equipment—to lie. No one can grasp that tragedy. Sometimes it's really awful.

SAJETAN Tragedy begins in the guts where it hurts. Those thoughts of yours, Mr. Prosecuting Attorney, don't penetrate to the nerve center—it's only the cortex of your brain that suffers painlessly and delightfully, holy mother of a slut. For us, from our point of view, that's pure fun, and those tragedies of yours—are nothing but pure pleasure: after a girl or two and some jellied plenckus, stretch out on a nice little bed, read a while, think about trash like we're discussing here, and then doze off, enjoying the thought that you're such an interesting man for some crud-crusted piece of tail. Oh, I wish I could have some fun with a tragedy like that! My God—what fantastic happiness that would be. What happiness—oh, if only the pain in my gut would go away for just a minute—I'm hurting for myself and for all mankind—oh, hey! (*He twists up into a knot. The Duchess laughs blithely.*)

SCURVY (*to the Duchess*) Don't laugh with such relish, you piece of tail, or I'll explode. (*Emphatically to Sajetan*) Now it'll have to be proved that your guts are really bleeding for all mankind. Maybe that never happens. (*A heavy silence for a very long time. Then Scurvy speaks over this background of silence, in which can be heard [sic] a distant tango from a radio.*) There's dancing at the Hotel Savoy in London. There they're really having fun. You'll excuse me a moment—I'm human too. (*He runs out to the left.*)

SAJETAN A guy like that can do anything he wants, whenever he wants to—but we can't even . . .

DUCHESS Quiet—don't make me laugh. The things you make up really tickle me.

SAJETAN (*suddenly moved*) Oh, my love, my dove! You don't know how lucky you are that you can work! We're so hot for work we can't keep our stinking fingers and legs from jumping; we're popping out all over to get at the only source of consolation, till we're ready to burst. But here there's nothing to do but stare at the bare gray walls and go mad. Thoughts come crawling in like bedbugs. And aching doubts swell from boredom dreadful as Mount Gaurizankar, stinking as the Cloaca Maxima, and Mount Excrement in the fantastic novel by Bulldog Mirkle—from boredom which bleeds like an ulcer, like a carbuncle—I'm running out of bitching words again, and yet I still want to go on yakking, like I'd like to do you know what. What's the point of yakking, anyhow? No one's going to understand it. I don't even have any proverbial blubber left in me. So why even try to express yourself? Why yell and scream, why rupture your gut, backward and forward? Why? Why? Why? "Why" is such a dismal word. It's the essence of emptiness and pain —so why bother? Since there's no work and nothing can come of it. (*He crawls up to the bars. To the Duchess*) Fair lady, my dearest, my own sweetheart, my transcendental pussycat, my metaphysical God-calf, so divinely mortal, and sweet, clever, and intelligent as a mouse—you don't know how lucky you are that you can work!— that's the only thing that justifies the existence of any living creature with all its wretched limitations, starting with the temporal-spatial ones.

DUCHESS Making work metaphysical is only a transitional phase in dealing with that question. The great lords of ancient Egypt didn't need it, any more than the men of the future will. He's howling for work, and work's what's tearing me in two, both spiritually and physically. That's how relative everything is—it's all due to Einstein —a long time ago I read . . .

FIRST APPRENTICE You ought to be ashamed, you contagious bitch virus! That's a lot of intellectual crap! Don't you know the theory of relativity in physics doesn't apply to ethics and aesthetics and dialectics and so on!—tum-tee-tum-tum-tum, dum-dee-dum-dum-dum! But I'll keep my mouth shut—it makes you vomit to listen to all that bilge. Hey, hey!—Sajetan—we won't talk about unimportant things any more—the way we used to—but what's left? We've talked about so many unimportant things, and now they've made work as appealing to us as a hooker from the tenderloin on a Sunday afternoon. I used that comparison because I don't even react at all, you know, sexually, to those really good-looking high-class broads—they're too good-looking, the frigging stuck-up bitches—too good-looking and too un-ap-proa-cha-ble! (*Repeats in despair*) And I've got the same kind of hankering for sewing boots as for simple, down-to-earth girls. (*With insane calmness*) Give me work, or there'll be trouble! (*With terrible resignation*) But who cares? I'm saying this with a hopeless sense of futility, unintelligible to anyone today.

SCURVY (*sings backstage*)

> I've grown quite bored with all the *femmes du monde*,
> And rage with mad desire for some cheap blonde.
> Today with strange new sights I'll be beguiled.
> Tomorrow I'll do something really "wild."

(*The Duchess listens very attentively.*)

SECOND APPRENTICE (*to the First Apprentice*) Don't talk to society the way you would to your mother or try to get anything out of it; it won't listen and, what's more, it'll give you a kick in the teeth for sucking up to it—hey!

SAJETAN Don't say "hey"—stop it, for Christ's sake! Don't remind me of those times, forever bygone!—"*o, ma mignonne*"—filthy and completely unaesthetic regrets rip my innards apart, making me dreadfully ashamed and disgusted with myself, as though I were a live cockroach in my own mouth. Hey, hey! (*Scurvy runs up to the lectern and buttons himself up somehow in a wild way [coat and so on] and rubs his hands. The Duchess watches him very penetratingly —almost ostentatiously.*)

SCURVY It's damned cold in all the toilets around here—a frost must be setting in. After all this, now I'll really enjoy some Mexican fried cuttlefish. (*A tango from the distance.*) But before that I'll go skating—there'll be waltzes. (*He sniffs in front of him.*) What a disgusting stink—their souls are rotting away in ghastly idleness and decomposing into a dead jam.

DUCHESS (*setting to work*) That's sadism—my sphere and domain.

SCURVY (*hysterically*) But I'm getting bored, damn it all to hell! If that's the way you're going to be, I'll have you all hanged without a trial! What's my power good for? I ask you? It would be a major event in the world of sports. Oh, power—what an abyss—how profound and fragrant are your temptations!

DUCHESS *(stops sewing the boots)* You know, Scurvy, my poor little nitwit Scurvykins, for the first time you're beginning to really appeal to me. I've got to live through everything, experience the worst, bedbug-infested corners of the soul and the crystal peaks, inaccessible on impenetrable moonlit nights . . .

SCURVY What a bitch of a style—it's really outrageous . . .

DUCHESS *(without becoming in the least embarrassed)* I'm a true aristocrat, nothing can faze me—that's one of our sterling attributes. Well, then: I've got to have you somewhere along the line, otherwise my life would be incomplete. But later when you've been imprisoned by them *(she points at the shoemakers with the boot which she's holding in her left hand)* and start to rot away in your cell, dying from lust for me—yes, for me: lust for somebody, that's the whole point—for a large beer and sandwiches from the Waldorf Astoria, I'll give myself to Sajetan who'll be at the height of his power, and then to those marvelous smelly boys—those, those shoemaking goo-spreaders straight out of this world—hey, oh, hey!! And at last, ah, I'll be happy, because then you'll give your whole life just to touch the hem of my dress and to have a bottle of beer from Heidelberg.

SCURVY *(numb with lust)* I'm utterly numb with infernal lust, coupled with other ideas in really dreadful taste. As a matter of fact, I'm like a glass filled to the brim; if I move, I'll overflow. My eyes are popping out of my head. I'm all puffed up like a full head of lettuce, and my brain is like cotton dipped in the pus of wounds from the world beyond. Oh, what a wild, elusive, unattainable temptation! The first injustice in the name of legal authority. *(Shouts suddenly)* Come on out of prison, you metaphysical piece of tail! Come what may: I'll have the time of my life for once, even if I have to die from remorse later on, like the criminals bred by the Duke des Esseintes in Huysmans!

DUCHESS We're talking just like ordinary people, not like idealists blinded by their own ideals. An average man won't voluntarily lower his standard of living, unless he's hit hard right in the face. And this applies to you too, my poor little Scurvykins. I'm not even talking about the idealistic side of the matter, only about the savage, snarling, basic layer of flesh and guts, which our personality crawls over like a poisonous cobra in the jungle.

SCURVY And you women aren't like that, I suppose . . .

DUCHESS Existence is hateful, try to get that through your head. It's only thanks to the illusions of a small segment of society in the total life of our species that anyone believes that there's any sense to life at all. It all comes down to the different classes eating one another up. The balance of power between fighting microbes makes our existence possible—if there were no struggle, as long as the food held out, a single species would have covered the entire surface of the earth in a few days with a layer forty miles thick.

SCURVY Oh, she's a clever one, you've got to admit that! It's driving me wild. Come to me as you are: unwashed, drenched in the stink of the prison air. (*The Duchess stands up, throws the boot down with a crash, and remains standing somewhat strangely lost in thought.*)

DUCHESS Somehow I've grown strangely pensive—the way a woman does—I don't think with my brain at all. The monster inside me does all my thinking for me. Maybe I won't give myself to you at all, Robert—it'll be better that way: more atrocious, but pleasanter for me.

SCURVY Oh no!—you can't do that to me now! (*He pulls off his purple robe.*) Now I'll really go mad. (*He runs to the bars and feverishly unlocks the door.*)

SAJETAN And while that crew—*eine ganz konceptionslose Bande*—is worrying about stuff like that and problems like that, we're dying like cattle for lack of work. Technical administrators for nonexistent little schemes—that's what you are! I've even lost my interest in women because of this pure desire to produce something, just anything at all.

THE APPRENTICES (*in chorus*) So have we! So have we!

FIRST APPRENTICE We've laid the problem of the machine aside for the moment: the machine's become too hackneyed—everybody knows about it—the futurists have run it into the ground—ugh . . . it makes you shudder just to hear the sound of the word "machine tool"!

SECOND APPRENTICE The machine is merely an extension of our own arms—that's the kind of acromegaly that's been growing up, you know—it's time to do some cutting down. Anyhow, a certain number of machines will be destroyed according to our plan of setting culture back. Inventors will be condemned to death after prolonged torture.

SAJETAN (*suddenly dazzled by a new idea*) I've just had a dazzling new idea. Hey, boys: let's knock down those puny little balusters and get right down to work like all hell broke loose. Get going! A hand-made boot race! Now or never! Hey! Hey!

FIRST APPRENTICE And then what'll happen?

SAJETAN For at least five minutes we'll live it up and work our heads off, before they chain us up and slaughter us. You only live once— why knock yourself out thinking? Workers commit rape on work —oh, hey!!

APPRENTICES At 'em! You either do—or you don't! Son of a prunt! I don't give a damn! What the hell! Hee, hee! (*and other similar exclamations. All three of them hurl themselves forward "like a shot," knock down the balusters, and hurl themselves like hungry beasts on the stools, shoemakers' tools, bundles of leather, and boots. They begin to work feverishly and furiously. In the meantime Scurvy throws his red robe over the Duchess' prison uniform—in which she looks exceptionally attractive—and they stand close together by the lectern. He holds her in his arms. They ogle each other.*)

SCURVY (*tenderly*) You're my little prosecuting attorney: now I'm going to kiss you to death.

DUCHESS (*with the Shoemakers panting in the background*) If that joke is any indication, you must be abominable when you're making love. At least shut up—I like it when it's performed as a silent ceremony of male degradation in absolute quiet—then I can hear eternity.

SAJETAN (*panting*) Here—give me the thread—hammer it in—here, like this . . .

FIRST APPRENTICE (*panting*) Here—take the hammer—Hey! Hurry up —here's a peg—give me the leather . . .

SECOND APPRENTICE (*panting*) Shove it in all the way—that's right— fasten it—stitch it—whack it—grease it all up—sock it in . . . (*There begins to be something lunatic about their work.*)

SCURVY (*emphatically*) Look, my dear: they're working too feverishly. There's something frightening about it. I can't say this emphatically enough; I want to stress this fact. Is this the beginning of a new era, or what the hell is it?

DUCHESS Quiet—let's watch—it's awful! I was part of that world only a minute ago. You saved me, my dear!

SAJETAN (*turning his head toward them, ironically*) They're working too feverishly! "Monkey face!" (*Said with a Russian accent.*) You've never understood what work is! (*Wildly inspired he pounds with his hammer. The others tear everything out of one another's hands; it all falls out of their hands. They moan dumbly and eagerly.*) Oh, work, work!—they remunerate, but they don't compensate! Down with it! What stupid prophetic jingles! I'm a realist.

Give me a nail—you got one. Oh, nail, strange visitor in the bottom of the shoe—who can comprehend the full extent of your strangeness? And work!—Is there anything stranger? Especially considering how horribly vulgar it is. Hammer! Pound! Your hands are burning—there aren't guts enough—cut it, grease it up, put it in the fire—then brag before they drag you in the mire. There go those blasted prophetic rhymes again—son of a bitch!

SECOND APPRENTICE Here—nail it in—hit it—pound it—bend it. Here's a boot! Oh, boots, boots—how beautiful you are! Worlds with their boots on! We'll put boots on the entire world—we'll work it over, we'll crap it up—it all comes out the same. Prison or no prison—work is irresistible. Work is the greatest miracle, it's the metaphysical unity of the plurality of worlds—it's the absolute! We'll work ourselves to death, to eternal life beyond the grave—if we're lucky! Who knows what's really at the bottom of work like ours!

FIRST APPRENTICE I'm shaking all over like a turbine with a million stallion-and-mare-power. Don't need girls, don't need beer—don't need radios, movies, or any kind of mental second-story men! Work for its own sake—that's the highest goal—*Arbeit an und für sich!* Hold it, pound it, thread it—jab it! Boots, boots—are rising up, emerging out of the nothingness of bootish slime, from the eternal, pure idea of the boot, looming up out of the abyss, ideal and empty as a hundred million barns. Hammer, hammer—well-hammered boots won't go to pieces—that's the truth, the absolute truth. There are as many kinds of truths as there are kinds of boots and as many concepts of the boot as a single Alpha accounts for the totality of all numbers. God—if only it could go on like this forever. Don't need broads—*Arbeit an sich*—like a dagger in the heart. Don't need beer—or my brains aired out through my ear. Happiness gushes out of one's own guts like a hidden stream among the reeds—it rushes and rushes. The hand-made boot trade hammers away in a hell of a hurry, hauling up everything out of us—but the wholesale boot supply can never keep pace with the whole world's needs—a miserable line but that's not the crucial matter: a boot is born, a boot is born!!

SCURVY Listen to that!—they've created a new metaphysics. Rena: it's a dangerous bomb—it's a new brand of missile from the nonexistent other world beyond. Rena, I'm afraid for the first time in my life. Perhaps this is actually, quote, "the solemn rite of initiation," end of quote, for the new epoch—yes: Solemn rite of initiation—"let the new age begin with a solemn rite of initiation"—as they used to say in the good old days. (*Completely stupefied*)

DUCHESS I'm gorging myself to the full on their delusions of happiness in the midst of the greatest agony—their agony, not mine—and their unparalleled stupidity—I'm becoming glutted, like a bear in the forest on honey. The two of us, two essentially criminal minds, inseparably joined in sexual embraces without the help of any artificial aids . . .

SCURVY But that's what'll happen, won't it? That's what'll really happen, won't it? What?—it won't? There won't be all that? Say there will, say there will, or I'll die.

DUCHESS Maybe today you'll get to know my complete emptiness—perhaps . . . (*The others are continually muttering and panting, working incessantly.*)

SCURVY Look—they're working more and more wildly. Something really frightening is finally happening here, which no economist in the world could ever have predicted. Look, my darling: I'm willing to die, today I want nothing but you.

DUCHESS That's just talk—it's only today that you're really beginning to live. But who cares anyway? Everything seems so petty to me. Oh—if only one could fill the whole world with oneself and immediately afterward die like a dog.

SCURVY More artistic problems—to hell with that filthy insatiable craving for form and content. Look: they're like wild animals, or rather work gone wild, excreted like the pure primitive emotions, like the instinct for feeding oneself and for procreation. Let's get out of here, or I'll go right out of my mind.

DUCHESS Look into my eyes.

SCURVY (*as though speaking to a child*) But dear, we have to put a stop to this deluge of work at all costs; it's really unheard of, and—if this psychosis spreads—they'll smash the world to pieces and destroy all the artificial floodgates. From under the rotting carcass of neo-ideologies, they'll drag out poor puny old mankind to be a laughing stock for apes, pigs, lemurs, and reptiles—our forefathers before the species degenerated.

DUCHESS What in the hell are you yakking about now?

SCURVY Mankind is a pitiful old thing, a frightful old thing! We've raised ourselves above it for one second of higher awareness of our own personal misery and the worthlessness of our feelings. In this never-to-be-repeated moment you have to stand by me, you yahoo!! (*He kisses the Duchess and whistles through his fingers. In rush Pugnatsy Jawbloatski's boys, the same as in Act I. Sajetan's son leads them.*) Grab them! Put them in solitary and idletary! Don't give them anything to do! I don't want to hear a peep out of them—

work's the greatest hidden threat to mankind. *Arbeit an sich*—it's a stick in the spokes of the wheels of progress. No tools at all!—understand?—even if they howl themselves to death. (*The Boys throw themselves on the Shoemakers. A dreadful fight in which the Boys become infected and begin working too: they simply become "shoemakerized." Sajetan falls into his son's arms, and they work together.*)

SCURVY Look, my pet—it's horrible. They've become "shoemakerized." My bodyguard no longer exists. It'll spread to the city and then caput.

DUCHESS You've completely forgotten about me . . .

SCURVY Even Pugnatsy Jawbloatski himself couldn't do anything to stop his boys from getting caught up in it, like in the gears of some infernal machine . . . And even he'll work himself to death, signing all those endless piles of documents . . .

DUCHESS But isn't this a magnificent background for our first and final night together!—our night, yours and mine—my poor little Scurvy-kins! *Di doman non c'è certezza!* Tomorrow I'll probably be "theirs"—I'm putting "theirs" in quotation marks—and you'll be rotting in a dungeon—such a poor rotten little rotter. With that thought in your soul, with that feeling of last-timeness, you'll be insane enough to inflame me today, so I'll burn like a star of the first magnitude suddenly appearing in the masculine firmament of underworlds belonging to the great Giant Carcass of Existence.

SCURVY I've really been had. (*The others go on muttering, of course during the pauses when no one else is speaking.*)

SHOEMAKERS AND BOYS Pound, sew, hammer, son of a prunt; the boot's the thing.

SAJETAN The boot as the ab-so-lute! (*incorrectly accented on the last syllable*) Do you understand this miraculous square root? The greatest symbol is the boot—let all illusions follow suit!

SCURVY (*to the Duchess*) That's tremendous—all this symbolism isn't half so stupid after all. I know I'm going to die, but I won't give in to you. Not unless I can kill you right now—on the spot. But that'd be a shame, a real shame—that body of yours, those eyes, those legs —and all those unbelievable moments together.

DUCHESS Come on then—son of a prunt. I wanted to have you just like this against a background of infernal work for work's sake. Where in the holy hell is that red glare coming from?

(*A red glare is, in fact, flooding the stage. Scurvy and the Duchess run out to the right. The work goes on like mad.*)

The End of Act II

ACT III

Setting as in Act I, but without the curtain and the small window. The semicircular boundary of the foreground is somewhat planet-shaped. All that remains is the tree trunk, on which red and green signal lights are shining. The floor is covered with a magnificent carpet. In the background down below a distant night landscape—lights from houses and full moon. Sajetan, in a magnificent colored dressing gown (beard trimmed and hair combed), stands in the middle of the stage, supported by the Apprentices, dressed in flowered pajamas with hair combed smoothly back and parted. To the right, Prosecuting Attorney Scurvy, dressed in a dog's or a cat's skin (with the exception of his head, he's entirely in the skin, and on his head he's wearing a little hood made of pink woolen yarn with a little bell attached to it) sleeps, rolled into a ball like a dog and chained to the tree trunk.

FIRST APPRENTICE (*sings in a hideous male voice*)
        I hear within myself strange singing,
        Listen to how our blood is singing—
        It's very vulgar, wild, and stinking,
        But hot, so hot they'll be forgiving
        And drain their very eyes with weeping.
SECOND APPRENTICE (*sings just like the First Apprentice*)
        In the storms the naked trees are dancing,
        Redness through glassy clouds is foaming,
        Something alone in my soul is singing
        Your eyes! I no longer remember your eyes.
FIRST APPRENTICE Whose eyes, whose eyes?
SAJETAN All right, all right. Leave off with those songs, they make you want to vomit. I understand everything now: my inner life is rushing past me like an avalanche—absolutely—like a herd of African gazelles. I'm an old man staggering on the edge of the grave, experiencing everything that has ever happened. I've taken an accelerated course covering all my own life, starting when I was about seven, and now everything's in a total state of confusion in my mind. I didn't believe that such changes could take place in such a short time, you know, in a man built the way I am.
FIRST APPRENTICE Ho, ho!
SECOND APPRENTICE Hee, hee!
SAJETAN For the love of God, just don't act as if you were in one of those ridiculous plays from the so-called "new theater" or, watch out, I'll throw up right here in front of you all over the rug. Now, as

I was saying before: to be able to endure existence without going mad, and at the same time understand a little of its essence, without being duped by religion or one's duty to society—that's an almost superhuman task. No point even talking about other things! I'm like a bedbug, drunk, not on the life blood of the bourgeoisie, but on a mixture of the raspberry juice of piddling ideals and the vitriol of everyday lies.

FIRST APPRENTICE Take it easy, boss—let's enjoy our own inner well-being, and live a life of comfort and ease within the confines of our own psyches—like jewels in a jewel case—hey!

SECOND APPRENTICE Isn't it only a delusion that we're really creating a new way of life? Maybe we're deluding ourselves this way simply to justify our own comfort? Maybe we're being governed by forces whose true nature we don't really know? And we're only marionettes in their hands. Why do we say "mary"-o-nettes, and not "ann"-o-nettes? Ha? No doubt that question will evoke little response throughout the world, but there's certainly something to it.

SAJETAN Sure there is. But I won't keep quiet, you lice eggs. Now that thought of yours, Second Apprentice as you're called, although now you're really Andrew Owlhootz, assistant to the chief in charge of creating the new . . . well, I won't get bogged down in titles, gentlemen: I simply say to you that that idea of yours occurred to me a long time ago and I suppressed it by a conscious effort of the will. We mustn't allow ourselves to have doubts like that—it's one of our old bad habits caused by years of poverty, degradation, and feeblemindedness. Now we have to catch up, and not dick around splitting hairs over whether we're nothing but seventeenth-century scrollherders, cripples who've sold out, false to our very guts— not even up to being bourgeois scum yet, just filthy fellow travelers slipping awkwardly on parquet floors made slick by hordes of democratic feet. And besides the stinking heap of beliefs in secret forces and organizations, masonic and otherwise—there's the remnants of religion and magic rattling around in our heads, too. But the really good guy will be the one who renounces his own standard of living, instead of constantly raising it higher and higher until it blows up. Why is it everything in history has to blow up and can't move smoothly into the future along the well-greased tracks of reason: the law of discontinuity.

SECOND APPRENTICE All that yakking's beginning to get me, greased mother of a prunt! But you've changed a lot, boss: you can't deny that. And you've changed along the same lines I have, although the actual changes are of a different kind. Isn't it true what the former prosecuting attorney said, that we're the way we are because we're on the other side, and when we cross over we'll become like them? And there are secret forces, and secret men around, although they're not any better or worse than those out in the open—that's how times have changed—hey!

SAJETAN Those are only shadows moving across a background of violent social change.

SECOND APPRENTICE (*calmly*) Wouldn't it be possible for you to drop that doggy, puffed-up, peasant, early-Polish-prophetic way of yakking, and above all else the number of words you use?

SAJETAN (*calmly, but firmly*) No. Just the same way Lenin, as a servant of his class—though as an individual he was a really good guy—was different from Alexander the Great, who was temperamentally a fanatic for power, so I'm different from that dog! (*He points to the sleeping Scurvy.*) But anyhow this is no time for yakking—we've got to do something—it won't happen all by itself, goddamn it three or four times that that's the way things are! The great days for ideologies have come to an end—you know, when you could stuff yourself with mayonnaise, and be an ideological bolshevik, and find consolation in utopian dreams even though you were down to your last bowl of soup, and feel that you're somebody even though you're rotting in excrementalia. No one individual is going to come up with a new utopia—the new social order will come about all by itself, by spontaneous combustion, explosion, eruption, forged out of the dialectical struggle of everyone's guts in the human boiler; we're sitting on the lid, right by the safety valve—former idiot sons of whores, but now creators in spite of ourselves, son of a daisy-digging bitch!

APPRENTICES (*together in unison*) That swearing's so boring it makes us want to howl. So that's local color, son of a bitch. We're speaking in unison intuitively, like one man—we could go on talking like this forever.

SAJETAN Stop it, for God's sake. That's enough, that's enough . . .

SCURVY (*stretching in his sleep, after murmuring a little*) I'd be thrilled to be a shoemaker to the end of my days. Oh, how delusive are those so-called higher aims we set for ourselves: they lead to heights from which we plunge headlong to the bottom and break our necks. Oh, and then to swim up to the great peaks which touch the sky, up to the great ding-dong—*ein Hauch von anderer Seite*—a breath from the other side. Metaphysics, which I've despised until now, now pounces on me from all the back alleys of existence. *Au commencement Bythos était*—the abyss of chaos! What a wonderful and unattainable thing chaos is! We'll never find out what it really is, even though the world is chaos, when you come right down to it.

Chaos! Chaos! But some kind of petty statistical order can always be imposed on our wretched compartmentalized society where we live like socialized cattle. Oh, what a pity I didn't develop my mind by appropriate readings in philosophy—it's too late now—I don't have the proper training to handle conceptual thought.

(The Shoemakers listen attentively. During Scurvy's disquisition, the First Apprentice comes up to him with a huge axe in his hands, which he has picked up off the ground where, as it just so happens, it has been lying at his feet, all gold.)

SECOND APPRENTICE Where are you crawling off to, you misplaced piece of dog crap?

FIRST APPRENTICE Let's finish him off while he's asleep. That way he won't suffer any more. Son of a gun, he's had much too nice a dream. It just so happens that there's an axe lying here next to me—gold from top to bottom—heeheehee . . . *(et cetera, and he goes on laughing too long, letting out trills of laughter until he almost busts a gut.)*

SAJETAN *(threatens him with a huge Mauser, which he has pulled out from under his dressing gown)* You're laughing too long letting out those trills of yours till you're almost ready to bust a gut. Not another step. *(The First Apprentice steps back.)* He's got to howl himself to death out of frustrated desire before our very eyes and give us full satisfaction as avengers of lust.

(The Duchess, dressed in a riding costume and jacket, enters from the direction of town, a little to the right side.)

DUCHESS I was doing a little shopping. I have all my intimate little things here in my bag, along with my make-up and other odds and ends. I'm so much a woman I'm ashamed, it positively stinks a little of something, you know, very indecent, but very enticing, you know. Ah—there's nothing more "abbominable" with three "b's" than a woman, as a certain composer quite rightly used to say, and nothing so sweet and tender at the same time. *(She strikes Scurvy as hard as she can with her riding crop; he springs up on all fours, then bristles and growls.)* Get up this minute and face the whole obscene mess—corkhead, cockhead, puffballbrain! I'll eat your brains spread on a little roll of the most exquisite tortures. Here's a pill for you which'll give you inexhaustible sexual power so you'll be eternally unsatisfied. *(Throws him a pill, which he eats immediately; then he lights a cigarette and from this point on smokes, always using his right paw. He doesn't stand up on only two paws ever again.)*

SCURVY Off to Babylon with that disciple of Satan!—that superbitch goddess, that sexy Circe, that notarized pair of grapefruits, that . . . *(He swallows the second pill which the Duchess gives him. She*

"squats," as they say, next to him, and he puts his head on her knees,
wiggling his rear end at the same time.)

DUCHESS *(sings)*

> Dream oh so sweetly of me, my pet,
> You won't get up on your two paws yet!
> I'll torture you sweetly, a tiny bit,
> 'Till you become quite "wild" with it.
> But now you'll never make love to me,
> Because your brain will simply be
> Like crap—another's, not even your own,
> In this lies the overwhelming charm.

(She strokes Scurvy, who falls asleep muttering.)

SCURVY That blasted witch—what a wonderful life I'd planned for
myself before I got to know her. I should have followed the advice
of those blasted homosexual snobo-pinheads and kept clear of the
female sex—"blood and viper are a woman's hunger, they feed the
ecstasies of sky-blue hangmen." Oh, oh—how can I overcome this
blasted, monstrous, invincible grief! My lust will be my death, oh, I
can't bear it.

DUCHESS *(stroking him)* Like this, like this. *(Looking at those present)*
I'm saying this and stroking him, the way you'd try to offer someone else the sky! *(To Scurvy)* That's it, my pet, my golden mutt—
without it, I'd be in a rut. *(Scurvy falls asleep.)*

SAJETAN How can we go on living without any more utopias to build
our hopes on? It's horrible, all we've got to look forward to is
emptiness and never-ending drudgery, and we can't even delude
ourselves any more about the value of work. You know what I
think?—it's really frightening: it was better to be a stinking shoemaker with your own little private utopias and think idealistic
thoughts about how to put them into practice in all that stink, than
to be like us now, all in silks at the height of our flunkey power—
and it is flunkey power, son of a sucking prunt. *(He stamps his feet;
he continues talking almost in tears.)* Roll up your paws, right up to
the neck, and give society everything you've got. It's boring as an
incurable disease, and it's too late for me to enjoy myself. I can't get
the stink out of those stinking years of mine. Your whole lives are
still before you. After you get through work, you can still lead your
own lives—but what about me? I can only get stoned, take dope,
what the hell else is there? I don't even want to swear any more. I
don't even hate anyone—I only hate myself—oh, horror, horror: to
the edge of what precipices and overhanging cliffs of the soul have I
been dragged by my vile ambition to be somebody on this round
little earth of ours, holy but incomprehensible!

DUCHESS This is the tragedy of what happens when the well-stuffed suppliers of happiness for all mankind get too stuffed themselves! Sajetan, baby, the world is an absurd gang of monsters fighting among themselves. If they weren't all devouring one another, some kind of bacilli would cover the earth in three days with a layer forty miles deep.

SAJETAN She's always harping on the same old thing—like some half-baked parrot. We know all that already. Lady, we got no time for a popular lecture series here—there's real tragedy going on. Oh, when will the individual lose himself in a mechanically perfect society? Oh, when will the end come at last to the suffering caused by the individual's own personality, eternally stuck out and left hanging on its own in the void like a transcendental rear end—God almighty, drugs are all we've got left!

FIRST APPRENTICE Up till now I've listened to you patiently, you bum, out of respect for your age—but I can't any longer.

SECOND APPRENTICE And I can't either, right in your girlicue ginker!

FIRST APPRENTICE That's enough! (*To Sajetan*) Boss, despite your past services, you're an old dodo—you don't understand a thing about the younger generation. We're not manure like you—we're the seeds of the future. I'm not saying it well, I'm not inspired—but why not let it all come pouring out any old way? Here's what I'd want to say: all you're doing is holding us back with all your old-fashioned useless, idiotic analytic philosophy, whose methods were created by those lackeys of the bourgeoisie, Kant and Leibniz. Throw 'em both out on a wun-swept dinghill—hey! hey!

SAJETAN Take it easy, you cherubs! So that's your new dialectics of the first waterbucket? I can hardly believe my ears! So I've got to go—like the stripped thread on an old screw, like a threadbare boardinghouse blanket, like a cracked, crumbling bidet? Is that it?

SECOND APPRENTICE (*categorically*) Yeah, you got to go. You're talking awful dirty, that bourgeois filth is rubbing off on you. You can't even yak straight any more the way you ought to. You're a disgrace to the revolution.

SAJETAN What's the world coming to! To think I'd live to see this!

FIRST APPRENTICE Take it easy!—now I know why that golden axe was lying there. We'll slaughter you like a sacrificial bull. I'm telling you, I've had it up to here with that son of bitching slob. I'm going to clobber him, I'm going to beat the living daylights out of him— Andy—hold my pajama top!! (*He pulls off his pajama top.*)

DUCHESS (*Extraordinarily aristocratic*) Bravo, Joe! That idea strikes me just the way the eye of a cat's needle goes to the dogs on camelback. I never knew I could have so much fun. Only take your time dying, Sajetan—you know, I like it slow, honored gentlemen. I'll show you how to beat him so he'll be mortally wounded, but die a lingering death—hee, hee.

SECOND APPRENTICE Listen, sister, quit yakking about things like that, you're driving me right out of my mind, everything's going black . . .

DUCHESS (*gently*) There, there, Andy.

FIRST APPRENTICE Well, boss, get ready to die, prepare to meet your maker or something like that—I've forgotten how to yak like a shoemaker. Stand straight, shoulders back! (*He says this like a military command.*)

SAJETAN But my dear Andrew, my dear first apprentice, really, it's the height of absurdity, it'll be a blemish on the unsullied body of our revolution, whose conception was practically immaculate. I promise I won't ask for anything more, I'll live like a mummy, not as the father of the revolution, but just its kindly old uncle. I'll stop yakking—I'll squat in the clothes closet like an embalmed symbol. I'll be quiet as a mouse squared under four brooms—I'm trying to soften you up by being funny—but something tells me that it isn't working very well, although after all, Boy kept cajoling society so long and hard that he finally got what he wanted out of them, son of a prunt if he didn't. I swear by all that's holy, I'll keep my trap shut, like a tight little rosebud with its sweet-smelling petals all folded up —only don't beat me, for God's sake!

SECOND APPRENTICE But what's sacred to you, dad, with that long tongue of yours, if you once decided to use your murky dialectics of senile emptiness to root out our most cherished illusions? What am I saying?—I could bite off my tongue for calling them illusions! —those ideas are the very basis of our philosophy, encompassing the entire existence of mankind.

SAJETAN I gnash my teeth at the very thought . . .

FIRST APPRENTICE Well, grind away, you old grindstone, it won't do you the least bit of good. Say your bourgeois prayers. You couldn't go on being our leader while you're still alive, you've petered out before your time with your damned papyrus scrolls and your uncontrollable yakking, so we're going to turn you into a holy mummy, but a dead one, Mr. Cat! Then we'll confiscate what's left of your influence and create a myth about you: but while you're still alive we're not going to let you disintegrate in front of everyone into dog pshit—the word comes from the ancient Greek—your influence has got to be safely preserved before it's too late, but with you as a corpse, baby, so that you won't have a chance to disgrace yourself—and us, too. Since you couldn't live out the rest of your days like other splendid—and splendiferous—old men in world history, special arrangements have to be made for you. Put your head down, boss, and let's not waste time yakking.

SAJETAN Where'd he pick all that up, the snot-nosed little bastard? I really won't say unnecessary things any more. I got one foot in the grave already, and I just wanted to talk with you, man to man, and right away they're ready to sock a guy in the head with an axe. (*Without being seen, someone draws the curtain from behind as in Act I.*)

DUCHESS (*voluptuously, with delight*) Oh, hit him right here: in the epistrophus—and then, Sajetan, you'll still be able to go on yakking for quite some time—that's the way I like it—it's better than Spanish fly! Let him have it!

SECOND APPRENTICE We'll let him have it, all right—so help me, whores. That isn't the greatest oath in the world, but what the hell. (*Suddenly accordion music is heard, and something begins to push its way in from under the curtain.*)

FIRST APPRENTICE Who's that? No one else was supposed to come here tonight. We've made a reservation with the girls from the Euphorion for 3:00 A.M. They're coming here after closing time for dancing and an orgy. (*The peasants, the old Peasant and the young Farm Hand, crowd their way in, pushing ahead of them a gigantic mulch—the Country Girl comes behind them, carrying a large tray. Dressed in Cracow peasant costumes.*)

SCURVY (*in his sleep*) And never to be able to play bridge again and say with that sense of imaginary self-importance: three hearts or double; never to be able to go to the Italia for a cup of coffee or even look at the cute young girls or her either; never to be able to read *The Courier* before going to bed; and never, never to be able to go to sleep! That's horrible—my nerves just can't stand it!—and nobody even cares! (*No one listens to him; everyone stares at the group at the left.*)

PEASANT (*sings*)
> There's just no point in talking with a fool,
> So shut your trap, and sit down on the stool—

FARM HAND (*picks up the tune, pointing to the Peasant*)
> But if by chance he wants to answer back,
> Don't let him yak, just give him one good whack.

FIRST APPRENTICE (*with clenched teeth*) Don't push your luck too far, you country bumpkins, you stubborn backward yokels, in other words, what's called our national peasant stock. Want to get your teeth knocked in? Hu-u-u-h?

FARM HAND (*"blusterously"*) Nevertheless, in the deep conviction that our mission is indeed a great one due to the downfall of the old nobility and the monstrous, cancerous aristocracy—who, it is said, wore checked trousers and dressed in the English style . . .

DUCHESS That's stale humor, à la Boy and Słonimski! Your jokes smell like the fish in the fifth-rate restaurant at the train station in Hickville. Get to the point, knuckleheads—you stuck-up, jackass peasants!

PEASANT Dear Lady, may you not come to regret in an hour of despondency those arrogant and swaggering words spoken out of season.

DUCHESS Shut your trap, you hick, or I'll throw up, you're so disgusting. Lechoń * wouldn't like me talking this way, he only knows duchesses who go to five o'clock teas at the Ministry of Foreign Affairs. But that's the way I am and always will be, with a rubstitch in your shiny pronker.

SAJETAN (*authoritatively*) Stop bickering! Thanks to you peasants, corrupted by pseudo-noble ambitions, I've regained my former position and am ready to sign a pact with you which will be almost princely. I have no intention of taking away your rights to your land. But you've only got to form a totally voluntary kolkhoz, said with a Russian accent of course . . .

PEASANT (*throwing up his hands*) We don't understand you, sir. We came here in good faith to have a talk with you, on an equal-to-equal basis. For remember what they say: whom God loves, his house is sweet to him, and he that is humble, ever shall have God to be his guide, and a plow that works, shines.

FIRST APPRENTICE What a backward race—it's as if we were hearing echoes of the landed gentry in Sienkiewicz' time. These characters are trying to get ennobled only now—it's outrageous—a really first-class evolutionary cake with obsolete social classes for layers.

FARM HAND I'll be brief: we brought Mr. Wyspiański's mulch with us. Even the fascists wanted him as the metaphysical-nationalistic basis for their joyful science of living life to the full and utilizing the state for the purposes of the self-defense of international investments of capital, and also . . .

SAJETAN Shut up, you hick, or I'll give you one right in the choppers!

FARM HAND You didn't let me finish, and what came out was goddam nonsense à la Witkacy. I know what you're going to say in advance

---

* Jan Lechoń (1899–1956), well-known Polish poet, prominent member of the avant-garde group "Skamander." When in 1926 actors in a Warsaw theater refused to take part in Witkiewicz' play *Tumor Brainard* and the performance had to be canceled, Lechoń and other writers defended Witkiewicz in print. [Translators' note]

. . . oh, what's the use! How about a little song—they'll get it better if it's got a tune—well, here goes:

> Here's our mulch and our naked heart.

(*The Girl moves forward to the front of the stage with her tray, on which a heart as large as a bull's is pulsating—a clock mechanism.*)

> We'll talk with Wyspiański's art
> And not like an odious modern churl—
> We've brought the famous "barefoot girl."

(*Speaks*) Only now she's put her shoes on to be respectable; after all, you can't go around barefoot in front of everybody—you know what I mean—hey! (*Continues singing*)

> She was supposed to save the world.
> With my scythe as my constitution
> I'll reap the harvest of revolution.

FIRST APPRENTICE Those symbols are obsolete! I got all the barefoot girls I want, the cutest dancing girls in town, and I can do whatever I want with their feet—and with their legs, too.

DUCHESS (*jumps up impetuously and pulls off her shoes and stockings. They all look at her and wait.*) I have the most beautiful legs in the world!

SCURVY (*waking up—he has hit his head on the floor*) Oh, don't talk like that! Oh, why, why was I so unlucky as to fall asleep! Waking up forces me to go through that torture all over again! I sound pompous, but I have nothing to lose—I'm not even afraid of being ridiculous.

SAJETAN Quiet over there, scum!—there are more important things here than your legs and your confessions. (*To the Peasants*) Well, what next?

FARM HAND Let's sing all together. (*They sing together*)

> Oh, lo God, the holy One,
> Let nothing evil happen;
> Oh, lo God, the holy One,
> Let nothing come of it.

(*To the Girl*) Sing *à tue-tête*, barefoot girl, with your shoes only temporarily on.

GIRL (*in a croaking voice à tue-tête*)

> Oh, lo God, the holy one,
> Let nothing come of it.

OLD PEASANT

> Oh, in the name of God's triple jewel,
> Can wisdom be stuffed in the head of a fool?

Let someone do it, tra-la-la,
And keep on stuffing it in—ha, ha!

SAJETAN (*in a horrible voice*) Scram, you lice eggs! (*All three of the Shoemakers hurl themselves at the peasants and throw them out. The peasants run away in panic, leaving the mulch behind standing to the left. The mulch slowly falls over and lies down. Exclamations like the following are heard: God help us! What's the world coming to! It's all up with us! Almighty Christ! Who in the world! Oh, Jesus! et cetera in profusion. The Sajetanites work the peasants over in silence; the only sound is their heavy panting. As soon as they return to the center of the stage, the First Apprentice shouts without paying attention to Sajetan's words.*)

SAJETAN (*returning slowly and panting*) That's the way we settle the peasant problem—hey!

FIRST APPRENTICE (*shouts*) To the center of the stage. Everybody, to the center of the stage! Let's get on with our work! The audience doesn't like such interludes, crap on them and their lousy taste.

SECOND APPRENTICE Hit him! Clobber him! Let the old son of a bitch know what he was living for in the first place! The martyr from here to cuckoldsnatchdom!

SAJETAN So you're getting all heated up about those miserable little peasants? So what's it all about, lice eggs, so not even a jot, nor a Greek iota—in middleclass talk they don't say jot, but iota—but who'd have thought I'd make up such rot when I'm on the spot on the edge of disaster—so you haven't changed your vile intentions not even one jotty-assed jot . . . Uuuuuuu!

(*The First Apprentice hits him in the head with the axe, and he falls to the ground howling. The Apprentices and the Duchess lay him down on the sheepskin sack [as in the House of Lords] which has been lying from the very beginning at the front of the stage, the devil only knows why. It's being done that way so Sajetan can have his say to his heart's content before he dies. In front of him, on a small table [which has been there all along too] lies the beating heart on its tray.*)

DUCHESS Put him down here, put him down here, I tell you, so he can have his say and get it all out of his system before he dies. (*Fidgeons rushes in.*)

FIDGEONS (*carrying a suitcase*) He's coming in here, like misfortune on the march, a dreadful superrevolutionary, a hyperworkoid—that's the only name for him—he's obviously one of the gang who are really running our lives—those puppets (*he points at the Shoemakers*) are only play-acting. He's got a bomb as big as a kettle and a whole pile of hand grenades; he's threatening everybody with them, and he's got his own life shoved up somewhere you shouldn't talk about—what I wanted to say was . . .

DUCHESS Cut the wisecracks! Have you got the costumes, Fidgeons? That's the most important thing . . .

FIDGEONS Of course I have—only I don't know whether we're all going to be blown to bits in a second. (*Frightful footsteps backstage—the joker's got shoes with lead soles.*) That worker's of a better make than the Wyspiański girl—he's a live, mechanized corpse. The Nietzschean Superman wasn't born among the Prussian Junkers, but among the proletariat, which some scholars quite unjustly consider to be the cesspool of humanity.

SECOND APPRENTICE (*to Fidgeons*) And why are you still going around all the time dressed like a lackey? Don't you know we've got freedom now? Huh?

FIDGEONS Well!—A lackey will always be a lackey no matter who's in power. (*In a Russian accent*) "What does it matter!" We're going to get blown to kingdom come any minute now!

SCURVY You can all run away—you're free men. But what about me? —half dog, half don't know what! I'm about to go out of my mind any minute now—there's no stopping it.

FIRST APPRENTICE You won't have time, you itchy scab! We're going to put on a little play for you that'll make you drop dead from insatiability two degrees higher on the Beaufort Scale than the ultimate cyclone of lunacy which would have been sheer pleasure compared to what's in store for you.

SCURVY (*whines and then howls*) That's a lot of stupid talk, but all the same—Mmmm oooh! Ah, ah, oooooooh! What agony to have to die like this, without ever having lived! I wanted to die from wasting away, like a handsome old man, noble down to his very toenails. Oh, now I know one life is all there is! Everything's swelled up inside me, a hump on my back, from this hideous rack. Now I realize the miserable lot of those I condemned to prison and death—that's trite, but it's the truth.

DREADFUL HYPERWORKOID (*entering; carrying a bomb*) I'm one of THEM (*frantic emphasis on "them"*). I'm Oleander Squintpease; you condemned me to life imprisonment, Mr. Scurvy. But I got smart and slipped out. I know that's a horrible way to put it, but I can't do nothing about the way I talk. Remember what you did to me, you sadist? Everything in me's been crushed and broken—understand? Literally everything: all my genes and gametes. But my soul, the other half of me that's attached to my body, is made out of raw oxhide, dipped into bubbling red-hot steel. I've got a bomb here, the most explosive F-bomb in the world, and I'm capable of throwing it at any moment. You're going to get it for all those sweet little abortions of mine who never got born because of you, you Kaffir! I wanted to have children! I'm talking crude—but that's the way it is. (*He hurls the bomb onto the ground. They throw themselves on the ground howling—everyone except Sajetan. Scurvy lets out squeals of animalistic fear. The bomb doesn't explode. The Hyperworkoid picks it up off the ground and says*) You bunch of meatheads—it's only a thermos full of coffee, see. (*He pours coffee from the bomb into the lid and drinks it.*) But in wartime it converts into a bomb in nothing flat. It's one of those symbolic comic routines, you know, in the old style—bores you to death—makes your bones ache out of sheer boredom. Ha, ha, ha! It's just as well you chickened out that way, we don't need any fearless daredevils in pseudo command posts, and what's more important: we don't like them. I'm making quite a point of this, who the hell knows why. Maybe I don't exist at all. (*Silence*)

SAJETAN (*without turning around to face the others, speaks directly to the audience*) Now I'll have my say. It's a good thing you murdered me; I'm not afraid of anything any more, and I can speak the truth: there's only one thing that's worth anything in the world—one's individual existence in decent material conditions. (*Until further notice, the others remain lying on the ground.*) Eat, read, mess around, screw, and fall asleep. There isn't anything else—that's the whole goddamn endomorph philosophy. And what are all your great social ideals worth anyhow? Not just for myself, but for everybody—that's just the point I've been trying to make. I'm not interested in talking about some future time you always read about in schoolbooks. It's only by doing something yourself for the sake of others, that even a small man can become great, when he couldn't any other way. This is the "greatness for everyone" theory—I put that in quotation marks, because in reality greatness lies only in the individual's expansive force and the degree to which it can mold reality: by sheer thought or will power enforced by a mailed fist—it doesn't matter which. And in this way on the universal level the small turns into the great in public affairs.—But what the hell's the use of this kind of philosophizing anyhow? . . . (*The Hyperworkoid comes up to him and blasts him in the ear with a large Colt. Sajetan goes on talking as if nothing had happened. They all get up, except Fidgeons, who still remains lying on the ground.*) And it doesn't matter whether the individual is a personal fanatic and maniac to the nth degree, or a servant and spokesman of some social class—it all comes out the same . . .

HYPERWORKOID (*to Sajetan*) "So you've changed sides again, Mr. Silver"—as Tom Morgan once said to Long John.

DUCHESS (*very aristocratically*) Get up, Fidgeons—these are just symbols—basic plane geometry for muttonheads; it's a deadly enthymeme whose only premise is that the whole human race has already gone to the dogs. It's only . . . (*Fidgeons gets up and pulls out of the suitcase a magnificent "bird of paradise" costume which he begins to put on the Duchess: he takes off her jacket, thus cutting short further effusions from her, and then dresses her in the things mentioned above. Only her legs remain bare—with a short green petticoat a little above the knees. The Duchess gradually quiets down as a result of being dressed, though still stammering for a while something unintelligible.*) brhmwbomxkatchnaho . . .

HYPERWORKOID Now our unpleasant comedy is about to begin; that's the kind most needed nowadays, although I shouldn't see it, naïve and innocent as I am. I spent fourteen years in a prison cell studying economics. (*To the Apprentices*) You lucky bastards, you two had the personal good, or bad, luck, not through any merit of your own, to be representatives of the cottage industries. As representatives of this class, you'll have a little pull, purely for show. It's a real break for you: you'll move in diplomatic circles with deputies of foreign powers that have gone temporarily fascist—that's the last gasp of capitalism expiring in putrid little holes all over the world—and you'll be eating langoustes and other doodlies with them—then suddenly a bullet through the head—death without torture—that's something in itself. And all the broads you want—I don't care what goes on inside your heads. (*He whistles through his fingers.*)

(*Enter Pugnatsy Jawbloatski—a monstrous walrus with huge bristling mustaches in the "aristocratic" style. Dressed in a Polish national costume made of gold lamé. He wears red boots and plumed cap; his saber frightens everyone; his wild popeyes can really snap.*)

JAWBLOATSKI (*he recites the preceding stage direction*)

I wear red boots and a plumed cap,
My saber frightens everyone,
My wild popeyes can really snap (*he makes cruel faces*),
That's what I'll be and what I am!
A Lady Killer or maybe a queer,
A Fascist or Socialist, it's not clear,
Like the worm in the cheese, I have no peer.

HYPERWORKOID That Wyspiański stuff is really getting contagious. Sit down here, you old fool, next to the corpse of the Great Saint of the last world revolution, who showed us the way to the Highest Truth by bringing the proletarian middle class into line. The poor old idiot, he's got to live forever—as a dead symbol, that is, and be for us what your saints and all your myths are for you, you pseudo-Christian Fascists; you've used them to turn the comedy of your pseudo-beliefs into something incredibly repulsive.

JAWBLOATSKI That's right—truth doesn't exist—Chwistek proved that.

HYPERWORKOID Shut up, jackass. Biological materialism, as the apex of the dialectical world view, can't even contend with the minor myths and mysteries. The real mystery is this: how a single living being can possibly exist, and how other living beings can form an inseparable part of it—in a dark, evil, and godless infinity.

JAWBLOATSKI Couldn't we do without these lectures for just a few minutes?

HYPERWORKOID (*coldly*) No. Here, on this scrap of earth, everything stands out as clearly as the Farnese Bull and will remain so, till the end of the world. (*He starts to leave, but actually doesn't; he turns around and continues speaking.*) Pugnatsy became converted to our beliefs—we've got to make use of even that old hunk of batshit. As that repulsive character the "thrifty housewife"—ugh—can tell you, nothing should go to waste. That's a special feature of our revolution. We'll use Pugnatsy as window dressing; all governments go in for that kind of folderol.

SAJETAN This feature is what gives hope to all kinds of scum that they'll survive the Revolution. But what about me? Do I have to die and those bastards live?

HYPERWORKOID You didn't draw a lucky number in the lottery, Sajetan. You've got to realize, once and for all, there isn't any justice and never will be—at least we've got statistics—that's something to be thankful for. (*He shoots him again with his Colt. Pugnatsy sits down on the sack next to Sajetan, looking vacantly through bloodshot eyes at the audience. He must be wearing a mask—a live human being couldn't look like that. Fidgeons, who meanwhile has finished dressing the Duchess, pulls off Pugnatsy's hat and topcoat and dresses him in old rags and a cap while he remains seated. The rags are covered with small white dots.*)

JAWBLOATSKI But what's all that white stuff?

FIDGEONS Lice.

SCURVY (*shaking all over, he's howling so hard*) I'm just shaking all over, I'm howling so hard for my lost life and happiness. Listen, Oleander, maybe you can do something for me this once? The noble dreamer's revenge—or doesn't the role appeal to you? Unleash me! Let me do good, honest, hard work! In any filthy old hole, on the mangiest scraps of a stinking life. I'll be a shoemaker and live in abject poverty—I'll change places with those two crooks in pajamas and pull their weight in the balance of social forces. (*He points to the Apprentices with his paw.*) Only not that, not what they're planning for me, the dirty rats: to let me howl myself to death out of remorse and desire! Aou! Aou! Aououououou! (*He howls and sobs.*)

HYPERWORKOID Yes, Scurvy, you're going to die just like that. What does scurvy mean? Your name is symbolic: you've been the scurvy of mankind which is suffering from a soul deficiency. (*To the Apprentices*) Well, you've got the power now, go ahead and govern —we're going to work on the technical machinery for the structural dynamics and balance of forces behind the governing game. Good-bye, as the English say!

JAWBLOATSKI (*grimly*) Good-bye! This is as boring as a scene of jealousy, as lessons for a special after-school study program, as an old aunt's nagging—or to synthesize the metaphor: as an old aunt's special after-school study program combining her nagging and her scenes of jealousy over another aunt. (*The board with the inscription:* "BOREDOM" *appears again.*)

HYPERWORKOID (*slowly*) Hogglewater. (*Exit stamping wildly with the lead soles of his shoes.*)

FIRST APPRENTICE (*ironically*) Hogglewater! Did you hear that!? Hey! Get things ready for tonight's orgy. Everything he said here was just a joke. There's no such thing as a whole hierarchy of secret governments, one on top of the other! (*To the Duchess*) Get dressed, you putanic superwhore!

SECOND APPRENTICE Joke or no joke, you weren't able to do him in either. It's still not clear what's really going on with all these secret governments. Perhaps even within the structure of our society there are secret . . .

FIRST APPRENTICE Things are all right the way they are! Better not to think at all—death from terror of oneself is lurking in every corner. Figment of the imagination or not, we'll survive just being window dressing better than they will—whether they actually exist or not. But at least it won't be boring, because ideas will have disappeared from the face of the earth, due to a total lack of any interest in philosophy. Hey! But all the same it's a little sad, son of a bitch! Let's get loaded; when the broads from the downtown dancehall get here and the teenagers from Disrespectful Delinquents Square and that awful crook who lives at No. 17 Szymanowski Street, we'll have a ball and forget about our terrible life, the last word in absurdity, the worst of all possible lives, because we're conscious of everything from start to finish. Oh, God, God! (*Falls to the ground and sobs*) Look at me sobbing my head off, and I don't even know why myself. That's bourgeois *Weltschmerz* for you, with your dingus dancing the tango. I'd like to crap on all of it. (*The Duchess whimpers, too; Scurvy howls protractedly and mournfully.*)

SAJETAN (*suddenly raises himself up, causing Jawbloatski to look at him in astonishment*) How about that? I got up on my two feet, and even you, the once great Jawbloatski, had to look at me in some astonishment. But I've got something new in mind. Look, don't slobber all over my last moments on this earth with your doggy blubbering, as Wyspiański put it. I've come to believe in metempsychosis—but just the "metem" part, not the rest. I've come to believe in the great BEYOND, and death doesn't mean anything to me since I couldn't go on living here like this any longer.

FIRST APPRENTICE The blasted old buzzard! There's no way of finishing him off. He's wallowing in his own filthy talk like a puppy in its excrement. *Une sorte de Rasputin,* eh?

SAJETAN Take it easy, you greasy ball of rancid bitch lard. You don't have a single witty or clever idea, son of a bitch! (*A placard: "Boredom getting worse and worse," appears in the place of the previous one, which disappears.*) And yet, say what you want—the world is full of infinite beauty. Every blade of grass, the tiniest little hunk of shit which gives life to the plants, each time you spit into an awe-inspiring sky piled high with clouds out of the East on a summer afternoon where they hold sway slowly right and left, bulging with the fury of inanimate matter which, being what it is, can never come to life.

JAWBLOATSKI That's enough—I'll throw up.

SAJETAN Okay—but I still feel miserable. Each blade of grass . . .

JAWBLOATSKI Cut it, or honest to God, I'll wring your neck. (*To the others*) I'm in charge of the propaganda pageants. The dress rehearsal is due to begin right away—the dancers will get here at three.

FIRST APPRENTICE You think so, do you? That'll be the day. So all right, that's the way it is—tough. You can't plug a hole in the sky with your finger. You can't jug the hair of the dog that bit you in a sick whore's canker sore.

SECOND APPRENTICE Oh, how he tortures me with that surrealistic cussing; it doesn't have any dynamic tension.

FIRST APPRENTICE That's it, that's it—it's so frightening, you don't even have the faintest, foggiest notion of what it's like. Dread, boredom, hangover, and terrible apprehensions about what's coming next. Somehow it's all gone to pot. (*Sings softly with a Russian accent*) "The coachman doesn't spur the horses on, there's no place any more for us to hasten." (*They both help Fidgeons finish dressing the*

Duchess, whose costume looks like this: bare feet, legs bare up to the knees. Short green petticoat through which you can see red drawers. Green batwings. Décolletage down to the navel. On her head a huge three-cornered hat, put on en bataille, *with a huge plume and green and white feathers. As the dressing progresses, Scurvy howls more and more loudly and begins to jerk the chain really frightfully, still just like a dog, but without stopping smoking cigarettes.*)

JAWBLOATSKI Don't writhe like that, Mr. Former Secretary of State; if you break the chain, I'll shoot you like a real dog. I'm working for them now—I've changed completely. Get that through your head, sweetie-pie, and quiet down. I've undergone a profound inner change and decided to spend the rest of my days eating poulardes, langoustes, vermouille, and papaverdi served with a good flamfari oblichanti. I'm cynical, right down to the dirt between my toes—I've stopped washing entirely and stink like a rotten flounder. I pshit on all of it.

FIRST APPRENTICE Did you say pshit?

JAWBLOATSKI Pshit enough to drown out one stink with something else that stinks worse. Men who've sold out find the noun useful, too—those who believe in democracy, for example: of the pshit, by the pshit, and for the pshit, and so on.

SECOND APPRENTICE Let's do it this way: if he can make a boot in a quarter of an hour, we'll turn him loose on her—if not, he'll just have to howl himself to death.

JAWBLOATSKI All right, Andy—go ahead! That appeases what's left of my now defunct sadistic desires—I can't do anything myself. (*He weeps quietly and ignominiously.*) Here I am all alone, weeping softly like a child, and I was once so enterprising and wild . . . I can't even write a good poem! A man like the late Tuwim * always had that consolation as a last resort, no matter what happened to him! But what about me? I'm just a poor orphan. I don't even know who I am—from the political point of view, of course. As far as life is concerned, I'm an old clown, flubbing up and dicking around: like trying to tack and yak at the same time, or fumbling slack and rummaging with one's finger where what's needed is a sharp instrument to give it the proper treatment and working over—I'll be that way until I die a pshitty death.

SECOND APPRENTICE (*who has listened attentively*) Well, then I'll look here for our old instruments here in this trash—what's left over from

---

* Julian Tuwim (1894–1953) prominent Polish poet, translator, lyricist, and satirist, cofounder of the poetic group "Skamander." [Translators' note]

what could be called our first revolutionary shoemakers' workshop
—holy mother of shit. But when was all that? How good things
were then. It'll be put in a museum to commemorate it forever.
(*Rummaging in the trash*) You're a gasbag, Jawbloatski—maybe
even a bigger one than our Sajetan. We'll be known as the Sajetanites or the Bruindinglerites—after the Bruindingler who fought with
Black Beatus, the Trundler, and whined at the sight of him. What
am I saying? Or did I just dream up something weird? (*To Scurvy,
who is whining like the last of the Whining-Agas on his way to the
workshop*) Here you are, Whining-Aga—you've got everything
you need—sew!

    (*Scurvy sets down to work feverishly, whining from nervousness
and haste. He whines more and more, and growing sexual excitement is "written all over" every movement he makes; nothing goes
right for him, and everything simply falls out of his hands, because
of his excessive state of erognosological excitement.*)

SCURVY Growing sexual excitement is "written all over" every movement I make, catiological pseudobourgeois that I am. Erognosologi-
cally speaking I'm almost a saint—a Turkish saint, I might add to
make it respectable, since I reek of cowardice and am a coward from
way back. I have to whine, or otherwise I'd burst like a child's
balloon. Oh, God!—ah, for what, ah—ah—it doesn't even matter for
what, if only I could get at her and then drop dead on the spot. I was
never so sad before in my whole life! Irina, Irina—you are nothing
but a symbol for all life now and what's more: Being, in the
metaphysical sense of the word!—something I could never understand before. You can only live once, and I've wasted my life! Those
I condemned to death could feel it when the rope . . . Oh, God! I'll
whine like a dog on a chain when it sees and sniffs—that's the most
important thing—racing by what's very accurately called the dog
wedding of free, happy dogs! (*He actually whines like that.*) The
bitch in front, the gentlemen dogs behind her, behind their one and
only!—a little black bitch or a beige one—oh, God, God!

SAJETAN Won't anything happen at the very last gasp of my life? Will
I die in the middle of this cancerous comedy, watching the disintegration of former highmuckymucks into a pulpy mass of regurgi-
tated words? For we're all cancers on the body of society in its
transitional phase, caught between greatness that has crumbled and
been pulverized and the true social continuum to come in which the
separate ulcers of individuals will flow together into one great
"*plaque muqueuse*" of absolute perfection in one universal organism.
Abscesses ache and hurt—that's what they're supposed to do—so be

it. This scab will just keep on itching delightfully until it heals. Then nothingness.

JAWBLOATSKI Jesus Christ—he keeps hammering away at us mercilessly with his dying lecture. (*The Duchess dances.*)

SAJETAN And do you think our own origin was any different? From the Greek hylozoists, through Giordano Bruno, by way of Leibniz, Renouvier, Wildon Carr—those last ones are lightweights, though —and later through Vailato and Kotarbiński, with his new version of reism presented in a lively way à la Diderot, and not à la Baron von Holbach, the blasted demon of materialism, who wanted to reduce everything to the billiard-ball theory of dead matter—a curious line of monadologues, or rather monadists, leads us to absolute truth, in which dialectical materialism, conceived of as a struggle among monsters, which results in existence, and so on and so forth . . . (*Sajetan's stammering from this point on becomes unintelligible. Signs of frenzied impatience grow in everyone. Scurvy goes raving mad on his chain. From now on everything is said against a background of unintelligible stammering by Sajetan, who keeps yakking until further notice. It will be specified where Sajetan's separate sentences are to be heard above this stammering.*)

SCURVY (*whining*) I can't sew these boots which the stars have vomited on three different times. I'm in such a hideous state of sexual excitement that I can't hold onto anything. I cannot go on, I know I won't be able to, but I keep on trying out of sheer despair; to die from such insatiability would be a gruesome gasconade on the part of fortune—a bit of braggadocio—or who the hell knows what! Oh —now I know what boots really are—what woman is, what life, knowledge, art, and social problems are—I know everything, but it's too late! Gloat over my anguish, you vampires! (*He begins to howl —not whine as before—he positively howls wildly and mournfully, and Sajetan yaks on incessantly and unintelligibly, making extravagant gestures.*)

SECOND APPRENTICE (*dressing the Duchess*) Absolute emptiness—nothing amuses me any more.

FIRST APPRENTICE Me neither. Something's cracked inside us, and we don't know why we go on living.

DUCHESS There, now you've got what you wanted, what we aristocrats have always had. You're on the other side now—enjoy it.

SAJETAN (*distinct words rise up out of the constant stammering and then are lost in it again*) . . . it's always like this high up on the peaks, my brothers, my desolate brothers in the void . . . (*In the background a red pedestal suddenly shoots up—it can be the prosecuting attorney's lectern from Act II.*)

DUCHESS Help me up on the pedestal, help me up on the pedestal as fast as you can! I can't live unless I'm up on the pedestal! *(Sings)*

> Hold me up on a pedestal,
> Hold me up, oh there!
> For all in a moment I'll come tumbling down,
> Flat on my face in despair!

(She runs up to the pedestal and stands on it in all her glory, with her batwings spread out, in the glare of a Bengal light and of other ordinary fireworks, which go off to the right and left, no one knows by what miraculous means. Scurvy lets out a howl like a lost soul in hell.) Here I stand in all my glory, on the mountain pass where two dying worlds meet!

SCURVY Forgive me, comrades in pain—no need to kid me—you're all suffering too—I'm not saying this to console myself, but because that's the way things really are—forgive me for howling like a lost soul in hell, bringing disgrace on the whole human race, but to tell the truth I really couldn't go on any more—I just couldn't go on any longer—*Schluss, finito. (He throws the boot away after several frenzied attempts at bending and sewing up a rough piece of leather —he does this while sitting down. Then he begins to crawl on all four paws toward the Duchess, howling more and more. When the chain holds him back, Scurvy's howling becomes really frightening.)*

JAWBLOATSKI I can't stand it here in this flat bidello—*(to himself)* as if there were curved ones. Even my fascist cut-ups were of a superior brand. And to top it all off there's my former secretary of state! Well, now, sir, this is scandalous—as they say in Galicia, this is the ultimate in degradation! But somehow it's having the same effect on me, too—I'd like a little whatchamacallit . . . *(Sajetan keeps on gabbling continually.)* Oh, son of a bitch! But what if I can't stand it any longer and start groveling too before that atrocious bagarina? *(After a pause)* Well, after all, that wouldn't be so terrible, my halo won't fall off. I'm utterly cynical—I sure am. *(He gets down off the sack and sways slowly to the right and left facing the audience.)*

SAJETAN . . . keep your balance, keep your balance, because once you've finally fallen, you won't be able to get out of it without worshiping her heart and soul . . .

DUCHESS *(calls out to them, with "unbridled fury," as the Russians say)* Here I'm calling to you with "unbridled fury," as the Russians say—there's no Polish word for it—with the voice of my superguts and galleries of my soul, born in these guts, now dead and gone: grovel before the symbol of the panmother—or rather the super-pan-oldbagiarchy! It'll burst out on the scene any moment. You men may suddenly rot: you may turn into a little pool of liquid putrefaction, like Mr. Valdemar in the short story by that unfortunate character Edgar Allen Poe. You men are turning into endomorphs! Your male schizoids are dying out, while our female schizoids are multiplying. The proof is that Sajetan got it in the head, but Jawbloatski will stuff himself on langouste—that's symbolic—as long as he can still open his mouth and turn the valves on in his stomach. Men are turning into women—women are turning into men in droves. The time may come when we'll begin dividing like cells, without even being aware of the metaphysical strangeness of Existence! Hurrah, hurrah, hurrah!

(*The Apprentices and Jawbloatski crawl toward her on their bellies. Scurvy tries to break his chain like a madman, amidst all the clatter and whining. Sajetan stands up and also turns toward her, like a Wernyhora.* Suddenly the mulch gets up and stands still. Slight consternation among the crawlers: all of them, without getting up, look at the mulch intently.*)

JAWBLOATSKI (*in a thundering voice*) We crawlers are in a state of slight consternation because the mulch stood up on his own two feet. What does it mean? Not in terms of reality—to hell with reality—but what does it mean in high poetic terms, according to Wyspiański and the whole post-Wyspiański tradition of national thought, with its swarms of phonies explicating literary works that don't mean anything at all and are just whims on the part of the artist: dynamic tension for the sake of Pure Form in the theater and nothing more—am I talking complete nonsense? (*The Mulch comes up to the pedestal. His mulch's costume falls off, and it turns out he's really a man-about-town in tails.*)

MULCH-ABOUT-TOWN (*ogling the Duchess*) Madame Irina, you've got the cutest laugh—how about us going somewhere and dancing—let's live it up—we'll dance a fabulous tango together—believe me . . .

SAJETAN Like Wernyhora I can still go on talking for some time yet. But where is she? The supreme chicknik is about to arise—the word's Russian-sounding: it ends in a provocative "nik"—she's appealing, I've got to admit that—if I don't manage to die before either night or the curtain falls, you may as well know that I won't be alive any more before you have time to get your coats from the crappy cloakroom—that's more than certain. I have a hole in my head made by an axe, and bullet holes in my belly and in my brain right through the ear . . . (*His gabble continues.*)

* Wernyhora, legendary Cossack of the eighteenth century, prophet of Poland's destiny, and a character in Wyspiański's drama *The Wedding*. [Translators' note]

JAWBLOATSKI She's beaten me, the snatchful bitch! I can't hold out any longer! (*He crawls.*)

SAJETAN (*full of admiration for the Duchess*) The Supreme Chicknik! The Supreme Chicknik! Oh, let's put this into that! Ah, this into that! And that into this! And who knows? Am I just a hick?— am I? I'm the ideal ruler, a cadaverous mummy, a stupid knucklehead. I've scrambled up to the full height of my fatal destiny—let someone else bail me out—I don't care, oh, put that into this and that's it! (*He tumbles to the ground and crawls toward the Duchess; the heart goes on beating.*)

SCURVY (*howls wildly and senselessly, then becomes quiet, and speaks in absolute dead silence*) Now's the time to go for a little walk; they don't have any idea at all any more what we're talking about.

TERRIBLE VOICE (*through a hypersupermegaphonopump*) THEY HAVE ABSOLUTE POWER NOW!

(*A wire cage for a parrot is lowered from above over the Duchess. The Duchess folds her wings.*)

SCURVY (*during the silence*) Oh, how my heart aches—it's from smoking too many cigarettes—the wreathed urns have been destroyed— rotten bulkheads—

> Are you the king of all my pain
> Come to get me on my chain?
> Physical pain—ah, that's the worst: (*brief pause*)
> To hell with it! My aorta's burst!

(*He dies and lies lengthwise, with the chain stretched its full length.*)

DUCHESS (*the tango is heard from a long way off*) He howled himself to death from desire. His heart burst, and probably everything else, too. Whoever wants me can have me—come and get me! I'm incredibly excited because he died from unsatisfied desire for me! Only a woman can . . .

(*Enter two men dressed in English suits. The Duchess goes on stammering something unintelligible. They speak to each other quietly, moving from right to left. They step unconcernedly over the crawlers and over the corpse of the prosecuting attorney. The Hyperworkoid follows them, carrying his copper thermos bottle.*)

ONE OF THE MEN: COMRADE X Listen, Comrade Abramovski: I'm abandoning the idea of nationalizing agriculture for the time being, not because I'm making any compromises . . .

THE OTHER MAN: COMRADE ABRAMOVSKI Of course not: you can justify it ideologically and make them understand that this is purely a provisional measure . . . (*The Duchess's stammering becomes unintelligible.*)

DUCHESS . . . I descend between God's shoulder blades like a tran-

scendental lotus flower . . . from the matriarchy of ultrahypercon-
struction . . .

COMRADE X Throw a cloth over that piece of tail and cover her up like
a parrot. Make her at least stop twittering and screeching. Up your
matriarchy. (*The dreadful Hyperworkoid runs up and throws a red
cloth, which Fidgeons hands him out of the suitcase, over the cage.*)
Well, now, listen Comrade Abramovski: so long as we keep them
at the very edge of despair . . . only as much compromise as is
absolutely necessary—understand: ab-so-lute-ly—necessary. Maybe
matriarchy will come into its own one of these days, but there's no
need to make a big fuss about it too much in advance.

COMRADE ABRAMOVSKI Of course not. It's too bad we can't be automatons ourselves. After the meeting, we'll take this piece of tail along
with us. (*He points to the Duchess, whose legs only can be seen
from under the cloth.*)

COMRADE X (*stretches and yawns*) All right—we can all go together. I
need a little rest and relaxation. I've been working too hard recently.
(*All of a sudden, like lightning, the iron curtain falls down.*)

TERRIBLE VOICE

> You've got to have a lot of tact
> To finish with the final act.
> It's no delusion—it's a fact.

End of the third and final act

March 6, 1934

Appendixes and Bibliography

Appendix I · On a New Type of Play

"On a New Type of Play" is the last section of An Introduction to the Theory of Pure Form in the Theater, *which first appeared in 1920 in numbers 1, 2, and 3 of* Skamander, *a leading Polish avant-garde literary magazine of the 1920's and 30's. Coming to the theater from painting, and strongly influenced by nonrepresentational modern art, Witkiewicz was able to develop a complete aesthetic theory of nonrealistic drama early in his own career as a playwright. His quest for "pure form" in the theater makes Witkiewicz part of the avant-garde European reaction against the realistic, psychological drama and social problem play which had dominated the stage since the 1890's.*

Before the First World War, Jacques Copeau, the guiding force behind modern French drama, attacked the socially constructive theater based on observation of real life as philistine and bourgeois, an adjunct of journalism, not art. The aim of the theater, Copeau argued, is not to make the spectator think, but to "'make him dream,' by evoking and suggesting the multiplicity and mystery of life." [1] *By the middle twenties, Gabriel Marcel suggested that "the future belongs to the theater of pure fantasy,"* [2] *and Benjamin Crémieux talked of the idea of "pure theater," which like pure poetry would have a technique of its own that would free it of the social content of realistic drama and give it independent life as pure movement.*[3] *In the 1930's, Antonin Artaud, in the manifestoes collected in* The Theater and Its Double, *formulated his theory of the theater of cruelty which rejects psychology and logic for violence, dreams, and the internal world of "man considered metaphysically."* [4]

Witkiewicz anticipated many of these ideas and quite independently came to conclusions similar to those of his Western European contemporaries. It is important to note that Witkiewicz' idea of pure theater is inclusive; he does not wish to rid the theater of reality, but to transpose it into a new dimension. Pure Form can absorb all kinds

[1] Jacques Copeau, *Critiques d'un autre temps* (Paris: Editions de la Nouvelle Revue Française, 1923), p. 230.

[2] Gabriel Marcel, "La crise de la production dramatique," *L'Europe Nouvelle*, No. 39 (September 29, 1923), p. 1255.

[3] Benjamin Crémieux, "Chronique dramatique," *Nouvelle Revue Française*, XXVII (August 1, 1926), 233–37.

[4] Antonin Artaud, *The Theater and Its Double*, trans. M. C. Richards (New York: Grove Press, 1958), p. 92.

*of material; the internal arrangement is simply freed from traditional
discursive and didactic demands.*   [Translators' note]

THEATER, LIKE POETRY, is a *composite art,* but it is made up of
even more elements not intrinsic to it; therefore, it is much more
difficult to imagine Pure Form on the stage, essentially independent, in
its final result, of the content of human action.

Yet it is not perhaps entirely impossible.

Just as there was an epoch in sculpture and painting when Pure
Form was identical with metaphysical content derived from religious
concepts, so there was an epoch when performance on stage was
identical with myth. Nowadays form alone is the only content of our
painting and sculpture, and subject matter, whether concerned with
the real world or the fantastic, is only the necessary pretext for the
creation of form and has no direct connection with it, except as the
"stimulus" for the whole artistic machine, driving it on to creative
intensity. Similarly, we maintain that it is possible to write a play in
which the performance itself, existing independently in its own right
and not as a heightened picture of life, would be able to put the
spectator in a position to experience metaphysical feeling, regardless of
whether the *fond* of the play is realistic or fantastic, or whether it is a
synthesis of both, combining each of their individual parts, provided of
course that the play as a *whole* results from a sincere need on the part
of the author *to create a theatrical idiom capable of expressing* metaphysical feelings within purely formal dimensions. What is essential is
only that the meaning of the play should not necessarily be limited by
its realistic or fantastic content, as far as the totality of the work is
concerned, but simply that the realistic element should exist for the
sake of the purely formal goals—that is, for the sake of a synthesis of all
the elements of the theater: sound, décor, movement on the stage,
dialogue, in sum, performance through time, as an uninterrupted whole
—so transformed, when viewed realistically, that the performance
seems utter non-sense. The idea is to make it possible *to deform either
life or the world of fantasy with complete freedom so as to create a
whole whose meaning would be defined only by its purely scenic
internal construction, and not by the demands of consistent psychology and action according to assumptions from real life. Such assumptions can only be applied as criteria to plays which are heightened
reproductions of life.* Our contention is not that a play should necessarily be non-sensical, but only that from now on the drama should no
longer be tied down to pre-existing patterns based solely on life's

meaning or on fantastic assumptions. The actor, in his own right, should not exist; he should be the same kind of part within a whole as the color red in a particular painting or the note C-sharp in a particular musical composition. The kind of play under discussion may well be characterized by absolute freedom in the handling of reality, but what is essential is that this freedom, like "non-sensicality" in painting, should be adequately justified and should become valid for the new dimension of thought and feeling into which such a play transports the spectator. At present we are not in a position to give an example of such a play, we are only pointing out that it is possible if only foolish prejudices can be overcome. But let us assume that someone writes such a play: the public will have to get used to it, as well as to that deformed leg in the painting by Picasso. Although we can imagine a painting composed of entirely abstract forms, which will not evoke any associations with the objects of the external world unless such associations are self-induced, yet it is not even possible for us to imagine such a play, because pure performance in time is possible only in the world of sounds, and a theater without characters who act, no matter how outrageously and improbably, is inconceivable; simply because theater is a composite art, and does not have its own intrinsic, *homogeneous* elements, like the pure arts: Painting and Music.

The theater of today impresses us as being something hopelessly bottled up which can only be released by introducing what we have called *fantastic psychology and action.* The psychology of the characters and their actions should only be the pretext for a pure progression of events: therefore, what is essential is that the need for a psychology of the characters and their actions to be consistent and lifelike should not become a bugbear imposing its particular construction on the play. We have had enough wretched logic about characters and enough psychological "truth"—already it seems to be coming out of our ears. Who cares what goes on at 38 Wspólna Street, Apartment 10, or in the castle in the fairy tale, or in past times? In the theater we want to be in an entirely new world in which the fantastic psychology of characters who are completely implausible in real life, not only in their positive actions but also *in their errors,* and who are perhaps completely unlike people in real life, produces events which by their bizarre interrelationships create a performance in time not limited by any logic except the logic of the form itself of that performance. What is required is that we accept as inevitable a particular movement of a character, a particular phrase having a realistic or only a formal meaning, a particular change of lighting or décor, a particular musical accompaniment, just as we accept as inevitable a particular part of a composition on a canvas or a sequence of chords in a musical work. We must also take into account the fact that such characters' thoughts and feelings are completely unfettered and that they react with complete freedom to any and all events, even though there is no justification for any of this. Still, these elements would have to be suggested on the same level of formal necessity as all the other elements of performance on the stage mentioned above. Of course, the public would have to be won over to this fantastic psychology, as with the square leg in the painting by Picasso. The public has already laughed at the deformed shapes on the canvases of contemporary masters; now they will also have to laugh at the thoughts and actions of characters on the stage, since for the time being these cannot be completely explained. We believe that this problem can be resolved in exactly the same way as it has been in contemporary painting and music: by understanding the essence of art in general and by growing accustomed to it. Just as those who have finally understood Pure Form in painting can no longer even look at other kinds of painting and cannot help understanding correctly paintings which they laughed at before as incomprehensible, so those who become used to the theater we are proposing will not be able to stand any of the productions of today, whether realistic or heavily symbolic. As far as painting is concerned, we have tested this matter more than once on people who were apparently incapable of understanding Pure Form at the beginning, but who after receiving systematic "injections" over a certain period of time reached a remarkably high level of perfection in making truly expert judgments. There may be a certain amount of perversity in all this, but why should we be afraid of purely artistic perversity? Of course, perverseness in life is often a sad affair, but why should we apply judgments which are reasonable in real life to the realm of art, with which life has essentially so little in common. Artistic perversity (for example, unbalanced masses in a pictorial composition, perversely tense movements or clashing colors in a painting) is only a means, and not an end; therefore, it cannot be immoral, because the goal which it enables us to attain—unity within diversity in Pure Form—cannot be subjected to the criteria of good and evil. It is somewhat different with the theater, because its elements are beings who act; but we believe that in those new dimensions which we are discussing even the most monstrous situations will be no less moral than what is seen in the theater today.

Of course, even assuming that a certain segment of the public interested in serious artistic experiences will come to demand plays written in the style described above, such plays would still have to result from a *genuine creative necessity* felt by an author writing for the stage. If such a work were only a kind of *schematic nonsense*, devised in cold blood, artificially, without real need, it would probably arouse nothing but laughter, like those paintings with a bizarre form of subject matter which are created by those who do not suffer from a real "insatiable pursuit of new forms," but who manufacture them for commercial reasons or *pour épater les bourgeois*. Just as the birth of a new form, pure and abstract, without a direct religious basis, took place only through deforming our vision of the external world, so the birth of Pure Form in the theater is also possible only through deforming human psychology and action.

We can imagine such a play as having complete freedom with respect to absolutely everything from the point of view of real life, and yet being extraordinarily closely knit and highly wrought in the way the action is tied together. The task would be to fill several hours on the stage with a performance possessing its own internal, formal logic, independent of anything in "real life." An invented, *not created*, example of such a work can only make our theory appear ridiculous, and, from a certain point of view, even absurd (for some, even infuriating or, to put it bluntly, *idiotic*), but let us try.

Three characters dressed in red come on stage and bow to no one in particular. One of them recites a poem (it should create a feeling of urgent necessity at this very moment). A kindly old man enters leading a cat on a string. So far everything has taken place against a background of a black screen. The screen draws apart, and an Italian landscape becomes visible. Organ music is heard. The old man talks with the other characters, and what they say should be in keeping with what has gone before. A glass falls off the table. All of them fall on their knees and weep. The old man changes from a kindly man into a ferocious "butcher" and murders a little girl who has just crawled in from the left. At this very moment a handsome young man runs in and thanks the old man for murdering the girl, at which point the characters in red sing and dance. Then the young man weeps over the body of the little girl and says very amusing things, whereupon the old man becomes once again kindly and good-natured and laughs to himself in a corner, uttering sublime and limpid phrases. The choice of costumes is completely open: period or fantastic—there may be music during some parts of the performance. In other words, an insane asylum? Or rather a madman's brain on the stage? Perhaps so, but we maintain that, *if the play is seriously written and appropriately produced*, this method can *create works of previously unsuspected beauty;* whether it be drama, tragedy, farce, or the grotesque, all in a uniform style and unlike anything which previously existed.

On leaving the theater, the spectator ought to have the feeling that he has just awakened from some strange dream, in which even the most ordinary things had a strange, unfathomable charm, characteristic of dream reveries, and unlike anything else in the world. Nowadays the spectator leaves the theater with a bad taste in his mouth, or he is shaken by the purely biological horror or sublimity of life, or he is furious that he has been fooled by a whole series of tricks. For all its variety, the contemporary theater almost never gives us the other world, other not in the sense of being fantastic, but truly that other world which brings to us an understanding of purely formal beauty. Occasionally something like this happens in the plays of writers of previous ages, plays which after all have their significance and greatness that we certainly do not want to deny them with any fanatical fury. This element which we are discussing can be found in some of the plays of Shakespeare and Słowacki, for example, but never in its purest form, and, therefore, despite their greatness, these plays do not create the desired effect.

The climax and the conclusion of the kind of play which we are proposing may be created in a complete abstraction from what might be called that debasing feeling of pure curiosity about real life, that tension in the pit of the stomach, with which we watch a drama of real life, and which constitutes precisely the one and only appeal of plays today. Of course we would have to break this bad habit, so that *in a world with which, on the realistic level, we have no contact,* we could experience a metaphysical drama similar to the one which takes place among the notes of a symphony or sonata and only among them, so that the *denouement* would not be an event of concern to us as part of real life, but only as something comprehensible *as the inevitable conclusion of the purely formal complications of sound patterns, decorative or psychological, free from the causality found in real life.*

The criticism of absolute freedom made against contemporary artists and their works by people who do not understand art can also be applied here. For example, why three characters, not five? Why dressed in red, not green? Of course, we cannot *prove* the necessity for that number and color, but it should appear inevitable in so far as each element is a necessary part of the work of art once it has been created; while we are watching the play unfold, we ought not to be able to think of any other possible internal interrelationships. And we maintain that, if the work is to be created with complete artistic sincerity, it will have to compel the spectators to accept it as inevitable. It is certainly much more difficult with the theater than with other arts, because, as a certain expert on the theater has asserted, the crowd as it watches and listens is an essential part of the performance itself, and moreover the play has to be a box-office success. But we believe that sooner or later the theater must embark upon the "insatiable pursuit of new forms," which it has avoided up until now, and it is to be hoped that extraordinary works, within the dimensions of Pure Form, still remain to be created, and that there will not simply be more "renaissance" and "purification" or repetition ad nauseam of the old repertoire which really has nothing at all to say to anybody.

We must unleash the slumbering Beast and see what it can do. And if it runs mad, there will always be time enough to shoot it before it is too late.

Appendix II · Major Works by Witkiewicz

Written	Title	Published	Performances
1893	*Cockroaches.* Comedy in one act	1965	None
	The King and the Thief. Comedy in one act	1965	None
	Comic Scenes from Family Life	1965	None
	Menagerie, or *The Elephant's Prank*	1965	None
	Princess Magdalena and the Overinsistent Prince	1965	None
1918	*Maciej Korbowa and Bellatrix.* Tragedy in five acts with a prologue	1962	None
1919	*New Forms in Painting and Misconceptions on the Subject*	1919	
	* *The Pragmatists.* Play in three acts and four scenes	1920	Warsaw, 1921 Zakopane, 1925 Zielona Góra, 1967
1920	† *Mister Price,* or *Tropical Madness.* Drama in three acts written in collaboration with Eugenia Dunin-Borkowska	1962	Cracow, 1921 Katowice, 1965
	They. Drama in two and a half acts	1962	Wrocław, 1965 Warsaw, 1966 Cracow, 1967
	Tumor Brainard. Drama in three acts with a prologue	1921	Cracow, 1921
	* *The New Deliverance.* Play in one act	1922	Zakopane, 1925 Warsaw, 1926 Warsaw, 1933 Cracow, 1967
	The Terrible Tutor. A drama in four acts	1935 [1]	Cracow, 1935

[1] Acts I and II only; Acts III and IV now lost.

Note on symbols: On copies of some of his plays, Witkiewicz used symbols to indicate whether they were more realistic (†) or closer to Pure Form (*).

Written	Title	Published	Performances
1921	*The Independence of Triangles.* A play in four acts	1962	None
	† *In a Small Country House.* A play in three acts	1948	Toruń, 1923 Zakopane, 1925 Lwów, 1926 Warsaw, 1959 Koszalin, 1963 Zielona Góra, 1966 Wrocław, 1967
	* *Metaphysics of a Two-headed Calf.* A tropical Australian play in three acts	1962	Poznań, 1928
	* *Gyubal Wahazar,* or *On the Precipices of Nonsense.* A non-Euclidean drama in four acts	1962	Poznań, 1966
	* *The Water Hen.* A spherical tragedy in three acts	1962	Cracow, 1922 Warsaw, 1964 Florence, 1966 Cologne, 1967
	The Anonymous Work. Four acts of a rather nasty nightmare	1962	Cracow, 1967
1922	*The Cuttlefish,* or *The Hyrcanic Worldview.* A play in one act	1923	Cracow, 1933, 1956 Warsaw, 1966
	Sluts and Butterflies, or *The Green Pill.* A comedy with corpses in two acts and three scenes	1962	None
	† *Jan Maciej Karol Hellcat.* A drama in three acts without corpses	1962	Warsaw, 1925, 1966, 1967 Lwów, 1926 Gdańsk, 1966 Florence, 1966
	Aesthetic Sketches	1922	
1923	† *The Madman and the Nun,* or *There Is Nothing Bad Which Could Not Turn into Something Worse.* A short play in three acts and four scenes	1925	Toruń, 1924 Zakopane, 1925 Warsaw, 1926, 1942, 1959 Vienna, 1966 San Francisco, 1967
	Janulka, Daughter of Fizdejko. A tragedy in four acts	1962	None

Written	Title	Published	Performances
1923	The Crazy Locomotive. A play without a thesis in two acts and an epilogue	1962	Cracow, 1964 San Francisco (radio broadcast), Middlebury, Vt., Stanford, Calif., 1968
	The Theater: An Introduction to the Theory of Pure Form in the Theater	1923	
1924	The Mother. An unsavory play in two acts and an epilogue	1962	Cracow, 1964 Saarbrucken, 1966
1925	The Beelzebub Sonata, or What Really Happened at Mordowar. A play in three acts	1938	Białystok, 1966 Łódz, 1967
	A Superfluous Man. A drama	Lost	
1926	The Baleful Bastard of Verminston. A drama	Lost	
1927	A Farewell to Autumn. A novel	1927	
1928	The End of the World. A drama in three acts	Lost	
	The Rules of the S. I. Witkiewicz Portrait-Painting Firm	1928	
1930	Insatiability. A novel	1930	
1932	Nicotine, Alcohol, Cocaine, Peyote, Morphine, and Ether	1932	
1934	The Shoemakers. A theoretical play with "songs" in three acts	1948	Gdańsk, 1957 Łódz, 1961 Toruń, 1961 Bydgoszcz, 1961 Wrocław, 1965
1935	Concepts and Principles Implied by the Concept of Existence	1935	

Selected Bibliography

ENGLISH, FRENCH, AND GERMAN

Bereza, Henryk. "Bruno Schulz," *Polish Perspectives*, IX, No. 6 (June, 1966), 37–39.

Boy-Żeleński, Tadeusz. "Le Théâtre de Stanisław Ignacy Witkiewicz," *La Pologne littéraire*, No. 18 (March 15, 1928), p. 1.

Grabowski, Zbigniew. "S. I. Witkiewicz, A Polish Prophet of Doom," *The Polish Review*, Winter, 1967, pp. 39–49.

Milosz, Czeslaw. *The Captive Mind*, chap. i, "The Pill of Murti-Bing," pp. 3–24. New York: Alfred A. Knopf, 1953.

Milosz, Czeslaw. "S. I. Witkiewicz, a Polish Writer for Today," *Tri-Quarterly*, No. 9 (Spring, 1967), pp. 143–54.

Puzyna, Kostanty. "The Prism of the Absurd," *Polish Perspectives*, XVI, No. 6 (June, 1963), 34–44.

Tarn, Adam. "Plays," *Polish Perspectives*, VIII, No. 10 (October, 1965), 8.

Toeplitz, Krzysztof T. "Avant-Garde with Tradition," *Poland*, American Edition, No. 4 (April, 1965), pp. 28–31.

Wysińska, Elżbieta. "Theaterbericht aus Polen," *Radar* (Warsaw), Ausgabe Deutscher Sprache, No. 2 (1967), pp. 18–27.

POLISH

Błoński, Jan. "Powrót Witkacego," *Dialog*, No. 9 (September, 1963), pp. 71–84.

Kotarbiński, Tadeusz i Płomieński Jerzy E. *Stanisław Ignacy Witkiewicz Człowiek i Twórca*. Warsaw: Księga Pamiatkowa, Panstwowy Instytut Wydawniczy, 1957.

Mencwel, Andrzej. "Witkacego Jedność w Wielości," *Dialog*, No. 12, (December, 1965), pp. 85–98.

Micińska, Anna. "S. I. Witkiewicz, Iuvenilia," *Dialog*, No. 8 (August, 1965), pp. 15–17.

Puzyna, Konstanty. "Introduction" to *Dramaty*, by S. I. Witkiewicz. 2 vols. Warsaw: Panstwowy Instytut Wydawniczy, 1962. I, 5–43.

Wazyk, Adam. "O Witkiewiczu," *Dialog*, No. 8 (August, 1965), pp. 70–75.